THE DUTCH UNDER GERMAN OCCUPATION
1940–1945

WERNER WARMBRUNN

The Dutch
under
German Occupation
1940-1945

STANFORD UNIVERSITY PRESS
STANFORD, CALIFORNIA
LONDON: OXFORD UNIVERSITY PRESS

Stanford University Press
Stanford, California
London: Oxford University Press
© 1963 by the Board of Trustees of the
Leland Stanford Junior University
Printed in the United States of America
Published with the assistance of
the Ford Foundation
ISBN 0-8047-0152-0
Original edition 1963
Reprinted 1972

Foreword

Many books on the history of people in countries occupied by Nazi Germany or Fascist Italy which have been published in English have stressed the extremes of political collaboration with the occupying power on the one hand, or the activities of the Resistance movements on the other. Many publications after the war consisted of documents from German archives and records of political trials dealing with political collaboration. It was natural that the Resistance attracted attention. It furnished examples of self-sacrifice and courage under extremely dangerous circumstances and it was heartwarming to author and reader to dwell on this material.

The real life of the peoples of occupied Europe lay between the two extremes of collaboration and resistance. In each occupied country the great majority of the population came to terms with the reality of the occupation. This applies not only to Western Europe but also to eastern Europe and the Balkans, where the Third Reich pursued an even more barbaric policy than in the West. The real history of occupied Europe therefore has been less heroic than many observers supposed during and sometimes even after the war. Most people, against their wills, were caught in a social system which of necessity continued to function under the occupation, to some extent to the advantage of the German war economy. Unwilling adjustment was the rule—intentional resistance the exception.

This dilemma probably caused more anguish in the Netherlands during the years 1940–45 than in any other occupied country. This is a reason to welcome especially the publication in English of a scholarly study which attempts to give a sober and factual picture of the history of occupied Holland. Occupied Holland has not remained an unknown quantity to the Anglo-Saxon world. Innumerable people have read with deep emotion the moving diary of Anne Frank, or have seen the play or film based on the diary. In that diary only one aspect of the reality of the occupation is reflected. The reality itself was more complicated, contained more nuances, more shades of gray.

The Netherlands State Institute for War Documentation, which, since 1945, has been collecting on behalf of the Dutch government great quantities of data and documents dealing with the history of the Netherlands during the Second World War, has been happy to give access to its collections to Dr. Werner Warmbrunn and to assist him in every respect possible with his research. Dr. Warmbrunn had to limit himself in his study since an entire lifetime would not suffice to examine all the material collected by the Institute. If this book increases interest in the Netherlands and in a broad sense furnishes some insights into the much wider problems of life in an occupied country, the Institute will consider itself amply rewarded for the time taken in assisting Dr. Warmbrunn in his research. It goes without saying that he was free to conduct this research in complete independence.

Louis de Jong, Ph.D.
Director, Netherlands State Institute
for War Documentation, Amsterdam

Preface

During the Second World War millions of unwilling peoples were subjected to the rule of comparatively small foreign military and police forces. Germany and Japan each controlled populations larger than their own by the threat and use of violence, and with minimal reliance on the consent of the conquered nations. In many occupied countries a substantial proportion of the available work force allowed itself to be employed in support of the war machine of the occupying power, while at the same time a few individuals and groups resisted the conqueror. This difference in response to enemy occupation raises questions about the origins of resistance and about distinctions between individuals and groups which led to differential responses to the occupation.

The German occupation of the Netherlands offers an opportunity for a study of these problems. Conditions for such a study are relatively favorable. The German occupation of much of Holland* lasted throughout most of the war. The small size of the country facilitates a coherent description of events under German rule. Abundant documentation is available on the occupation period, since the written word was one of the foremost weapons of the Dutch Resistance and since an excellent center for war documentation was established in Amsterdam in 1945.

The aim of this study is to present the story of the German occupation of the Netherlands in such a way as to provide a background for discussion of the origins and nature of the Dutch reaction to the

---

* In this book, the term "the Netherlands" will be used to refer to the Dutch state. In most other instances the more graceful term, "Holland," is used interchangeably with the formal designation. In Dutch parlance, however, "*Holland*" refers to the two western provinces of Noord-Holland and Zuid-Holland, while the term "*Nederland*" is applied to the country as a whole.

German regime. Part One provides information about antecedents of the German invasion and outlines the main events of the war and occupation. Part Two describes the German administration and the Dutch National Socialist Movement. Part Three presents the reaction of the Dutch people to the occupation regime. Part Four contains a summary of German actions and the Dutch response and my conclusions on the origin and nature of the Dutch response to the occupation.

Since some of the judgments in this study may be controversial and since no "scientific" validity is claimed for them, it may be well to say at the outset that there is no intention to condemn the Dutch people, for whom I hold a deep affection, or Dutch individuals or groups for what hindsight informs us may have turned out to be errors in judgment. Least of all is there a desire to condemn the Jews, German or Dutch, who paid so dearly for whatever mistakes they or their leaders made.

Instead, in the final chapter I attempt to "test" the response of groups and individuals to the occupying power against the premise that "any collaboration with the absolute evil represented by National Socialist principles, policies, and institutions backed by the police power of the totalitarian state was bound to corrode the good intentions of all collaborating individuals and groups." This procedure hopefully yields observations of some relevance to the judgments which groups or individuals who are confronted with totalitarianism in one of its many shapes are required to make. In a very small way, using a limited localized situation, this study thus hopes to make a contribution to our insights into the basic problem of the individual's responsibilities in his confrontation with society and the state.

This inquiry makes use of a preliminary study by the author which dealt in greater detail with the first nine months of the occupation. The present study was originally completed as a Ph.D. dissertation in 1955 but was revised between 1960 and 1962.

Since this book has been long in the making, many persons have contributed to its evolution. Harold H. Fisher, then Chairman of the Hoover Library at Stanford University, originally suggested that I use the library's newly arrived Dutch materials for research on the Dutch Resistance. David Harris and H. Stuart Hughes made helpful suggestions as departmental supervisors of the study during its period of gestation as a doctoral dissertation. I also want to express my profound gratitude to Joan Strong Warmbrunn, who rigorously edited the original version of the dissertation and thus started me on the long, slow road toward learning to write English.

Encouragement to revise the dissertation with a view to possible publication was given by Leon E. Seltzer, Director of the Stanford University Press, and Hubert R. Marshall of the Political Science Department at Stanford. The revision was made possible by financial support from Stanford University and from the Rockefeller Foundation, given through the Stanford Committee on Research in Public Affairs.

Foremost of all, I wish to acknowledge a major debt of gratitude to Louis de Jong, Director of the Netherlands State Institute for War Documentation in Amsterdam, for his help with the revision of the study, which took place between the summers of 1960 and 1962. Dr. de Jong made the facilities of the Institute fully available to me, including access to the collections of the Institute, an office for study, and the services of his staff. In addition, Dr. de Jong took many hours from his multifarious duties to read the revised manuscript and to suggest modifications in the light of his incisive insights and profound familiarity with the history of the occupation. Without Dr. de Jong's generous criticism and patience with the inadequacies of the study it would have been difficult to complete the present revision.

I also wish to express my thanks to Dr. de Jong's associates at the Institute: Professor Jacob Presser of the Municipal University of Amsterdam, who read the material on the persecution of the Jews; Mr. B. A. Sijes, who reviewed the section on the labor draft; and Mr. and Mrs. Edouard Groeneveld, respectively librarian and head of the indexing department of the Institute, whose help and friendship were invaluable. A. H. Paape, Peter G. Rijser, C. J. F. Stuldreher, J. Zwaan, N. Stroeve, M. M. Wolthaus, and E. S. R. Swerissen also helped in different phases of research or preparation of the manuscript.

Final and very special thanks go to Ellen Croson Warmbrunn, who edited and typed the revised version of the study and prepared the Index. Her encouragement and help provided much of the incentive to complete the present revision.

While I was the beneficiary of valuable advice which has been incorporated in this study, the responsibility for the final product and its imperfections is entirely mine. This applies especially to the conclusions in Part Four, with which some of my Dutch friends and associates may not find it possible to agree. I am offering them in the hope that an outsider's view can furnish perspectives that may be of some use in the work of those who lived through the occupation or those who are more deeply immersed in specialized materials than limitations of location and time have permitted me to be.

Contents

THE NETHERLANDS

NORTH SEA

WADDENZEE

TEXEL

AFSLUITDIJK

N

Den Helder

WIERINGERMEER

Schoorl
Alkmaar

Beverwijk
Ijmuiden
Haarlem

NOORD-

HOLLAND
Zaandam

Amsterdam
Hilversum

Leiden
Wassenaar
Scheveningen
s'Gravenhage

Delft
Rotterdam

ZUID-

HOLLAND

Schoonhoven
Dordrecht

Heusden

Moerdijk
Vught
Haren

Roosendaal
Bergen op Zoom

Breda
Tilburg

Eindhoven

Walcheren
Middelburg

ZEELAND

Vlissingen

Delfzijl

GRONINGEN
Groningen

Leeuwarden

FRIESLAND

Westerbork

DRENTE

Meppel

Zwolle

Ommen

OVERIJSEL
Almelo

Hengelo

Deventer
Enschede

Zutphen

Putten
Barneveld
Apeldoorn

Soest

Utrecht
Amersfoort

UTRECHT

GELDERLAND

Wageningen
Winterswijk

Arnhem

LEK R.

Nijmegen

MEUSE R.

s'Hertogenbosch
St. Michielsgestel

NOORD-
BRABANT

LIMBURG

Venlo

Roermond

RHINE R.

Maastricht

BELGIUM

GERMANY

MILES

0 5 10   20   30   40   50

PART ONE

Introduction

CHAPTER ONE

Before the Occupation

GOVERNMENT AND FOREIGN POLICY

In the years between the First and Second World Wars, Holland enjoyed stable government. Dutch cabinets were coalition governments since no party had a majority in the Second Chamber.* Frequently cabinets had to rely on shifting support from different parliamentary combinations for each legislative issue. This was possible because most political leaders realized that parliamentary government had to be carried on somehow. Therefore they granted sufficient support to the cabinet in power to ensure stable government. This arrangement was fairly successful because the existing distribution more or less accurately represented the social structure and allegiances of the Dutch people rather than a temporary trend in public opinion. Consequently *Katastrophenpolitik* was not in the interest of any of the democratic parties, for none of them had much to gain from new elections.

The nucleus of these interwar cabinets was formed by the Christian parties. As war approached, the Social Democrats pulled closer to the policies of the government then in power.

Hendrik Colijn, the leader of the Antirevolutionary Party, the largest Protestant party, was the dominant political figure in the years between the wars. He headed the cabinet from 1933 until August 1939, when he was replaced by D. J. de Geer, the head of the Christian Historical Union, the second largest Protestant party. The De Geer cabinet was a broad national coalition government, and the

* See Glossary for listing of Dutch political parties and Dutch terms. Modern Dutch spelling, which was adopted officially after the Second World War, is used throughout this study.

first Dutch government in the history of the Netherlands to include representatives of the Social Democratic Party. The Antirevolutionary Party did not participate in the cabinet officially, but one of the members, Professor P. S. Gerbrandy, became Minister of Justice, albeit without the approval of his party. This broad representation was a singularly fortunate development because it meant that the government-in-exile had the backing of all democratic political groupings.

In the interwar years appreciation of the Queen had been less than universal, especially because the Socialists feared that court circles on which she was believed to rely had a reactionary influence on the conduct of the government. Left-wing elements resented the use of troops in labor disturbances, and many stories were circulated about the remoteness of the Queen, although she was generally conceded to be an experienced and capable ruler.

In 1937 the marriage of Crown Princess Juliana to a German prince, Bernhard of Lippe-Biesterfeld, made the royal family the center of friendly attention. The subsequent birth of children to the royal couple further contributed to the popularity of the House of Orange. In 1937 the Social Democratic Party accepted in principle the rule of the House of Orange, abandoning its aim to turn the Netherlands into a republic. At the beginning of the war, the ruling dynasty and the monarchy found more widespread acceptance than it had for many years.

After the virtual collapse of the policy of collective security in the mid-nineteen-thirties, Dutch foreign policy was designed to maintain the neutrality that had served the Netherlands so well during the First World War. The Netherlands depended on the maintenance of good relations with neighboring powers, especially with Germany and England, since trade with the German hinterland and with the Dutch East Indies—the security of which required the support of Great Britain—was the mainstay of the Dutch economy. The Netherlands also made an effort to establish closer collaboration with other small countries of northwestern Europe, particularly neighboring Belgium.

Official relations between the Netherlands and Germany had been good up to the Nazi seizure of power. Common interests in the carrying trade on the Rhine made cooperative relations mandatory. When international tension began to increase after the German occupation of the Rhineland in 1936, the German Foreign Office repeatedly assured the Netherlands government that the Reich would respect Dutch neutrality. An explicit declaration to that effect was delivered in the last days of August 1939, just before the outbreak of hostilities.[1]

On August 28, 1939, the Dutch government ordered the mobilization of the armed forces in anticipation of the outbreak of war.[2] Immediately after the invasion of Poland on September 1, the Dutch government issued a declaration announcing the intention of the Netherlands to stay out of the European conflict.[3] The mobilization was maintained until the invasion.

The state of war existing between Germany and the Allies imposed a heavy economic burden on the Netherlands, quite apart from the expense of mobilization. Transit trade with Germany practically ceased as a result of the British blockade. War conditions made it more difficult to secure raw materials for Dutch industry. Dutch ships were sunk by mines in the English Channel and elsewhere. As a result of these conditions, the total volume of industrial and commercial activity decreased. Unemployment rose despite the fact that approximately 300,000 men were mobilized. The cost of living increased by about 10 percent between August 1939 and May 1940.[4]

THE INVASION

In November 1939 an incident in the best cloak-and-dagger tradition occurred at Venlo* near the German border. The British Secret Service thought it had established contact with German military leaders who, it was hoped, were ready to precipitate a revolt against Hitler.[5] Actually, the British were negotiating with German counterintelligence agents, who proposed a meeting between Captain S. Payne Best of the Secret Service and the German general on whose behalf they claimed to operate.[6] Major General J. W. van Oorschot, Chief of the Dutch Military Intelligence Service, had stipulated that a member of his staff be present at all meetings between the British and the Germans.[7] The meeting with the German general finally

---

[1] Numbered notes (primarily source citations) will be found at the back of the book, on pp. 285–311.
* Most of the place names mentioned in the text can be located on the map at the front of the book.

was set for November 9, 1939, at Venlo in a café on the Dutch side of the border. The Anglo-Dutch party was seized by German agents and abducted across the border. The Dutch liaison officer was critically injured and died in a German hospital, after having been interrogated by German officials.

It appears that this incident grew out of a routine espionage contact initiated by a German agent. The Germans were delighted with this opportunity to secure statements which they could use after the invasion to accuse the Netherlands government of violating Dutch neutrality. In addition, Hitler apparently believed that Payne Best and his associates had instigated the November 9 bomb attack on his life at Munich, and he attempted to coerce the captured British agents into admitting their responsibility.[8]

In the same month Dutch intelligence received reports that the invasion was to begin on November 12, and the army was placed in a state of readiness. On November 11 German plans were reported canceled and November 12 passed quietly, as did subsequent reported dates for the attack.

In the months before the invasion finally took place, Dutch intelligence discovered the existence of a system of espionage involving, among other things, the smuggling into Germany of Dutch uniforms and of information regarding Dutch defense installations.[9] In April, twenty-one prominent Dutch Nazis were arrested and the Government declared a state of siege in order to be able to deal more efficiently with German espionage without the impediment of normal court procedures.[10]

The Netherlands government was prepared to face all these trials with comparative equanimity as long as Dutch neutrality was respected. Since it was well aware that the ultimate decision rested in the hands of German leaders, it maintained a scrupulous neutrality. Actually, the German High Command, at the insistence of the Air Force, had decided as early as May 1939 to attack in the West through Holland and Belgium.[11] Adolf Hitler justified the violation of Dutch and Belgian neutrality on the basis of a need to protect the Ruhr Valley and to gain air bases for the coming attack on England.[12] The German High Command repeatedly reconsidered these plans and the timing of the invasion, partly because of weather conditions.[13]

In the spring of 1940 signs began to multiply that the Dutch desire to remain neutral was to be of no avail. Early in May, intelligence reports indicated that the invasion was about to commence. The army was alerted, and on May 9 the Dutch military attaché in Berlin warned the Defense Ministry: "Tomorrow at dawn. Hold tight."[14]

On May 10 at three o'clock in the morning, German troops started to cross the border. German planes bombed Dutch airfields and dropped parachute troops near strategic locations. A few hours later, the German ambassador delivered a declaration in the name of his government, stating that German troops had entered the Netherlands to protect Dutch neutrality against an impending Allied invasion aimed at the Ruhr Valley. The German note urged the Netherlands government not to offer pointless resistance, but to place itself under the protection of the Reich. In that case only, it said, would Germany guarantee the monarchy and the independence of the country.[15] Similar declarations, handed to the Dutch minister in Berlin, contained accusations with regard to the allegedly unneutral attitude of the Netherlands.[16]

Actually, the Reich leadership knew very well that these accusations were spurious. In a briefing of his top command, Hitler had stated brazenly that "a breach of the neutrality of Holland and Belgium is meaningless. Nobody will question that when we have won . . ."[17]

The Dutch government rejected the German allegations. It declared that the Netherlands would offer military resistance and asked the Allies for military assistance.[18] The Queen issued a proclamation repudiating the German assertions and branding the invasion as a breach of international law and decency.[19]

In the meantime, the German air offensive wore relentlessly on. The German air force succeeded in destroying most Dutch military planes on the first day of the attack and in occupying a number of airfields around The Hague and Rotterdam, where German air-borne troops were landed. A small party of parachutists was dropped on the Moerdijk bridge across the estuary below the confluence of the Rhine and the Maas, which separates the northern and southern parts of the country. This unit succeeded in cutting off Allied relief troops from the central part of the country. On the fourth day of fighting, the Germans captured the entire Moerdijk bridge intact.[20]

Most of the parachutists around The Hague, who had been

dropped for the purpose of capturing the Queen and the Government, were eliminated on the first day. But the Germans did not relinquish their hold on the airfields, and, despite strong Dutch opposition, they succeeded in consolidating their position in the neighborhood of Rotterdam.

Dutch strategy had been based on plans calling for the uncontested surrender of the northeastern and southern sections and for a concerted defense of "Fortress Holland," the central section of the country, which was protected by inundations and fortified defense positions. The German success in landing and firmly lodging airborne troops inside Fortress Holland, and the severance of Dutch communications with Belgium, portended the failure of these plans.

German land armies in the north drove up to the Ijselmeer without encountering much opposition. Bitter fighting developed along Dutch defense lines, which ran from the Ijselmeer to the Big Rivers, but the Germans did not stage any decisive breakthrough in that area. They did succeed, however, in driving across the southern provinces of Limburg and Noord-Brabant into Belgium and, most important, in advancing along the Big Rivers toward Rotterdam. On the fourth day of the fighting they linked up with their air-borne troops in the neighborhood of Rotterdam.[21]

Early in the invasion it became apparent that the German advance was unexpectedly successful, and that the invaders were attempting to capture the Queen. Therefore, on May 11 the cabinet recommended to the Queen that she take measures to ensure the safety of the royal family. On May 12, Crown Princess Juliana, her children, and her husband went to England on a British destroyer. Prince Bernhard returned immediately to join Dutch troops fighting in Zeeland. On the next day the Commander in Chief of the Dutch Armed Forces, General H. G. Winkelman, advised Queen Wilhelmina that he could no longer be responsible for her safety. At her request she was taken to another British destroyer, which conveyed her to England after her intended port of disembarkation in the province of Zeeland had been bombed by the Germans.[22] The Government followed her later in the day. Only the ministers went to England, leaving behind the Secretaries-General[23] (as the permanent heads of government departments were called) of all the Ministries except Justice and Finance.

Upon arrival in London, the Queen released a statement explaining the reasons for her departure from the Netherlands. She declared that she had come to England to protect the interests of her country, to retain her freedom of action, which she would have lost had she fallen into the hands of the enemy, and to safeguard the independence of the Dutch East Indies. She vowed that from London she would conduct the fight against the invader to the best of her ability and strength until victory was achieved.[24]

Despite the section in the Constitution which stated that the seat of the government could not be placed outside of the Netherlands,[25] the Queen proclaimed London the seat of government. By doing so, she assured the continued legal existence of the Netherlands and made it possible for her country to continue the war in the ranks of the Allies.*

By Tuesday, May 14, the military situation had become manifestly hopeless. The Germans had cut off Fortress Holland from Belgium and established themselves solidly near Rotterdam. They threatened to bomb the cities of Holland, starting with Rotterdam. Consequently, General Winkelman, who had become the highest governmental authority in the Netherlands after the departure of the Queen and the Government, authorized surrender negotiations to avoid the threatened bombing of Rotterdam. The negotiations dragged on beyond the deadline stipulated in the German ultimatum. Apparently through faulty communications with their own aircraft, the German officers in charge of surrender negotiations failed in their attempt to stop one squadron of airplanes. Starting at approximately 1:30 P.M. on Tuesday, it executed the bombing of Rotterdam.† The center of the city, including one-eighth of its total area,

---

* In September 1940 Professor P. S. Gerbrandy, a member of the Antirevolutionary Party, succeeded De Geer as Prime Minister, since De Geer had begun to advocate a policy of negotiated peace.

† A controversy over the responsibility for the bombing of Rotterdam broke out in 1940 and continued after the war. The Commandant of Rotterdam, Colonel Scharroo, asserted in 1948 that the Nazi leadership had wanted the destruction of Rotterdam for an ulterior reason, such as to terrorize the Western Allies into submission by a demonstration of Nazi determination to destroy entire cities in the West as in the East in pursuit of German victory ([19], 1-C, 645). A German scholar, Hans Adolf Jacobsen, writing in 1958 blamed the bombing primarily on Dutch delaying tactics and on faulty communications between the German commanders on the ground and their aircraft ([181], p. 284). On the other hand, Jacobsen admits that general strategic considerations designed to

was destroyed. Approximately 900 persons were killed and 78,500 were made homeless.[26] Rotterdam, along with Warsaw and Coventry, became a wartime symbol of Nazi ruthlessness. Later in the afternoon, General Winkelman announced his decision to surrender. On the following morning, he signed the capitulation for all Netherlands troops except those fighting in the province of Zeeland.[27]

Thus the Dutch had to give up the fight against an enemy who had planned a modern war for which the Netherlands were even less prepared than France or Great Britain. Dutch casualties in manpower had not been heavy,[28] but the superior technology and greater resources of the invader had rendered further resistance useless. The people of Holland entered the five years of occupation after a five-day war which had been so brief that most citizens had not fully grasped what had happened.

---

force Holland to capitulate also played a part (*ibid.*). A reply to Jacobsen's article by a Dutch scholar, J. L. Hartog, suggests a deliberate double-cross by Goering, who is suspected of having withheld a message from the field commanders to the air squadron ([178], pp. 240–41). The fact that one-half of the German aircraft understood and obeyed the red warning signals fired from the ground (testimony of Squadron Commander Hoehne [181], p. 282) forces this writer to doubt Hartog's hypothesis and to assume that the bombing was due to a failure in communication. This position in no way denies that Goering and his generals were more willing to take the risk of bombing Rotterdam "unnecessarily" than to pursue a more cautious policy which might have delayed the Dutch capitulation.

CHAPTER TWO

Survey of the Main Periods
of the Occupation

THE LONG WAIT: MAY 1940–AUGUST 1944

During the five years of German rule Nazi occupation policies underwent a number of modifications in response to events inside and outside the occupied territory. It is possible to distinguish four phases, closely linked to military events.

The first period lasted from May 1940 until the spring of 1941. Its first few months, at least, may be called the "honeymoon" of the occupation. Hitler allowed Dutch prisoners of war to return to civilian life. At this time German leaders were confident that they could conquer, without much additional military effort, those sections of the European continent that were not yet under their control. They established a German supervisory civilian administration for the occupied territory, headed by Dr. Arthur Seyss-Inquart. This administration undertook the first tentative steps which were to lead to conflict with the population in subsequent years. Rationing of food and other goods was established gradually. Employment services began to recruit labor for work in Germany, but did not yet physically force Dutch workers to accept employment in the Reich. German police arrested a number of hostages in reprisal for alleged mistreatment of Germans in the Dutch East Indies. The hostages were treated well in captivity and several were later released.

In the realm of politics, the German administration subordinated the Socialist parties to a Dutch National Socialist commissioner, but allowed a measure of political expression to the Liberal and denominational parties. The Dutch National Socialist Movement (N.S.B.)

was given a free hand in the staging of public demonstrations and the dissemination of propaganda. These activities of the National Socialist Movement led to increased friction with the population at large. In February 1941 a strike broke out in Amsterdam in response to the anti-Jewish actions of the N.S.B. and the Germans. The first anti-Jewish regulations, including the registration of persons of Jewish ancestry, were initiated in these early months.

During the second phase of the occupation, lasting from the spring of 1941 to the spring of 1943, the conflict between the German administration and the population of the occupied territory became more pronounced. This conflict resulted in part from the breakdown of the conciliation attempt, as evidenced by the February strike in Amsterdam and the severe punishments administered by the German occupation authorities. In the second place, the entry of the Soviet Union and the United States into the war against Germany during 1941 created the practical prerequisites for an Allied victory. The growing likelihood of such a victory was bound to encourage the spread of Dutch resistance. In the third place, the increased conflict was related to the radicalization of German policies after the invasion of the Soviet Union. Rationing measures became increasingly strict. Compulsory registration for all unemployed labor was established in 1942, and selected groups of specialists were more or less forced to work in Germany. In the spring of 1942, the Wehrmacht reinterned the professional officers of the former Dutch armed forces. The German police took hostages to be held responsible in the event of future sabotage.

After the invasion of the Soviet Union, political parties were dissolved. This was the period of the maximum German effort to impose National Socialist ideas and institutions on the Dutch people. Dutch National Socialists were placed in administrative positions wherever possible. In this period German authorities concentrated on the establishment of National Socialist organizations in all realms of public life, corresponding to comparable organizations in the Third Reich. Much conflict developed over this attempt to nazify Dutch life.

From the summer of 1941 on, German authorities intensified their efforts to segregate and concentrate the Jewish population. In July 1942 they began to deport Jews to Poland.

During the third phase of the occupation, which lasted from the spring of 1943 until September 1944, the conflict between the occupying power and the Dutch population was intensified as a result of German measures following military defeats at Stalingrad and in the Mediterranean. In March 1943, Hitler declared a state of total war mobilization for all territories under German control and appointed Himmler Minister of the Interior. Within the German National Socialist Party, the balance of power shifted toward the radical wing. German measures aimed at avoiding defeat became more harsh and direct. In Holland, this tendency became most apparent in the heavier penalties imposed by the German courts, and in the area of labor recruitment, which became one of the main preoccupations of the German administration.

In late April 1943 nationwide strikes broke out in response to a decree ordering the reinternment of Dutch army veterans. Thousands of veterans went into hiding to avoid reinternment. Additional young men went underground as German authorities called up entire age groups for work in Germany. Extensive resistance organizations sprang up to support the people in hiding. Open warfare broke out between these resistance groups on the one hand and the Dutch National Socialists and the police on the other hand. A number of assassinations and counterassassinations occurred during 1943 and 1944.

During this third phase of the occupation, the German authorities admitted to themselves that they had failed to win over the Dutch people. Consequently it became less important to indoctrinate them, or to treat them gently.

The German administration attempted to secure labor for the Reich through a series of special actions, including the calling up of certain age groups, selective draft through a review of manpower in each branch of commerce, industry, and agriculture, and the issuance of new ration books. During the same period rationed goods available for distribution decreased significantly.

The German police in this period almost completed the deportation of the Jewish population to Poland. Except for thousands of Jews in hiding, only small groups of Jews remained in a few camps in the Netherlands.

The final phase of the occupation commenced with the approach of the Allied armies during the first days of September 1944, after the liberation of Belgium. Although the southern provinces fell into Allied hands, the remainder of the country went through great hardship and tragedy during the remaining months of the war. The Germans now acted on the assumption that they were occupying enemy territory and that they were facing a hostile population willing to give aid to the enemy whenever possible. Dutch men of military age were drafted or arrested primarily for fear they might assist the Allied forces. No longer did the Germans attempt to use Dutch factories and other productive facilities, but they removed to Germany as much machinery and equipment as possible.

Dutch resistance grew to unprecedented heights, evidenced in intelligence and sabotage activities, the railroad strike, the burgeoning of the underground press, and the assistance given to people in hiding. More than ever before, resistance activities were directly related to the progress of military operations.

In the summer of 1944, while the Allied Expeditionary Forces established themselves in France and liberated most of that country, life in the Netherlands continued as before. Toward the end of August, however, the left wing of the Allied armies rapidly conquered northwestern France. On the third of September, Allied troops crossed the Belgian frontier and entered Brussels. Antwerp fell on the fourth of September. At first it seemed that the headlong Allied advance would continue, and that the Netherlands would also be liberated.

After the fall of Antwerp, however, the Allies interrupted their progress in order to eliminate remaining German garrisons on the Belgian coast and to prepare an assault on the Albert Canal.[1] On the northern front, no important advances were scored until after the middle of September. In the south, the first Dutch city, Maastricht, fell to units of the United States First Army on September 14.[2]

On September 17 the Allied High Command started the great offensive, designed to bring the war to a quick conclusion by driving toward Berlin through the Netherlands and the northwest German plain. A key element of this operation was to capture intact the bridges near Nijmegen and Arnhem and to force a crossing of the rivers Maas and Rhine through the use of parachute troops. On the afternoon of September 17 American parachute troops were dropped near Nijmegen while British and Polish parachutists landed near Arnhem on the east bank of the Rhine. At the same time, motorized troops advanced from Allied positions in Belgium near the Albert Canal, and drove to Nijmegen on a narrow front. In support of this operation, the Netherlands government-in-exile ordered Dutch railroad workers to go on strike, to impede German troop movements.

The American parachute troops succeeded in seizing intact the bridge near Nijmegen, but British and Polish air-borne troops near Arnhem failed to establish a firm foothold. During the night of September 25 they had to be evacuated, with heavy losses, to the western bank of the Rhine.[3]

The failure of the Allied enterprise at Arnhem doomed hopes for a speedy liberation of the entire Dutch territory. Opening the port of Antwerp and establishing a solid front line along the Maas and Rhine became the next objective of the Allied High Command. Therefore the Allies had to drive the Germans from the mouth of the Scheldt river. This objective was achieved substantially by the end of the first week in November.

Farther south, the Allies advanced slowly toward the river Maas, which was reached at almost all points by the beginning of December. By November 15 a large portion of the provinces of Zeeland and Noord-Brabant and much of the province of Limburg had been liberated.

By the middle of November, most fighting in the Netherlands had stopped. The Germans shifted their troops south for the coming offensive in the Ardennes, and the Allies moved theirs for the assault on the Rhine in Germany proper.[4]

During the winter of 1944–45, both German and Allied strategists realized that northwestern Holland was no longer strategically important, since the Allies had succeeded in approaching the lower Rhine. By the tenth of March, 1945, the Allies had reached the Rhine at a number of points and established the Remagen bridgehead. Concurrently, the Allied Air Force started to soften up German positions in the eastern Netherlands, which blocked the Allied advance to the northwestern corner of Germany. The land attack started on

March 21 with a parachute crossing of the Rhine near the Dutch frontier. In the following weeks, Allied troops advanced through the eastern provinces. On April 10, Canadian troops liberated the city of Deventer, and during the following week the dike across the Ijsel-meer (Afsluitdijk) was reached and almost all of the northeastern Netherlands was liberated.

During the middle of April Canadian units also began operations against German troops in the province of Gelderland. Arnhem finally fell on April 14, and Apeldoorn on April 17. By April 21 the German garrison in the northwestern Netherlands was completely cut off from the Reich. The further advance of the Allies against the main German defense line, the Grebbe line, was stopped since surrender negotiations were then in process.[5]

In the spring of 1944 the German administration took precautions against the moment when the Netherlands might become a theater of operations. During the summer, earlier curfew hours were an-nounced, food rations were decreased drastically, and the rationing of utilities based on coal, such as electricity and gas, was made much more strict. Telephone and telegraph communications and the sched-ules of electric trains were cut sharply.

In an attempt to break the railroad strike, the Germans in October imposed an embargo on movements of foodstuffs from the eastern Netherlands to the western section of the country. Partly as a result of the embargo, food rations decreased to starvation levels during the winter and spring. In the big cities, the struggle for food and fuel became the dominant preoccupation of the people at large.

With the approach of Allied armies, Dutch resistance forces be-came more active. In September the Dutch government announced the establishment of the Netherlands Forces of the Interior (Neder-landse Binnenlandse Strijdkrachten) with Prince Bernhard as their Commander in an attempt to achieve more coordination within the Resistance.[6] Members of recognized resistance organizations were declared to be soldiers of the Forces of the Interior, and became subject to Prince Bernhard's orders and those of his subordinates.

In the final weeks of the occupation, armistice negotiations took place between the German authorities and the underground Com-mittee of Representatives of the Government (College van Vertrou-wensmannen der Regering), a group of patriots which had been appointed by the government-in-exile in August 1944 to serve as the governmental authority during the transition from German to Allied rule.[7] On April 3, 1945, its chairman, L. H. N. Bosch Ridder van Rosenthal, received a report to the effect that the German authorities might be willing to negotiate with the Allies and to stop executions, demolition actions, and inundations while negotiations were in progress. He passed on this information to the London government. On April 12, a conversation took place with the High Commissioner, providing assurance that the military authorities were in accord with the negotiations.[8] The Dutch government, however, was unable to empower its representatives to make firm commitments, because it had no such authorization from the Supreme Headquarters of the Allied Expeditionary Forces in Europe (SHAEF). On April 25 SHAEF took over the conduct of the surrender negotiations. After a preliminary staff conference on April 28, Seyss-Inquart conferred with General Bedell Smith, General Eisenhower's Chief of Staff, near Apeldoorn on April 30. Prince Bernhard attended this conference as Commander of the Dutch Forces of the Interior.[9] The general surrender of all German troops in northwestern Europe on May 4 took place before definite arrangements for an armistice in Holland could be completed, but the meetings near Apeldoorn resulted in an agreement on the movement of foodstuffs into the occupied territory. The Germans also gave permission for Red Cross famine teams to enter the occupied territory to prepare emergency aid for victims of acute starvation.[10] The effect of these negotiations was to slow down the pace of the German police terror in the weeks before the German surrender. On May 5 the surrender of German troops in Holland went into effect at eight o'clock in the morning.[11] Holland was free at last after five years of enemy occupation.

PART TWO

The Germans and
the N.S.B.

CHAPTER THREE

The Establishment of the New Administration

NATIONAL SOCIALIST GOVERNMENT AND IDEOLOGY[*]

When the Nazis assumed power in Germany in 1933, they promptly began to adapt the existing machinery of government to their purposes. At the outbreak of the Second World War, the real power mechanisms had been transformed beyond recognition, although the Weimar Constitution was never formally repealed.

Dominant Nazi theory held that the state should serve as a means for the promotion of the race, and that this purpose required the introduction of the leadership principle into all levels of the administration. This trend was exemplified by the position that Hitler occupied as the "Leader and Chancellor" (Fuehrer and Reichskanzler) and, after 1939, as the "Leader" (Fuehrer). The Fuehrer was the ultimate authority within the state as well as in the Party. The basis of that authority was never clearly stated, although it was sometimes technically derived from the original appointment of Hitler as Chancellor, and from the Enabling Act of March 1933. The real source of the Fuehrer's authority could not be defined in rational terms but rested on the assertion that the leader possessed qualities lacking in ordinary human beings.[1]

In his position of unlimited power, Hitler was the head of the state, the government, the army, the judiciary, and the Party. The ministries of the national government were reduced to a large extent

[*] This section will discuss only a few special aspects of National Socialist government and ideology which are particularly pertinent to the development of German occupation policy in the Netherlands.

to technical boards exercising their duties on behalf of the Fuehrer. The Nazis succeeded in destroying the independent purposes and powers of nearly all institutions or organizations which might have served as foci of resistance to the charismatic leader. Only a mandate from Hitler could create authority in the Third Reich.

The Nazi Party (Nationalsozialistische Deutsche Arbeiterpartei, or N.S.D.A.P.) was expected to provide ideological leadership but theoretically was not to interfere with the actual operations of public administration or of private business. In effect, however, the distinction between party and state became blurred. A number of party leaders who also occupied government positions, such as Rosenberg, Goebbels, and Bormann, derived most of their actual power through their influence in the Party and with the Fuehrer.

Only in the police, through the S.S. (Schutzstaffel), was the Party clearly superior to the government. Himmler, as head of the police, was technically subordinate to the Minister of the Interior, prior to his own elevation to that post in 1943. But in actuality, Himmler's power greatly exceeded that of his superior. Essentially, it was based on his personal control of the S.S., which had been amalgamated with the professional police in 1936.[2] The S.S. even established a military branch, the Waffen-S.S., which was subordinated to the military commanders for tactical purposes, but served as a political check on the armed forces.

While all the power in the Third Reich was derived from the Fuehrer, German government at home and in the occupied territories was by no means the functional, streamlined hierarchy it claimed to be. Many agencies had overlapping areas of competence. A struggle for power went on among various individuals, factions, and offices, to be resolved in the final instance by Hitler, who retained for himself in this fashion ultimate control of all party and government officers and of all major decisions.[3] These internal tensions often interfered with the setting of policy and the conduct of business. In the last year of the war the approaching defeat of Germany caused the antagonisms between the Wehrmacht, the Party, and the S.S. to become more pronounced.

The motives for changing governmental structure and practices must be sought chiefly in the peculiar nature of National Socialist ideology. National socialism proclaimed that the main goal of nature and therefore of human activity lay in the procreation and perfection of biologically higher forms of life. On the human plane, this meant that all individual and collective endeavor must be directed toward advancing and increasing the most valuable races of mankind. The Nazi concept of race defied scientific definition. For our purposes, it suffices to point out that the National Socialists recognized two main racial groups: first, the Aryan race, represented by what the linguists call the Indo-European peoples, and second, all other races such as the mongoloid, negroid, and Semitic peoples.

The Nordic and Germanic peoples were considered the most valuable races and were described as the creators of all important civilizations and the founders of all powerful states. Therefore national socialism claimed that the enhancement of the growth and power of the Germanic races was one of its main tasks. This task was to include an increase in the Nordic racial strain in the population of the Reich.

Nazi race scholars held the racial qualities of the Dutch people in high respect. Hitler himself told Mussert that the best representatives of the Germanic race could be found in the Netherlands and in Norway.[4] The German leaders were particularly pleased with the racial purity of the rural population and showed great confidence in the character of the Dutch peasants.[5]

National Socialist doctrine asserted that the Aryan races had an implacable enemy in the Jewish race, the "Anti-Race," which, it was charged, tried to destroy the substance and achievements of the higher races, through deceit and parasitical exploitation of the host nation. In order to eliminate this danger, Nazi leaders proclaimed their intention to drive all Jews from positions of power in Europe, to segregate them, and eventually to remove them from the continent.

As early as the nineteen-twenties, Hitler wrote in *Mein Kampf* that in order to fulfill its mission, the Germanic race needed more living space. He felt that overseas colonies could not satisfy the demand, because they were not contiguous to the home territory, and because they did not lend themselves to the agrarian colonization which the best interests of the race required. Only in eastern Europe was such territory to be found.[6] Preceding or accompanying the colonization of eastern Europe, the Nazis wanted a union with Germany, by force if necessary, of all Germanic nations on the continent, especially of the Scandinavian countries and the Netherlands, and an alliance with Great Britain.

Since the original decision to invade the Netherlands as part of a general Western offensive was based on strategic considerations, the German High Command of the Army (Oberkommando des Heeres) had assumed at first that a military administration would be established in the occupied Netherlands. In the instructions to its field commanders, the High Command stipulated that German authorities should avoid anything which might arouse suspicion that Germany intended to annex the Netherlands. The High Command insisted that the rules of international law be strictly observed.[7]

Hitler's decision to establish a civilian administration in the Netherlands, headed by Dr. Arthur Seyss-Inquart, came as an unpleasant surprise to German military leaders.[8] It indicated to some Dutch observers that Hitler had political designs on the Netherlands,[9] although throughout the war the German administration officially claimed it had no intention of annexing the Netherlands.

There were a number of reasons for this policy. At least until December 1941, German leaders hoped to preserve the Dutch colonies, especially the East Indies, for the "New Europe" by keeping the Netherlands ostensibly independent.[10] Furthermore, the High Commissioner wanted to create a minimum of trouble during the initial period of adjustment. He recognized that only a minute percentage of the Dutch people favored annexation to Germany. Also Seyss-Inquart wanted to use Mussert and the Dutch National Socialist Movement, which would not have been possible had the German authorities come out frankly for annexation.

The real thinking of Hitler and his associates was governed by their vision of a postwar Europe. Three major interrelated considerations were at work. Of primary importance was the race theory, probably one of the factors responsible for the establishment of civilian administrations in the Netherlands and Norway. Hitler wished to utilize the superior stock of the Dutch and Norwegian peoples to improve the racial composition of the German nation.[11]

The second factor was Hitler's romantic-historical vision of a reconstitution of the Holy Roman Empire. In *Mein Kampf* he stated that the borders of 1914 would not be adequate, but that the nation would need all the soil and territory to which he considered it entitled.[12] In a secret speech given in 1937 before a school for prospective party leaders, he reiterated this vision of a "Holy Germanic Empire of the German Nation."[13] Before 1648, the Netherlands had formally been a part of the Holy Roman Empire.[14]

In the third place, geopolitical considerations seemed to make it desirable for the Reich to control the mouths of the Rhine and the Maas, and to expand its port facilities through possession of the great harbors of the Lowlands, which carried much of the overseas trade of Germany.[15]

Within the German administration in the occupied territory two divergent tendencies became increasingly pronounced. The High Commissioner and his associates, while publicly asserting that the Netherlands would remain independent, hoped to postpone the entire issue until the end of the war. On the other hand, the German S.S. propagated the view of the race scholars that the Dutch were a Germanic people and therefore should become members of the Reich at once. Goering himself, although not an ally of the S.S., told Mussert that he could not see any difference between the Germans and the Dutch.[16] In 1942 the Dutch Secretary-General of Justice, J. J. Schrieke, was informed by high German officials that the Netherlands would be annexed completely (*"mit Haut und Haaren"*) to the Reich.[17]

Apart from these plans to absorb the Netherlands territorially, a number of schemes were under consideration to transfer the Dutch to the conquered eastern territories. Before the invasion of the Soviet Union, Hitler and Himmler apparently toyed with the idea of transplanting all or part of the Dutch population to the East, possibly as punishment for the February strike in Amsterdam.* In

---

* See *The Memoirs of Doctor Felix Kersten* ([108], pp. 83–92). Kersten was a Finnish physiotherapist who had treated the husband of Queen Wilhelmina and other highly placed persons in Holland and Germany. His tale of how he singlehandedly prevented Himmler from carrying out the contemplated transfer of the Dutch population sounded so fantastic that this writer did not take it seriously at first. But Kersten's story did stand up in the investigations of the Special Commission of Inquiry of the Ministry of Foreign Affairs in 1950 ([19], 6-B, pp. 179–84), and of the Parliamentary Commission of Inquiry of the Second Chamber (*ibid.*, 6-A, 337–38). In 1950 the Dutch government officially acknowl-

1942, at the instigation of Alfred Rosenberg, the Commissioner for the Eastern Territories, plans were drawn up for Dutch settlers to be sent to the Baltic countries.[18] To accomplish this, the East Company (Oost-Compagnie) was organized in Holland to provide capital and other assistance for Dutch settlers going to the East.[19] One Dutch Nazi writer expressed the hope that five million Dutchmen would find new homes there.[20]

There seems little doubt that Hitler himself planned to tie the Netherlands to Germany as closely as was politically feasible after a German victory. In 1942 he told an intimate group of collaborators that he was happy that the Queen and the Government had fled to England because their absence would make it easier to dispose of the Netherlands after the war.[21] He firmly refused to allow Mussert to control the armed Netherlands S.S. troops because he recognized that this would strengthen the Dutch spirit of independence.[22] In 1941 and 1942, when Mussert tried to induce the Fuehrer to commit himself to Dutch postwar independence, Hitler consistently evaded the issue. He compared the Dutch unwillingness to join the German Reich to the unwillingness of the German states to join the Reich in 1871, and drew a parallel between his delaying tactics and those employed by Bismarck during the earlier period. In December 1942 Hitler pointed out to Mussert that it had been necessary for him to destroy the independence of his own fatherland, Austria, for the

---

edged Kersten's alleged wartime services to the Dutch people by awarding him a high rank of the Order of Oranje-Nassau (*ibid.*, pp 346–47). The well-known British historian and specialist on the collapse of the Nazi empire, H. R. Trevor-Roper, accepted the conclusions of the Dutch commissions and the claims that Kersten made in connection with the rescue operations during the final days of the war, which have been generally attributed to Count Folke Bernadotte ([225], pp. 69–76). Doubts about Kersten's role and the validity of the outcomes of the inquiries cited in this footnote continue to exist among some Dutch historians, partly because it has not been possible so far to gain access to all papers in Kersten's possession at the end of the war. Kersten's career, one of the more mysterious sidelights of the Second World War, deserves an objective appraisal sometime in the future. (Achim Besgen, *Der Stille Befehl* [241], is the latest treatment of Kersten's career accepting Kersten's story without qualifications.)

Regardless of Kersten's role in the prevention of the (allegedly) proposed deportations of all or part of the Dutch people to eastern Europe, this writer is inclined to believe that some such plan, among many others, constituted the subject of discussion between Hitler and Himmler in 1941. Whether the deportation would ever have been carried through, even without Kersten's intervention, is doubtful, although it must be admitted that other equally irrational schemes were executed by the Nazis.

sake of strengthening the Greater German Reich.[23] In the final analysis, Hitler, if victorious, probably would have annexed the Netherlands unless unforeseen political conditions had made annexation unprofitable.

THE OFFICE OF THE HIGH COMMISSIONER

With the departure of the Queen and the cabinet on May 13, 1940, the Supreme Commander of the Dutch Army, General Winkelman, became the highest governmental authority in the Netherlands. With the surrender his authority was transferred to the German government and was exercised by the High Command of the German Armed Forces. On May 18 Hitler issued a decree establishing a German civil government in Holland. The Fuehrer assigned the supreme civilian authority in the occupied territory to a High Commissioner (Reichskommissar für die besetzten niederländischen Gebiete) who was directly responsible to the Fuehrer. He appointed Dr. Arthur Seyss-Inquart to the office of High Commissioner.[24] On May 26 Seyss-Inquart and some of his associates had an audience with the Fuehrer, who lectured them on Dutch history. Hitler expressed confidence in Seyss-Inquart and with some minor modifications approved the High Commissioner's proclamation to the Dutch people.[25]

On May 29 Seyss-Inquart gave his "Inaugural Address" in the historic Ridderzaal where formerly, at the beginning of the session of the States General, the Queen delivered the "Speech from the Throne." In his address the High Commissioner claimed that the Germans did not have imperialistic designs on the Netherlands and did not wish to force their political convictions on the Dutch people.[26] In July 1940 the High Commissioner again characterized the occupation as being exclusively military, involving no claims on Dutch territory in Europe or overseas.[27]

The High Commissioner assumed all civilian functions and powers exercised by the Crown and the Government under the Constitution of the Kingdom. With the exception of the German Armed Forces, all German and Dutch agencies were supposedly under his jurisdiction. The High Commissioner's office was intended to supervise rather than replace existing Dutch agencies. All laws were to remain in force until further notice.[28]

Within a month after the surrender, Seyss-Inquart organized the High Commissioner's office in the basic form that it retained throughout the occupation. The High Commissioner governed through four German Commissioners-General (Generalkommissare), who, as quasi-ministers, were to supervise the Dutch administration. The Commissioner-General for Administration and Justice took charge of the Departments of Internal Affairs, Justice, and Education, Arts, and Sciences, and of related activities. The Commissioner-General for Security controlled security and police affairs and the German and Dutch police forces. The tasks of the Commissioner-General for Finance and Economy were indicated by his title. The Commissioner-General without Portfolio functioned as a political adviser to the High Commissioner, with special responsibility for nongovernmental organizations.[29]

In addition, Seyss-Inquart appointed German "Representatives of the High Commissioner" (Beauftragte) who supervised provincial and local governments.[30] The High Commissioner assumed the right to issue laws by decree and to review the decrees of subordinate agencies. The regulations prepared by the High Commissioner were to be published in the *Journal of Decrees* (*Verordnungsblatt für die besetzten niederländischen Gebiete*).[31]

Throughout the five years of the occupation, a flood of decrees appeared in the *Journal of Decrees,* commencing as a veritable torrent in 1940 and 1941 when the German administration was being organized and slowing down to a trickle in 1944 and 1945. In the beginning, German decrees were implemented with a measure of effectiveness, since German power was comparatively unchallenged, but from 1943 on many German regulations increasingly remained empty paper gestures frustrated directly or indirectly by the Resistance, patriotic officials, and the population at large. Therefore, a wide and ever-growing gap existed between impressions gained from the *Journal of Decrees* and the reality of procedures and conditions of life in the occupied territory.

The High Commissioner and his associates did not design the basic German policies that determined the course of the occupation. In the main, the High Commissioner's office simply executed such policies as the economic exploitation of the Netherlands, the labor draft, and the deportation of Jews, which were decided by Hitler on the advice of his closest political and military advisers. Nevertheless, the German leaders in the occupied territories occasionally could modify such directives through negotiations with Reich authorities or through their mode of executing such orders. They also had considerable independence in the conduct of day-to-day affairs. Hitler relied heavily on Seyss-Inquart's judgment, especially with respect to internal political developments.

Seyss-Inquart was not a colorful man. He was rather tall, somewhat lame in one leg, balding, and he wore thick horn-rimmed glasses. A lawyer by profession, he was a retiring and cultured person in private life. Being intelligent and systematic, he would have made a conscientious civil servant in any chancellery. He claimed that outside of military affairs he was personally cognizant of every important German action taken in the Netherlands.

Like many other high Nazi leaders, Seyss-Inquart grew up on the fringe of German settlement in Moravia, a region where Slavs formed the majority of the population. His early experience as a member of a minority group developed in him a strong pro-German nationalism, and he worked with nationalistic organizations when he moved to Vienna to practice law. He belonged to a generation that had difficulty in coming to terms with the civilian world of economic disintegration and lack of purpose into which it returned from the First World War.

When Hitler rose to power in neighboring Germany, Seyss-Inquart saw in his ideology the solution to the troubles of the German peoples, especially in central Europe. His close association with both nationalists and National Socialists projected him into the Austrian Ministry of the Interior in the last Schuschnigg cabinet. He played an important part in arranging the Anschluss in March 1938. His role in this historic event, through which Hitler's homeland became a part of the Reich, recommended him to the Fuehrer. In line with common practice, Seyss-Inquart was given a high rank in the S.S. After the Polish campaign, he was appointed second in command to Hans Frank, the Commissioner of the conquered Polish territory.

Within the framework of a complete acceptance of national socialism and of unswerving obedience to orders from the Fuehrer, Seyss-Inquart was a "moderate." He was willing to compromise in order to achieve his ultimate ends, and to listen to advice. He consulted his associates on important measures in weekly "cabinet meetings," and he saw things more realistically than did some of the fanatical members of the Nazi hierarchy. Hitler and Goebbels admired his diplomatic and supposedly conciliatory techniques of dealing with the Dutch people.[32] Especially during the early years, the S.S. attacked Seyss-Inquart for his "soft" policies.[33]

The High Commissioner also developed a proprietary interest in his domain. He did not approve of some of the more extreme measures ordered by the Reich authorities, such as the reinternment order, the big raids of 1944–45, and the mass shootings of hostages. Occasionally he tried to soften such policies.[34] But in the final analysis he loyally obeyed the Fuehrer and carried out his directives regardless of their impact on the Dutch people. In his political testament, Hitler rewarded this loyalty by appointing Seyss-Inquart Foreign Minister in the Doenitz cabinet.[35]

At the Nuremberg Trial, Seyss-Inquart was one of the few defendants who acknowledged responsibility as a cabinet member for the actions of the Reich government.[36] He never publicly turned against Hitler, although in his final moments he did accuse the Fuehrer of ruining Germany.[37] He was sentenced to death and hanged in October 1946.

The most influential German official in the Netherlands, apart from Seyss-Inquart, was the Higher S.S. and Police Leader Hanns Albin Rauter. The position of "Higher S.S. and Police Leader" (Höherer S.S. und Polizeiführer) had been created throughout Germany late in 1939 in an attempt to increase the influence of the more "elite and revolutionary" S.S. vis-à-vis the Party, the army, and the government machinery.[38] These posts were filled with aggressive S.S. officers whose main function was political.

Rauter, also an Austrian, had been appointed chief of police by Hitler, upon the recommendation of Himmler, without prior consultation with Seyss-Inquart.[39] The High Commissioner assigned Rauter a place in the hierarchy of the civilian administration by appointing him Commissioner-General of Security. To complicate the situation, Rauter was chief of all S.S. troops, including the Waffen-S.S., that were stationed in the Netherlands, and he was Seyss-Inquart's superior in S.S. rank. Rauter's position was anomalous (as was not uncommon in the German hierarchy) since, in his capacity as S.S. and Police Leader, he received his orders directly from Himmler, although he was supposed to clear them with Seyss-Inquart. After the war, Rauter claimed that he was simply the subordinate of Seyss-Inquart, and that Hitler and Himmler had told him so.[40] On the other hand, the Chief of Staff to the Commander of the Armed Forces in the Netherlands reported that Rauter had at one time denied that Seyss-Inquart had any authority over him.* Others, including some of Rauter's subordinates, also believed that Rauter frequently had better access to Hitler, through Himmler, than Seyss-Inquart.[41] The latter could give orders to the police via Rauter, who would execute them if they were compatible with Himmler's directives.[42] Actually, conflicts concerning the severity of punishments and a number of executions did occur, which were resolved only after much discussion in The Hague and at the Fuehrer's headquarters.

A veteran of the First World War, Rauter had joined the nationalistic "free corps" of that period. He became a National Socialist in the nineteen-twenties, and served as a member of the Nazi underground in Austria for many years. After the Anschluss he attracted Himmler's attention and was employed in police work in Poland.

Rauter was a tall, tough-looking person of little charm, and rather formal in his contacts with Seyss-Inquart and his colleagues. With his subordinates he was a stern disciplinarian. He was a fanatic and radical National Socialist and possessed tremendous energy and an overriding sense of duty. During the occupation he rarely left his post, and, unlike Seyss-Inquart, he was always on hand during the great crises of the occupation.[43]

Rauter was more a soldier than a politician. The happiest time of his life came, apparently, when he took part in repelling the British air landings near Arnhem.[44] He had strange and contradictory ideas about the people he ruled. He never comprehended that the occupation in itself was unacceptable to the majority of Dutch citizens. On the other hand, he admired the resistance movement as containing the best racial elements, although he executed members of the Resistance by the hundreds and assigned thousands to death in concentration camps.[45]

In the great discussion regarding the political future of the Netherlands Rauter was the local protagonist of the extreme S.S. faction. He opposed the idea of entrusting the government of Holland to Mussert, whom he called *"einen kleinen Spiesser."* He reproached Seyss-Inquart for championing the N.S.B. in order to please Martin

* *". . . dass er ihm garnichts zu sagen habe . . ."* Memorandum of Heinz Helmut von Wuehlisch, November 12, 1946, [179], p. 47.

Bormann, the Secretary of the Fuehrer, who attended to the interests of the German National Socialist Party at the Fuehrer's headquarters. In November 1942 he submitted his plans for postwar Holland to Seyss-Inquart. The Netherlands were to become part of the Greater German Reich and to be divided into *"Reichsgaue,"* territorial units replacing the existing provinces. These *"Gaue"* were to be administered by reliable S.S. men, preferably veterans of the Russian campaign.[46]

After the parachute landings near Arnhem on September 17, 1944, Rauter was given command of a number of German and Dutch units called the Kampfgruppe Rauter. On February 6, 1945, Rauter and his *Kampfgruppe* were assigned a sector of the front on the Rhine. This last excursion into military affairs lasted only one month.[47] On March 6, 1945, the car in which he was traveling was attacked by a resistance group near Apeldoorn.[48] His companions were killed and he was so badly wounded that he spent the remainder of the war in a hospital. The British captured him in May 1945, in Germany, and handed him over to the Netherlands government. In 1948 he was brought to trial by the Dutch and was sentenced to death. He appealed, was turned down, and was executed in February 1949.[49]

The second Commissioner-General with a definite political role was Fritz Schmidt. He was born in Westphalia, and was the only non-Austrian among top German civilian officials. This accident of origin may have made it somewhat easier for him to understand the psychology of the Dutch people. Schmidt was made Commissioner-General without Portfolio, his field of responsibility including public opinion and Dutch politics. He was close to Seyss-Inquart. In Holland he represented the power and the interests of the N.S.D.A.P. as opposed to those of the S.S.

Schmidt was an ambitious, intelligent, and somewhat unbalanced person. Recognizing the attitude of the Dutch majority toward the Germans and the N.S.B. more clearly than did most other German officials, he tried to compromise between the requirements of the Nazi rulers and the consciences of their subjects. In the battle over the political future of the Netherlands he promoted the interests of Mussert and the N.S.B., possibly because he hoped that the ineffectiveness and unpopularity of a Mussert government would make the Dutch more amenable to annexation to the Reich.[50]

When Schmidt was killed by a fall from a train in June 1943, it was generally thought that Rauter and the S.S. had assassinated him, but suicide or an accident seems a more likely cause of death.[51] His successor, Wilhelm Ritterbusch, was a colorless party official without an independent policy. Therefore Schmidt's death was a stroke of luck for Rauter and his associates.

The Commissioner-General for Finance and Economy, Hans Fischboeck, a former bank president from Vienna, was a capable and clever official who did not seek the limelight during the occupation. Together with the representatives of the German Four-Year Plan, he presided skillfully over the utilization of Dutch resources for the German war effort. His special contribution was the elimination of the currency frontier between Germany and Holland, enabling the Reich to drain Dutch resources more effectively.[52]

Dr. Friedrich Wimmer, another Austrian, was in charge of the Departments of Internal Affairs and Justice. He occasionally backed requests of old-time Dutch administrative officials. He was opposed to the S.S. wing of the German administration and, with Schmidt, attempted to follow a comparatively conciliatory policy. In contrast to Schmidt, however, he was a rather weak person.[53]

Starting in 1943, administrative offices were moved to Apeldoorn, and to other cities in the interior of the country. Seyss-Inquart, however, remained in The Hague. During the last months of the war, military authorities and the police tended to assume overall direction, and the High Commissioner played a less important role, except in connection with the surrender negotiations of April 1945.

THE COMMANDER OF THE ARMED FORCES
IN THE NETHERLANDS

On May 20, 1940, two days after issuing the decree establishing the office of the High Commissioner, Adolf Hitler created the position of Commander of the Armed Forces in the Netherlands (Wehrmachtsbefehlshaber in den Niederlanden). The new official was to be the military counterpart of the High Commissioner. As coordinating Commander of the three branches of the Wehrmacht, he was responsible to the High Command of the Armed Forces (Oberkommando der Wehrmacht) and to the Fuehrer. At the suggestion of Air-Marshal Goering, Hitler appointed Friedrich Christian Christiansen, a general in the air force, to this post.

The son of a Protestant minister, Christiansen was born in northwestern Germany. He became an officer in the merchant marine and served on transatlantic liners. While he was an aviator during the First World War, he met Hermann Goering. After the Nazis seized power in 1933, Goering put Christiansen in charge of all German aviation schools. Until the outbreak of the war in 1939, Christiansen was chiefly concerned with training young aviators. His appointment as Commander of the Armed Forces in the Netherlands came to him as a surprise, since he had had little military training and had never been a member of the General Staff.

Although Christiansen technically was a coequal of the High Commissioner, he carried much less influence than Seyss-Inquart. In the first place, he was a rather weak person, no match for the superior intelligence and political skill of the High Commissioner. In the second place, as the protégé of Goering, whose influence was on the wane after the Battle of Britain, he could achieve little with Hitler when he came into conflict with the High Commissioner, or with Rauter, who had Himmler's support. The High Command of the Armed Forces also failed to back him on such occasions. Furthermore, Christiansen did not have the military background necessary to acquire and hold the professional respect of his subordinates. Although he was the tactical Commander of all German forces in the Netherlands, actual control of military operations from September 1944 on was in the hands of his Chief of Staff, Lieutenant General von Wuehlisch, or of unit commanders stationed in the Netherlands.[54]

Christiansen personally was not a fanatic or extremist, but his training had not prepared him to deal with essentially political situations.[55] Therefore, he ordered such actions as the shooting of hostages in August 1942 and the destruction of the village of Putten in October 1944[56] without a full awareness of the moral and political impact of these decisions. He was brought to trial for these crimes in July 1948 and sentenced to twelve years in prison.[57]

THE DUTCH ADMINISTRATION

For practical reasons Seyss-Inquart decided to utilized the existing governmental structure of the Netherlands to the fullest possible extent. He knew that it was virtually impossible to replace existing

Dutch agencies and that the Dutch Nazi movement did not include enough technically qualified members to take over administrative jobs if these should be vacated by a great number of public servants at one time. Specifically, Seyss-Inquart was eager to retain the permanent department heads because he correctly assumed that the transfer of raw materials and supplies to Germany and the imposition of rationing and security regulations would proceed more smoothly if they could be issued over the signatures of the Secretaries-General.[58]

On the other hand, the High Commissioner was quick to modify those features of the Dutch government that were likely to conflict with the reorganization of the country along totalitarian lines. The elective legislative bodies had no place in the new scheme. It was also necessary to control the organs of public opinion. The new rulers accomplished this objective quickly, first through informal measures, then by a reorganization of journalistic and cultural institutions. Furthermore, certain duplications of function within the Dutch administration, particularly in its police apparatus, had to be eliminated to establish a more functional totalitarian control. Various sectors of public life which had been left primarily to private initiative in a democratic Holland (insurance, radio, cooperatives, etc.) were placed under the direct control of Dutch government departments.

After the first few months of the occupation, the German administration began to discharge officials who were thought to be unreliable. The dismissal of approximately 2,500 Jewish officials in November 1940 was justified in this fashion.[59] Since too few faithful Nazis had the needed technical and administrative qualifications, the occuping power never succeeded in its attempt to nazify completely the Dutch administration.

Upon taking over the government, Seyss-Inquart decided to eliminate General Winkelman as soon as it was practicable. After the surrender Winkelman served as head of the Dutch administration, issued orders to the Secretaries-General, and headed an army of almost full mobilization strength. He had become a popular hero and received enthusiastic ovations in public. First the Germans relieved Winkelman of all his functions except those concerned with the demobilization of the Dutch armed forces. Because Winkelman continued to lay blame for the bombing of Rotterdam on the Germans and to oppose other German propaganda claims, he was arrested on July 2, 1940, and taken to an internment camp in Germany as a prisoner of war.[60]

With considerable skill the High Commissioner proceeded to secure the cooperation of the Secretaries-General, the permanent "civil service" heads of the ministries. He asked the Dutch officials whether they would be willing to stay on, saying that it was their privilege to resign without prejudice if they felt they could not endorse specific measures they were asked to implement. Loyal cooperation, however, was expected of them if they should decide to stay. After consultations with General Winkelman, the Secretaries-General decided to continue in office.[61]

Apart from the reorganization of the police forces, the separation of the Department of Education, Arts, and Sciences into two departments was the only major reorganization effected by the Germans. The new Department of Education, Science, and Protection of Culture (Opvoeding, Wetenschap en Cultuurbescherming) took charge of the various aspects of formal education and youth care. The Department of Propaganda and Arts (Volksvoorlichting en Kunsten), a replica of Goebbels' ministry in Berlin, was designed to implement the nazification of the Dutch through its control of public media, and of literature and the arts.[62]

The Department of Foreign Affairs was dissolved after the surrender. Its internal functions eventually were distributed among other departments.[63] In 1941, the High Commissioner created the Department of Special Economic Affairs under Rost van Tonningen, which was designed to increase National Socialist influence in economic life. In effect, however, this new department mostly concerned itself with new ideologically inspired projects such as colonization of the eastern territories.

While leaving most departments intact, the Germans gradually introduced authoritarian principles into the government machinery. In the first place, they gave the permanent department heads increased regulatory powers. In the second place, they appointed National Socialists to government posts whenever possible.

The first major step toward "government by decree" was taken in June 1940, when the Secretaries-General were empowered to issue decrees having the force of law and carrying the penalties of imprisonment and fine for violations.[64] The Secretaries-General also assumed the veto right over the ordinances of lower administrative echelons.[65] Under these regulations the Secretaries-General became virtual ministers who made policy under German supervision.

As part of the institution of an authoritarian regime the Germans were determined to eliminate elective bodies. In June 1940 the High Commissioner suspended the activities of the States-General, as the Dutch parliament was called.[66] In the ensuing months he issued a number of regulations limiting the operations of provincial parliaments and municipal councils. Finally, in August 1941, the High Commissioner published a decree codifying previous administrative regulations. His decision to suspend rather than dissolve the States-General and other representative groups was considered a conciliatory gesture toward Dutch politicians, enabling them to continue receiving certain remunerations.[67]

The legislative functions of the municipal and provincial representative bodies were to be assumed by the mayors and the provincial commissioners respectively. These executives were to appoint advisory councils.[68] Sometimes the former municipal councils were reorganized as advisory groups. In other instances it proved impossible to organize complete advisory bodies because not enough citizens could be found who were willing to serve.

A number of semi-independent governmental bodies, such as postal services[69] and employment offices,[70] were integrated into the department hierarchy. Only the Water Districts, special local government units formed to maintain pumping installations for low-lying lands, were left undisturbed, even though their offices were elective.[71]

The policy of placing N.S.B. members and other pro-German persons in government service was most successful in the higher echelons. By September 1943 the High Commissioner had replaced eight of eleven provincial commissioners and the mayors of all major cities with "reliable" men.[72]

The replacement of mayors was of great importance because of their local influence, especially since their powers had been expanded considerably through the authoritarian reorganization of the administration. There was a great shortage of qualified candidates, and the N.S.B. gave quick brush-up courses for prospective mayors. A special effort was made to find Nazi candidates for all major towns. In July 1944, 52 percent of the population lived in municipalities administered by National Socialist mayors, while 34 percent of the mayors then in office were members of the N.S.B.[73]

Although he placed as many Dutch National Socialists as possible in responsible positions, the High Commissioner did not give governmental power to the N.S.B. as a party organization. He was concerned primarily with placing individuals in government positions who were loyal to the occupying power. Naturally he found few such persons outside the N.S.B.

THE ADMINISTRATION OF LAW

In July 1940 the Germans instituted a separate German court system independent of the Dutch judiciary. The new courts were to try cases involving German nationals, and non-Germans accused of anti-German activities. The German judicial hierarchy consisted of two tiers, the one-judge District Court (Landesgericht), which could impose a maximum sentence of five years' imprisonment, and the High Court (Obergericht), composed of a panel of three judges, which could impose unlimited sentences.[74]

The judges were German civilians who generally attempted to be fair to the defendants. They had to steer a careful course, however, since the police often would send the defendant to a concentration camp if the sentence conflicted too much with its judgment. In the civilian courts Dutch lawyers were permitted to assist Dutch defendants. A person accused of a crime against Germany was fortunate if tried by one of the civilian courts rather than by a military or police court, since the latter were more politically motivated.[75]

The High Commissioner held the right to review sentences by the German courts.[76] He availed himself of that right conscientiously, and frequently mitigated sentences passed by the courts.[77] This procedure was necessary partly because German law did not include the principle of a suspended sentence or of parole.[78] Nevertheless, even a short-term sentence might mean death if it was served in a penal or concentration camp, or if the police would not release a prisoner at the end of his term.

The occupying power left a large part of the Dutch judicial system undisturbed, notably in those areas where the Germans had no special concern. As a result, law was administered in a traditional manner in most cases that did not involve politics. But some alterations in basic legal philosophy and in the structure and administration of the judicial system were made.

The most profound interference with traditional legal philosophy was the introduction of the principle of analogy in June 1943. This addition to the criminal code stipulated that "if the basic intention of a law, but not its actual formulation, applies to a crime, the corresponding penalty should apply, if, according to sound legal sentiment, the deed should be punished."[79] This is, of course, the legal formulation of the principle "no crime without punishment," which national socialism substituted for the time-honored principle of Roman law, "no punishment without a law that covers it (specifically)" (*nulla poena sine lege*).

In order to be able to deal with political offenses in the spirit of national socialism, Seyss-Inquart established "Peace Courts" for political offenses that did not fall under the jurisdiction of the German courts. The lower courts were one-man chambers (Vrederechter), while the appellate court in The Hague (Vredegerechtshof) had three members.[80] The Germans and the N.S.B. saw a need for these courts because in their opinion the regular Dutch judges often dealt too lightly with patriots and too severely with Dutch Nazis in cases with political implications. These new courts were to base their decisions on "sound folkish sentiment" (*gesundes Volksbewusstsein*), rather than on the letter of the law.

According to the Nazis, the function of folkish law was to educate the people of Holland in the ideology of national socialism and to promote cooperation with the Reich. In dealing with political offenses, the intent of the action was deemed of paramount importance. Hence a member of the N.S.B. could be excused for beating up an opponent if he had done so in the spirit of winning Holland for national socialism. On the other hand, a patriot who had called a National Socialist a traitor was sentenced severely because his insults betrayed his opposition to national socialism.[81]

In order to deal with increasing thefts and violations of economic regulations such as rationing and price controls, special "eco-

nomic judges" (*economische rechters*) were designated.[82] No appeal
of their decisions was possible, but many of these judges tried to protect defendants from more severe measures which might be taken
against them by the Germans.[83]

Some minor modifications in the administration of justice are
worth mentioning. Dutch military courts were abolished and military cases were assigned to civilian courts supplemented by military
officers.[84] In order to create more opportunity for the appointment
of pro-German judges, the retirement age was lowered from seventy
to sixty-five.[85] In order to avoid politically undesirable trials and to
protect Dutch National Socialists, the High Commissioner deprived
the courts of the right to initiate prosecution.[86] Judgment was pronounced "in the name of the law" rather than "in the name of the
Queen."[87]

Despite these changes in the administration of justice, the attempt
of the occupying power to ensure the subservience and cooperation
of the population and to discourage opposition was implemented not
so much through these dual judicial systems as through the extra-
legal terror of the police, especially through the practice of sending
patriots to concentration or extermination camps without legal procedures, or in addition to legal sentences pronounced by the courts.

THE POLICE SERVICES

From the beginning the Germans brought their own police apparatus with them to function parallel to, and in command of, the Dutch
police services. It was necessary for the administration to establish a
distinct police organization, since the new laws and the very presence
of the Germans created new categories of crimes and punishments
which the Dutch police were neither organized nor prepared to enforce.

The German police apparatus in the Netherlands was a direct extension of the organization obtaining in the Reich. One branch, the
Security Police (Sicherheitspolizei), had the task of preventing and
detecting crimes against German interests. This branch included the
Criminal Police, the Secret State Police, and the Security Service.
The Criminal Police concerned itself with the detection of criminals
guilty of acts falling within German jurisdiction but not necessarily

committed for political reasons. The Secret State Police (Geheime Staatspolizei), commonly called the Gestapo, was assigned to prevent and punish political crimes. The Security Service, or S.D. (Sicherheitsdienst), was the heart of the German police state. The S.D. grew from an intelligence service of the S.S. into the central investigative agency of the Reich which directed the S.S. and police activities against the German people and against foreign nationals. The S.D. concerned itself mainly with internal subversion and occasionally with counterespionage.[88] It operated through hundreds of Dutch undercover agents, called V-men (Vertrauensmänner), who infiltrated underground organizations.

The Order Police (Ordnungspolizei) formed the executive branch of the service. Since its members wore green uniforms, they went by the name of "Green Police." The Green Police carried out arrests, mass raids, deportations, actions against strikes, and executions. Therefore it became the incarnation of the German police terror.

The Commander of the Security Police was the second in command after Rauter. The personality of the Commander of the Security Police had considerable influence on the conduct of the German police. Up to 1943 Dr. Wilhelm Harster, a professional police officer, was in charge. Under his direction the German police carried on its business of detecting and apprehending suspects in a comparatively "conservative" manner, although third-degree methods and outright torture were used even then. Harster's successor was Erich Naumann, who served from October 1943 to June 1944.[89] Naumann had previously served as commander of one of the special commandos (Einsatzgruppen) in Poland which engaged in the wholesale shooting of Jews and alleged Communists. Partly as the result of his experience in Eastern Europe and partly in response to the deteriorating political and military situation, Naumann introduced an intensified police terror including reprisal murders. He had a number of conflicts with Rauter and in 1944 was transferred at the latter's request.[90] His successor, Dr. Karl Georg Schoengarth, accelerated this terror and granted far-reaching independence of action to his local commanders. From September 1944 on, Schoengarth was the virtual head of German police services.[91]

The German police had its own courts, not only for enforcing internal discipline, but also for trying persons accused of serious crimes against the German state. Unless the defendants were acquitted, these courts usually passed out death sentences only.[92] This system, of course, exemplified the totalitarian state. The police acted as prosecutor, witness, judge, jury, and defense, all in one.

In view of the tensions which he knew to be ahead, Rauter increased the personnel of the Dutch police in July 1940 by recruiting additional men from the army, then in the process of demobilization, the majority being assigned to the big cities.[93] In order to overcome limitations inherent in the somewhat archaic organization of the Dutch police,* the Germans established a centralized State Police headed by a Director-General of Police responsible to the Secretary-General of Justice. The country was divided into five police districts headed by district presidents. Some large cities had police administrations headed by police presidents. In municipalities without State Police units, the mayors retained their traditional role as chiefs of police, but were subordinated to the central police authorities.[94] In the case of patriotic mayors, this arrangement involved serious conflicts of conscience.

Rauter also founded a special police school at Schalkhaar, where Dutch recruits were trained according to the German S.S. pattern.[95] The Schalkhaar police became a byword in occupied Holland because of its ruthlessness and cruelty.

---

* Before the war Dutch police forces consisted of the national police, which were responsible to the Minister of Justice, and municipal police forces, responsible to the mayors, which ranged from a one-man village police to large metropolitan police forces headed by commissioners of police. The national police were divided into two small, sometimes competing organizations of fewer than 2,000 men each, the State Constabulary (Rijksveldwacht) and the Royal Mounted Police (Koninklijke Marechaussée), which was trained and equipped by the Ministry of War.

CHAPTER FOUR

German Political Activities
in the Occupied Netherlands

The Germans' desire to ensure the close collaboration of the Dutch people during the war and after victory induced them to establish National Socialist institutions and organizations in the Netherlands. Although Seyss-Inquart never intended the Dutch people to have a free choice in the final analysis, he hoped, for tactical reasons, to achieve cooperation by persuasion and indirect pressure.[1]

These hopes were doomed to failure. In the first place, political events inside Holland during the summer of 1940 demonstrated that patriotic sentiments had revived quickly after the shock of the unexpected invasion and defeat, and that the Dutch people used the opportunity for political activity primarily to express their enmity toward national socialism.[2] This development forced the Germans to rely more or less exclusively on Dutch National Socialists in their search for political allies. In the second place, the successful defense of the Soviet Union and the entry of the United States into the war in 1941 made German victory progressively less certain, and thereby encouraged patriotic resistance.

From the beginning the German leadership realized that patriotic loyalty to the royal family presented an obstacle to the close association of Holland with the Reich. After some early hopes that the Dutch people had abandoned the Royal House, it became apparent that the House of Orange was becoming a vital rallying point for the Dutch. As a reaction to a demonstration which had taken place on June 29, 1940, Prince Bernhard's birthday,[3] Seyss-Inquart declared that demonstrations for the royal family would henceforth be considered as directed against Germany and would be dealt with accordingly.[4]

The occupying power continued its battle against the dynasty by replacing postage stamps bearing the picture of the Queen,[5] and by eliminating the title of "Royal" from a number of governmental and semigovernmental organizations and institutions. Pictures of the Queen were removed from government offices,[6] and references to the Royal House were eliminated from newly printed textbooks. Another regulation abolished street names referring to living members of the House of Orange.[7]

When the Queen declared the Netherlands to be an ally of Soviet Russia, in June 1941,[8] Seyss-Inquart designated the Queen as an enemy alien and confiscated her property. However, he refused to award it to Mussert, despite the latter's insistence.[9]

After 1941 the issue of the House of Orange was settled, as far as the Germans were concerned. The Queen had committed her fate and that of her government to the Allied cause, and the outcome of the military struggle would decide between the House of Orange and the Nazi Reich.

In July 1940 the High Commissioner began to suppress political parties by placing the Communist and Social Democratic parties under the commissionership of M. M. Rost van Tonningen, one of the chief radical members of the N.S.B. The German administration justified this action by pointing to the anti-German attitudes and the international connections of the Marxist movement.[10] A follower of Rost van Tonningen, H. J. Woudenberg, was made Commissioner of the Netherlands Association of Trade Unions, the largest Dutch labor union.

At first, the German attitude toward traditional parties of the center and the right was one of watchful waiting, but after the invasion of the Soviet Union, Seyss-Inquart dissolved all parliamentary parties, except the N.S.B., and confiscated their property.[11] A number of prominent party leaders were included among the hostages taken in 1940 and 1942, an action designed partly to make clandestine party activities more difficult.[12]

The years 1941 and 1942 comprised the period of the most intensive effort to remake Holland in the German image. In order to establish a totalitarian society with all power emanating from one source, the German administration replaced existing voluntary associations with authoritarian groupings under the supervision of the state. Usually the pertinent governmental department would appoint a Dutch Nazi as leader of the organization concerned. Sometimes only members of new organizations were permitted to exercise their professions. The head of the group could refuse membership at his discretion, thereby depriving an applicant of his livelihood.

In order to implement this transition, Seyss-Inquart appointed a Commissioner for Noneconomic Organizations.[13] This official had the power to prohibit the founding of new associations, and to dissolve existing ones and confiscate their property. In the first year of the occupation the Germans dissolved such groups as the Masonic Lodges, the Rotary Club, the Salvation Army, the Boy Scouts, and Jehovah's Witnesses.[14] Many local groups of these organizations, and of many other small associations, continued to meet informally throughout the occupation. The Germans simply did not have enough personnel to control such activities, and frequently took no notice as long as no security problems were involved.

The new organizations, or "Chambers" as they were frequently called, covered the entire range of professions. The Culture Chamber (Cultuurkamer) was established in November 1941 to include persons active in cultural fields, such as writers, journalists, artists, musicians, and architects. Individuals in each of these areas of cultural activity were organized in guilds, or occupational groups (*Gilden*).[15] Similar chambers were set up for veterinarians, dentists, pharmacists, and physicians.

Reorganization also extended to the economic sphere. The organization for farmers, the Netherlands Land Estate (Nederlandse Landstand),[16] was an outstanding failure because of its ineffectiveness and corruption.[17]

Seyss-Inquart moved more slowly in replacing the shell of the old labor movement, already under Woudenberg's control. In April 1942 he finally established the Netherlands Labor Front, on the model of the German Arbeitsfront.[18] The peak enrollment of the Netherlands Labor Front probably amounted to fewer than 200,000 members, as compared with almost 800,000 organized workers before the war.[19]

The Germans also tried to harness the humanitarian impulses of their subject peoples in their attempt to remodel society. In October 1940 Seyss-Inquart established the "Foundation Winter Help Netherlands" (Stichting Winterhulp Nederland), which was supposed to secure a monopoly in the field of charity.[20]

The German administration likewise introduced a Labor Service on the German prototype. After the surrender, General Winkelman collaborated with the German Commissioner for the Demobilization of the Dutch Armed Forces in setting up a temporary "Construction Service" (Opbouwdienst), largely to avoid a rise in unemployment due to the sudden demobilization of the Dutch army.[21] The main assignment of the organization was to remove the destruction wrought by war. Its staff, including its commandant, Major J. N. Breunese, was drawn mostly from the professional army officers' corps and its personnel from the demobilized armed forces. During the few months of its existence it remained a fairly nonpolitical organization. In July the Construction Service reached its maximum enrollment of 64,000 men. Thereafter it rapidly decreased in numbers.[22]

During the autumn and winter months the new administration laid plans for a future permanent labor service which would replace the temporary Construction Service. In May 1941 the High Commissioner established the Netherlands Labor Service (Nederlandse Arbeidsdienst), dissolving the Construction Service at the same time.[23] Major Breunese became the first commandant of the new organization.

Seyss-Inquart's decree made six months' labor service compulsory for all Dutch citizens upon completion of their eighteenth year. Actually the Labor Service continued to draw largely on volunteers until 1943. Girls were never required to serve, but volunteer women's camps were established, filled mainly with National Socialists.[24]

The work of the Labor Service consisted of all kinds of manual labor, such as soil conservation, road building, and harvesting. In addition to such work, the program included athletic activities and instruction in first aid, agriculture, and social studies.[25]

At first the Labor Service was not a strictly National Socialist institution. Major Breunese was not a member of the N.S.B., and he hoped to keep the organization free of political influences. In the autumn of 1941, when it became apparent that this would not be possible, he resigned. Pressure for the introduction of National Socialist instruction and practices continued to increase in 1942 and 1943, and the Labor Service definitely became an instrument of National Socialist indoctrination.[26]

In the attempt to influence education, the German administration tried to gain control of the appointment of teachers. In April 1941 public and private schools were required to secure the approval of the Secretary-General for appointments and dismissals of teachers. Many denominational schools ignored this regulation. The right to veto dismissals was designed to protect National Socialists.[27] In 1942 the Department assumed the power to dismiss teachers and administrators.[28] On the whole, Nazi authorities met with little success in their attempt to nazify teaching personnel. Until the Liberation in 1945, the majority of teachers remained loyal patriots, although higher administrative echelons were staffed with collaborators.

The new Secretary-General also made some minor changes in the curriculum. German became the first foreign language, while French was relegated to an inferior place.[29] More time was devoted to language, history, physical education, and vocational instruction, and a decree was passed, but not implemented, making the eighth year of elementary school compulsory.[30]

The Germans met special resistance in schools under the control of religious bodies. Seyss-Inquart almost closed Catholic schools in 1941, as a reprisal for the anti-Nazi pronouncements of the episcopacy, but finally he contented himself with nuisance measures against the teaching clergy.[31]

THE CHANNELS OF COMMUNICATION

The nature of the totalitarian state and the desire of German leaders to convert the Dutch people to national socialism made it imperative for occupation authorities to establish firm control over the media of communication. In line with Seyss-Inquart's initial assurance that the Dutch people could make their own political decisions, the German authorities at first pretended to exercise only advisory guidance of press and radio.[32] They did not institute a preventive censorship or engage in wholesale suppression of publications. From the day after the capitulation, newspapers were published "as usual."

In place of preventive censorship, general directives were issued and it was required that the first printed copies of each issue be submitted to the German Press Division. Under the general supervision of Commissioner-General Schmidt, daily press conferences were held in which the Germans made "recommendations" as to the choice of topics and manner of presentation.[33] Within a few months these recommendations had become orders regulating the daily press to the least minutiae, including such details as page assignments for certain photographs and speeches and the censorship of birth announcements and obituaries.[34] Subsequently the Press Division of the Department of Propaganda and Arts conducted these press conferences.[35]

In the first months, occasional "indiscretions" occurred, with which the censors dealt by suppressing the newspaper in question, or by other equally effective if less obvious means.

In August 1940 the authorities established the Netherlands Journalists Association,[36] and in May 1941 membership in this group was made compulsory.[37] Most journalists joined the association, but there were a few notable exceptions, such as D. J. von Balluseck, editor in chief of the prominent *Algemeen Handelsblad.* Some of the journalists unwilling to join eventually became editors of clandestine periodicals.

The number of publications and newspapers began to decrease rapidly under Nazi pressure. At first certain selected papers were suppressed, especially those of the extreme left wing and the Catholic press. During the first two years the Nazis used the paper shortage as a pretext for eliminating approximately half the dailies and about 80 percent of the periodicals. Many publications then pooled equipment and working forces in order to continue operations.

This reorganization eliminated the majority of denominational and provincial publications, which had been the most difficult to supervise. In addition, a genuine paper shortage developed, which forced the Germans to ration paper allotments strictly in July 1942.[38] The size of the dailies also decreased, until in the last months of the war they appeared as two-page tabloid editions, carrying primarily official announcements, such as rationing news.

In addition to acquiring control of the Dutch press, the Germans started a daily newspaper of their own, *Deutsche Zeitung in den Niederlanden*. This daily became the official mouthpiece of the office of the High Commissioner.

The occupying power also instituted controls over other media of communication. Before the war a number of private associations reflecting the religious and political divisions of Holland had controlled the Dutch radio. After the Social Democratic Party was placed under custody, its radio association fell into the hands of Rost van Tonningen. This solution was not, however, entirely satisfactory to the Germans, who wanted uniform control of all programs. In December 1940 the Secretary-General for Propaganda and Arts therefore appointed a commissioner for the reorganization of the Dutch broadcasting system.[39] Finally, in March 1941 the High Commissioner ordered the complete unification of radio services. Seyss-Inquart's decree transferred all Dutch broadcasting facilities, and the property of private radio organizations, to the state.[40] The new regulations also introduced a compulsory radio fee, which had been traditional in Germany. This measure involved, incidentally, the registration of existing radio sets.

The number of radio sets in use rose immediately after the occupation because people were eager to listen to foreign broadcasts. However, participation in the radio hook-up, which channeled programs into homes via electric circuits, decreased because people were not interested in the censored programs of official radio stations. After the confiscation of radio sets in May 1943, the number of wired connections increased rapidly. By September 1944 it was twice as great as it had been in 1941.[41]

The quality of official radio programs deteriorated considerably, since many experienced broadcasters were unwilling or were considered unfit to cooperate. The Catholic hierarchy enjoined priests and Catholic laymen to refuse cooperation with the nazified radio service.[42]

The film industry was also quickly brought under control. In October 1940 the entire motion picture industry was reorganized and placed under the Department of Education, Arts, and Sciences. Membership in the Netherlands Film Association (Nederlandse Bioscoopbond) became compulsory for all producers, distributors, and exhibitors.[43] This decree exemplifies the earliest instance of the type of corporative organization through which, in succeeding years, the Germans attempted to organize the whole of Dutch cultural, social, and economic life.

In July 1941 moving picture operators were required to show certain films at the behest of the authorities.[44] Under this regulation the Germans imposed propaganda films and newsreels on their "captive audience." In August 1941 the final comprehensive regulation of the film industry stipulated that theaters must keep seats available for official supervisors or censors.[45]

The variety and number of films shown decreased because of the exclusion of French, English, and American films, which had formed a large portion of prewar movie fare. After frequent incidents during the showing of Dutch newsreels, which were full of Nazi propaganda, the Germans prohibited departure from the theater during the showing of a newsreel.[46]

An attempt on the part of the N.S.B. to make films failed. The Germans operated the facilities of the Dutch film studios in Amsterdam until 1944. After the Allied invasion of Holland, they removed the film-making equipment to Berlin.[47]

Press, radio, and films were only the most obvious propaganda vehicles. Wide circulation was also given to speeches of German and Dutch National Socialist leaders, and in 1944 Seyss-Inquart himself published a collection of his addresses under the title *Vier Jahre in den Niederlanden.*[48] German organizations and the N.S.B. distributed a large number of pamphlets, often beautifully illustrated. At the beginning of the occupation, German propaganda agencies flooded the Netherlands with an illustrated book consisting of photographs of Hitler, designed to counteract the "false" democratic propaganda of prewar days.[49]

Seyss-Inquart was personally interested in a close cultural alliance between Germany and the Netherlands. He hoped that a cultural and artistic *rapprochement* might serve as the start of a closer political alignment of the Netherlands with the Reich.[50] To serve that purpose, he founded the German-Netherlands Culture Association (Duits-Nederlandse Cultuurgemeenschap) and the German Theater in The Hague. The Culture Association presented readings of Dutch and German writers and performances of music and exhibitions of paintings by German and Dutch artists.[51]

National Socialist propaganda also made ample use of posters. Themes were constantly readapted to the changing needs of the occupation policy and to shifts in the conduct of the war. In 1940 it stressed the faults of prewar Holland: its many divisions, its unemployment, and the inability of the former Government to protect the Dutch people. The Nazis also emphasized the inevitability of German victory and the fact that, in the last analysis, the only chance for survival lay in cooperation with Germany. Plutocratic England was violently attacked. In 1940, after air raids by the R.A.F. in which Dutch victims had fallen, the Germans put up a poster with the caption "English fliers have no pity on peaceful citizens,"[52] which aroused much sarcastic comment among a population familiar with the German bombardment of Rotterdam.

The hate campaign was stepped up after the attack on the Soviet Union. The Nazis portrayed the Bolshevists as devils incarnate, against whom they were defending Europe. On their posters the Soviet soldier was portrayed as a Neanderthal man, with blood dripping from his bayonet as he went about his business of killing women and children. Coupled with this campaign went an appeal to young Dutchmen to join their German comrades in the defense of Europe against bolshevism. Apart from this specific appeal, the Nazis kept up a continuous campaign to persuade the Dutch people to join Nazi organizations of all descriptions.

In 1943 the defensive theme became stronger. The underground press had started drawing comparisons between 1918, the year of the collapse of the German Empire, and the year 1943, which, it was hoped, might also turn out to be the year of German defeat. The Germans picked up this theme and tried to prove in articles, radio talks, and posters how much stronger the Germany of 1943 was than the Germany of 1918.[53]

This defensive theme also found expression in the concept "Fortress Europe," which developed after the German defeat at Stalingrad and the Allied successes in the Mediterranean. German propagandists attempted to persuade the Dutch people that the Reich was defending Europe against the dual threat of atheistic bolshevism and plutocratic capitalism represented by the United States and the other Western Allies. During the autumn and winter of 1943, this theme was stressed increasingly. With it went a stepped-up attempt to recruit Dutch men for military service.

In 1943 and 1944 German propaganda tried to dampen the popular spirit of expectation of, and hope for, an early establishment of the Second Front. German propaganda portrayed in lurid colors the destruction and tragedy that would result if Western Europe and the Netherlands were to become combat territory. One poster showed a small child bending over his dead mother, asking: "Mother, is this the Second Front that daddy used to talk about so often?"[54]

After September 1944, German propaganda efforts slackened because military problems became all-important.

POLICE AND SECURITY MEASURES

Throughout the occupation, maintenance of public order and security remained a primary task of the German administration in the occupied territory. Especially after September 1944, security criteria overrode all other considerations.

In order to control the Dutch population more closely, the German administration required each inhabitant of the occupied territory over fifteen years of age to carry an identity card (*persoonsbewijs*).[55] This card became the cornerstone of the German police rule. It bore the photograph, signature, and fingerprints of the owner. Jews had the letter "J" stamped on their cards. From 1942 on, the police frequently checked identity cards in trains, theaters, and other public places.

By the middle of 1943 it became apparent that the identity card no longer provided an adequate control of the population. Too many persons had gone underground or carried falsified documents. Therefore Rauter developed a new scheme to be carried out in conjunction with the issuance of new ration books. This scheme, as he wrote to Himmler, would have the result that "the army of 'divers' [people in hiding] will be driven to desperation because it will not get anything to eat."[56]

To accomplish this aim, Rauter proposed that the new ration book be available only to those reporting in person and presenting an identity card. He suggested that a special stamp be placed on the identity card before a new ration book was issued. All persons not having such a stamp on their identity cards would be suspect. The new ration book was to be provided with a seal which had to be replaced every six months. Thus Rauter hoped to effect a complete reregistration of the entire adult population on a periodic basis. In order to avoid all possibilities of sabotage, he had the books and stamps printed in Vienna. In early January 1944 he informed Himmler that he still had confidence in the success of this scheme.[57]

From the start, it was apparent that this measure was directed against people in hiding. Therefore underground organizations cooperated with officials in the rationing services and the Bureaus of Population Records (Bevolkingsregisters) to thwart Rauter's plans.[58] Cards, stamps, and seals were forcibly removed or secretly smuggled out of government offices, and thousands of extra cards came into the hands of the Underground.[59] Finally Rauter changed his mind, supposedly because he did not want to exert any further pressure on the people in hiding for fear of causing more unrest, but more probably because he realized that the Resistance had wrecked his scheme. He eventually promised that the police would not check persons asking for new ration books.[60] At any rate, the measure failed to rout out people in hiding.

The German police also restricted the freedom of movement of the population. In October 1940 the High Commissioner declared a curfew from midnight to 4:00 A.M.[61] Unauthorized travel across the borders of the occupied territory was outlawed,[62] and at various periods of the occupation, travel to or from certain designated sections of the country was prohibited.

In 1942, as part of the defense preparations against the expected Allied invasion of the continent, German military authorities ordered the evacuation of thousands of residents from coastal regions where fortifications were to be built. The first major evacuation took place on the island of Walcheren in the province of Zeeland, but the largest number of people were removed from a neighborhood in The Hague located near the beach. On other parts of the coast individual residents also had to leave their homes, which frequently were demolished to make room for fortifications.[63]

In the autumn of 1944 the German army evacuated the inhabitants of a few towns in the southern part of the country, such as Venlo and Roermond, which lay in the path of advancing Allied armies. The almost 100,000 residents of Arnhem were removed a week after the Allied air landings. Most evacuees were relocated in the eastern and northern provinces of the Netherlands.[64]

Naturally the German police took care to prevent unauthorized contacts with persons abroad. Foreign mail was censored and from March 1943 on, letters to persons abroad had to be delivered to the post office by the sender.[65] The possession of carrier pigeons and transmitters was outlawed.

It was particularly important for the Germans to cut off the Dutch population from Allied broadcasts. Technically it was easy for the Dutch to tune in on British radio programs. From July 1940 on, the Dutch government in London sponsored a daily quarter-hour radio program called "Radio Oranje," broadcast over the facilities of the British Broadcasting Corporation. The British radio also had news broadcasts in the Dutch language. In 1940 the German administration prohibited listening to radio stations outside of Germany and the occupied territories, and imposed increasingly stiff penalties for the violation of this regulation.[66] It also regulated the sale or transfer of radio receiving sets.[67] Rauter realized that all these measures were of little avail, since the danger of discovery was quite small. In 1943 the May strike provided him with the pretext for ordering the confiscation of all radios, except those of members of the N.S.B., who could obtain permits for keeping their sets.[68]

In its determination to suppress opposition and active resistance, the German administration continued to extend the variety of activities for which punishment was threatened and to increase the severity of penalties for these activities. Death sentences were pronounced so frequently that the police did not execute all persons condemned to die but sent them to concentration camps, which in many instances meant deferred death. Most persons caught in resistance activities were sent to concentration camps without ever being brought to trial.[69]

From the beginning of the occupation, heavy punishments had been threatened for actions directed against the armed services, such as espionage, sabotage, and attacks on soldiers. The early sentences in 1940 for actions of unorganized sabotage, largely committed by juveniles, were, however, comparatively light. After the February strike in Amsterdam, the High Commissioner issued a decree threatening a minimum prison term of one year for strike activities.[70] In July 1941, after the invasion of the Soviet Union, activities on behalf of disbanded political parties, participation in anti-German demonstrations, publication and distribution of clandestine newspapers, and reception or distribution of news from foreign radio stations became punishable by imprisonment up to five years.[71] In October 1941 a decree dealing with acts of sabotage set the death penalty for any act "which is designed or likely to threaten . . . public order . . ."[72] In May 1942 the death penalty was fixed as a possible punishment for activities in underground organizations.[73] In January 1943 the High Commissioner codified the preceding regulations affecting public order and security in an omnibus decree called the Decree for the Protection of Public Order 1943 (Ordnungsschutzverordnung 1943).[74]

The events surrounding the February strike of 1941 induced Rauter to ask for the creation of a legal basis for an administrative state of siege which would enable him to take quick measures in the event of future unrest. In March 1941, in response to Rauter's request, Seyss-Inquart issued a decree establishing an administrative state of siege (*Verwaltungsstandrecht*), during which all disobedience to orders of the police was punishable by death.[75] In the decree of January 1943 the administrative state of siege was changed in name only to the police state of siege (*Polizeistandrecht*).[76] The police state of siege was invoked for the first and only time during the May strikes of 1943.

In May 1944, in anticipation of the approach of military operations, the High Commissioner authorized the declaration of martial law (*Ausnahmezustand*) upon the request of the Commander of the Armed Forces in the Netherlands. Under martial law, the death penalty was mandatory for practically any action against the occupying power, especially work stoppages, collaboration with the enemy, and interference with the movement of supplies.[77] The High Commissioner declared the Ausnahmezustand to be in effect on September 5, 1944.[78]

Certain security decrees emanating from the Fuehrer or the High Command of the Armed Forces provided for even swifter and harsher penalties than did Seyss-Inquart's regulations. One of these decrees was the "Night and Fog Decree" (Nacht und Nebelerlass) issued by Field Marshal Keitel in December 1941. This decree stipulated that no persons in the occupied territories suspected of having committed sabotage should be brought to trial unless it was certain that the court-martial would sentence them to death. If there was no assurance that a death penalty would be imposed, such prisoners were to be sent to German concentration camps under special conditions of secrecy and harsh treatment, where it could be assumed that they would perish in time.[79]

On July 30, 1944, Adolf Hitler issued another order in which he stipulated that persons of enemy nationality in the occupied territories who were caught in the act of committing sabotage should be shot on the spot. Those who were apprehended afterwards were to be handed over to the Security Police rather than brought before a court. The police were to execute them without formal trial.[80]

Considerations of security induced the German administration to engage in a number of mass actions against large sections of the population. The isolation and deportation of the Jews was camouflaged as such a security measure.[81] In May 1942, after the completion of a sabotage trial of seventy-two Dutch citizens, many of whom had been professional officers, General Christiansen reinterned all the commissioned officers he could seize, with the exception of a few members of the N.S.B. This reinternment was executed in a particularly treacherous manner. The officers concerned were called up for a regular inspection, the second one since the demobilization. They were even issued round-trip tickets. When they had gathered in the barracks where the inspection was supposed to take place, German troops and police suddenly closed in on them and they were taken to Germany. Christiansen asserted that the participation of former army personnel in anti-German activities made this action necessary. He threatened reinternment of reserve officers and professional noncommissioned officers if these anti-German conspiracies continued.[82] However, despite German pretense to the contrary, security considerations played only a minor part in the decision to reintern all army veterans in 1943.[83]

By contrast, the large-scale raids on Dutchmen carried out in the autumn and winter of 1944–45, which were disguised as a labor draft, were chiefly security measures, although the need for labor played a subsidiary role. The German military knew that arms had been dropped by the Allies, and, after recent experiences in France and Belgium, it was feared that the Forces of the Interior might aid Allied troops at critical moments.[84]

The German administration was not content with the punishment of persons who actually had engaged in anti-German activities; it also held people responsible for the actions of others. This principle was employed for the first time in July 1940, when the Germans arrested a few hundred prominent Dutchmen as a reprisal for the alleged mistreatment of German nationals in the Dutch Indies. These "Indian Hostages" were to ensure better treatment of German nationals interned in the Indies.[85]

In 1941 the High Commissioner issued a decree stating that individuals, groups, and municipalities could be held responsible for anti-German activities with which the German authorities believed them to sympathize. He authorized the imposition of fines and compulsory services on communities where anti-German actions had occurred.[86] At Rauter's trial, the prosecution claimed that fines were imposed fifty-eight times during the occupation.[87]

In another application of the principle of collective responsibility, the German police and Wehrmacht frequently required local citizens to perform guard duties to protect German or public property. The death penalty was threatened for deliberately unsatisfactory execution of such guard duties.[88]

The principle of punishing people for actions they had not committed found its extreme application in the execution or murder of third parties in retribution for acts of sabotage and assassinations in which they had not been involved. In the spring and summer of 1942, on orders from the High Command of the Armed Forces, the German police arrested approximately 1,000 prominent Dutch citizens in two separate raids, and announced that they would serve as hostages in the event of further sabotage.

When an attempt was made in Rotterdam to blow up a German troop train in August 1942, Rauter had five prominent Dutch citizens executed, four of whom were taken from the group of internees. The fifth was selected because he was closely connected with the royal household, and German authorities felt that his death would hurt the

Queen personally.[89] Later it turned out that the act of sabotage had been committed by a Communist, who, according to Rauter's postwar statements, expressed joy over the fact that the Germans had executed five "reactionaries."[90]

In November 1942 the German police executed another group of hostages in retribution for a number of sabotage actions in the Arnhem region, including setting fire to stores of grain and other agricultural products. In announcing this sentence the German military commander threatened future arsonists with the gallows.[91]

Another reprisal execution occurred in January 1943 when a German soldier from the Medical Corps was shot down in Haarlem, where a number of assassination attempts and sabotage actions had taken place in the preceding weeks. At the request of the High Command of the Armed Forces, ten persons were executed from among the arrestees of the Haarlem region. This measure was based on a Wehrmacht order of December 1941 requiring that a minimum of ten civilians be shot for each attack on a soldier.[92]

In the wake of the assassinations of prominent members of the N.S.B., which started in February 1943,[93] the German police organized a new kind of counterterror, which involved the unofficial murder of admittedly innocent people. In September 1943 Rauter authorized the secret killing of patriots in retribution for the assassination of Dutch National Socialists.[94] Three patriots were to be killed for each Nazi. When an assassination had taken place, the German Security Police would pick the names of patriots living in the same town or region who were to be murdered. Special commandos of the (Dutch) Germanic S.S., dressed in civilian clothes, would then carry out the killing, usually under cover of darkness. The German police would make arrangements to prevent the discovery of the Nazi assassins by the Dutch police. This procedure was christened "Operation Silver Fir" (Aktion Silbertanne). In 1943 and 1944 approximately forty-five Dutch citizens were killed in this manner, according to Rauter's own statement.[95]

From the autumn of 1943 on, as a variation of this method of reprisal, German police frequently shot a certain quota of persons who had been arrested after an attempt on the life of National Socialists or Germans had been made. Such arrestees were declared to have been shot while attempting to escape (*auf der Flucht erschossen*).[96]

After the Normandy invasion the German police began to execute Dutch patriots in its prisons in reprisal for anti-German actions. Under the stringent regulations then in force, prisons were full of men subject to execution by virtue of having been caught in anti-German activity. When certain acts of violence took place, the police made a habit of executing a number of these prisoners and publishing their names. Rauter considered the execution of these death candidates (*Todeskandidaten*) only "phony reprisals" (*Scheinrepressaillen*), since the prisoners were "under sentence of death" anyway.[97]

After September 1944, in the face of the Allied advance and the growth and arming of the Netherlands Forces of the Interior, German police tactics became harsher than ever. Police General Schoengarth admonished his men "to demonstrate to the Dutch population that the Security Police is acting with special vigor [*hart zuschlägt*] under present circumstances . . ."[98] Moreover, from August to November Rauter could not exercise full control over executions since most of his time was to be devoted to military affairs.[99] This and the deliberate policy of General Schoengarth to leave a free hand to subordinate commanders may have been partly responsible for the increasing ruthlessness of local police officers.

Even in this period of climactic ruthlessness a few actions gained special notoriety. The first of these occurred after the air landings at Arnhem. An underground group attacked an army vehicle near the village of Putten, killing one German officer and wounding another. In retribution for this attack, General Christiansen, through his Chief of Staff, Lieutenant General von Wuehlisch, ordered the destruction by fire of Putten and the arrest of all male inhabitants.[100] Actually only a portion of the village was burned, but most of the men were sent to a concentration camp in the Reich. Out of the 590 men who were taken to Germany, approximately 540 died.[101] Although it is not yet entirely clear why such a large proportion of the prisoners perished, it seems that the deterioration of conditions in German camps during the final months of the war was largely responsible. Moreover, the Putten men were taken completely by surprise and did not have the mental preparedness and sense of purpose that frequently helped imprisoned resistance workers to survive the ordeal of the concentration camp.

Another major reprisal took place in Amsterdam in October 1944, when an official of the Security Police was murdered by the Resistance. In retaliation, Amsterdam police shot twenty-nine prisoners on the spot where the attack had taken place and blew up a number of adjoining houses.[102]

In response to the attack on Rauter near Apeldoorn on March 6, 1945, General Schoengarth had over 250 prisoners executed.[103] This was the largest number of persons executed in any one reprisal during the occupation.

Perhaps the most senseless and inexplicable German action during the last winter of the war occurred in the town of Heusden in the province of Noord-Brabant. In the early morning hours of November 5, 1944, a military demolition squad blew up the city hall, in which a number of civilians had sought shelter. One hundred thirty-four adults and children were killed in the explosion or died of injuries.[104] Not all of the circumstances surrounding this disaster have been explained, but the demolition team must have known that the explosion would endanger the lives of civilians in the basement shelter. No reasonable motive for this action has been uncovered, nor has it been possible to locate those responsible for the tragedy.[105]

According to official Dutch estimates prepared in May 1960, 2,000 to 3,000 persons were executed in Holland,[106] 600 died in concentration camps within the Netherlands, and approximately 20,000 perished in prisons or concentration camps in Germany. None of these figures include casualties from military hostilities, the labor draft, or the persecution of the Jews.[107]

These figures indicate that most deaths attributable to German police actions occurred in concentration camps and prisons. Outright executions accounted for only a small portion of the total loss of life, and probably at least half of these executions occurred in the final eight months of the war, as shown by the following table:

	Number of persons executed[108]	
Year	Men	Women
1940	0	0
1941	35	0
1942	292	0
1943	317	3
1944	570	11
1945[109]	1,560	19

In order to house arrestees and deportees the German police established a number of internment and concentration camps in Holland, although most political prisoners were sent to Germany. The installations at Haren and St. Michielsgestel were internment camps.[110] They contained the original groups of hostages chosen from among the intellectual and political leaders of prewar Holland.[111] The Jewish transit camp at Westerbork was a special kind of camp. An unusually large part of its internal administration was managed by inmates, especially by German refugees. Families were allowed to remain together and occasionally inmate officials were permitted to visit Amsterdam. Camp Erika at Ommen, in the province of Overijsel, was used as an overflow camp for prisoners convicted by Dutch courts, especially black-market operators. The camp at Amersfoort served chiefly as a transit camp for political prisoners destined to be taken to Germany and, from 1941 to March 1943, also for regular arrestees. The Vught concentration camp in Noord-Brabant, built by Rauter, served as an overflow camp for Jews, comparable to Westerbork, as well as a permanent concentration camp for others.[112] It had a special women's section. Some of its prisoners worked in nearby factories. The Vught camp became the scene of a major scandal in 1943, when its commandant had a group of seventy-four women locked in a small cell for a night, as punishment for their maltreatment of a fellow prisoner. The next morning, ten women had died of suffocation and others had gone insane. News of this event spread throughout Holland via the clandestine press. Rauter prosecuted the commandant, and Himmler personally consigned him to a hero's death on the eastern front.[113]

THE TREATMENT OF THE JEWS

Abandoning earlier plans for a forced emigration of European Jews to some place such as Madagascar, Hitler decided in 1941 to concentrate the European Jews under his control in the eastern territories and to exterminate them physically.[114] He entrusted the execution of this policy to Himmler, who in turn delegated it to Adolf Eichmann of Section IV B of the Main Security Office of the German Police (Reichssicherheitshauptamt).[115] Early extermination methods included mass executions by special police squads (*Einsatzgruppen*) and decimation through hard labor and starvation. The decision to use poison gas was made sometime during the first six months of 1942.[116]

At the beginning of the occupation of the Netherlands, the Germans pretended they would leave the Dutch Jews alone until the end of the war. Commissioner-General Wimmer told Secretary-General Frederiks that as far as the German administration was concerned, no Jewish problem existed in the Netherlands. Soon thereafter, however, orders arrived from Berlin to introduce anti-Jewish legislation and to begin segregation of the Jewish section of the population.[117]

Administration of the anti-Jewish measures involved a number of German agencies. General directives for deportations came from Himmler and the Main Security Office in Berlin. The Main Security Office in Berlin considered the Commander of the Security Police to be its "Commissioner" for Jewish affairs, but Seyss-Inquart appointed his special representative in Amsterdam, Senator Boehmcker, the former Mayor of Luebeck, as his own deputy in this field.[118]

Basic problems of the Jewish question were discussed in special staff meetings (*Judenkonferenzen*), which were held every five or six months, with Seyss-Inquart presiding. The conferences included the Commissioners-General, the Commander of the Security Police, the representative of the German Foreign Office (Senator Boehmcker), and others. At his trial Rauter claimed that in cases of disagreement, the High Commissioner had the last word.[119] Although this is doubtful, it is certain that Seyss-Inquart eventually was cognizant of and gave his consent to measures taken against the Jews.

The High Commissioner's Office was responsible for segregating the Jews within the Netherlands and for taking them to Westerbork and Vught. This assignment was delegated to Rauter as Commissioner-General of Security. Commissioner-General Fischboeck supervised the economic measures against the Jews. The Commander of the Security Police, under direct orders from the Main Security Office in Berlin, was responsible for the deportation of Jews from Westerbork and Vught to the East. The Security Police also dealt in the first instance with Jews who were guilty of infractions of German regulations, especially persons who had been caught in hiding.[120] Nevertheless, it is clear that Rauter, by virtue of his energy and aggressiveness, took a dominant part in most aspects of the persecution of the Jews,* even in areas where the Security Police supposedly received its orders directly from Berlin.[121]

German treatment of the Jews may be divided into four stages. During the first of these, lasting until the summer of 1941, the Germans began to eliminate Jews from public life and from positions of influence. They introduced a series of petty annoyances, such as the dismissal of Jewish members of the air-raid protection services, the prohibition of ritual slaughter, and the confiscation of radio sets. They began separating Jews and Gentiles by excluding Jews from recreational facilities, hotels, and restaurants. A special registration for Jews was held in January 1941.[122]

In 1940 the High Commissioner also ordered the registration of Jewish business establishments and authorized the appointment of German administrators. In March 1941 he established procedures for the compulsory sale of such enterprises.[123] In May 1941 the registration and sale of agricultural property owned by Jews was made mandatory.[124]

Although physical persecution of the Jews did not start in earnest during this first phase, future deportations and their outcome were foreshadowed by two mass arrests of young Jews. In February 1941, in retribution for actions of self-defense by Amsterdam Jews, Himmler had approximately 400 young Jews arrested and sent to the extermination camp at Mauthausen in Austria. In June 1941 another group, mostly young German refugees, was arrested as a reprisal for the planting of a time bomb in Amsterdam, and 230 young men were taken to Mauthausen.[125] There they underwent inhuman treatment including heavy labor at the quarries and other measures designed to annihilate them. At the end of 1941 only eight of these young men were still alive, and only one of the entire group survived the war.[126] At his trial Rauter claimed that this high rate of deaths induced him to send no additional prisoners to Mauthausen.[127] Large groups were indeed no longer sent from Holland, but individuals were. Transfers from other camps also continued to arrive in Mauthausen up to the last months of the war.[128] In addition, the threat of deportation to the camp was used repeatedly after 1941.[129]

In February 1941 the Germans established a new Jewish organiza-

---

* At his trial, Rauter asserted that he had very little to do with anti-Jewish measures ([24], p. 46).

tion, the Jewish Council (Joodse Raad, or Judenrat), in connection with the Amsterdam riots. In effect, the establishment of the Council was part of a Europe-wide scheme to designate Jewish leaders whom the Germans could employ in their administration of Jewish affairs. These Jewish Councils were modeled after the Prague Judenrat, which had been in existence for centuries.[130]

The two main leaders of the Council were A. Asscher, a prominent Amsterdam businessman who had been active in the Liberal party, and D. Cohen, Professor of Ancient History at the Municipal University of Amsterdam. The latter had been chairman of a committee that had assisted refugees from Germany since 1933. Asscher was an outgoing and popular person. A simple and brusque individual, he possessed a good deal of personal courage. Cohen was an intellectual and a scholar, and a more subtle and complex personality than Asscher. Both men were essentially humanists and philanthropists who accepted the responsibility of serving as chairmen of the Council in the hope that they might be able to help their people in a time of crisis.[131]

They remained in Amsterdam until September 1943, but were deported subsequently to Westerbork and Theresienstadt (Bohemia), from where they returned after the war. Asscher died in 1950. Cohen resumed his post at the University, but was suspended temporarily, pending an inquiry into his wartime conduct. He finally became emeritus in 1953 and is still living at this writing.

The Germans insisted that the Jewish Council be organized on the basis of the leadership principle. Asscher and Cohen were empowered to make whatever decisions were required. This arrangement was an ideological extension of the Nazi leadership principle to the Jews, and served to isolate the chairmen from their associates and therefore make them more pliable instruments in the hands of their German masters.

The second phase of the German policy against the Jews lasted from the invasion of the Soviet Union in June 1941 until the beginning of the deportations in July 1942. It was characterized by further isolation of the Jews and preparation for the deportations. In September 1941 a branch of the Main Security Office of the S.S. and Police, called the Central Agency for Jewish Emigration (Zentralstelle für jüdische Auswanderung), was established in Amsterdam to direct the deportations.[132]

In order to isolate the Jews, Jewish students were excluded from non-Jewish educational institutions,[133] and Jews were required to resign from all non-Jewish organizations.[134] In April 1942 Jews were required to wear the Star of David in public.[135]

During this period the German administration ordered Jews to deposit their money in blocked accounts at a designated bank managed by German officials. Jews were allowed to withdraw from these accounts only small monthly allowances.[136] They also were forced to register their real estate under German supervision and to dispose of it eventually.[137] The Germans authorized employers to discharge Jews and prohibited Jews from exercising certain professions.[138] Unemployed and later even employed Jews were sent to labor camps within the Netherlands.[139]

The third phase of the persecution of the Jews lasted from the start of the deportations to the virtual completion of the removal of the Jews from the provinces and Amsterdam in September 1943.

On June 26, 1942, the Zentralstelle informed the Jewish Council that the Reich had decided to put Jews to work in Germany under police supervision (*polizeilicher Arbeitseinsatz*).[140] This announcement caused great consternation, especially since the first group was to leave before the middle of July.

In preparation for the deportations, the Security Police issued, over Rauter's signature, a series of decrees aimed at further isolation of the Jews. Jews had to hand in their bicycles and were forbidden to use public transportation. A special curfew from 8:00 P.M. to 6:00 A.M. was established.[141] They had to do their shopping at special hours and were no longer allowed to use telephones.

The Zentralstelle selected Jews for deportation from files furnished, originally, by the Bureau of Population Records (Bevolkingsregister) and based on the special Jewish census conducted in 1941 at German behest. The Jewish Council could propose exemptions from each deportation, which the Zentralstelle might or might not respect. Individual Jews also could apply for exemptions through the Council.

From Amsterdam, Jews usually were sent to transit camps at Westerbork or Vught. In some instances Jews living outside of Amsterdam were forced to move to Amsterdam, but in others they were rounded up and sent to transit camps. In special circumstances they were deported directly to the East.[142]

At Westerbork and Vught the process of selection for final de-portation to the East began all over again. On the final journey Jews were usually put into sealed freight cars.[143] Upon their arrival at an extermination camp, such as Auschwitz, the S.S. would segregate Jews capable of work and consign those unfit for work, including old people and mothers with small children, to immediate extermination. This latter contingent was told to undress in preparation for a shower. They were then ordered into so-called shower rooms, the doors were closed, and poison gas was injected into the chamber. After approxi-mately half an hour, the doors were opened and special commandos, made up of camp inmates, hauled the bodies out for cremation, after removal of gold teeth and other valuables.[144] Other extermination camps employed variations of the Auschwitz method.

In order to induce the Jews to submit more readily, the German police employed an elaborate system of temporary exemptions from deportation. The largest group of Jews exempted were the em-ployees of the Jewish Council and their families, who were allowed 17,500 temporary exemptions at the peak period.[145] At first, thou-sands of textile workers were also exempted from deportation, as were other workers in war industries.[146] Jews married to Gentiles generally were not deported,[147] although the details of German poli-cies for this group changed from time to time. In 1943 the Germans offered sterilization as the alternative to deportation for Jews in mixed marriages without children. Women were sterilized only in rare instances, but approximately 600 men were sterilized. A far larger number of Jewish men in mixed marriages refused to submit to the operation, despite the risk of deportation.[148]

Apart from these comparatively large exempted categories, some smaller groups enjoyed a tenuous postponement of deportation. Com-missioner-General Schmidt allowed Secretary-General Frederiks to draw up a list of a few hundred prominent Jews whom he promised to protect. These people, and their families, were taken to a castle at Barneveld where they remained until after Schmidt's death. In September 1943 the Germans sent them to Westerbork, despite Schmidt's earlier promises to the contrary. In 1944, the "Barnevel-ders" were deported to Theresienstadt, Hitler's showplace of a Jewish community, from which most of them returned after the war.[149]

Also temporarily exempted were the people on the "Calmeyer

list." These were persons who claimed they had registered as Jews by mistake. They filed requests for recognition of their Aryan ancestry with the pertinent section of the High Commissioner's office, headed by a Dr. Calmeyer. This official was willing to give some applicants the benefit of doubt, and a number of this group survived the war.

The Portuguese Jews (Sephardic Jews) in 1942 submitted a memorandum to the German authorities explaining that, racially speaking, they were not really of Jewish but of Mediterranean extraction and therefore they should be exempted from deportation. The Germans continued to investigate these claims until 1944, but eventually this group was deported and exterminated.[150]

Other Jews in privileged positions included persons who held permits to enter Palestine and Jews of dual or foreign nationality. Most persons in this category were eventually taken to the concentration camp of Bergen-Belsen in northwestern Germany, where many perished from exhaustion, malnutrition, and disease.

Apart from these "genuine" exemptions, other "lists" were established for a number of purposes by various German agencies. These lists raised false hopes and induced the persons concerned to comply with German orders rather than go into hiding.

The fourth phase of the persecution of the Jews lasted from October 1943 to the end of the occupation. It was characterized by deportation of the Jews still in transit camps and prisons and of individuals on special "lists" such as the "Calmeyer list" and the "Portuguese Jews." During this period the German police also attempted to catch as many as possible of the Jews in hiding.

After the major groups were deported from Westerbork, only a skeleton crew was left. Most of the remaining Jewish affairs which had been managed by the Council were entrusted to exempted Jews in mixed marriages.

In 1941 approximately 140,000 persons registered as full Jews under the Nuremberg Laws.[151] Of this group 18,886 persons were listed as living in mixed marriages,[152] but this figure appears to be too high for reasons that are not entirely clear at this writing.[153] It may be assumed, however, that between 8,000 and 10,000 persons were exempted from deportation because they were married to non-Jews.[154] Approximately 8,000 Jews survived by remaining underground in Holland, and 900 remained in Westerbork.[155] Another estimated 2,000 Jews who lived in Holland in 1941 survived in other occupied territories,[156] and a few hundred proceeded to Allied territory with or without German consent.

Approximately 110,000 Jews were deported to the East. Latest estimates indicate that 5,450 returned after the war. Therefore, between 104,000 and 105,000 deported Jews perished in the East.[157]

CHAPTER FIVE

The Exploitation of the Netherlands

GENERAL POLICIES

From the outset the German authorities considered the economic utilization of the occupied territory to be one of their major objectives,[1] but they did not exploit the Netherlands as ruthlessly as the territories conquered in eastern Europe. In June 1940 Hermann Goering promised the Dutch people that their standard of living would not fall below that of their German neighbors.[2]

Three distinct phases can be noted in the German economic approach to the Netherlands. In 1940 and 1941 planning was directed primarily toward the long-term economic integration of the occupied territory into the unified European economic structure, which German economists thought they were building at the time.[3]

In 1942 the unexpected continuance of the war in the East forced the German leadership to readjust its aims. From the spring of 1942 to the summer of 1944, exploitation of the labor power and productive capacity of the occupied territory was increasingly emphasized. From the middle of 1943 on, Albert Speer, whom Hitler entrusted with the overall direction of armament production, stressed better utilization of the productive capacity within the Netherlands.[4]

From September 1944 on, German economic policies turned to acts of outright spoliation involving the wholesale removal of manpower, machinery, and rolling stock to Germany.

Commissioner-General Fischboeck supervised the economic exploitation of the occupied territory, carried out by two major German agencies. The economic branch of the High Command of the

Armed Forces, called the Armaments Inspectorate Netherlands (Rüstungsinspektion Niederlande), supplied the needs of the military. The civilian coordinating agency was the Central Order Agency (Zentralauftragsstelle), which was a branch of the Reich Ministry of Economic Affairs (Reichswirtschaftsministerium). These agencies usually addressed their requests to the appropriate office in Fischboeck's department, or placed their orders directly with industry. Frequently Fischboeck's department asked the Dutch administration to issue economic regulations implementing German requirements over the signatures of the Secretaries-General.[5] From 1943 on, German demands became so harsh that German authorities could no longer count on the collaboration of Dutch officials.[6]

In a number of instances agencies of the Reich operated directly in Holland, though generally in consultation with the High Commissioner's office. Gauleiter Sauckel's effort to recruit skilled industrial labor, and the total labor mobilization of the winter of 1944–45, were among these instances. Frequently these Reich agencies (military and civilian, local and central) worked at cross purposes, and their conflicts were settled only after much controversy.[7]

SUPPLIES, MANUFACTURED GOODS, AND
AGRICULTURAL PRODUCTS

In June 1940, in order to stop the unlimited hoarding of goods in which many people engaged immediately after the surrender, German authorities ordered a registration of all supplies at the wholesale level. They also began moving to the Reich the raw materials and foodstuffs which the Dutch government had stockpiled as a precautionary measure. Seyss-Inquart intended to leave only enough supplies in the Netherlands to keep industry going for six months.[8] By the end of that period he hoped to achieve the integration of Holland into the German war economy. He succeeded so well in this latter aim that, according to official figures, the value of exports to Germany doubled in 1940 over the level of 1938, and more than tripled over 1938 for the four subsequent war years.[9]

Apart from this wholesale removal of supplies, the German authorities engaged in a number of special requisitions in support of the war effort. In 1941 surplus metal goods had to be delivered. In

December 1941 winter clothing was requisitioned for German soldiers in Russia.[10] In the same month, to bolster the supply of scarce metals, Fischboeck introduced zinc coins as replacements for old copper, nickel, and silver coins. In September 1942 the administration required delivery of all coins which had been withdrawn from circulation.[11]

In 1942 the Wehrmacht conducted large-scale bicycle raids in the streets or on the garages where Dutch city-dwellers stored their bicycles. The 1942 raids netted more than 100,000 bicycles for the German military.[12] These raids continued through the last winter of the occupation.[13]

During the final winter of the war the occupying power imposed a textile requisition.[14] After the evacuation of Arnhem in September 1944 the Wehrmacht ordered the removal of all furniture and household goods for the use of bombed-out Germans.[15] Confiscation of furniture had been practiced earlier on a smaller scale in connection with evacuations from coastal areas and as punishment for certain types of offenses.[16]

As the occupation wore on, an ever-increasing share of the industrial production of the Netherlands went to Germany. The percentage of goods going to Germany was highest in plants manufacturing products most urgently needed for the war effort, such as metals and electric equipment. The manufacture of consumer goods, such as clothing and shoes, rose in 1943 and 1944 as a result of Speer's new policy.[17]

The total quantity of industrial production, however, dropped throughout the occupation until in 1944 it was less than half that of 1939.[18] This drop in production was caused in part by the reduction of the skilled labor force, brought about by the labor draft, for which utilization of previously unemployed labor did not compensate. Labor efficiency was decreased further by poor food and deteriorating health, and by the deliberate slow-down and sabotage practiced in many plants. In the mining industry, for example, the loss of man-hour efficiency was almost 40 percent.[19] Finally, supply problems, poor fuel, and the inability to replace worn-out machinery contributed to the drop in total production.

After September 1944 most factories ceased operations for lack of fuel, transportation, and workmen willing to endanger themselves by appearing in public. It has been estimated that in January 1945 the level of production was only 25 percent that of 1938.[20]

In order to feed the Dutch population and to export as much food as possible to Germany, the agricultural economy had to switch from the production of high-quality dairy and poultry products, requiring the importation of vast amounts of grain, to the production of such crops as potatoes, grains, and plant proteins. This policy entailed a decrease in farm animals, amounting to a reduction of 90 percent of the poultry and two-thirds of the hogs.[21] Fortunately, the reduction of cattle stock was not so drastic. By 1944 it amounted to only 22 percent of the 1939 level. The number of farm horses actually increased, since they were needed to do the work of tractors and trucks for which no gasoline was available.[22]

In order to raise the production of foodstuffs, the Department of Agriculture and Fisheries offered inducements to farmers to plow up acreage previously used for pasture, and imposed penalties on farmers refusing to cooperate. Until 1943 the use of additional land for raising crops more than compensated for the loss of acreage yield due to soil exhaustion, use of poorer lands, lack of fertilizer, and the deterioration of farm machinery. After the harvest of 1943, however, the nonanimal agricultural output which was officially registered began to decrease. This was at least partly the result of increased clandestine sales, particularly of vegetables.[23] During the season of 1944–45, agricultural production was less than half that of the year 1938. To a large extent this decrease was the result of combat activities and inundations which interfered with cultivation of the land.[24]

THE LABOR DRAFT

Since the German war machine needed more and more manpower as the war dragged on, the Germans drafted labor from all over Europe for work in the Reich. Goering, as Commissioner for the Four-Year Plan, was formally responsible for the overall direction of the labor draft. In March 1942, when it became apparent that the war would continue for some time, Hitler appointed Gauleiter Fritz Sauckel as Plenipotentiary for Labor Mobilization (Generalbevollmächtigter für den Arbeitseinsatz).

Supervision over policies of labor utilization in Holland rested with Commissioner-General Fischboeck until April 1942. Commissioner-General Schmidt, as representative of the N.S.D.A.P. in the occupied Netherlands, was given responsibility for coordinating that policy in April 1942 after Sauckel took over in Germany.[25] The Office of Social Administration (Hauptabteilung Soziale Verwaltung) directed and supervised operations of the Dutch labor exchanges.[26]

In order to marshal and deport labor more efficiently, the Germans replaced existing municipal labor offices by a centralized State Employment Office (Rijksarbeidsbureau) in May 1941. This Office was located in the Department of Social Affairs.[27] The Office of Social Administration assigned a German official to each of the local labor offices of the State Employment Office to supervise Dutch personnel. Despite a minor reorganization in 1943, the State Employment Office remained in charge of the labor draft until September 1944. At that time the Germans established a special office in Groningen, under the authority of Goebbels, whom Hitler had put in charge of total war mobilization. This office employed the police, the S.S., and the army as its executive branch.[28] Its activities were restrained to some extent by local German and Dutch agencies.

The exploitation of Dutch labor went through three major stages. From 1940 until March 1942 the Germans tried to round up labor for the Reich through so-called "voluntary" methods, using all kinds of pressure short of outright force. From March 1942 to September 1944 they established a legal obligation, backed by penalties and police enforcement, to work in Germany, but relied in the main on their administrative machinery to assign Dutch workers to the labor draft. After September 1944 the occupying power attempted to seize all men of military age through a variety of direct methods, such as mass raids, a general registration with German labor offices, and general proclamations. Administrative action was largely replaced by police action in this final phase.

Immediately after the surrender in May 1940 the authorities had to cope with the problem of temporary unemployment due to the closing of factories, general labor dislocation, and the release of men from the Dutch armed services. As one of the first major steps, the administration offered inducements to unemployed labor to work in Germany by promising good wages and working conditions including regular vacations.[29] It increased the pressure on the unemployed by refusing to pay unemployment insurance to those unwilling to accept work in Germany.[30]

In March 1941 the High Commissioner provided the legal basis for a compulsory labor draft by authorizing employment offices to put citizens to work at assigned locations within the Netherlands. Employment offices could also require employers to release workers for reassignment.[31] The clause in the decree limiting such compulsory employment to the Netherlands was eliminated in March 1942[32] in preparation for the Sauckel Action of that year, the turning point in the history of the labor draft.

In February 1942 all unemployed persons between the ages of eighteen and forty were required to register with the employment services.[33] In March 1942 employers were required to secure permission for the hiring of workers under forty years of age.[34] To ensure a fuller exploitation of Dutch labor, German authorities introduced a minimum work week of forty-eight hours. In 1943, a work week up to seventy-two hours could be authorized upon application by the employer.[35]

In April 1942 the Sauckel organization started sending special task forces to Holland to draft skilled workers for German armament industries. These task forces went into the factories to make selections from among the personnel.[36] The German police placed Dutch workers unwilling to go to the Reich in special camps or transported them to Germany. In 1942, according to official statistics, 162,000 workers were deported to Germany. This was the highest number sent to the Reich in any one calendar year.[37]

The results of all these efforts did not satisfy Reich authorities. After Stalingrad, they initiated additional compulsory measures as part of their program of total mobilization in Germany and in the occupied territories.

In March 1943 the German authorities issued a decree requiring the closing of certain nonessential enterprises (as they had in the Reich), but this order was generally sabotaged.[38] On April 29 Christiansen ordered the approximately 300,000 army veterans of May 1940 to report for reinternment. Christiansen's proclamation asserted that reinternment was a punishment for the widespread anti-German activities of Dutch veterans.[39] Actually, the measure had been conceived by Himmler as a means of drafting additional labor for the war effort, while punishing the Dutch for their resistance activities, which had flared up early in 1943.[40] Resistance to this reinternment order was so great that only 8,000 persons reported.[41]

On May 6, 1943, Commissioner-General Schmidt ordered all males between eighteen and thirty-five, with the exception of certain categories, to register with the State Employment Office for work in Germany.[42] On the basis of this registration, the Employment Office called up men born in the years 1922 through 1924 and canceled exemptions for these age groups, except those given to students and mine workers. This time even agricultural workers were included. In June and July of 1943 alone, about 65,000 young Dutchmen were deported.[43] Despite this initial success, only 148,000 Dutchmen were taken to Germany in the entire year 1943, according to official statistics.

Partly because of objections raised by the Dutch civil service and partly because of poor results, the Germans did not expand the system of deporting entire age groups.[44] Instead they established an elaborate system of exemptions in August 1943, aimed at registering employees and workers and culling out for deportation those not performing essential war work.[45] However, through the cooperation of the Resistance, employers, and patriotic officials in government services, the preparation and filing of these exemption records were delayed and confused to such an extent that the so-called ZS-campaign (Zurückstellungsverfahren) failed.[46] It continued, industry by industry, until the summer of 1944, but only 20,000 new workers were deported to Germany from January to July 1944.[47]

After the German retreat from France and Belgium in August 1944, the emphasis shifted again. Now German policy was dominated by military considerations. Construction of defense fortifications against the advancing Allied armies required large amounts of local labor. Local German authorities ordered municipalities to furnish men for work on fortifications. From September on, the Germans conducted raids to get men for work of this sort, especially in the northeastern part of the country. In some instances they took local hostages to force men of working age to report. In Hengelo the police surrounded factories and abducted men working in the plants.[48]

In the large-scale raids of the last winter of the war, which were primarily security measures, the desire to recruit labor for work on fortifications and for the war industries in the Reich played a subsidiary part.[49]

The most successful of these raids was staged in Rotterdam on November 10 and 11, 1944. One the morning of November 10 the Germans sealed off most of Rotterdam with military units and police. They distributed handbills and dispatched sound trucks ordering all men between the ages of seventeen and forty to pack up their gear and wait in the streets where they would be picked up. The order threatened punishment and confiscation of property for men attempting to hide. The Germans threatened to shoot persons attempting to escape. Those holding exemptions from the labor draft were also required to report.[50] The controlling authorities respected few of these exemptions and even deported members of the N.S.B. When German task forces searched dwellings, they dragged along any men they could find. Thus the methods originally used to capture Jews slated for deportation were applied to the population at large.

During this raid the Germans claimed to have taken 54,000 prisoners out of the estimated 60,000–70,000 Rotterdam men between the ages of seventeen and forty. Of these, they deported 40,000 to Germany and put the remainder to work in the eastern section of the Netherlands.[51]

Subsequent raids of this type in Delft, The Hague, and other cities did not yield as many prisoners because the Resistance and Radio Orange admonished men to go into hiding, and because news of the Rotterdam raids gave people a chance to prepare a hiding place. After the Rotterdam raids, few males between the ages of seventeen and forty dared show themselves on the street unless they were reasonably confident the Germans would respect their exemptions.

In addition to continuing individual raids throughout the winter, Seyss-Inquart published a general order on December 24, 1944, requiring men between the ages of sixteen and forty to register for the labor draft between January 4 and January 7.[52] A new system of exemptions was to be based on this registration. Knowing that they could no longer rely on the Dutch Employment Service, the Germans assigned to their own personnel the job of registration and granting exemptions.[53]

The main purpose of this final effort was to register as many men as possible and to utilize them for military production, construction of fortifications, and the clearing of railroad lines which were under heavy Allied bombardment. In general, men from western Holland were to be taken to Germany while those in the eastern Netherlands were put to work on fortifications within the country.[54]

The Dutch government in London and the Resistance warned government agencies and employers against furnishing employment lists to the Germans and ordered individuals not to register. In the end, 50,000 out of an estimated potential 650,000 registrants reported and a few thousand were sent to Germany. Many were put to work in Holland. It has been estimated that the Germans deported approximately 100,000 men between November 1944 and April 1945.[55]

By the end of the war, between 300,000 and 400,000 Dutchmen were at work in the German Reich, exclusive of "genuine" prisoners of war and the deported Jews.[56] Of these Dutch workers, more than 5,000 perished in Germany.[57] The number of labor draftees represents the highest percentage of workers recruited for work in Germany from any occupied territory in the West, with the exception of Belgium.[58] This high percentage may be attributed in part to the fact that in 1940 a pool of skilled unemployed surplus labor existed which increased because of dislocations resulting from the occupation.

DESTRUCTION OF PRODUCTIVE CAPACITY

Until the Allied armies threatened to advance on Dutch territory in September 1944, the Germans had been eager to exploit the productive capacity and transportation facilities of the Netherlands. Once the Germans began to retreat from the occupied territories, however, Hitler ordered a "scorched earth" policy involving the removal to Germany or the outright destruction of industries and transportation facilities which might be of use to the Allies or to the reconstruction of Europe after a possible German defeat. He put the Wehrmacht in charge of executing this policy.[59]

Fortunately there was much resistance to this plan among the Germans, led by the Minister of Armaments and War Production, Albert Speer. Speer prevented complete execution of the destruction ordered by Hitler,[60] but German demolition and removal crews destroyed or shipped to Germany a large share of the industrial facilities and the transportation system of the Netherlands. It has been estimated that of the total quantity of goods and equipment taken to Germany during the five years of the occupation, about 70 percent in monetary value was taken away after August 1944.[61] Some of the worst demolitions took place in the harbor of Rotterdam, where, according to statements of the Netherlands government, approximately 40 percent of the total pier area and of the warehouse space was destroyed.[62]

After the outbreak of the railroad strike in September 1944, German authorities took most of the rolling stock of the Dutch railroads to the Reich. A postwar survey showed that between one-half and two-thirds of the country's passenger equipment had disappeared, while only 4 percent of its freight cars had been left behind.[63]

The large-scale inundations undertaken by the Germans, especially after the Normandy invasion, caused another serious, if temporary, loss of productive capacity. In instances where the authorities used fresh water, damage did not necessarily extend beyond one growing season. Where sea water was allowed to flood the land, reclamation of the soil was bound to take more time. In the final days of the war, the Germans also flooded the Wieringermeer, an area of fertile land in the province of Noord-Holland, located below sea level and reclaimed since the First World War. The inundations covered approximately 8 percent of the total agricultural acreage of the Netherlands. About one-third of the inundated soil was covered with sea water.[64]

According to estimates made by Dutch government sources after liberation, the total value of goods removed during the occupation totaled 3.6 billion guilders.[65] In 1945 the total cost of the German occupation was officially estimated to be 11.4 billion guilders (at the 1938 price level).[66]

DISTRIBUTION OF SUPPLIES

Responsibility for the issuance of ration books and the general management of rationing services rested with the Central Rationing Office (Centraal Distributie Kantoor) in the Department of Commerce, Industry, and Shipping.[67] The Department of Agriculture and

Fisheries administered the allocation of food supplies through its Service for Food Supply in Wartime (Dienst voor Voedselvoorziening in Oorlogstijd), entrusted to S. L. Louwes.[68] Both departments were headed by Secretary-General Hirschfeld.

After the surrender the population of the occupied territory engaged in a buying spree which stripped many stores of their supplies. It took the authorities some weeks to set up working machinery for comprehensive wartime rationing. During the summer and fall of 1940 they put the most important food items on the rationing list. By the end of the year 70 percent of the typical family diet was rationed. In August 1943, with the rationing of fruits and vegetables, 95 percent of the diet had come under rationing regulations.[69]

The average daily ration for adults from 1941 to the summer of 1944 was about half the average prewar consumption in terms of calories. It dropped by only about 15 percent during this period.[70] This average ration of between 1,500 and 2,000 calories, usually augmented by food secured outside of rationing channels, did not represent a famine level, but it led to the progressive weakening of human energy and resistance to disease.[71]

After September 1944 rationing was carried out on the local level. The size of the rations was related directly to the quantity of supplies at hand. Therefore rationing conditions varied widely from one region to another. The northeastern section of the country maintained a ration of approximately 1,300 calories.[72]

The heavily populated sections of the western seaboard, especially the big cities, suffered most during the final winter of the war. One factor responsible for the famine was the embargo on the shipment of food into western Holland imposed by Seyss-Inquart in an effort to break the railroad strike.* But even after he withdrew this embargo in October 1944, few carriers were available for shipping food into the western provinces, since barge owners were afraid that the Germans would confiscate their boats.[73] Dr. Hirschfeld, head of the Dutch economic administration, organized a special pool of barges by offering owners part of the food and fuel they carried and by promis-

---

* Seyss-Inquart's testimony, June 11, 1946, [10], XVI, 14; cf. Hirschfeld's testimony, June 14, 1946, *ibid.*, pp. 213–14. The Germans blamed the famine largely on the strike, but in fact a number of related factors were responsible for the distress.

ing protection against confiscation.[74] Unfortunately an unusually early and severe frost prevented Hirschfeld's efforts from bearing fruit in the autumn.

During the famine winter of 1944–45, public food services set up in 1940 for assisting needy persons assumed great importance in supporting the city population of western Holland. In Amsterdam, they served 300,000 people, or nearly 40 percent of the total population, during the peak of operations in March 1945. During the last weeks of the occupation, when the ration dropped below 500 calories in the big cities, supplies donated and shipped by the Swiss and Swedish Red Cross were distributed free through regular rationing channels.[75] Despite these efforts, the general health of the population in the cities of the western Netherlands deteriorated after October 1944, and serious illness and death from starvation occurred among people in institutions and among the old and the very poor.[76]

In the final months before surrender, the people of the cities of western Holland, especially children, women, and old men, scoured the countryside in an effort to barter with farmers for food. Some expeditions in search of food for the family took as long as two weeks. The black market flourished in the cities. A few days before the German capitulation, the Allies began to drop food from the air, to be distributed by regular rationing offices. This food, however, did not become available to the population until after liberation.[77]

Although food rationing was the part of the rationing program most vital to physical survival, practically all other consumer goods were also on the ration list. Many items such as clothing and shoes were unavailable by 1943. A variety of substitutes were invented for such items as tea, coffee, tobacco, and soap. Even these substitutes were rationed in 1943. Gas and electricity remained available until September 1944 at 75 percent of the prewar consumption. Until 1944 the authorities also succeeded in maintaining coal distribution at approximately two-thirds of the prewar level.[78]

Despite the vigorous attempts of the German and Dutch administration, many consumer goods found their way into the black market, which served German as well as Dutch customers. During the final winter of the war, reliance on the black market became a necessity for the urban population. During this period black-market prices rose to extraordinary heights, sometimes to more than one hundred times the official rate, and frequently barter arrangements had to be made instead of payment in cash.[79]

WAGES AND PRICES

In order to ensure an equitable distribution of goods and services, the German administration made an effort to keep price and wage levels reasonably stable. Otherwise inflation would have prevented the poor from buying the food to which their ration books entitled them. This stabilization was not an easy task because of the basic imbalance of the economic situation. The German war effort claimed an increasing share of the Dutch national product. German agencies paid Dutch factories and workers for services rendered, but they did not provide goods for which the Dutch people could spend their earnings. The total value of exports to Germany exceeded that of imports by 6.73 billion guilders between January 1940 and December 1944.[80] The circulation of paper money increased almost fourfold from April 1, 1941, to May 1, 1945.[81] Bank accounts and investments increased likewise.

Fiscal authorities attempted to curb these inflationary tendencies in three different ways. In the first place, they increased the rate of taxation in such a way that the annual income from taxation of the national government almost doubled from 1940 to 1944.[82] This method of siphoning off surplus purchasing power also helped to balance the national budget, which showed a marked deficit due to payments made to the occupying power.

As a second defense against inflation, the authorities set up machinery to control prices. After the surrender in 1940, they froze prices at the prewar level.[83] Later in the year they permitted limited price increases designed to pass on to the consumer the increased cost of production. In November 1940, Seyss-Inquart established the Office of the Price Commissioner, whose chief function was the enforcement of existing price regulations.[84] In 1942 the Commissioner, a National Socialist, took over complete policy control of price adjustments.[85]

On the whole, German and Dutch authorities succeeded in preventing a runaway inflation for legal purchases. By June 1944 the average cost of living computed for eight cities had risen by approximately 50 percent over the base year 1938–39. The cost of food rose by about 60 percent during the same period.[86] This increase did not constitute a severe threat to the Dutch consumer, since a larger proportion of the family budget could be allocated to food purchases, inasmuch as few other goods were available.

Control of wages constituted the third check on inflation. In 1940 German officials froze wages as soon as they took over. After a temporary preoccupation with the prevention of wage and salary cuts due to war dislocations, the administration set up a procedure for orderly wage increases. In November 1940 it assigned to the Commission of Labor Arbitrators the authority to grant wage raises.[87] In October 1942 Seyss-Inquart appointed a Labor Commissioner vested with complete authority over working conditions in Holland.[88]

As a rule, wages did not rise quite proportionately to the increase in prices, although conditions varied widely in different occupations. The Germans used the power to fix wages as a means of directing the flow of labor. Therefore white-collar wages increased least while agricultural wages showed the greatest increase (90 percent) between the fiscal year 1938–39 and May 1945. The increase of industrial wages between 1939 and the first half of 1945 averaged between 35 and 50 percent.[89] Thus a fairly orderly adjustment of wage and price levels was accomplished, although certain population groups, such as older persons living on fixed incomes, and others who did not receive wage or salary adjustments commensurate with increases in the cost of living, found it difficult to make ends meet.

CHAPTER SIX

The National Socialist Movement
of the Netherlands

The National Socialist Movement of the Netherlands (Nationaal-Socialistische Beweging der Nederlanden, or N.S.B.), under the leadership of Anton A. Mussert, had been founded in 1931. In the 1937 elections for the States General, 4.2 percent of the total vote cast went to the N.S.B., a significant drop from the 7.9 percent obtained in the 1935 elections for the provincial parliaments. In the provincial elections of 1939, the N.S.B. popular vote decreased further.[1] In 1939 the N.S.B. held four seats in the Second Chamber.

THE MIDWAY POSITION OF THE N.S.B.

During the occupation, the National Socialist Movement of the Netherlands occupied a dual position. In one sense it was the passive object of German machinations, a tool to be employed while useful and to be discarded when its services were no longer needed.[2] In this respect, Dutch National Socialists may be regarded as merely another segment of the Dutch people, exploited by the occupying power for the special purpose of achieving the ideological integration and political compliance of the Dutch nation and of obtaining assistance for the war effort.

In another sense, however, the N.S.B. was a real force in the life of the Dutch community, and its activities were often the focus of more attention than were the activities of the German authorities. The latter view of the N.S.B. is most pertinent to this study, since during the occupation it was uppermost in the minds of the Dutch people. The majority of the population viewed the N.S.B. as a party of traitors which collaborated with the German authorities for its own selfish ends.[3] This popular view of the N.S.B. makes it preferable to discuss the National Socialist Movement together with the German administration as part of the enemy rule to which the population responded.

THE LEADER: ANTON ADRIAAN MUSSERT

To a large degree, the character of the N.S.B. was colored by the personality and ideas of its founder. Anton Mussert was born in 1894 of middle-class parents, whom he lost at an early age. He married his aunt, who was fifteen years his senior.[4] After one year of volunteer service in the Dutch army during the First World War, he studied and later practiced engineering. At the age of thirty-three he was appointed to the position of chief engineer in the public works department (Waterstaat) of the province of Utrecht. He held this position successfully until his dismissal for political activity in 1934.[5]

In 1931 Mussert founded the N.S.B. From 1934 on, he devoted himself exclusively to his political activities. He did not stand for election, but supervised operations of the N.S.B. from his headquarters in Utrecht. He was arrested in May 1945, placed on trial the following November, and sentenced to death for treason. After his appeal had been turned down, he was executed on May 7, 1946.[6]

In 1940 Mussert was a balding, heavy-set man with a square head and slightly protruding eyes. He liked to strut about stiffly and to strike histrionic poses reminiscent of Mussolini, whom he resembled considerably even in body structure and height. Mussert was not a dynamic and incisive person. He did not always command the respect or control the actions of his associates,[7] and he failed to cope with opposition to his policies within the N.S.B. It is to be doubted that he understood the full implications of the doctrines he preached, or the ultimate results of his almost complete compliance with the wishes of the occupying power. On the other hand, he was not a cheap opportunist. Toward the end, he dared to confront the German administration with its broken promises, and he remained faithful to certain basic principles in his ideology, even though on specific issues he usually yielded to German demands.[8]

Mussert's nationalism was the mainspring of his actions. In 1940 he envisioned a Greater Netherlands (including Belgian Flanders), with a population of fourteen million people, to be ruled by him.[9] He fervently opposed the annexation of Holland to Germany and wished to preserve the cultural and political identity of a Greater Netherlands allied with the Reich, as attested by the following entry in his diary, dated June 9, 1940:

> It became apparent to me [in a conversation with S.S. General Gottlob Berger] that the highest S.S. leadership considers the Dutch people Germans. It is terrible! What will come of it? If I resign I play the game of those who want to annex our people. . . . May God permit that I can reach the Fuehrer.[10]

Throughout the occupation Mussert tried to achieve this goal of eventual independence for the Netherlands by submitting to Hitler's every demand. There is every reason to assume that Mussert was genuine in his opposition to the annexation of the Netherlands to Germany, especially since annexation would have frustrated his personal aspiration to become the leader of an independent nation.

In 1940 Mussert submitted to Seyss-Inquart a plan designed by his legal adviser, J. H. Carp, to place Mussert at the head of the Dutch state through dismissal of the existing Council of State, the body charged by the Constitution with the appointment of a regent in the event of a vacancy.[11] A new Council of State made up of National Socialists and others sympathetic to Mussert could then appoint Mussert regent, since, according to Carp's interpretation, the position of head of state had been left vacant by the departure of the Queen.

Seyss-Inquart declared this plan too far-reaching,[12] but this did not prevent Mussert from reviving it in 1942 in his quest for power.[13]

THE DOCTRINE

The ideas and principles of the N.S.B. originally were more closely related to those of Italian fascism with its restorative tendencies than to those of German national socialism with its essentially nihilistic dynamism.[14] During the years immediately preceding the outbreak of the Second World War, however, the Party increasingly drifted toward the German Nazi ideology. The party platform of the N.S.B. called for a "strong government, national self-respect, discipline, order, and solidarity of all classes of the population and the precedence of the national interest over that of groups, and that of groups over the self-interest of the individual . . ."[15]

Such a government was conceived as deriving its power from the will of the leader rather than from the consent of the people as expressed in an election. It was supposed to serve as an arbiter of social and economic conflicts, and to organize industry and labor into corporative organizations, with final decisions left to the government. The national economy was to be planned by the government in the interests of labor and industry, which were conceived as harmonious. This arbitration and planning was considered to replace the class struggle as a method of resolving conflicting interests.[16]

The party platform emphasized a traditional patriotism based on pride in Dutch historical accomplishments, especially during the seventeenth century, the Golden Age of Holland. For instance, the N.S.B. adopted an expression used by seventeenth-century Dutch sailors, *"Houzee"* ("Hold steady"), as its official party greeting.[17] This sense of patriotism prevented Mussert and the Party from committing the treasonable acts and widespread fifth-column activities during the five days' war in 1940 which popular belief had attributed to them. In fact, Mussert expelled from the Party a few leaders, domiciled in Germany, who organized assistance for the German invasion.[18] The Party also officially opposed the use of N.S.B. members as undercover agents of the German police, because it was felt that they should not inform against their countrymen. Nevertheless, many members of the N.S.B. did serve the German police in that and in other capacities.[19]

The party platform included a statement in favor of freedom of religion. It recognized Christianity as one of the foundations of Dutch national existence.[20] Mussert, not a practicing Christian himself, did not acknowledge fundamental contradictions between Christianity and his brand of national socialism.[21] However, the National Socialists did not want churches to concern themselves with social and political affairs.[22]

During the early years the party platform contained no reference to race theories. The N.S.B. accepted Jews in its ranks, though many N.S.B. members were anti-Semites. As German influence increased, the Party began to adopt race theories and to attack the Jews as a group. After the invasion, the N.S.B. became openly anti-Semitic.[23] It applauded, and its members assisted, the persecution of the Jews.

THE ORGANIZATION OF THE MOVEMENT

The National Socialist Movement of the Netherlands operated independently of the German National Socialist Party (N.S.D.A.P.), although the two organizations sometimes had common meetings and activities.[24]

The Leader (De Leider) stood at the head of the Movement, assisted by a headquarters staff located in Utrecht. Most persons on the staff were loyal to Mussert personally and represented his views.

Territorially, the N.S.B. in the Netherlands was divided into fourteen districts, one for each of the eleven provinces, and one for each of the three big cities, Rotterdam, Amsterdam, and The Hague. It also had two districts in Germany and one in Belgium. Seventy-two "circles" (*kringen*) were designed to conform to regions with common historical backgrounds. "Groups" forming the next tier in the administrative hierarchy usually covered territories with between 7,000 and 15,000 inhabitants. The smallest units were "blocks," including between 100 and 500 people.[25]

Membership in the N.S.B. carried an obligation to pay dues assessed on the basis of personal income. All party members were required to contribute to such causes as the Winter Help and the National Socialist Welfare Organization. They also were expected to give generously of their time to party duties. Vending the party publication was considered one of the most important tasks of party members.[26] The common form of address between party members was that of "comrade."

The Movement also had its own basic literature, presenting its doctrines. Among its major publications was Mussert's pamphlet *De Bronnen van het Nederlandse Nationaal-Socialisme* ("The Sources of Dutch National Socialism"), published in 1937. The weekly *Volk en Vaderland* was considered Mussert's personal mouthpiece and his editorials were the current guideposts of the Movement. Two selections from these editorials were published as separate brochures. The N.S.B. daily *Het Nationale Dagblad* was edited by one of Mussert's opponents within the Party, Rost van Tonningen, until the latter's removal from the editorship in November 1940. The official party history was C. van Geelkerken's *Voor Volk en Vaderland*, first published in 1941, on the occasion of the tenth anniversary of the founding of the N.S.B.[27]

In its propaganda the N.S.B. almost always supported German policies. In the summer of 1940 it echoed German assertions that the pre-invasion government had failed to maintain its neutrality by leaning toward the Allies.[28] Mussert maintained that the dynasty and the former government had ceased to exist after the desertion of its members to England,[29] and that the state of war between Germany and the Netherlands had ended with the surrender of May 14, 1940. He tried to impress the Dutch people with the fact that the acceptance of national socialism and of his own leadership was a precondition of cooperation between Holland and the Reich,[30] and pointedly cited Czechoslovakia as an example of what had happened to a country unwilling to read the signs of the times.[31]

Throughout the occupation the N.S.B. attempted to direct a stream of propaganda at the Dutch people, designed to persuade them to join the Movement. Posters in public places praised the cause of the N.S.B. and encouraged enlistment in one of the formations of the Party. The publications of the N.S.B. were sold aggressively, often by calling on people in their homes.

Like the German Nazi Party (and other totalitarian organizations) the Movement held public meetings designed primarily to impress party members and the public with its strength. On such occasions stage effects were planned carefully.[32] A sea of flags, careful blending of different uniforms, and operations of claques applauding the leader all were ingredients of successful meetings. The Movement held an annual rally in the country in May or June. These meetings usually culminated in demonstrations of loyalty to Mussert, who was carefully placed in the spotlight, while other prominent leaders often were deliberately excluded. Mussert's speech to his followers was the climax of the event.

Despite all these efforts the N.S.B. did not grow into a true mass movement. Soon after the beginning of the occupation, it launched a drive to increase its modest membership of 33,000 adherents. According to its own public claims, the N.S.B. had a peak membership of 100,000 or more.[33] At his trial, however, Mussert placed the figure at approximately 80,000.[34] Postwar investigations indicate a membership of 50,000 by the end of 1940.[35] This was a weak basis for the national government which Mussert aspired to establish.

AUXILIARY ORGANIZATIONS

The Party had a number of auxiliary organizations, many of which were of a paramilitary character. The largest of these was the Defense Troop (Weer-Afdeling, or W.A.). In August 1941 membership in the Defense Troop was made compulsory for all male members of the N.S.B. between the ages of eighteen and forty.[36] This organization was modeled upon the German S.A., and supposedly designed to protect individual party members and their property as well as party meetings and offices.[37] Frequently the W.A. was used to terrorize political opponents,[38] and to demonstrate the might of the N.S.B., particularly during the first year of the occupation. Even Rauter considered the aggressiveness of the W.A. excessive.[39]

After the shooting of a W.A. man in September 1940, Mussert established the Netherlands S.S. (Nederlandse S.S.),[40] supposedly to protect party members against armed attacks,[41] but actually in response to pressure from Himmler and Seyss-Inquart.[42] Many members of the S.S. served on a full-time basis and subsequently transferred to military units which fought on the Eastern front and elsewhere.[43]

Its leaders conceived of the Netherlands S.S. as an integral part of the German S.S., which they considered to be the advance guard for the establishment of the Greater German Reich. The Netherlands S.S. advocated the racial theories of Himmler and Rosenberg, and required its members to prove their Aryan descent back to the year 1800, as did its German counterpart. Although the Netherlands S.S. formally was a part of the N.S.B., and therefore was subject to Mussert, its members were obliged to swear an oath of allegiance to Hitler as the Greater German Leader.[44] Actually, Mussert had practically no control over the S.S., and the organization became the base of operations for his radical opponents within the Party.[45] The Commander (Voorman) of the Netherlands S.S. was J. H. Feldmeyer, who served in the German campaign in the Balkans in the spring of 1941 and, later, on the Russian front. He became one of Mussert's chief antagonists within the N.S.B. He was killed in an attack by Allied planes in February 1945.[46]

In November 1943 Seyss-Inquart and Mussert established the Netherlands Home Guard (Nederlandse Landwacht), supposedly to protect party members against assassination. The Home Guard, headed by an Inspector-General, carried arms provided by Rauter. Its members used the German salute and swore an oath of loyalty to Adolf Hitler. Mussert's second in command, Van Geelkerken, was appointed Inspector-General. The Home Guard began its activities in March 1944.[47]

The Home Guard occupied a dual position with respect to the N.S.B. and the German administration. In the original decree, Seyss-Inquart characterized it as a defensive organization of the N.S.B. After the war, Mussert declared that he had intended to use the Home Guard exclusively for the protection of party members. From the beginning, however, Rauter used it as an auxiliary police force, as the initial decree authorized him to do.[48] In the last winter of the war[49] he even tried to employ it as a combat troop.* Mussert was most unhappy about this development since it deprived him of all control over the organization. In December 1944 he asked Van Geelkerken to resign as Inspector-General. When Van Geelkerken refused, Mussert dismissed him from the N.S.B. But Rauter, with Seyss-Inquart's backing, and after temporarily suspending Van Geelkerken, continued to keep him in command in spite of Mussert's protests.[50]

Soon after its creation, the Home Guard became notorious for reckless conduct, especially for looting. Members of the Home Guard often became objects of assassination attempts. But at his trial, Seyss-Inquart praised the effectiveness of the Home Guard in preventing further assassinations of members of the N.S.B.[51]

The N.S.B. also encouraged its members to join military units

---

* In April 1945 a few hundred Home Guard members rebelled against their use for military service. After a brief internment in Amersfoort concentration camp, they were released with the promise that they would be employed against "internal enemies" only.

other than its own paramilitary organizations. The earliest of these was the S.S. Standarte Westland, a volunteer unit of the Waffen-S.S., formed in 1940.[52] In July 1941 General H. A. Seyffardt, a former Chief of the General Staff of the Dutch Army, established the Netherlands Volunteer Legion (Vrijwilligerslegioen Nederland) to fight under Dutch officers and its own national flag.[53] Actually, it turned out that the assurances of autonomy were empty promises. The Commander of the Legion was a German, and so were many of the other officers. Eventually, the Legion was dissolved and its units integrated into the Waffen-S.S.[54]

The N.S.B. also assisted in recruiting for the Territorial Guard (Landstorm), established in March 1943. This was a military formation designed to defend the occupied territory against internal and external enemies.[55] Despite promises that the Territorial Guard would be used only within the Netherlands, it saw service in Belgium, in September 1944, during the Allied advance to the north.[56]

By 1943 a sizable proportion of N.S.B. members of military age were in the service of the German war effort. In a note written in August 1943 Van Geelkerken claimed that out of 35,000 men under forty-five years of age who were party members, 23,700 were participating in the war effort.[57] After the war the total number of volunteers in combat service was estimated to have been over 25,000, one-third of whom were killed.[58] A 1960 estimate places the number of volunteers who lost their lives at 10,000.[59]

THE RADICAL WING OF THE PARTY

Within the ranks of the N.S.B. a numerically small but influential group of men opposed many of Mussert's policies. This minority was headed by M. M. Rost van Tonningen, an economist by training, who had worked for the League of Nations in the thirties.[60] Rost was a brilliant and hard-working radical who despised Mussert's moderation and mediocrity. Somewhat unstable, he had great ambitions and hoped eventually to replace Mussert with German help.[61] Within the German administration, Rost had the backing of Rauter and Himmler. Even Seyss-Inquart characterized him as "ideologically perfectly adequate and adjusted to the Germanic idea."[62]

In 1940, in his attempt to supersede Mussert, Rost van Tonningen tried to build up a National Socialist labor movement. When Seyss-Inquart appointed him Commissioner of the Socialist and Communist parties in July 1940,[63] it turned out that Rost was unable to secure sizable support. Therefore the German administration, partly at the insistence of Commissioner-General Schmidt, decided to work with Mussert and the N.S.B. rather than with Rost and his associates. Rost van Tonningen's political influence with the High Commissioner decreased in the sense that he never again was seriously considered for the highest political office. Nevertheless, Seyss-Inquart continued to use his considerable talents.[64]

In November 1940 Rost van Tonningen had to give up the editorship of the *Nationale Dagblad,* the daily publication of the N.S.B. When the Socialist and Communist parties were dissolved in 1941, Rost's function as their Commissioner ceased. In March 1941 Rost was appointed successor to L. J. A. Trip, Acting Secretary-General of Finance and President of the Netherlands Bank.[65] He even may have had ambitions to become eventually the Reich Minister for Economic Affairs.[66]

Throughout most of the war, Rost continued to intrigue against Mussert and remained a power within the Party. In February 1943, for the sake of appearances, Mussert appointed him to the Secretariat of State.[67] In 1944 Rost van Tonningen volunteered for service with the Landstorm and received training with the Waffen-S.S. After a few months' service, he resumed his civilian career.[68] In the winter of 1944–45 he came out openly for annexation, and Mussert dismissed him from the Party.[69] Rost was arrested after the Liberation, and in June 1945 succeeded in his second attempt to commit suicide.[70]

Apart from the conflict of personal ambitions, two major points of ideological difference separated Mussert's "moderate" majority from Rost van Tonningen's "radical" minority. In the first place, the "radicals" opposed the establishment of an independent Dutch government under Mussert. Instead, Rost van Tonningen and his associates advocated complete integration of the Netherlands into the Greater German Reich and the introduction of German language, culture, and institutions.[71] Members of the S.S. group ridiculed the national pride which Mussert attempted to foster.

The second major point of difference was the rejection by the radicals of Mussert's concept of an authoritarian government, bound by law and guaranteeing freedom of religion. Instead, the radicals subscribed to Himmler's brand of dynamic mysticism which subordinated law and government to the biological maintenance and improvement of the superior race. Like Himmler and Rosenberg, the "radicals" despised Christianity as a softening and corrupting influence, interfering with the creation of the new Nordic man. Because of its racial concepts, the S.S. faction was especially uncompromising in its anti-Semitism. Its weekly *Storm* became the foremost mouthpiece of anti-Semitic propaganda in the Netherlands.

In the German camp each of the two factions had its spokesman. Mussert was backed mainly by the German party organization (the N.S.D.A.P.), represented in the Netherlands by Commissioner-General Schmidt and his successor Ritterbusch, and at the Fuehrer's Headquarters by Martin Bormann. Rost van Tonningen and his associates had the backing of the German S.S., with Rauter as its local representative and Himmler as its supreme leader. On the whole, Seyss-Inquart backed Schmidt and Mussert, although Mussert felt that the High Commissioner gave the N.S.B. insufficient support.[72] At any rate, whatever the outcome might have been in the event of a German victory, the German civilian administration in the Netherlands continued to cooperate officially with Mussert and the N.S.B. This was true in spite of the fact that the radical leaders of the Home Guard and the Germanic S.S. retained their influence with Rauter and their control over these organizations.

MUSSERT AND HITLER

In order to present his views to the Fuehrer, Mussert secured four interviews with Hitler between 1940 and 1944. In preparation for the first of these meetings, which took place on September 23, 1940, Mussert drew up a plan for a League of Germanic Peoples composed of Germany, the Scandinavian countries, and the Greater Netherlands, including Flanders. Hitler was to be the head of the League, but each member would have its independent National Socialist government and its own military establishment.[73]

During the interview Hitler expressed his interest in this plan, but carefully avoided any promise of eventual independence. Conversion of the Dutch people to national socialism was to be Mussert's main job. Hitler promised that the German administration in Holland would assist him in this task and would prepare the way for Mussert's seizure of power.[74] This was quite a concession (if it was meant sincerely) in view of the fact that Seyss-Inquart had characterized Mussert as a liberal nationalist with a capacity below that of the average *Gauleiter*.[75]

For this part, Seyss-Inquart carried out his assignment of assisting the N.S.B. In January 1941 he authorized a monthly subsidy to the N.S.B. "for uniforms."[76] The abolition of all other parties in 1941, including Fascist and National Socialist splinter groups, provided the N.S.B. with a political monopoly. In return Mussert faithfully supported the war against the Soviet Union and urged his followers to serve in the Netherlands Volunteer Legion and in other military units.[77] He administered to such volunteers[78] the oath of allegiance to Adolf Hitler, and in December 1941, during his second interview with Hitler, he personally swore the following oath of loyalty: "I swear to you, Adolf Hitler, as Germanic leader, loyalty unto death, so help me God."[79]

In 1942 Mussert made another major attempt to be named head of government, this time with support from Seyss-Inquart and Schmidt.[80] However, he was refused again in his third interview with Adolf Hitler, which took place in December 1942 in the presence of Bormann, Himmler, and Seyss-Inquart. Hitler pointed to the difficulties of the Quisling government in Norway, which had to impose unpopular measures on the Norwegian people, as an additional reason for keeping the reins of government in German hands.[81] He did say, however, that he considered Mussert the leader of the Dutch people. He also promised that no German agency in Holland would be allowed to oppose the policies of the High Commissioner. This was meant as an assurance that Himmler and Rauter would stop their open advocacy of annexation.[82] Even before this conversation Seyss-Inquart formally announced the recognition of Mussert as the "Leader of the Dutch People."[83] In order to implement his new function, Mussert formed a "cabinet" called the Political Secretariat of State of the N.S.B. (Staatspolitiek Secretariaat der N.S.B.).

On January 30, 1943, Seyss-Inquart ordered the German administration to consult with the Secretariat of State on all important administrative measures, especially on the matter of new appointments,[84] and authorized an annual contribution of one million guilders for operation of the agency.[85] The Secretariat of State, however, had no operational authority over Dutch government agencies.[86]

In reality, recognition of the Secretariat of State was only a token concession. As a matter of fact, Mussert's influence began to wane from the middle of 1943. The death of Commissioner-General Schmidt in July 1943 deprived Mussert of his strongest advocate within the German hierarchy. Himmler's appointment as Minister of the Interior led to an increase in the power of the S.S. in the Reich and in the occupied territories. Furthermore, the need for increasing exploitation of the Netherlands as part of the intensified German war effort and the revelation of the temper of the occupied nation in the May strike cooled German eagerness to convert the Dutch people to national socialism with the help of the N.S.B.

In his final interview with Hitler in December 1943, Mussert failed to obtain additional concrete promises of independence. The Fuehrer merely assured Mussert that he would not impose German culture on the Dutch people and that he was prepared to maintain freedom of religion. He was more vague than ever about the final political solution.[87]

After this last interview, Mussert became increasingly aware that, with the worsening of the war situation, exploitation of Holland for the war effort had become the overriding objective, and that the Germans cared less than ever about the feelings of the Dutch people and the N.S.B. In public, however, Mussert continued to back the German war against the Allies. In December 1944 he submitted to Adolf Hitler another memorandum dealing with a revised concept of his League of Germanic Peoples.[88]

During the September 1944 panic he showed courage and integrity. As a result, his personal prestige with the German administration increased, though his actual power did not.[89] After Hitler's death and just before the Liberation, Mussert drew up a last declaration of loyalty to Adolf Hitler, which was never published.[90] At his trial he continued to maintain that "Hitler did not favor the imperialistic policy of annexation, but the men around him did, and his entourage pushed this imperialism through against his will."[91] He never admitted, and perhaps never knew, how wrong his estimate of Hitler was, and how the Fuehrer would have dropped him with little consideration in the event of a German victory if such a move had suited his purposes.[92]

Mussert never fully understood the nature of the forces behind German national socialism with its mysticism and essential nihilism. Like Mussolini and other Fascist dictators, he represented restorative forces which sought to achieve their own objectives through alliance with a dynamic movement which was bound in the end to destroy all independent values.

PART THREE

The Response of
the Dutch

CHAPTER SEVEN

The Response of the People at Large and the Two Great Strikes

It is necessary to use caution in attributing specific attitudes or actions to a nation of more than eight million men, women, and children. Few comments made with regard to such a group apply to all members. But such statements as "The American people were shocked by the Japanese attack on Pearl Harbor" or "The Dutch people rejoiced at the liberation of their country from the German rule" are meaningful descriptions of an actuality, even though they are neither inclusive nor literally correct. Such a generalized description is needed, along with a discussion of the reaction of special groups to German policies because, as in the case of the two great strikes, no one group can be assigned responsibility for certain attitudes and actions.

A description of the responses of the people at large requires reference to Dutch family life because family values played an important role in determining individual attitudes and reactions to the occupation regime. In the years before the Second World War, Dutch family life seemed to have yielded very little to the disintegrating influences of twentieth-century civilization. The cohesion of the family was reinforced by the tendency of Dutch people to live in the towns where they were born.[1] The high average age at marriage (twenty-nine for men and twenty-six for women)[2] illustrated the importance of the family, even for its grown-up children. For this reason Dutch civilization has been called a "living-room culture."

The Netherlands was the only country in Western Europe where the birth rate did not decline in the decade before the Second World

War. Consequently, even urban families were relatively large. Moreover, employment of married women was not very common, especially during the period of unemployment in the decade before the outbreak of the war. Most mothers stayed at home and devoted themselves primarily to their families. Children also tended to live at home, at least until they married.

The strong ties between parents and children contributed to the acceptance of inherited values and mores by the young, even though they themselves frequently grew up in an increasingly modern industrial environment, the physical features of which seemed to put the validity of many inherited principles into question. This persistence of "old-fashioned" values often inhibited and frustrated the more adventurous young people. But on the positive side, the individual frequently found security and sympathy in his home, the lack of which is characteristic of a more mobile society.

DAILY LIFE IN THE OCCUPIED TERRITORY

The effects of the occupation on the daily lives of the Dutch people varied widely from one section of the population to another. Some continued in their normal daily routines until the final months of the war. In the early years particularly, day-to-day physical life, at least for the majority, remained much as it was during prewar days, except for changes imposed by rationing and curfew regulations. Gradually more citizens were affected by the measures of the occupying power until, by the last winter of the war, conditions created by the occupation and by the conduct of the war dominated the lives of nearly all inhabitants of the Netherlands.

As a rule, farmers and others living in rural areas were less exposed to the new regime than were their urban compatriots. Many people in the country seldom met German soldiers or policemen. Conversely, those living in the largest cities had more personal contact with German officials than did the populations of rural areas or of medium-sized and small towns. City-dwellers saw the N.S.B. in action oftener, and they suffered more from rationing because they could not secure supplementary food directly from producers.

Personal family situations also influenced the pattern of popular reaction to the occupying power. Jews, Communists, and families of young men forced to work in Germany were threatened most directly from the beginning. Relatives of persons engaged in clandestine activities, or arrested as hostages, had similar concerns. But the majority had little reason to fear for the safety and well-being of fathers, husbands, or sons until the intensified labor draft in 1943.

Material shortages brought about the most tangible changes in daily routines, particularly in the cities. Life became even more family-centered than before the war. Blackout and curfew kept people at home. Travel became more difficult since tires wore out and bicycles were hidden, trains were overcrowded, and streetcars did not run after dark. Moreover, the variety and quality of commercial entertainment decreased, although attendance at moving picture theaters and athletic events almost doubled from 1941 to 1943,[3] despite admonitions of the clandestine press to stay away from such public affairs and to boycott Nazi films. The need for escape was too great.[4]

Within the home itself living conditions became more crowded. In the winter more families than before the war would live in one room to save fuel. Families often had to share living quarters because of evacuations and the growing housing shortage.

The new emphasis on home life caused an increase in the sale of books, until in 1942 the paper shortage forced a reduction in publications. Historical and travel literature and textbooks were much in demand.[5]

The scarcity of goods, combined with a lack of desirable employment, led more persons into criminal activities. These were usually economic offenses, such as thefts. In 1942, for instance, almost three times as many criminal offenses were brought to the attention of the district courts as were noted in 1939.[6]

Material shortages also made housekeeping difficult, since shopping took more time and available goods were of poor quality. Meal planning required more effort and ingenuity. Soap and other household items became scarce, as did luxury items such as tobacco and alcohol. Mending became more important because of textile rationing. Many families began to raise their own vegetables to supplement rationed foods.

In some ways, children and teenagers were less affected by the occupation than were adults. Most schools continued as usual until the winter of 1944–45, and many young people were able to carry on their customary youth activities in church or athletic organizations. Even groups such as the Boy Scouts, which had been dissolved by occupation authorities, continued to meet informally. On the other hand, many youngsters from urban low-income families became victims of wartime demoralization, especially if their fathers worked in Germany.

Even the relative protection of young people from hardships of the occupation broke down during the final winter of the war, when many schools closed and teenage children frequently had to share the responsibility of finding food for their families. From June 1944 on, breakdown of the ordinary facilities of life affected people of all ages, particularly in the northwestern section of the country. Telephones were cut off after the invasion. Railroad schedules were limited, and eventually trains and streetcars ceased to operate. People stayed at home as much as they could, but those with business in nearby towns usually walked, tried to hitch rides on German army trains, or traveled by boat. The use of gas and electricity was progressively restricted until during the autumn and winter of 1944 these utilities were completely cut off in many areas.[7]

Meanwhile, the official fuel ration dropped to approximately one-third of that of 1940–41, and most families received only a fraction of their official allocation.[8] In desperation, people in the cities cut down trees in parks and streets, tore out streetcar ties, wrecked abandoned houses, such as those vacated by deported Jews, and stole any wood they could find.[9] During this period, nearly all the energy of the urban population went into securing food and fuel to ensure physical survival.

To many people in the occupied territory, declining health conditions presented an additional worry. The incidence of contagious diseases and of fatalities resulting from them increased throughout the war. In 1943 an epidemic of poliomyelitis swept the country. Tuberculosis become more prevalent, despite an expanded X-ray program. In 1944, diphtheria caused many deaths, since a virulent variety of the disease had been introduced from Germany.[10]

The death rate increased substantially in 1944 and early 1945, owing to the cumulative effect of undernourishment and the frequency of contagious disease. In Amsterdam so many people died that it became impossible to bury all corpses promptly, in view of the lack of transportation and coffins.[11] As a result of the famine of 1944–45, approximately 15,000 persons succumbed in the northwestern part of the Netherlands alone. The total number of deaths in 1945 was nearly twice that of 1939. At the same time, however, the birth rate mounted until 1944 and was only temporarily affected by the deprivations of the final months of the occupation. Consequently, the population of the Netherlands increased by almost half a million, or by about 5 percent, between January 1, 1940, and December 31, 1945, even though approximately 240,000 persons perished as a result of war and occupation.[12]

ATTITUDES BETWEEN THE SURRENDER AND
THE FEBRUARY STRIKE OF 1941

The attitudes of the Dutch population underwent a rapid change during the first few months of the occupation, when the German administration tried to follow a conciliatory course.

During the first days of the occupation, the population in general remained calm and undemonstrative toward German officials and soldiers. When German troops entered the cities after the surrender of May 14, the people usually lined the streets silently, without any particular show of feeling. As a rule, individual Dutch citizens did not fraternize with German personnel, but dealt with their conquerors in a businesslike manner when necessary. At first some Dutch citizens boycotted their German acquaintances who had been residents of the Netherlands before the war, because it was thought that German residents had given aid to the invading troops.[13] German soldiers often were disregarded or cold-shouldered by the population.

This passive attitude remained typical of the first weeks after the surrender, partly in reaction to the shock of unexpected invasion, the quick capitulation of the Dutch army, and the subsequent Allied collapse on the continent, and partly because the Germans did not seem too objectionable. Fear of arrests, searches, and deportations, which had led some people to take their own lives and others to burn anti-Nazi books during the night of the surrender, appeared to have been groundless.[14] There seemed reason to hope for mutual accommodation. However, general apathy lasted only a few weeks. In the middle of June the first violence between patriotic citizens and members of the N.S.B. flared up,[15] and the earliest widespread demonstrations of a new mood among the people occurred on June 29, the birthday of Prince Bernhard.

On that day, people all over the country demonstrated their allegiance to the House of Orange. In The Hague, thousands flocked to the Royal Palace, among them General Winkelman, to enter their names in the birthday register. Flags were displayed from private residences, bouquets were laid before royal statues, and many people wore carnations, Prince Bernhard's favorite flower, or orange-colored flowers in honor of the Prince. Carnation Day (Anjerdag), as the event was afterwards called, represented an early turning point in the attitude of the people toward the German regime and the N.S.B.[16] and may be considered the first major act of "symbolic resistance" in a period when "real" resistance appeared impossible.[17]

During the summer and autumn of 1940, patriotic activity increased. The tremendous influx of members into the Netherlands Union was a manifestation of growing anti-Nazi sentiment.[18] Street fights between patriots and members of the N.S.B. became frequent. The working class with its Socialist tradition was in some ways less subject to moods of defeatism than were some political leaders.[19] Its activity was attested by an N.S.B. report of a march through a working-class neighborhood in Rotterdam: "It rained tiles . . . and flowerpots and some other unmentionable household articles, with contents, from the windows. Here the words of Schiller become true: 'Da werden Weiber zu Hyänen' . . ."[20]

The Royal House became even more popular during the second half of 1940. Although there were no major demonstrations on the birthday of the Queen, August 31, which had been a national holiday before the war, the people invented new ways of demonstrating their loyalty. For a while, many wore pins made of coins bearing the picture of the Queen. Householders grew gardens displaying orange flowers or the three national colors, which were frequently destroyed by adherents of the N.S.B. Many newborn children were given the names of living members of the House of Orange.

Almost the entire population began to listen to Radio Orange, a quarter-hour broadcast in Dutch over the facilities of the B.B.C., introduced in July 1940 with a radio address by the Queen.[21] From this time on, the Queen's occasional speeches provided a source of inspiration, and Radio Orange became a force in shaping Dutch public opinion. Listening to the B.B.C. or to Radio Orange was in itself an act of resistance. By hearing the voices of the Queen, Churchill, and members of the government-in-exile, citizens could identify with the Allied world beyond the borders of the occupied territory.[22] Even occasional British bombing attacks failed to turn the population against the Allies.[23] This acceptance of the need for bombing German installations in Holland, and of the occasional mistakes made by Allied aviators, persisted throughout the war despite the fact that thousands of Dutch citizens became victims of these attacks.[24]

The rejection of the Nazi-inspired charity organization, Winterhulp Nederland, by the population was another illustration of growing anti-German and anti-Nazi sentiment during the first winter of the occupation. When the Winterhulp Nederland was established by the High Commissioner in October 1940 as a direct copy of the corresponding organization in the Reich, the Germans had succeeded in enlisting the support of many "respectable" Dutch officials and private individuals, including three Secretaries-General, the Director of the Netherlands Bank, all provincial commissioners, and some of the mayors.[25] Despite this support from official quarters, the population at large viewed the Winterhulp action as one more attempt to impose National Socialist institutions and practices. Therefore Winter Help drives were boycotted with increasing effectiveness, despite a variety of pressures employed by the organization. Thus boycott of the Winterhulp, like demonstrations on Carnation Day or joining the Netherlands Union, became a feasible form of protest against the occupying power and national socialism.

For three major reasons the mood of the population became more antagonistic toward the occupying power during the late autumn and winter of 1940–41. In the first place, the N.S.B. provoked antagonism. This was especially true of W.A. members who went about systematically stirring up trouble. In the second place, initial German measures against the Jews aroused resentment and frequently deep emotional revulsion and hatred of the Germans. Student strikes at Delft and Leiden protesting the dismissal of Jewish professors were symptoms of this sentiment, and, in turn, stimulated popular imagination.

Finally, the determination of the British to continue the war, and the British success in repelling the Nazi air attack in the autumn of 1940, provided some encouragement.

Other factors also induced greater antagonism toward the occupying power. The population was aware of the seizure of the "Indian Hostages,"[26] and of preventive arrests. Many were indignant over the imposition of rationing, since it was felt that the Dutch people were being deprived for the sake of the Germans. The working class in the major cities, at least, was particularly restless, partly because of Communist and Socialist influence and partly because the rise in the cost of living affected workers more severely than it did the wealthier citizens. Also there was much unemployment, and pressure to accept jobs in Germany was applied chiefly to the working class during this period. Illegal returnees from Germany spread stories about the poor conditions and warned their friends to stay out of the clutches of the Germans.[27]

By the beginning of the new year, even the German police recognized that "the Dutch population, which has been stirred up for months through pamphlets, handbills, chain letters, Radio London, and an organized whispering campaign, is drifting more and more into a dangerous anti-German and anti-N.S.B. attitude . . ."[28] It remained for the actions of the W.A. and the German police to set off the spark which led to the first major explosion.

THE FEBRUARY STRIKE

By early 1941 Amsterdam had become the center of political restiveness. The largest concentrations of Jews and of Communists could be found in the capital, and these groups were potential nuclei of opposition to the N.S.B.

The W.A. in Amsterdam, recently placed under a new Commander, engaged in blatantly provocative actions. In January the W.A. took upon itself to force owners of hotels and restaurants to display signs stating that Jews were not wanted as customers. Early in February National Socialist rowdies attempted to drag Jews from streetcars. A few days later, an effort of the W.A. to evict Jewish customers from a restaurant in the center of Amsterdam led to riots which spread all over the city.[29]

For self-protection, young men among the Jewish population started to form Action Groups (Knokploegen, or K.P.'s) which made contact with left-wing groups in the proletarian neighborhood located near the Jewish section, one of the few instances when Jewish and Gentile groups acted in concert during the occupation. At the same time, Senator Boehmcker, Seyss-Inquart's representative in Amsterdam, ordered the Commandant of the W.A. to stay out of the Jewish quarter.[30]

Despite these orders, a group of about forty W.A. men was sent into the Jewish quarter on February 11. The Nazis were badly beaten by a Jewish Action Group, and one of them, Hendrik Koot, died of his wounds. Rauter reported to Himmler that a Jew had bitten through Koot's jugular vein and sucked out his blood,[31] an obvious allusion to ritual murder.

The atmosphere in the capital remained tense during the ensuing days. On the day after the Koot incident, German authorities shut off the Jewish quarter and established the Jewish Council as a device for maintaining order among the Jewish population.[32] On February 15 demonstrations and incidents occurred in a variety of locations including one of the main thoroughfares of the capital.

On February 19 German police raided a Jewish ice-cream parlor which had been the headquarters of an Action Group. According to German reports, Jewish defenders sprayed the police with acid and it was alleged that a shot had been fired. From the German point of view, this was the most serious incident yet, because members of the German police had been attacked for the first time.[33]

In a consultation between the High Commissioner, Rauter, and Himmler, it was decided to arrest 425 young Jewish men between the ages of eighteen and thirty-five. These arrests were carried out by the Order Police on February 22 and 23 in two raids on the Jewish neighborhood. The brutality of these raids aroused widespread indignation in Amsterdam, as stories circulated about the humiliations inflicted on the arrestees and on others who happened to get in the way of police action.

This indignation was quickly utilized by the clandestine organization of the Communist Party. The Communists had been looking for ways of stirring up the working people of the country, especially in Amsterdam. In the autumn they had organized a successful agitation among the unemployed in public works projects (*werkverruim-ing*). The Communists had also been the organizing force behind the public demonstration of February 15. They had been leaders of another strike of Amsterdam shipyard workers on February 17 and 18, which had forced local German authorities to abandon the plan of deporting workers to Germany against their will.

When the arrests of the young Jews became known on Saturday, February 22, the local leadership of the Communist Party decided to organize a protest strike. In preparation for this, the Communists mimeographed thousands of pamphlets exhorting Dutch workers to cease work for one day in protest against the maltreatment of the Jews. The authors appealed to Gentile families to take Jewish children into their homes and to assist their Jewish countrymen wherever possible. Workers were urged to organize their neighbor-hoods against the W.A. The pamphlets also called for wage increases and for a raise in unemployment payments, and attacked members of the Jewish Council for collaboration with the Germans. This col-laboration was said to have sapped the defensive strength of Jewish workers.[34]

Strike leaders began agitation for a protest strike on Tuesday morning, February 25. They concentrated on the workers and em-ployees in the municipal services, which included a fairly large percentage of Communists. A special attempt was made to persuade streetcar conductors and drivers to go on strike, since it was felt that failure of the streetcars to make their daily runs would spread news of the strike. There was some hesitation among streetcar operators, but many cars never left the shed that morning, while others returned after their first run. By noon, all streetcar traffic had ceased. Word of the work stoppage spread quickly to other municipal shops and of-fices, and by the end of the day almost half of the municipal per-sonnel was on strike.[35]

The strike, however, was not limited to municipal enterprises. The first men in private industry to join the walkout in large numbers were metal and shipyard workers from large establishments in the northern section of Amsterdam who had taken part a week earlier in the successful conspiracy which obliged German authorities to abandon their plans for a forced labor deportation. By midmorning, practically all activity in these plants had ceased.

During the forenoon the strike spread to many other private establishments. It included white-collar workers as well as manual laborers. The absence of streetcars had given notice to the population that something unusual was in progress. Some people stayed at home, others walked to work. Later in the morning hundreds of those who were not working circulated in the center of Amsterdam, challenging others to join the strike. They also threatened streetcar operators who had taken out cars at the request of their superiors, and forced them to return to their barns.

During the late morning and early afternoon a number of demonstrations involving hundreds of people occurred in the center of Amsterdam. However, no serious incidents took place because the Dutch police did not interfere before noon. Even then the police used moderate methods in dispersing the crowds.

The outbreak of the strike took the German authorities completely by surprise. Seyss-Inquart, not expecting any trouble from the arrests in Amsterdam, had gone to Vienna, leaving Rauter in charge. After taking stock of the situation on Tuesday morning, Senator Boehmcker, Seyss-Inquart's representative in the capital, tried to persuade the Mayor of Amsterdam and the Acting Commissioner of Police to take energetic steps to suppress the strike, but did not receive the cooperation he wanted. Boehmcker also called A. Asscher of the Jewish Council and threatened further arrest of Jews if the strike did not stop the next morning. Asscher notified some of the major employers of this threat. At the same time Rauter prepared German police units for use in Amsterdam. Toward evening he began to move troops into the city. Some patrols used firearms and wounded a few persons. Rauter also had posters displayed to explain the arrests. The murder of Koot and the attack on the German police on February 19 were given as reasons for the action. The Commissioner-General ordered all inhabitants of the city to be indoors by 7:30 P.M. This curfew was generally obeyed, and the streets were deserted by early evening.[36]

Despite German threats, the strike did not end on Wednesday, February 26. Only in the municipal offices and installations in Amsterdam did the majority of workers return to their jobs. This was the result of an announcement by the Mayor, threatening dismissal and punishment for all persons who did not resume their work by

Wednesday morning. Even so, when streetcars started running again in the morning, the crowds interfered. Regular operations were resumed in the afternoon, when a policeman was stationed on each car.

The total number of strikers did not diminish, since additional citizens in private employment laid down their work on Wednesday. The strike also spread to towns outside of Amsterdam. Large crowds continued to demonstrate within the city. These constituted a serious threat to the occupying power, which could not tolerate a display of popular strength in defiance of its orders.

By Wednesday morning the German authorities felt that ruthless and quick action was needed, including the establishment of a state of siege during which harsher punishments would be meted out by summary courts. At that time civilian officials had no legal authority to declare a state of siege. Therefore the executive power in the province of Noord-Holland was transferred to the Commander of the Armed Forces in the Netherlands, who immediately declared a state of siege. Himmler authorized third-degree methods and the arrest and deportation of 1,000 strikers. After noon German police and S.S. troops began to patrol the streets of Amsterdam in greater numbers, making frequent use of firearms. Some persons were wounded when the police raided a meeting of street cleaners, called by the director of that service. Altogether, seven persons were killed in Amsterdam on the second day of the strike.[37]

The proclamation of the state of emergency and the ruthless actions of the German police made it obvious to most strikers that continuance of the strike would lead to much bloodshed. Furthermore, the organizers had spoken originally of a one-day protest strike, and employers had been urging their men to return to their jobs. Consequently, normal activities were resumed everywhere in Amsterdam by Thursday morning. But in some of the outlying towns it was noon before everyone had returned to work.[38]

In retaliation for the strike, the German police arrested over 100 Communist workers and others who were suspected of having instigated the action.[39] The German administration imposed fines on Amsterdam and on other municipalities where large numbers of work stoppages had occurred. Seyss-Inquart also dismissed the mayors of Amsterdam, Haarlem, and Zaandam, and other Dutch officials accused of making insufficient efforts to suppress the strike.

The February strike demonstrated the attitude prevalent in at least one section of the country toward the German administration, and specifically toward its anti-Jewish policies. The Communist leadership had been successful beyond expectations because the call for a protest strike appealed to many citizens who had no sympathy with the Communist Party. To those who had participated, the strike provided a sense of relief, since it represented an active repudiation of the German regime. Furthermore, the fact that the strike had developed into a protest against injustice inflicted on others, and was not aimed at the fulfillment of selfish demands on behalf of the strikers, lent a particular dignity to the action. The February strike demonstrated that "the race demagoguery of the Germans as well as the lies and party propaganda of the N.S.B. were a complete failure . . . [The Dutch] people knew how to judge . . . the lies about the Jews, the sanctimonious patter about the 'New Order' and the babbling about German 'socialism.' "[40] In the strike the working population of Amsterdam had discovered its own identity in defiance of the occupying power.*

Yet the strike also taught quite different truths. In the first place, the strength of the German police apparatus was clearly shown. It became apparent that open opposition to the enemy was not feasible if the occupying power chose to use force. This insight was one reason why no major popular demonstration occurred again in Amsterdam for the remainder of the occupation. In the second place, the strike failed to deflect the German administration from its anti-Jewish policies, but merely induced the authorities to publicize their anti-Jewish activities to a lesser extent.[†]

---

* On the other hand, the success of the strike also helped to reinforce Marxist illusions about the power of the working class under the occupation. (See [66], p. 7.)

† There has been some controversy over the role the Communist Party played in the February strike. The preceding presentation is based to a large extent on the work of B. A. Sijes, *De Februari-Staking* [208], published in 1954 in the series of monographs sponsored by the State Institute for War Documentation. Its author has been accused by conservative groups of giving too much credit to the Communist Party for the organization of the strike (interview with Hendrik Houthakker, August 1, 1954). On the other hand, the Communist Party attacked Sijes in 1954 for having given insufficient credit to the Party in his work on the February strike [246], pp. 22–23, and *passim*). In the absence of available evidence to the contrary, this writer is willing to accept Sijes' thesis that Communist workers provided the original impetus for the strike movement. The majority of strikers, of course, were not Communists but Socialists, or simply patriots who used this opportunity to protest against the German regime.

THE GROWTH OF ANTI-GERMAN SENTIMENT
MARCH 1941–MARCH 1943

In the two years after the February strike the sentiments expressed during the unrest in Amsterdam spread throughout the country. The sense that it might be possible to compromise with the occupying power faded as it became obvious that the fiction of a military occupation had been dropped and that the German administration was trying to impose the institutions of the Third Reich on the Netherlands. Repressive German actions taken in 1942 such as mass executions, the deceitful internment of army officers, and the start of Jewish deportations intensified anti-German sentiment.[41]

Despite this growth of hostility, fewer open expressions of popular sentiment occurred in these two years than in the ten preceding months. Total repression of political opinions outside of those represented by the N.S.B. made it impossible for opposition to be legally voiced. But while the majority of the population now tended to become increasingly antagonistic toward the occupying power, few people were willing to run serious risks through participation in "dangerous" clandestine activities. Furthermore, active opposition was discouraged by Allied defeats during 1942, when Allied fortunes were at their lowest ebb. Present and future seemed gloomier and more hopeless in Holland in 1942 than at any other time during the occupation, except for the last famine winter in western Holland.

During that year, Dutch hostility was expressed predominantly in acts of resistance which did not greatly endanger the perpetrators. Increasing numbers read and passed on to friends the underground papers, which were growing in number and scope. The population almost universally sabotaged the delivery of metal. Only between 5 and 10 percent of the coins in circulation were turned in.[42] In many factories working for the Germans, labor and management became more ingenious in practicing slow-downs.[43] In small ways, such as through monetary contributions, the population assisted victims of Nazi persecution, but it remained extremely difficult to find hiding places for Jews threatened by deportation. Patriotic employers and employees began to develop methods of protecting workers from the labor draft. A few local work stoppages occurred, such as the refusal of Limburg mine workers to work on Sunday.[44]

Thus a definite change in popular attitude toward the occupying power took place below a relatively placid surface. Since there was no longer any legitimate outlet for resentment and hatred, the problem now was how to oppose the German regime as vigorously as possible, within the bounds of reason and prudence. To many Dutch citizens, resistance became necessary in order to maintain self-respect, because the moral indefensibility of German policies had become manifest.

Intensification of the labor draft after Stalingrad threatened new sections of the population and faced them with the alternatives of submission and resistance. Recognizing this crisis, the underground press called upon patriots who previously had taken a passive attitude: "The time is ripe. It won't be many weeks before Hitler has his Black Marias ride again, or jumps on the youth of Holland in some other way to weld it into his infernal war machine . . . Then the moment will have come for us to pit our 'Total Resistance' against Hitler's 'Total War' . . . "45

THE APRIL-MAY STRIKE OF 1943*

This moment arrived on Thursday, April 29, when General Christiansen issued his proclamation ordering Dutch army veterans to report for reinternment in Germany.46 In an atmosphere of increasing tension this order precipitated the strike of 1943, perhaps the strongest demonstration of popular resistance during the occupation.

The strike started in the town of Hengelo, in the eastern province of Overijsel. This section contained a substantial concentration of industry, although even the largest plants had only a few thousand workers. Most of the factories had been unionized before the war, and former union officials continued to exercise considerable authority.47

At about noon on Thursday, General Christiansen's proclamation was distributed to the newspapers and to other news media. By the time Hengelo workers returned from lunch, a local printer's shop had posted the announcement in its window. Among the employees of

---

* It may be more appropriate to speak of the "April-May strikes" than of one strike, since work stoppages occurred in widely separated parts of the country. This terminology has been adopted by Professor P. J. Bouman in his authoritative treatise on the subject [195], on which this section is based to a large extent.

the largest Hengelo plant, the Stork Company, the news caused great unrest, particularly since the proclamation did not mention any exemptions for workers in armament industries. Directors of the Stork Company tried to find out by telephone whether their workers would be exempted, but could not secure a definite answer. The excitement was so intense that in most shops work was not resumed at all.

After the reinternment report had been confirmed, many workers began to leave the factory spontaneously, without direction from labor leaders. In one or two places encouragement from former union officials who believed this to be the moment to strike sufficed to induce people to lay down their work. The management did not make any effort to stop the exodus.

Word of the strike spread quickly throughout the town, especially since most industrial installations in Hengelo were located close together. Soon workers in other plants joined the walkout. By the middle of the afternoon practically all factories in Hengelo, except for one operated by Germans, had stopped working. Other local services, including municipal offices, followed suit. Strikers returning to their homes in surrounding villages spread the news through the countryside.[48]

People in other parts of the country heard of the strike by telephone. As early as Thursday afternoon, there was much agitation within several widely separated regions, such as the Limburg coal district and the Philips factories of Eindhoven. By Thursday night news of the strike had reached all but the most isolated parts of the Netherlands. On Friday morning work stoppages occurred in most sections, with the notable exception of Amsterdam, the heavily settled coastal regions, and the islands of Zeeland, Noord-Holland, and Friesland. The strike movement was strongest in the outlying provinces and weakest in the central regions, especially in the large cities and the province of Utrecht.

Friday, April 30, was the peak day of the walkout in urban areas. At that time, several hundred thousand persons were on strike, with the heaviest work stoppages occurring in the northeastern part of the country, in Limburg, and in the regions south and east of Rotterdam where industry and agriculture intermingled, as in Twente. On Saturday, the strike spread to a few new sections such as the island of Noord-Beveland in the province of Zeeland, and became more general in the easternmost portions of the provinces of Drente and Friesland.[49]

On Friday and Saturday the movement spread to agricultural regions. Peasants and milk truck drivers refused to deliver milk to the factories. On Friday, milk deliveries to cooperative dairy plants in the province of Friesland dropped by about one-third. On Saturday a little more than one-tenth of the normal quota was sent to the creameries.[50] In Friesland and other rural sections, some people, often teenagers, interfered with milk deliveries and poured out the milk they found on delivery trucks.

The outbreak of the strike in Twente caught the German police by surprise. Since Seyss-Inquart was away, as in February 1941, Rauter was left to deal with the situation by himself. When the extent of the movement became apparent, Rauter proclaimed a "police state of siege" (*Polizeistandrecht*). The regulations of this state of siege, threatening strikers and demonstrators with capital punishment, were brought to the attention of the population through thousands of posters. As a rule, Rauter did not arrest or sentence patriots, except in Twente, until after posting the emergency decree. When the posters had been put up, the German police proceeded to use force unless strikes ended immediately. The police made a considerable number of arrests and placed a few arrestees before police summary courts (*Polizeistandgerichte*). The summary courts usually sentenced the defendants to death, and the sentence was promptly executed. Executions were announced at once, a procedure that proved an effective means of intimidation. When such announcements seemed to impress the strikers, the German police sometimes released the remaining arrestees, or promised mercy for persons condemned to death if all strikers would return to work at once.[51]

Rauter also sent patrols into the smaller towns and rural areas. These forays intimidated townspeople more readily than they did strikers in rural districts where patriots gave warning by telephone that patrols were approaching.

At first the German police concentrated their forces on the most important strike centers. Since the walkout had started in Hengelo, Rauter immediately sent a unit of about 200 men there to patrol the city. After a number of conferences with the German authorities on Friday, plant directors and strike leaders saw little point in continu-

ing the walkout, and advised the personnel to this effect. By Saturday morning, work was resumed in all the large factories in Hengelo.[52]

In most other cities the strike movement was also on the wane by
Saturday. Many government officials returned to their offices at that
time. By Monday, May 3, work was resumed in most urban areas.

The Philips factory at Eindhoven, whose workers were considered
by Reich authorities to be especially anti-German, was a notable exception. The strike had started at Philips as late as Friday afternoon,
partly because the clandestine leadership had waited to ascertain
the intentions of railroad and postal employees. But on Saturday the
strike had spread throughout Eindhoven, despite the proclamation
of the police state of siege. Workers from Philips and other plants
even demonstrated on the streets. On Monday comparatively few
workers showed up at the plant. In order to suppress the strike
quickly, the German police set up a summary court in the office of
the Philips factories and sentenced seven persons to death. These
measures succeeded in getting many workers back to their jobs on
Tuesday, although even then there were a considerable number of
absentees.[53]

In two rural areas the strike continued after Monday, May 3. One
of these areas was Friesland, especially its northern seaboard, where
the strike was fairly general even on Monday, and where normal
work was not resumed until Friday, May 7. The other strike center
was an isolated section along the Big Rivers, in the province of Noord-
Brabant. In this region the strike sometimes had the appearance of a
revolt, with crowds demonstrating and attempting to liberate prisoners. Not until Saturday, May 8, were conditions back to normal in
this part of the country.[54]

In their suppression of the strike the German authorities proceeded with effectiveness. They carried out only as many executions
as they deemed necessary to intimidate the population of a given
section or town, but did not engage in large-scale acts of reprisal,
except for a number of random shootings by police patrols in the
northeastern provinces. Despite this "moderation," the German police executed approximately eighty patriots and killed about sixty
persons in random shootings.[55]

A comparison of the April-May strike with the February strike of

1941 shows a number of outstanding differences and similarities. Both strikes were conflagrations caused by an accumulation of resentment against the oppressive behavior of the occupying power. But by 1943 so many citizens had been affected by the measures of the German authorities that the strike reached a much larger number of people. This fact explains the almost nationwide character of the second work stoppage, which involved perhaps half a million people spread over many sections of the country.

Other differences between the two outbreaks are shown in the economic groups involved, in the motivation of those groups, and in the targets of strike action. Whereas in 1941 the bulk of the strikers had been industrial and municipal workers, in May 1943 the rural population played a significant part. In 1941 Communist and Socialist loyalties played an important role, but in 1943 much of the spontaneous motivation was provided by accumulated Calvinist and Catholic indignation at the injustice and godlessness of the German regime, particularly in agricultural regions. Unlike the 1941 strike, the strike of 1943 was directed primarily against the occupying power, with animosity against the N.S.B. playing only a subordinate role.

Similarities between the two strikes can also be cited. On both occasions factory workers set off the original spark, and both walkouts were aided by the sympathy of employers, especially in 1943. In factories run by German managers, the strike movement usually did not make much progress in either year. Like the earlier action, the strike of 1943 had tragic consequences for individual patriots. In May 1943 the German police again proved itself master of the situation and made it obvious that no uprising could prevail against the occupying power without external military assistance.

The events of April–May, 1943, showed that, after three years of German rule, the people of Holland had retained their patriotic identity and had not fallen victim to National Socialist propaganda. This sense of unity encouraged a rapid expansion of the resistance movement and the underground press. It supported young people who wanted to escape the labor draft. It also stimulated political awareness in the rural regions. Many more farmers began to offer shelter to people who wanted to go into hiding.

Yet the most significant outcome of the strike was its spiritual impact on the Dutch people themselves. In the words of an underground publicist, the April-May strike was "the greatest event since the capitulation. . . . For a few moments the fear psychosis was broken and we did not feel like subjects of a terror regime, but like courageous and liberated people suddenly pushed on by an invisible mutual bond."[56]

Even the German administration recognized the strike of 1943 as a proof of its failure to win over the Dutch people. In response to an inquiry from the High Commissioner, all provincial Representatives (*Beauftragte*) told Seyss-Inquart that in their opinion the population would render active support to Allied troops in the event of an invasion. Among German ranks this realization aroused considerable fear of a "stab in the back," an attitude significant in the shaping of German policies after the Normandy invasion.

ATTITUDES DURING THE LAST TWO YEARS OF THE OCCUPATION

The April-May strike marked a distinct change in the attitude of the Dutch population toward the German regime. After the uprising it was no longer acceptable to many patriots to collaborate with German actions such as the labor draft. Whereas very limited numbers had engaged in active opposition to the occupying power before, tens of thousands now resisted, if they could do so without excessive personal risk.

This "minor resistance," or refusal to collaborate further, was demonstrated in many ways. Only a few thousand veterans reported for reinternment.[57] Seventy percent of all university students refused to go to work in Germany.[58] In the middle of July, Rauter estimated that one out of five radios was hidden instead of being delivered to the authorities. Many persons had handed in their old sets and kept their good ones.[59] Compliance with labor draft calls in the summer of 1943 was spotty. After the autumn of 1943 even fewer people than before reported voluntarily. In the summer of 1944 only half of the eighteen-year-olds called up for their terms with the Netherlands Labor Service reported for duty.[60] A rapidly increasing number of patriots went underground.

The belief that it was unethical for patriots to collaborate with the German labor draft was strengthened by a declaration from the London government-in-exile forbidding government officials and others to assist the Germans in their hunt for labor.[61] The consequent growth of popular resistance made it possible to frustrate to a large extent the two major German attempts of 1943 and 1944 to ferret out persons in hiding and to cull out nonessential workers from Dutch industries.[62] The Germans themselves recognized that they could no longer rely on Dutch government agencies and police services in this matter without close supervision by German officials.

Throughout the summer months of 1943 the population closely followed events in the theaters of war, especially those in the Mediterranean, and hopes were high for an early invasion of the continent. The fall of Mussolini in August 1943 was known within hours of the announcement over the British radio, and a mood of guarded optimism spread throughout the Netherlands. In June 1944 the invasion of Normandy aroused further hopes for liberation, since it was generally believed that the Allies would also land in Belgium or the Netherlands. The height of expectancy and subsequent disappointment came on September 5, 1944, the day noted in occupation history as "Mad Tuesday" (Dolle Dinsdag).*

On September 4 the London radio erroneously reported that the Dutch city of Breda had been liberated. This news spread quickly through the Netherlands. Expecting an early Allied advance, many Germans left for the eastern part of the country, and members of the N.S.B. rushed their families to the eastern Netherlands and Germany. In the big cities, news circulated to the effect that the Allies were nearby and that liberation was impending. Some people started to celebrate while waiting for the Allies to arrive. Flags were displayed, and children sang patriotic songs in the streets. By evening, when no troops appeared and the radio reports again sounded vague, the festive mood began to fade and the population resumed its cautious attitude.[63]

Reports of the Allied air landings near Arnhem and Nijmegen once more raised the hope for an early liberation. When it became

---

* The term "Dolle Dinsdag" was first coined by a German-sponsored counter-propaganda periodical, *De Gil* [154]. It subsequently became the commonly accepted term for September 5, 1944. See [157], I, 13 (October 3, 1946), p. 2.

obvious that the Allied attempt had failed, a long winter of hunger and suffering descended on the people in the territory that remained occupied.

During the final winter of the war the unusual hardships of hunger, cold, and other privations tended to disintegrate the moral fiber of the people. In the last months before liberation, different segments of the population became more antagonistic toward each other. Animosity between urban and rural groups became pronounced as city-dwellers turned to the peasants for food. Hatred of black-market profiteers who took advantage of the general distress was widespread.

On the other hand, the winter of 1944–45 saw more overt resistance than ever. Particularly after the establishment of the Netherlands Forces of the Interior and the arrival of Allied forces on Dutch soil in September 1944, an increasing segment of the population felt itself to be part of a belligerent nation. Compliance of the railroad personnel with strike orders issued by the London government-in-exile on September 17 was the outstanding demonstration of this attitude.[64] During the air landings of Allied parachute troops near Arnhem and Nijmegen in September 1944, patriots assisted the Allies by serving as guides, supplying food and drink, and aiding and hiding wounded personnel and soldiers who were cut off from their units.[65] During the gradual Allied advance from September 1944 to May 1945, patriots continued to aid Allied troops as scouts and in actual fighting.[66] Many more persons than before participated in the manufacture and distribution of the burgeoning clandestine papers and news sheets.

Not all Dutch citizens were prepared to participate in resistance during these last months of the occupation, as demonstrated by the success of the surprise raids in Rotterdam. But even so, to a greater extent than ever before, hatred of the Germans now had taken hold of the Dutch people,[67] and Dutch and Germans faced each other as belligerents committed to fight to the finish.

CHAPTER EIGHT

The Reactions of Special Groups

THE SECRETARIES-GENERAL AND THE NATIONAL ADMINISTRATION

After the capitulation of May 1940, officials had to decide whether they would remain in office and serve the occupying power. In 1937 the Colijn government had prepared a set of somewhat vague secret instructions for the conduct of civil servants in the event of a military occupation.[1] These "Directives of 1937," as they were called, assumed that the occupying power would respect the rules of the Hague Convention. Essentially, the Directives of 1937 urged government officials to continue their work if by so doing they served the welfare of the population. Should the benefit of their service to the enemy and its war machine be deemed larger than the advantage derived by the population from their continuance in office, officials were advised to resign.[2]

Unfortunately, the instructions were couched in such general terms that they were not very useful, since they left decisions to each individual involved. Moreover, the authors simply did not foresee the moral climate of an occupation by a ruthless totalitarian enemy bent fanatically on the achievement of certain ideological objectives. In May 1943, therefore, Bosch Ridder van Rosenthal, the former Commissioner of the Queen for the province of Utrecht and a leading Resistance leader, published a clandestine "Commentary" in the underground press, in an attempt to make the "Directives" more specifically applicable to the realities of the occupation.

Officials were enjoined to practice passive resistance to actions in conflict with the interests of the population, and to wait for possible dismissal for their failure to implement "illegal" German orders. The assumption was that the German authorities might not dismiss all officials practicing such passive resistance. The Commentary declared it impermissible to assist in the following programs: the requisitioning of raw materials and goods beyond the needs of the armies of occupation, the labor draft, the recruitment of Dutch men into German military service, the taking of hostages, and political arrests and deportations. The Commentary re-emphasized that the government-in-exile remained the legal government of the Netherlands. It reminded officials that they were individually responsible and would have to render legal account of their actions after the Liberation.[3] In October 1943 Prime Minister Gerbrandy endorsed the Commentary over the radio and stated that no government official had the right to add his own interpretation.[4]

Unfortunately neither the original Directives nor the Commentary of 1943 solved the moral problem posed to individuals by the occupation. Consequently, most government officials remained in office, frequently at the price of participation in projects forbidden by the Commentary of 1943. Such officials were assured by the National Socialist Secretary-General of Justice, Schrieke, that they could plead duress in the event of an Allied victory.[5] The clandestine periodical *Het Parool* countered this argument by stating that officials could claim duress only if they were personally threatened by "disproportionately severe punishment." General announcements, such as threats of vague penalties for entire categories of officials, were said not to constitute duress.[6]

In this situation the attitude of the Secretaries-General was of supreme importance. When they decided to stay on in June 1940, their example was followed by most of their subordinates. The German administration, however, soon made demands to which some Secretaries-General could not agree. In the summer of 1940, C. Ringeling, Secretary-General for Defense, opposed the use of armament factories for the German war effort and was removed by Seyss-Inquart.[7] Sooner or later, most of the Secretaries-General resigned or were removed, until by the end of 1943 only three of the eleven Secretaries-General serving under the De Geer cabinet remained in office.[8]

One of these was K. J. Frederiks, permanent head of the Department of Internal Affairs. He was a conservative civil servant with a limited horizon. His loyalty to the House of Orange was above suspicion. He collaborated to a considerable extent with the Germans because he believed that his failure to do so would lead to his replacement by a National Socialist. After the war he took the position that the government had told him in May 1940 to remain in office and that it was his duty to do so until he received orders to the contrary. He believed that nobody but himself was in a position to judge his specific actions, and he resented the fact that the government-in-exile was critical of his performance. He also bitterly resented the attacks of the Resistance.[9]

Frederiks felt he had to collaborate "loyally" with the occupation power as long as he remained in office. He therefore opposed administrative sabotage, at least until 1943. Admitting that new developments in warfare required total utilization of the resources of the occupied country, he collaborated with such measures as the labor draft (while attempting to decrease the numbers who would be drafted), the authoritarian reorganization of the Dutch administration in provinces and municipalities (which remained largely on paper), and the recruitment of workers for defense works in Holland, as well as with many other German projects. In return for this cooperation, he obtained, in his opinion, a number of concessions from the Germans, such as protection for the Barneveld group.[10] He could support mayors when they refused to obey certain orders from local German authorities. He succeeded in delaying or weakening the execution of certain German measures, such as the projected loyalty declaration by all government officials, and frequently he succeeded in having especially repugnant actions performed by German agencies rather than by his own officials.

After 1943 Frederiks' attitude changed somewhat as German policies became harsher. He refused to sign the order instituting a new rationing system because he realized that it was designed primarily to catch persons in hiding.[11] In September 1944, after an attempt to assassinate him, Frederiks himself went into hiding.[12]

Another important department head who worked with the German administration until the end of the occupation was Hans Max Hirschfeld, Secretary-General of the Departments of Agriculture and Fisheries, and Commerce, Industry, and Shipping. He played a part in initiating the surrender negotiations of April 1945 and was a witness at the Nuremberg trial. Hirschfeld was an intelligent and capable official who did his best to prevent the complete collapse of the Dutch economy. He was respected by his staff and by the Germans, who kept him in office even though they knew he had a Jewish father.[13]

Like Frederiks, Hirschfeld remained in office because he felt he could serve the Dutch people best in that way. He realized from the beginning that the German administration would use the productive apparatus of Holland to the fullest possible extent. To the Resistance and the London government it seemed that Hirschfeld went even farther than Frederiks in his willingness to collaborate with the occupying power. In December 1943 he signed the decree instituting the new rationing system. He warned his subordinates against going into hiding. He exhorted them not to pay attention to the comments of the underground press, even if they were attacked personally.[14] He maintained that political problems should not play any part in the economic administration of the country.[15] After the Liberation, he was suspended from office because of his role during the occupation, and was eventually given an honorable dismissal.[16]

In recent years the judgment of Hirschfeld's policies has become more favorable than it was in the immediate postwar period. It now appears that Hirschfeld played his cards close to his chest and that he stubbornly and consistently followed a line of conduct which he believed best served the interests of the population and the prospects of postwar survival of the Netherlands as an economically and socially viable state.

The Acting Secretary-General of the Department of Social Affairs, A. T. Verwey, also deserves special mention. He was appointed acting department head after the resignation of his predecessor in August 1940 and remained in this post until the end of the occupation.

Like Frederiks and Hirschfeld, Verwey was prompted by humanitarian and patriotic considerations. By no means a National Socialist, he was a devout Christian, and religious motivations played a large part in his policy.[17] He wanted to preserve public health and maintain and improve social welfare to whatever extent he could under the occupation, and to stave off hunger, disease, and death. There is also evidence that he hoped to use the interlude of freedom from the limitations of administrative action under a parliamentary regime to put into effect certain measures close to his heart which would improve existing social welfare programs.[18]

Like his colleagues, he had to compromise on many counts with German policies in order to stay in office and retain a degree of effectiveness. Since the labor draft fell within the scope of his department, he became the focal point of one of the most important areas of conflict between the Germans and the Dutch, and soon was a prime target of patriotic attacks for his collaboration with the Germans. The underground press designated him the "Number One Bootlicker."[19] After the war he claimed it was a miracle that he was not assassinated during the occupation, since he considered himself misunderstood by both the Germans and his own countrymen.[20]

To many observers of the occupation it appeared that Verwey went further than was necessary or justified to please the Germans. He endorsed the gradual extension of the work week to seventy-two hours, but at a lower echelon this policy was sabotaged.[21] He collaborated with the labor draft even more closely than Frederiks. He ordered Population Records offices to furnish the Germans with data for the labor draft. He authorized the designation of members of his department for deportation to Germany in a set of instructions that displayed the worst possible class prejudices, surrendering persons who had less education and came from lower strata of society to the clutches of the Germans.[22] In January 1945 he permitted his department heads to issue exemption certificates (*Ausweise*) to their staff, disregarding instructions from London.[23]

There were limits, however, to his collaboration. He joined the other non-N.S.B. Secretaries-General in refusing continued service if Mussert were appointed head of the government, and he threatened to resign on at least two other occasions.[24]

He also could take credit for a number of useful accomplishments. He claimed after the war that he had been able to save individual Jews.[25] He kept certain unemployment insurance funds out of the hands of the Netherlands Labor Front.[26] He prevented church property from being sent to Germany.[27] And he postponed the issuance of a "Labor Book" (a document like a passport containing a worker's employment record), which he had advocated before the war, because he realized that such a document would provide the Germans with another tool to make the labor draft more effective.[28]

In summary, like Hirschfeld and Frederiks, Verwey collaborated with the Germans because he felt that he could do some good by remaining in office. Once this basic assumption was made, it became necessary to compromise further and further, so that Verwey, despite basically humanitarian motivations, emerged as one of the most submissive and collaborating non-Nazi Secretaries-General of the occupation.

Frederiks, Hirschfeld, and Verwey were targets of violent attacks by the underground press and by many patriots. All three bitterly resented what they considered to be uninformed and unjustified counsel from London and irresponsible comments on the part of the underground press.[29] Yet there is no doubt that the tenor of their advice encouraged their subordinates and officials in other government departments to collaborate with the Germans in ways that were prohibited specifically by the Commentary of 1943.

The mayors also held a key position in the national administration, especially in small towns and villages. There they acted as heads of local police forces and were responsible for the administration of population records (Bevolkingsregisters) and of rationing offices, including issuance of Rauter's new ration cards in 1944. Many of these men played their part in frustrating this plan by protecting patriots in their offices who engaged in administrative sabotage.

Patriotic mayors were in a difficult position, because while they had to be sufficiently cooperative with the occupying power in order to retain office, they also had to keep the people's confidence. Their situation was made more difficult by the fact that they were obliged to deal with local German authorities, civilian or military, who sometimes did not have the civilized veneer of the higher German officials.[30] Despite their wish to compromise in order to protect their people, many administrators eventually refused cooperation with German attempt to seize divers* and other evaders of the labor draft. Sometimes they themselves went underground.

Secretary-General Frederiks claimed that he protected the loyal mayors as much as he could. In 1943 he backed their refusal to supply data from the population records for the labor draft. Frederiks tried to persuade the Germans not to require these officials to arrest any but those suspected of offenses against regular Dutch laws. He

---

* A colloquial term for persons in hiding.

claimed that after the middle of 1943 Dutch administrators were no longer required to make political arrests.[31]

Of all the government services the police had the largest number of National Socialist or pro-German officials, since Rauter took special pains to make the police ideologically reliable. In many instances the Dutch police, patriots and collaborators alike, were required to assist German authorities in their political activities, particularly in the early years of the occupation. In February 1941 Dutch officers and men had to lend a hand in the raids on Jews in Amsterdam. They also were used for seizing persons in hiding and for suppressing the April–May strike of 1943. After 1943, patriotic police officials had to make fewer political arrests, since the German administration depended increasingly on ideologically reliable units such as the Schalkhaar police and the Home Guard. But patriotic officials continued to be assigned to guard offices containing rationing and population records.

Opposition of the patriotic Dutch police to the German administration was constantly demonstrated. Especially in the smaller communities where people could rely on each other, the police often forewarned local citizens of impending arrests. In a few instances they refused to arrest Jews slated for deportation. At times they made prior agreements with resistance groups to be "overwhelmed" during attacks on government offices. One high police official in Rotterdam operated a falsification service in his own office.[32] The story of a soccer game between a police team and a team of divers was widely believed.[33] In some cases entire police units went underground after May 1943. The disappearance of policemen with their weapons became such a problem that Rauter ordered the arrest of families of police officials who had deserted with their firearms.[34] The German lack of confidence in the loyalty of the officers and men concerned was shown most clearly in the disarming of Dutch police units in 1944 and 1945.

Throughout the occupation most Dutch courts continued to do business as usual,[35] but the Dutch judiciary could not completely ignore the political problems of the times. As early as November 1940, the highest court in the land, the High Council (De Hoge Raad), was faced with the need to make a vital decision. In that month the German administration dismissed its President, L. E. Visser, along with all other Jewish government officials. Supposedly on the advice of Visser himself, the Court did not take a public stand on that occasion. Later an apologist for the High Council justified this silence by accepting the German argument that the occupying power had the right to remove hostile officials and that all Jews were bound to be hostile.[36] As additional vacancies occurred, the Germans filled them with members of the N.S.B. or with pro-German individuals. But the pro-German elements never obtained a majority in the Court.

The moment of critical decision for the High Council came in January 1942 when, in reviewing a case on its docket, it had to pass on the legality of the decrees of the occupying power. This suit presented the Council with an opportunity to stipulate that German decrees were bound to conform to the Hague Convention, to which the Reich was a party. Instead of doing so, however, the High Council refused to review the case in question.[37] This decision was based on the reasoning that, as in Great Britain, the Dutch courts could not test the validity of legislation, but that the States General, like the British Parliament, were the final judges of the Constitution. The Germans and many people in the occupied territory considered that this narrow legalistic decision provided a legal justification for decrees passed by the occupying power.[38]

Throughout the remainder of the war the High Council continued its routine business without formally opposing the occupying power. It did not even take issue with the introduction of the analogy clause into Dutch law. But some members of the Council supposedly decided to resign if Mussert was made head of the government.[39]

In the autumn of 1944 the government-in-exile suspended the activities of the High Council, pending an inquiry into its conduct. It dismissed all judges appointed by the Germans and suspended a number of others.[40] The chief criticism of the government was leveled at the court decision of January 1942, which seemed to justify German actions.

One reason for the decision of the High Council to continue its normal operations without challenging the German regime was the conviction of its majority that a resignation of the High Council would have been followed by the resignation of the lower courts. In that case, members of the N.S.B. and pro-Germans would have taken over the entire judicial machinery. In short, the High Council claimed that it maintained its silence in the interest of the people of the Netherlands, to avoid their being thrown at the mercy of a judicial system completely nazified in spirit and personnel.[41]

In one instance, at least, some of the lower courts did not follow the lead of the High Command in its policy of ignoring the abuses of the occupying power. Conditions in Camp Erika, which had been established near Ommen in June 1942 to absorb the overflow from regular prisons, had become notorious. Frequently prisoners were so badly treated that they died.[42]

Early in 1943 a few Amsterdam judges took it upon themselves to investigate the situation personally. In disguise they visited the Ommen hospital and interviewed the prisoners. At a meeting of the members of the district courts in February 1943, a report of those investigations was read. Subsequently the report was given to a representative of Seyss-Inquart.[43] On March 15 the Amsterdam judges requested the Secretary-General of Justice to close the Ommen camp or to turn it over to regular officials of the Department of Justice. It was also suggested that all sentences passed by the Dutch judiciary should be served in Dutch prisons only.[44] In the following months the Amsterdam bench was informed that the Ommen camp would be closed and that other demands would be met as far as possible.[45]

In the meantime, other judges had reacted to the situation in Ommen. They also had realized that the police often failed to release prisoners at the expiration of their terms. Therefore they had imposed short sentences or had acquitted defendants to protect them from imprisonment for an indefinite term or from mistreatment in the Ommen camp. This had been happening for some time without German interference.

In February 1943 the Leeuwarden Court of Appeals reduced the sentence of a lower court to time served, which meant that the defendant was to be released. The Court based its decision on the fact that the remainder of the original sentence was to be carried out in a penal camp where the prisoner would have to undergo the heavy hardships described above, and would not be assured of release at the end of his term.[46]

The Leeuwarden judgment was circulated throughout the country and was reprinted in the underground press. It was welcomed by patriots everywhere as an instance of courageous denunciation of National Socialist policies and practices. But the High Commissioner considered the judgment an act of insubordination and dismissed the judges responsible for it.

POLITICAL PARTIES

The democratic parties represented in the 1940 legislature did not play a very active part in the year before their dissolution in July 1941. Those of their leaders who sat in the De Geer cabinet had gone to London, and many others were arrested. Before the end of the war one quarter of the Second Chamber had been imprisoned or interned.[47]

Nevertheless, party organizations continued to accept new members in 1940. The Protestant and Liberal parties actually increased their membership during the summer of 1940, and held several large meetings to discuss postwar reform of the political system in an attempt to combat National Socialist ideology.[48] But on the whole, party leaders took the position that the resumption of normal political activities would have to await return of the legal government. The Antirevolutionary and Social Democratic parties managed to maintain an unofficial network of communications with their members across the country.[49] Most parties managed to maintain informally a skeleton organization throughout the war.

The Social Democratic leaders refused to cooperate with Rost van Tonningen after his appointment as Commissioner of the Party in July 1940.[50] They told him that in their opinion political democracy was a precondition of socialism.[51] Many lower party officials also refused to cooperate or resigned at that time and the party machinery ceased to be useful to Rost van Tonningen for any practical purposes.[52] The contacts and friendships of individuals who had been associated with the Social Democratic Party became an effective basis for developing underground activities.

The Catholic Party remained rather inactive,[53] although individual members played a role in establishing the Netherlands Union. Catholic leadership during the occupation, however, was exercised through the episcopacy and, secondarily, through Catholic trade unions and lay organizations, rather than through the Party.

Some individual party leaders remained politically active even though their organizations did not function normally. Koos Vorrink, chairman of the Social Democratic Party, considered his work in the Resistance to be so important that in 1943 he apparently refused to accede to the Queen's request to come to London.[54]

Of all the prewar politicians, Hendrik Colijn, head of the Anti-revolutionary Party and former Prime Minister, played the most publicized role during the summer of 1940. He had a brilliant political mind and great personal ambitions, supported by a rather autocratic and self-confident temperament. Although he was an arch-conservative and harbored some confused sympathies for the authoritarian features of the Fascist and National Socialist systems, there could be no doubt of his patriotism and loyalty to the monarchy.

After the surrender it seems that Colijn wanted to stage a comeback in politics. He had an interview with Seyss-Inquart soon after the latter's arrival in Holland, in which he evinced a willingness to cooperate with the occupation authorities.[55]

In June 1940, after this interview, Colijn published a pamphlet entitled *Op de Grens van twee Werelden* ("On the Border between Two Worlds") in which he excused Hitler's foreign policies on the basis of the injustices inherent in the Treaty of Versailles. He attacked the "evils of democracy," such as interference in economic affairs and excessive dependence on the will of the electorate, and advocated re-establishment of the supremacy of the cabinet over the elected Chamber, through abolition of the principle of ministerial responsibility.

In addition, Colijn advised his countrymen to work out a compromise with the Third Reich, since he considered German hegemony a certainty. He acknowledged the fact that the Netherlands might not retain complete independence of action, and that it might be necessary to remodel some national institutions after the pattern of Germany, provided the House of Orange could be retained. Finally, Colijn called for the organization of a directorate made up of party leaders with sufficient authority to confer with the Germans, although he claimed that this group was not designed to replace the London government.[56]

The pamphlet naturally produced much comment, but it was repudiated within a few weeks by the author himself, who was flooded by protests from his own followers.[57] Furthermore, German intentions to support the N.S.B. soon became more apparent. By August 1940 Colijn withdrew his demand for a new government and ceased to advocate accommodation to the Germans.[58] From this time on, he was no longer allowed to hold public meetings, but he continued to confer regularly with a group of Antirevolutionary leaders. After the invasion of Russia, he was arrested and later taken to Germany, where he died in September 1944.[59]

D. J. de Geer, head of the Christian Historical Union and Prime Minister at the time of the invasion, played a more seriously defeatist role. During the summer of 1940 it became evident to his associates in London that he really hoped for a compromise with Germany. Consequently he was persuaded to resign his office in September 1940, and Professor P. S. Gerbrandy became his successor. In defiance of the orders of the Gerbrandy government, De Geer managed to return to the occupied Netherlands with German approval.[60] Upon his return, he composed a pamphlet entitled *De Synthese in de Oorlog* ("The Synthesis in the War"), in which he advocated collaboration with Germany and surrender of Dutch independence. The booklet was endorsed by German authorities before publication.[61] De Geer's work represented a worse indiscretion than Colijn's pamphlet because it was published in 1942, when German intentions had become more obvious.

Of all the non-Fascist parties represented in the States General, the Communist Party played the most active role during the occupation. It was better equipped to do so than the other groups because it was prepared to operate illegally if necessary, in line with its revolutionary traditions and its character as an action group.

When Rost van Tonningen was appointed Commissioner of the Communist Party on July 20, 1940, an underground party organization headed by an executive committee of three was established. The clandestine party was like a pyramid of small cells, each consisting of a few men and having a minimum of contact with one another. Propaganda and political instruction were carried on through these cells.[62] In the beginning of 1941 the Party was said to have approximately two thousand members, more than half of whom lived in Amsterdam.[63]

The German police pursued the Communists ruthlessly. After the invasion of the Soviet Union, the S.D. arrested approximately six hundred party members, but the national leaders escaped. When two of the three members of the executive committee were arrested in 1943, it became necessary to reconstitute the group completely.

According to a postwar statement of the surviving member of the original executive committee, only a very few of the prewar party leaders survived and over 60 percent of the members of the Party lost their lives during the occupation.

After June 1941 the Party fervently supported Allied warfare and called for an early establishment of a Second Front. It advocated cooperation among the resistance groups in the occupied Dutch territory, but was careful to preserve its own identity. Until the end of the occupation, Communist propaganda usually stressed the anti-German theme and played down ideological differences among the patriotic groups in the occupied territory.[64]

Despite its pleas for postwar political unity of all workers, the Communist Party was the first political party to be re-established in the liberated territory.[65] In the postwar era it continued to echo the policies of the Soviet Union.

THE NETHERLANDS UNION

Soon after the surrender it became apparent that the traditional parliamentary parties could not operate effectively during an occupation by a totalitarian power. Therefore a number of prominent Dutchmen, who were disappointed with parliamentary government and had corporative leanings and shared some of the defeatism characteristic of the temper of the summer of 1940, looked for a new political organization that could unite the patriotic elements of the population.

These men, many of whom were appointive officials, wished to counter the claim of the N.S.B. that it should be allowed to form a government because it represented the Dutch people. Because they could not know how loath the German administration was to entrust the N.S.B. with governmental power, they believed that some unity movement, showing the strength of patriotic and anti-National Socialist sentiment among the Dutch people, was needed to deter the occupying power from establishing a government headed by Mussert.

Seyss-Inquart was willing to allow the more conservative patriotic elements to form a movement which pledged itself to loyal coopera- tion with the occupying power. He wanted at least the temporary support of Catholic and Protestant politicians, and he believed that a measure of political self-expression would make it easier for the Dutch people to adjust to the new situation.[66]

After unsuccessful preliminary negotiations with some of the old party leaders, including Colijn, three prominent citizens, J. Linthorst Homan, Commissioner of the Queen for the Province of Groningen, Professor J. E. de Quay of the Catholic Party, and L. Einthoven, Po- lice Commissioner of Rotterdam and a member of one of the Liberal parties, founded the Netherlands Union (Nederlandse Unie). In its founding proclamation, issued on July 24, the triumvirate stated the basic purpose of the new organization as follows: " . . . to gather all patriots . . . in loyal attitudes toward the occupying power." The Union declared itself as standing for the preservation of national independence and the principle of Christianity as well as for tolerance and freedom of religion, education, and speech. The platform repudi- ated the past, with its class divisions and its materialism, and called for a new system of government embodying a stronger principle of leadership. The platform also envisaged a corporative economic structure guaranteeing the right to work, with the obligation to work as its corollary. In deference to the wishes of the German authorities, the platform failed to mention the House of Orange.[67] This omission had been the main reason for Colijn's refusal to participate.

The Union soon recruited a large membership. By February 1941 it had 800,000 members as compared with the peak membership of 100,000 claimed by the N.S.B.[68] Judging from the great influx of members, a heterogeneous group of people was attracted to the Union. The majority joined primarily as an act of protest against the N.S.B.[69] The authoritarian theories of the Union leaders did not in- fluence its membership to any great extent.

Publication and the street sale of the weekly *De Unie* was one of the most important activities of the Union. In its weekly, the Union stated its views refuting the Dutch Nazi claim that the N.S.B. alone represented the people of Holland.[70] The street sale of *De Unie* demonstrated that the publications of the N.S.B. and the W.A. had an effective competitor. During the period when street sales were permitted, fights and brawls took place frequently throughout the country. In the larger cities the Union established clubhouses and stores with reading materials, designed to compete with those of the N.S.B.

In its weekly journal the Union discussed the whole range of issues before the people of Holland. On a number of questions it interpreted the views of its own majority and of the people of Holland. Having originally admitted Jewish citizens to membership in 1940, the Union deplored the first measures taken against the Jews in the fall of that year, but showed signs of weakening on the Jewish issue under Nazi pressure.[71] On the whole, the Union disclaimed any intention of making fundamental changes in the governmental structure until the peace settlement.

On the other hand, the Union was unable to disregard its basic assumption that collaboration with the German regime was feasible, and that certain concessions had to be made in the interest of such collaboration. Consequently, Union members were warned against joining underground activities[72] and were asked to support the Labor Service and the Winter Help.[73] In 1941 the Union excluded Jews from full membership and exacted an oath of total obedience from its members.

None of these concessions helped in the final analysis. In 1941 the leaders of the Union came to realize that collaboration with the Germans was possible only at the price of complete surrender. In March 1941 the Union restated its determination to wait until the end of the war for political changes, and asked the Germans to remember that the Netherlands was still at war with the Reich.[74] This statement resulted in the prohibition of the street sale of *De Unie*. After the invasion of Russia, the Union refused to call for a crusade against bolshevism on the grounds that Soviet Russia was the ally of the Kingdom of the Netherlands.[75] In retribution, the Germans suppressed the weekly for six weeks and subjected it to preventive censorship at the end of that period. Thereupon *De Unie* stopped publication and the organization was disbanded. Many of its most active members joined the Resistance,[76] in which contacts established during their work for the Netherlands Union provided a valuable nucleus of underground cooperation.[*]

It was inevitable that the Germans and the N.S.B. would try to secure control over Dutch labor. Free labor unions with elected leadership had no place in a totalitarian society.

The largest Dutch trade union was the Netherlands Association of Trade Unions (Nederlands Verbond van Vakverenigingen), which was allied to the Social Democratic Party. Before the invasion it had 319,000 members. Next came the Roman Catholic Workmen's Association (Rooms Katholiek Werkliedenverbond) with 186,000 members, which had close ties with the Roman Catholic Party. The third largest trade union was the Christian National Trade Union (Christelijk Nationaal Vakverbond), an organization of Protestant workers with 119,000 members. The total of all organized workers approached 800,000, approximately one-quarter of all those gainfully employed.[77]

The trade unions did not limit their activities to the role of collective bargaining agents. They administered social insurance systems for their members with the aid of government funds and operated many social, educational, and cultural programs. They published their own newspapers and periodicals and ran rest homes, sanitariums, sports clubs, youth groups, travel organizations, and other social agencies. The preservation of these auxiliary institutions, associations, and programs was an important concern of labor officials, who had a vested interest in their operations.

The Netherlands Association of Trade Unions (N.V.V.) was the first large labor organization to be taken over. When J. H. Woudenberg was appointed Commissioner of the N.V.V. in July 1940, the leading functionaries cooperated with the new Commissioner. A

---

[*] A postwar commission of inquiry appointed by Prime Minister Schermerhorn concurred in the conclusion that the Netherlands Union made a valuable contribution to the resistance movement ([242], II, 108–8). See also [19], 7-A, 186, for the comment of the official Commission of Inquiry, criticizing the Union for lack of faith in democratic parliamentary institutions, but praising the huge membership sign-up as a powerful anti-German and anti-N.S.B. demonstration.

few high officials threatened to withdraw, but the threat of reprisals sufficed to make them change their minds. A few staff members resigned and some of the constituent unions, especially in the eastern part of the country, refused to cooperate with Woudenberg.[78] The rank and file were not quite so cooperative. By October 1941 almost one out of four members had resigned.[79]

The compliance of union leaders must be related to the vested interest of these officials in their careers and in the preservation of the auxiliary social services provided by the unions. It must also be borne in mind that they had to make their decision in the climate of the summer of 1940, when the Germans had not yet betrayed the full scope of their political intentions. By the spring of 1942, however, when German authorities established the Netherlands Labor Front, the far-reaching nature of German designs had become apparent. Ninety-five percent of all salaried union employees and most other officials resigned, and within a few months about two-thirds of the membership of the N.V.V. withdrew to avoid induction into the Netherlands Labor Front.[80]

In the summer of 1940 the denominational labor unions also decided to continue their activities and to accept a German liaison official. Despite some minor conflicts with the German administration, the unions managed to carry on for another year.

When it became evident in July 1941 that the Germans would not allow the continued independence of denominational unions, leaders of the Catholic union decided to refuse collaboration. As soon as Woudenberg was appointed Commissioner of the Catholic union, all officials, including those in affiliated organizations, resigned.[81] In a pastoral letter, the episcopacy designated the Union, now under Woudenberg's commissionership, as a National Socialist organization.[82] This declaration forbade Catholics to remain in the Union, on penalty of being refused the Holy Sacraments.

The resignation of membership was so complete that within two weeks after Woudenberg's appointment the Union ceased to exist for all practical purposes. Therefore Woudenberg dissolved the organization and urged its former members to join the N.V.V. By the end of the year, less than 5 percent had done so.[83]

The Protestant union, the Christian National Trade Union, received the same treatment as did the Catholic union. Most of the leadership likewise resigned, but a larger number of members transferred to the N.V.V.

The Netherlands Labor Front remained an empty shell. Its functionaries were ineffective and most workers refused to collaborate. The organization had no influence, even over its own members. This became abundantly clear during the April-May strikes of 1943, when Labor Front functionaries usually did not even try to oppose the strike.

Despite failure of the Labor Front to win the workers' loyalty to national socialism, most Dutchmen who had been members of trade unions in May 1940 were working for the German war effort by 1942. In some war industries both labor and management attempted to practice deliberate slow-downs, to misunderstand directions on purpose, and to decrease productivity as much as could be done safely. But opportunities for sabotage varied greatly. They were especially limited in the larger factories, where the Germans frequently placed informers.

Certain groups of workers were particularly effective in slow-downs and sabotage. The mineworkers of the province of Limburg were one example. The strong anti-German sentiment which had developed in this Catholic region could be expressed through action, because the common religious background of the miners provided effective social cohesion. This attitude was demonstrated in a refusal in 1942 to work on Sundays and in a determined slow-down and lowering of output.

The personnel of the Philips factory in Eindhoven furnished another example of relatively effective resistance. There, also, the Catholic background of many workers, which made them impervious to National Socialist ideology and threats, contributed to the spirit of independence. In 1941 the celebration of the fiftieth anniversary of the Philips factories became the occasion for a major demonstration of loyalty to the House of Orange.[84] German authorities nicknamed the Philips plant "Fortress England" and considered deporting its workers to Germany.[85]

THE RAILROAD STRIKE

It was, however, among the railroad personnel that the most effective and spectacular labor action during the occupation was achieved.

The organization of the Dutch Railroads (Nederlandse Spoorwegen) was a tight, highly centralized structure with more than 30,000 permanent employees.[86] Railroad employees were organized into five unions. The largest union was Socialist and a member of the Netherlands Association of Trade Unions (N.V.V.). Two were denominational. The two smallest unions were the white-collar employees and an autonomous nondenominational group.

Relationships between the management and the unions were channeled through an elective Personnel Council (Personeelraad). Unions were represented on the Council in proportion to their membership. The unions themselves, like the rest of the Dutch labor movement, had lost the revolutionary fervor of the early twentieth century. The last major railroad strike had occurred in 1903.[87] Union officials and the rank and file did not have close contact, since a union bureaucracy had come into existence which was closer in mentality to the management than to its own constituency.[88] Nevertheless, the Personnel Council had retained the confidence of the membership to a considerable extent.

Management policy was basically determined by W. Hupkes, who became Acting Director of the Railroads after the internment and subsequent dismissal of Professor J. Goudriaan, President of the Railroads, by the Germans.[89] Hupkes worked closely with G. Joustra, Chairman of the Personnel Council.

After the surrender, the management made an agreement with the Germans promising loyal collaboration, provided the Railroads could continue under their own (Dutch) management. Hupkes' main goal throughout this period was to prevent infiltration of the system by Germans and Dutch Nazis on the one hand, and by left-wing radical elements on the other.[90]

The Germans supervised the Dutch Railroads by attaching to the management in Utrecht representatives of the German railroad system and military transportation services. In effect, the German representatives helped the management to resist political infiltration of the system, since their major concern was to maintain the flow of traffic without interference.[91]

When the denominational unions were dissolved in 1941, their representatives were retained on the Personnel Council.[92] But when the Germans, in 1942, imposed the Netherlands Labor Front on railroad employees, Woudenberg appointed his own Personnel Council.

The management, however, refused to have any dealings with this new group and threatened to resign if the issue were forced. Since the Germans wanted to avoid chaos, a compromise was adopted which in effect reinstituted the old Personnel Council. The Council was placed on the railroad payroll, but was promised full independence by the management.[93]

The overriding objective to keep the railroad organization intact and free from major Nazi infiltration was responsible for the decision to render many services to the occupying power. The Dutch Railroads repaired and manufactured German equipment, ran trains in German border regions, and permitted the use of railroad personnel and equipment for the progressive plunder of Holland, and for the deportation of Jews, political prisoners, and labor draftees. The management also advised railroad personnel against joining the February and April-May strikes. Small groups of local employees did join these strikes spontaneously, but only for brief periods.[94] On the other hand, the management protected from German reprisals a group of central office workers who had walked out briefly in April 1943.[95] The management was successful in keeping the men on their jobs because the railroad personnel had been traditionally dependent on directives from the Utrecht central office, and continued to be so during the occupation.

Responses to questions asked after the Liberation indicated that not much thought was given at the management level to the ethical implications of this collaboration,[96] although individual workers, especially locomotive engineers, seem to have been troubled by the necessity of serving the enemy to this extent, especially in connection with the deportation of Jews. In isolated instances, engineers apparently reported sick to avoid running trains with Jewish deportees, but replacements could always be found.[97]

The specific idea of a massive railroad strike in support of Allied troops seems to have been discussed seriously for the first time during the April-May strike. It appears that a major underground organization, the Council of Resistance (Raad van Verzet), was the first to suggest this project to the London government.[98] Gerbrandy passed the suggestion on to Allied authorities, who responded favorably. Subsequently, the concept of a strike was accepted by the railroad management and patriotic members of the Personnel Council.

Hupkes and Joustra personally fully supported such a massive strike, provided it was ordered by the London government. The management made a determined attempt to keep the conduct of the strike in its own hands.[99]

In 1944 preliminary preparations were made for the organization of the strike. Individuals in local stations were designated as contact men by Joustra. He tried primarily to select reliable former union leaders. In these preparations, and in consultations with the Resistance and London, it was always assumed that a few days' warning would be given so that the strike could be properly organized from Utrecht.[100]

In May 1944 workers and employees were given one month's advance salary, to be used in an emergency such as an invasion.[101] The Germans heard of this "invasion money" and required that it be returned. The funds were then left in the safe of each station master, with the understanding that the month's salary was to be paid on orders from Utrecht.

Early in September 1944, British military authorities in London informed the Dutch Minister of War, Van Lidth de Jeude, and the Dutch intelligence service (Bureau Inlichtingen), that parachute landings would take place soon in Holland and that a railroad strike in support of impending military operations in the Netherlands would then be desirable.[102] In the middle of the night of September 16–17, C. L. W. Fock of the Dutch intelligence service was instructed to ask Prime Minister Gerbrandy to order a general railroad strike in support of the parachute landings, which were scheduled for noon the following day. Fock had difficulty in locating Gerbrandy and Van Lidth de Jeude.[103] Therefore strike orders were not issued until the evening of September 17, six hours after the initial parachute landings, in a radio broadcast asking the entire population to support the railroad men. These instructions and the prearranged code message ordering the strike were repeated in subsequent broadcasts.

Since the railroad management in Utrecht had not received advance notice, it could exercise little influence on the actions of personnel in the initial phase of the strike. Therefore, response to the strike call depended to a large degree on local conditions.[104]

The strike was most successful in the central and western parts of the country and in the provinces of Friesland and Overijsel. It was least successful in the provinces of Groningen and Drente and in the southern regions near the front. Sufficient numbers, however, went on strike to bring practically all trains to a halt, with the exception of those in the border provinces of the northeast and the south and those run by German personnel.

Local leadership was of crucial importance in setting the course of action at each station. The station chiefs, considered the main authorities by employees and workers, and the contact men of the Personnel Council played key roles. In a number of instances the designated authorities were ineffective, and other individuals spontaneously assumed leadership of the strike.[105]

Considerations affecting the attitudes and actions of workers and employees were complex. On the one hand, the desire to deal a blow against the Germans and to contribute to the patriotic cause was conducive to participation in the strike. There was a general expectation that the strike would be short and liberation at most a few weeks distant. Then, too, heavy bombings of railroad facilities by the Allies and threats from the Resistance made it seem safer to stay away from work.

On the other hand, the traditional sense of duty (*Beamtengeist*) made it difficult for many to embrace the concept of a strike. Then there were many practical problems, such as fear of German reprisals against strikers and their families and property, and the need to have a hiding place and be assured of an income and food for the duration of the strike. Out of these considerations the final decision emerged, usually strongly influenced by the reactions of local superiors and fellow workers.

When the failure of the Allied offensive disappointed hopes for an early liberation, it became necessary to decide whether to continue the strike, since it no longer served a direct strategic purpose. Allied authorities informed the Dutch government that they could approve resumption of traffic in the western part of the country but that the strike should be continued in the north and east.[106] The government-in-exile decided that it would be impractical to order a partial cessation of the strike, because this would undermine the morale of the strikers.[107] Therefore, in October 1944, it urged continuation of the strike. This issue was again considered in London in January 1945 in connection with the critical food shortage in the western part of the country, but the decision to continue the strike was reaffirmed and new instructions to that effect were broadcast at the request of the Resistance.[108]

The management and the Personnel Council in Utrecht did their best to encourage continuation of the strike, partly because they wished to keep control of the strike movement in order to be in a position to resume leadership after liberation. The desire to salvage their patriotic reputation, which had been tarnished during the long years of collaboration with the Germans, also played a role.[109]

Relations with the Resistance remained tenuous during this period, partly as a result of the antagonism that had developed before September 1944 and partly because of conflicting leadership aspirations. Better relationships and divisions of functions were worked out gradually. Communications with London and the location of hiding places were generally handled by the Resistance.

A major conflict developed over the method of distribution of financial aid to the strikers. Once it became obvious that the strike would have to be continued for a longer period than had been originally envisioned, the "Banker of the Resistance," the National Assistance Fund (National Steunfonds),[110] offered its services. This offer was accepted by the railroad management with some hesitation. The railroad management wanted the money turned over to the Railroads for distribution and postwar accounting. The Fund, on the other hand, wanted to distribute financial aid itself, following its usual accounting procedures. The leaders of the Fund pointed out that the Railroads no longer had an apparatus for distribution, and that the Fund itself had to account to the government for its disbursements. The reluctance of the Fund leaders to turn over money to the Railroads stemmed partly from an unwillingness to strengthen the position of the management and of the Personnel Council because of the previous record of collaboration and partly from their suspicion of the way in which the Railroads were handling the money.[111] Finally a compromise was worked out. The Railroads were to disburse financial aid and keep the receipts, but the Fund was to control local distribution and to take over where the Railroads did not have proper machinery for making payments. This arrangement was characterized as one in which the Railroads were given "the glory" but the Fund the actual control.[112]

A second conflict between the Railroads and the Resistance occurred over the amount of financial aid for strikers. The Railroads wanted their personnel to receive regular wages, including even overtime payments and Christmas bonuses. The Resistance felt that railroad workers should make some financial sacrifice and that stipends should be designated to cover only subsistence needs. In this conflict the Railroads' point of view prevailed generally, although local practices varied.[113] In Roermond, for example, railroad employees who had joined the strike from the beginning were given full stipends, whereas those who had ceased work later were paid only fractions of their regular incomes.[114] On the whole, there was less difficulty between the Railroads and the Resistance at the local level than at the top.[115]

German reaction to the strike was not as severe and violent as might have been expected, although a few railroad men were arrested and executed or sent to concentration camps. As a rule, the Germans did not make a systematic attempt to ferret out strikers in hiding. Instead, Seyss-Inquart attempted to force resumption of work through the imposition of the food embargo. The Germans also attempted unsuccessfully to persuade Hirschfeld and his associates to encourage the strikers to return to work to save the food situation.[116]

In the northern and eastern sections of the country, especially in localities where the strike was slow in getting started, local German authorities applied more pressure on strikers than in the west. The uneven efforts of the Germans to break the strike can be explained at least partly by the fact that the police had more important worries at the time. Moreover, the strike did not affect military operations as seriously as Allied air attacks. Rauter even claimed to have welcomed the strike, asserting that it did more damage to the work of the Resistance by cutting its communications than to the Germans, who could maintain essential communications through their own personnel.[117]

It is difficult to assess the practical effect of the strike on the Germans. The unavailability of Dutch trains during the first week of the strike, while fighting around Arnhem was in progress, handicapped the Germans, despite claims to the contrary. Furthermore, the strike forced the Germans to use their own personnel to a greater extent than if the Dutch had stayed on the job. Eventually 5,000 German railroad men were employed in Holland[118] and 500 became casualties from bombing and sabotage.[119] It therefore appears that the strike caused the Germans difficulties and interfered with their traffic to some extent but that it did not substantially affect the outcome of military operations.

In practical terms, the Dutch, too, paid a price for the strike. It was one of the factors, but by no means the only one, responsible for the famine of the final months of the occupation. It provided a reason for Seyss-Inquart to impose a food embargo; and in conjunction with the early heavy frost of that winter it deprived the Dutch of an alternative way of moving food supplies from the surplus areas of the northeast to the west. In addition, the strike interrupted the dispatch of Red Cross parcels to internees and prisoners in Germany, and this may have meant the difference between life and death for an unknown number of deportees.[120]

The railroad management and its associates on the Personnel Council derived great benefits from the success of the strike. This success gave the management and the Personnel Council an opportunity to recoup ground lost in the preceding years, in the eyes of the Resistance and of public opinion. Hupkes and Joustra made good use of this opportunity, and were able to reassert their control of the Railroads after liberation.[121]

Although the military usefulness of the strike and the balance of benefits reaped by and injuries inflicted upon patriots and the enemy may be uncertain, there can be no question that the strike represented a great ideological and spiritual accomplishment. For one thing, it raised the prestige of the Dutch among the Allies. But beyond that, it was a successful act of resistance to the Germans, in which large sections of the population participated by rendering aid and assistance to railroad workers. After long years, in which the Dutch population had been the victim of German oppression and during which the Germans had managed to crush each large-scale protest, a group of Dutchmen finally presented a successful defiance of the Germans in the closing days of the war.

It appears that the postwar Commission of Inquiry was correct when it concluded that the railroad strike, ". . . intended as a strategic operation as part of Allied warfare [became] a spectacular act of resistance of the Dutch people, an act of which the psychological significance in particular cannot be overestimated."[122]

In 1939 there were four public universities in the Netherlands: Leiden, Utrecht, Groningen, and the Municipal University of Amsterdam. In addition to these, the Technical Institute at Delft and the Agricultural Institute at Wageningen were administered by public authorities. The Free University of Amsterdam was a Calvinist school, while the Catholic University at Nijmegen and the Catholic Economic Institute at Tilburg were governed by Catholic corporations. The Netherlands Institute of Economics in Rotterdam was a private, nondemoninational institution. In 1939, in contrast to the situation in elementary and secondary schools, only about 10 percent of the total university enrollment of 11,201 was registered at the three denominational institutions. Only one out of every five students was a woman.[123]

Like other continental institutions of higher learning, Dutch universities resembled American graduate schools in most respects. They were essentially professional schools, since it was assumed that formal liberal or general education terminated with graduation from secondary school. At the same time, Dutch universities accepted first-year students for their twelfth or thirteenth year of schooling, the average age of the youngest group being around nineteen years. Therefore, social life bore some resemblance to college life in America, although student activities were carried on outside the university. At most institutions there were social clubs corresponding to fraternities. Since membership in these clubs was comparatively expensive and somewhat exclusive, a definite cleavage existed between members of the clubs and "independents."

On the whole, the student body lived in a world apart from the community even though most students resided with their parents or in rented rooms. Before the war, students showed limited interest in political action, partly because most were under voting age,[124] but under the occupation students and faculty members of Dutch universities kindled and spearheaded ideological resistance to national socialism. At crucial junctures, particularly in November 1940 and

April 1943, some universities, through their actions, alerted broader segments of the population to the need to resist national socialism on grounds of principle.

Dutch university resistance was not planned on a grand design, but developed in response to specific German actions. Many German officials would have gladly postponed the ideological housecleaning of universities until the end of the war, but they found themselves embroiled in conflict with students and faculty either as a by-product of broader policies (such as the persecution of the Jews and the labor draft) or as the result of pressure from Dutch Nazis who wanted to place their own men on the faculty and tighten their ideological grip on university youth.[125]

Before the war, student associations had been mostly social in nature. After the start of the occupation, students became progressively aware of their obligation to serve as leaders in the struggle against the nazification of their country. They were reinforced in this attitude by a number of clandestine study groups and publications, of which *De Geus onder Studenten* was the most important. Many students joined the resistance movement once legal opposition had become impossible. A great many paid with their lives for their underground activities. The number of student casualties (approximately 400 out of 14,807 students registered in 1940–41) was high. One German source is said to have asserted that as many as one-third of the persons executed were students.[126]

While student organizations remained in operation, close contacts were maintained with those faculty members who were determined to resist German encroachments. Later, as student organizations were dissolved and many of these faculty members were arrested, the gulf between students and faculty widened. This was particularly true of relationships with the more cautious faculty members who chose to remain in office after May 1943. A black list of collaborationist faculty members was published in *De Geus onder Studenten* alongside a similar student list.

The first opportunity for the universities to speak up came in October 1940, when it became known that the German authorities planned to dismiss Jewish officials. A group of university professors, under the leadership of Professor Paul Scholten of Amsterdam, sent a petition to the High Commissioner. This "Scholten Petition" asserted that no Jewish problem existed in the Netherlands and that belief in religious and racial tolerance was one of the basic values cherished by the Dutch people. It requested the High Commissioner not to introduce anti-Jewish legislation.

The petition could not deflect Seyss-Inquart from his course. The so-called ancestry forms were sent to all government officials. Despite student objections, they were filled in by the great majority of faculty members, though many registered protests orally or in writing.

In late November, when German authorities announced the dismissal of Jewish officials, including university professors, student strikes broke out at the University of Leiden and the Technical Institute of Delft. At other universities, largely through the persuasion of the faculty, students restricted themselves to individual oral or written statements.

At Leiden, Professor R. P. Cleveringa, Dean of the Law School, was assigned the classes of Jewish professor E. M. Meijers, a respected and renowned scholar. On the morning of November 26, Professor R. P. Cleveringa addressed the students of Professor Meijers' customary class,* augmented by many others who had heard that a special event was about to take place.[127] He eulogized the former teacher and bitterly denounced the action of the German authorities as a violation of international law. Following the address, the students went on strike.[128]

Professor Cleveringa's speech electrified the country. Thousands of typewritten and mimeographed copies were circulated. The emotion felt by his immediate audience was shared by those who read the text, because it was the most outspoken statement yet made in defiance of the conqueror. In the words of a clandestine communication of that time: "The courageous and noble words of Professor Cleveringa came as a liberation from the oppression [of having to submit passively to all German measures]. With relief we heard of the truly Dutch reaction of the students of Leiden and Delft who went on strike."[129]

German authorities responded quickly to the events at Leiden and Delft. They discontinued classes at both institutions and arrested

* So many students showed up that a special hall with a public address system had to be opened up.

Professor Cleveringa. In December they disbanded student fraternities and clubs at the closed universities because they considered
them centers of student resistance.[130]

Removal of Jewish students from the universities in the autumn
of 1941 did not precipitate a protest of the scope aroused by the dismissal of Jewish professors. However, student organizations at Amsterdam and Groningen dissolved themselves when ordered to exclude Jewish students from their ranks.[131]

The University of Leiden remained officially closed to students
for the remainder of the war, although they were permitted to take
certain examinations for a few months in 1941.[132] Most of the students registered elsewhere, more than half of them at the Municipal
University of Amsterdam.[133] The faculty remained on duty until
1942, when the authorities precipitated another conflict.

In the autumn of 1941, Van Dam, Secretary-General of the new
Department of Education, Science, and Protection of Culture, announced his intention of replacing some of the incumbent Leiden professors with National Socialists. The faculty informed him that it
would resign if the authorities carried out these plans. Thereupon
Van Dam dropped the project for the time being. In the spring of
1942, however, the authorities dismissed Professor R. Kranenburg, a
leading authority on Dutch constitutional law. Thereupon the patriotic majority of the faculty decided that this was the moment to refuse all further cooperation with the Germans. Eighty percent of the
faculty resigned by May 1942. Many of these were arrested as hostages in July.[134] From May 1942 on, Leiden ceased to exist as a university.[135] A plan of Commissioner-General Wimmer and Himmler
to reopen the institution as a National Socialist university, primarily
for army and S.S. veterans, had no tangible results.[136]

In contrast to the shutdown of Leiden, classes at the Technical
Institute at Delft were resumed in April 1941 because German authorities wished to train engineers. The university suffered a serious
blow in 1941 when two faculty members and a number of students
were arrested and executed as part of a sabotage group of seventy-
two belonging to the Ordedienst, one of the earliest resistance groups.
These arrests weakened the will to resist at Delft.[137]

The faculty of the Municipal University of Amsterdam took a different position from that of the majority at Leiden. The Amsterdam

University Senate thought it advisable to continue regular activities, supposedly for two main reasons. In the first place, the faculty pointed out that it could protect young men from the labor draft by continuing instruction. Second, the faculty asserted that it was important for Holland to have a supply of trained young men and women for postwar reconstruction.[138]

Therefore most professors at the Municipal University in Amsterdam stayed on, even when some of their colleagues were arrested and National Socialists were appointed to the staff. Only once did the faculty of the Municipal University threaten to close the institution. This occurred when Rauter expressed his intention to take students and professors as hostages in reprisal for the explosion of a time bomb in the clubhouse of the Nazi student organization.

Toward the end of 1942, German authorities began to consider ways of including university students in the labor draft, from which they had been exempted thus far. In early December, Van Dam asked the heads of the universities to prepare lists from which a quota of 7,000 men could be assigned to work in Germany, but all the university rectors except one refused to comply.[139] Word of this request spread quickly and caused unrest in some institutions. The office of the Registrar at the University of Utrecht went up in flames,[140] and the University was shut down for Christmas vacation four days early in order to avoid further commotion. The administration also closed the Free University of Amsterdam, allegedly because of the fuel shortage.[141] As it became obvious to the Germans that a wholesale draft would lead to the shutdown of all universities, they dropped their plan. Van Dam informed the universities accordingly.

The final crisis in higher education, however, was precipitated by German reactions to the wave of intensified resistance activities early in 1943. In retribution for the assassination of General Seyffardt, which was believed to have been planned by student circles, Rauter arrested about 600 students in simultaneous raids on the universities in Amsterdam, Delft, Utrecht, and Wageningen.[142] As a result of these raids, instruction stopped everywhere. Negotiations began between the parties concerned in the dispute. The moderate faction among the authorities, led by Secretary-General Van Dam, tried to work out a compromise which would satisfy German demands for additional labor and provide assurance that students would not participate in resistance activities, and at the same time protect universities against a repetition of the February raids.

The solution to this dilemma was the famous loyalty pledge. On March 10 the Secretary-General required that students who wished to continue their studies take a loyalty pledge. The pertinent section of this pledge read:

> This signatory . . . herewith declares solemnly that he will obey existing laws, decrees, and other rules in all honor and conscience. He will refrain from all actions directed against the German Reich, its armed forces, or the Dutch authorities, as well as from actions and utterances that will endanger public order at the universities and technical institutes . . .*

At the same time, the authorities limited the total number of students in the interest of "the European struggle against bolshevism." After termination of their studies, students were under obligation to work in Germany for six months.[143] Consequently, signing the loyalty pledge implied an agreement to work in Germany. The German authorities further declared that they would consider students refusing to sign the pledge unemployed and therefore subject to the labor draft.

The students had one month in which to decide whether to sign. They received a great deal of advice in the matter. The majority of the faculty at Delft advised them to sign,[144] although it voted a formal motion of regret at this decision in June 1944.[145] It may be assumed that the students' parents usually did likewise out of fear of reprisals. At the University of Amsterdam the professors left the decision to each student.[146] At the denominational universities the faculty advised against signing and did not provide students with the necessary forms. The underground press, particularly the student publication *De Geus onder Studenten,* urged students not to sign and to go into hiding after the April 10 deadline. Underground student organizations formed special teams to convince fellow students. The Minister of Education, Arts, and Sciences in the government-in-exile, G. Bolkestein, ordered students not to sign under any circumstance.

---

* [8], 28/1943. A similar loyalty declaration had been required of all new government officials since September 1940, but had not been imposed on incumbents [165], pp. 36–37, 120–23.

He declared in 1944 that the government would make certain that students who consented to sign the loyalty pledge would be at a disadvantage after liberation.[147]

In the end, only about 15 percent of all students signed the loyalty pledge. The Technical Institute at Delft had the highest percentage of signers (26 percent), whereas at the Catholic University at Nijmegen only two students were reported to have signed.[148]

On May 5, Rauter called up all male students who had not signed the pledge.[149] He promised to place students in work related to their studies, a promise that was not kept except in the case of medical and pharmaceutical students. The German police threatened reprisals against the families of students who failed to report. Consequently, students were under enormous pressure to do so, especially since the state of emergency declared in connection with the April-May strike was still in force. Thirty-one percent of all nonsigning students reported for deportation.[150] The rest went into hiding or merely waited for the German police. Actually, it seems that the Germans did not usually make special attempts to arrest individual students for failing to report.

Imposition of the loyalty pledge marked the virtual end of university instruction for the remainder of the occupation, except at Delft. Denominational universities and the University of Leiden remained closed. Other public universities carried on after a fashion, and most faculty members gave in to the heavy German pressure and threats and continued their lectures, although they resented having to teach students who had signed loyalty pledges. A number of faculty members went into hiding. During the academic year 1943–44, about 1,500 students, or a little more than 10 percent of the regular enrollment, continued their studies.[151] In many cases, professors clandestinely administered examinations to students in hiding. These examinations were recognized after the Liberation. At the start of the academic year 1944–45, university life came to a complete standstill.

Throughout 1943, reports on the poor conditions of student camps in Germany circulated in Holland. The underground press published the names of students who had succumbed in the Reich.[152] Professor J. Oranje of the Free University of Amsterdam made a secret inspection tour of student camps in Germany. He helped set up an escape route which was so effective that most students were said to have returned to Holland before the Liberation.[153] Upon completion of his inspection tour, Professor Oranje reported to his colleagues. A petition was drawn up describing the poor living conditions and the excessive physical work required in Germany. In March 1944 the petition was signed by the heads of seven universities and forwarded to the Secretary-General.[154]

THE MEDICAL PROFESSION

Early in 1941 it became apparent that the German authorities and the N.S.B. would attempt to control the medical profession. Therefore, physicians decided to prevent the N.S.B. from gaining control of their professional organization and imposing National Socialist concepts on individual practitioners.

As in the case of the universities, the immediate ideological conversion of the medical profession was of secondary concern to the Germans. They were primarily interested in the preservation of public health. The N.S.B. physicians rather than the German authorities were the driving force in the ensuing conflict.

The conflict started when the German authorities forced the Board of Directors (Hoofdbestuur) of the Netherlands Society for the Advancement of Medicine (Nederlandse Maatschappij tot Bevordering der Geneeskunde), the Dutch equivalent of the American Medical Association, to accept Dr. C. C. A. Croin, Assistant Leader of the N.S.B. Medical Front, as one of its members, with the understanding that Dr. Croin would have the task of bringing professional practices into line with the concepts of National Socialist medicine.[155] During the summer of 1941 it became apparent that the majority of the Society's members were unwilling to submit to the proposed arrangement, and disapproved of the decision taken by the Board of Directors. In protest, certain local groups began to advise their members to leave the Society, and they established contacts across the country, inviting colleagues to do likewise. The movement spread quickly. By the end of the summer, most members had withdrawn. Thereupon the Board of Directors resigned at the end of September.[156]

During the agitation for country-wide resignations, a number of patriotic physicians had established contacts in August 1941 which led to the formation of an underground medical organization called the Medical Contact (Medisch Contact). This group was organized somewhat like the Society for the Advancement of Medicine. It was headed by the Center (Centrum), which numbered seven members at first. The Center managed to work closely with local physicians through eleven district representatives. Each district covered approximately one province.[157] Local cells, consisting of five doctors each, were organized in such a way that members supposedly knew only the head of their respective groups, but not their fellow members. This system was worked out so well that the German police never succeeded in seriously interfering with the organization.

Much of the success of the Medical Contact must be attributed to its excellent communications system. Messages issued by the Center were taken to the districts by couriers, and passed on in the same manner to the lower tiers. The mails were used only rarely. Later in the war, the Medical Contact generally used girl couriers.[158]

Because of its emphasis on nonviolent resistance and its intention to help prevent the ideological contamination of Dutch society, the Medical Contact kept in close touch with the churches, especially with the Catholic Church. The episcopacy frequently supported the directives of the Medical Contact in its instructions to Catholic physicians and in its pastoral letters.[159]

In the autumn of 1941, when it became known that German authorities were about to set up a National Socialist physicians' organization with compulsory membership, the Medical Contact began its first major action. It drew up a letter to Seyss-Inquart asking him to abandon his plans. This letter, signed by over 4,000 physicians, was presented to the High Commissioner early in December 1941 by representatives of the Medical Contact. Although the letter did not deter the German administration from its course, it encouraged subsequent resistance, since the German administration had not taken reprisal measures against the petitioners.[160]

In the middle of December, the High Commissioner established the Physicians' Chamber (Artsenkamer) and appointed Dr. Croin as its chairman. All Dutch physicians were declared to be members of the Chamber automatically. The Medical Contact advised its followers to ignore the new organization and not to pay contributions or fill in its questionnaires. Thousands of physicians endorsed a letter to Dr. Croin, the text of which had been suggested by the Medical

Contact, setting forth the reasons for their resistance to the Chamber.

During 1942, only collaborationist physicians joined the Chamber. Dr. Croin did not yet force patriotic physicians to participate but laid the groundwork for doing so by issuing disciplinary regulations which authorized the imposition of fines on noncooperating physicians.

In March 1943 Dr. Croin finally precipitated a crisis. He fined approximately eighty physicians for their failure to enroll in the Chamber. He had unlimited authority to increase these fines to the point where he could break the resistance of the doctors concerned. Therefore the Medical Contact advised its members to "resign" their practice by "giving up" the title of "physician," which was made possible by the wording of one paragraph in the original decree establishing the Physicians' Chamber. Over 6,000 doctors sent their letters of resignation to Dr. Croin and taped over the title of "physician" on their office signs. The German authorities, considering this action a political demonstration, ordered the physicians to resume their practice and restore their office signs, but it was clear that they did not wish to provoke a major crisis. In negotiations with Commissioner-General Wimmer, it was decided that, in return for the doctors' promise to continue to practice and to remove the tape from their office signs, the Germans would not force physicians to join the Chamber.[161]

Matters were not allowed to rest at this point, however. At the end of May, Seyss-Inquart issued a decree that prohibited persons who had taken an oath of office from resigning without permission.[162] This new decree was obviously designed to close the loophole in the original regulation and to force the physicians to join the Chamber. Thereupon the Medical Contact in June 1943 advised its members to send another protest letter to the High Commissioner. The final paragraph of this letter summed up the case of the medical profession:

> . . . [the] medical oath which ties us to medical and ethical norms can make it impossible for us in the future to satisfy your demands. If it should come to the point where unacceptable demands should be imposed on us physicians, then it could happen that we must throw freedom and life into the balance despite your threats. We expect that you will spare us this conflict and will allow us to continue our work in liberty and peace, according to our consciences. The future course of events will depend on you. . . .[163]

The High Commissioner considered this letter to be an open defiance. In retribution, the German police arrested 360 physicians. Many others promptly went into hiding to avoid anticipated arrests. For a time it looked as if the entire practice of medicine in the occupied territory might come to a standstill.

Once again, personal contacts were made with German authorities. When the High Commissioner declared that he felt insulted by the letter, representatives of the Medical Contact drew up a letter of apology, stating that the communication had not been intended as a political action or as a defiance of the High Commissioner. The German authorities, for their part, made it clear that they would require Dr. Croin to abandon his efforts at making physicians join the Chamber. The arrested physicians were gradually released, and the Chamber passed into oblivion.[164] With the letter of apology, the Medical Contact had provided a face-saving device for the German administration while gaining an actual victory.

The events of the spring and summer of 1943 brought to a climax the struggle of the medical profession. Other small actions, however, continued. Throughout the occupation, the Medical Contact successfully advised its members against collaboration with the labor draft. Physicians were warned against asking for exemptions or assisting with the medical selection of labor deportees. The Medical Contact also advised its members against going to Germany on any pretext, since they would be forced in the long run to serve the German war effort there. The management of hospitals and other institutions was urged not to surrender Jewish patients to the police. Physicians were urged not to betray their professional secrets or to report persons with wounds, as required by German decrees. In 1944 and 1945 the Medical Contact protested against food conditions in the occupied territory and confronted the German administration with its responsibility for the general decline of public health.

THE CHURCHES

In 1930 three Christian denominations had sizable numbers of adherents. Catholics were the largest group, with 36.4 percent. Next came the two large Protestant denominations, the Dutch Reformed Church (Nederlands Hervormde Kerk) with 34.4 percent, and the

Reformed Churches (Gereformeerde Kerken) with 8 percent. Only 14 percent of the population did not belong to any church, approximately one-fourth of the percentage so listed in the United States in 1926.[165]

In the sixteenth and seventeenth centuries, the Calvinists had played a dominant role in the struggle against the Spaniards. They had organized the Dutch Reformed Church, which became the state church, along Presbyterian lines. Its supreme ruling body was the National Synod, which was indirectly elected by the local consistories, made up of preachers, elders, and deacons from the several congregations. After the Kingdom of the Netherlands was founded in 1815, the new ruler, William I, brought about a reorganization of the Church, which resulted in centralization and in a weakening of the Presbyterian principle.[166] Thus it lost some of its flexibility and power to inspire its members.[167]

The congregations organized in 1892 under the name of "the Reformed Churches" had seceded from the Dutch Reformed Church during the nineteenth century because many orthodox Calvinists felt that the parent church allowed too much tampering with doctrine. The Reformed Churches represented the more aggressive and fundamentalist section of protestantism. Their main strength lay with the lower middle class and the farmers.[168]

After their emancipation in the wake of the French Revolution, the Catholics became increasingly influential. In 1853 a Catholic episcopate for the Netherlands was established. The country was divided into five dioceses. The archbishop of Utrecht became the head of the Dutch Catholic Church. The Catholic hierarchy exerted a more specific and better enforced discipline among its faithful than did the pastors of other denominations.

During the twentieth century, the episcopate consistently urged its communicants to enlist in Catholic parochial social, cultural, and political organizations. This appeal was highly effective, particularly as the Church backed it up with a prohibition against joining many nonparochial organizations, and generally barred from the sacraments Catholics who enrolled in groups advocating or believing in Communist, Socialist, liberal, or agnostic principles. Membership in the Socialist Netherlands Association of Trade Unions was prohibited under this clause. After the rise of national socialism in Holland, this ban was extended to most communicants joining the National Socialist Movement.

The religious division of the Dutch people extended into all walks of life. Protestants and Catholics had founded numerous organizations covering practically every phase of group action, for members of their respective faiths. These parochial organizations were founded in addition to corresponding nonsectarian bodies. Thus parallel Catholic, Protestant, and nondenominational unions, parties, educational institutions, newspapers, radio stations, recreational clubs, and numerous other groups existed in greater profusion in Holland than anywhere else in Western Europe.

The abundant growth of parochial groups had its roots in the formative years of the Dutch republic, when Calvinism made its strong imprint on Dutch civilization. Calvinist doctrine held that the Church should more or less directly control the entire life of the faithful. When the Catholic Church rose to a position of influence in the nineteenth century, it found itself in thorough harmony with this doctrine.*

Because of the pervasiveness of religious divisions, an analysis of public opinion and motivations for action must place considerable emphasis on religious motives and stratification. Ministers and priests, professors, and professional men in general played a more important part in shaping public opinion than they did in such countries as the United States and Germany, and to a large extent they were the interpreters of national ideals.

The pluralism created by the existence of thousands of different and often locally autonomous associations, independent of and often unknown to the government, greatly contributed to the stability of the social structure. By the same token, in times of peace denominational divisions made cooperation more difficult for the separate segments of the Dutch population.

Because of these pervasive religious divisions there was little cooperation between the episcopate and the Protestant churches before the occupation. Moreover the Protestant denominations even among themselves stressed differences in theological doctrine. But in poli-

---

* This was the natural outcome of the fact that Calvinism, as well as Catholic dogma, maintained the medieval theory of the supremacy of the militant church over the secular community.

tics the members of the Christian parties often united in common parliamentary action. This tradition provided the framework for the cooperation between the churches during the occupation.

This resistance extended to three general areas. First, the churches provided guidance to their members on ideological issues and practical matters arising from occupation policies. This was done in sermons and pastoral letters, through individual counseling furnished by the clergy, and through those denominational lay groups that continued to exist legally or underground during the German occupation. Second, the churches acted as spokesmen for the conscience of the entire community. At first their comments were hesitant, but from 1941 on, they angrily denounced the actions of the occupying power. The churches spoke their mind in pastoral letters, in interviews with German and Dutch authorities, and in communications addressed to government dignitaries. Third, some churches virtually became resistance organizations, protecting affiliated lay groups and individuals who were threatened by German measures. They collected funds, used lay groups to conceal clandestine organizations, and encouraged or allowed individual pastors and priests to work in the underground movement.

This preoccupation with mundane political matters did not represent as great a departure from the past in Holland as it might have in Germany or Scandinavia. Out of the common medieval concept of the supremacy of church over society and state, the Calvinist and Catholic churches had traditionally guided their communicants in moral and public matters. The Dutch Reformed Church, with its Presbyterian leanings, had been less inclined than the Catholic and orthodox Calvinist churches to concern itself with political matters, but its General Synod decided as early as July 1940 that the Church had a special responsibility to uphold Christian tenets in public life against the expected onslaught of national socialism. Most other Protestant denominations followed this example, although some of the smaller groups were more cautious in the beginning since they were more vulnerable. The Lutherans, with their German ties and their state church traditions of submissiveness to the powers that be, were the most hesitant of all in their actions. In order to consult with one another, and to coordinate actions, the Protestant churches established an interdenominational council (Interkerkelijk Overleg).[169]

Perhaps the most important aspect of church resistance was the attempt to furnish spiritual and ideological guidance for communicants. Catholic and Protestant churches became increasingly emphatic in their denunciation of National Socialist institutions. In January 1941 the Catholic Church reiterated in a pastoral letter its prewar prohibition against joining the N.S.B. or any National Socialist organization.[170] This circular reassured many that during the occupation the Catholic Church would maintain its opposition to Nazi organizations. The Catholic Church also prohibited its communicants from joining many of the new semipublic organizations which were gradually established in Holland. It advised students against signing the loyalty oath,[171] and preferred to have Catholic universities closed rather than have their students submit on this point.

The Catholic Church and the Reformed Churches were willing to enforce their prohibitions by the imposition of religious penalties. Both authorized exclusion of members of the N.S.B. and its auxiliaries from the sacraments, although these instructions contained a variety of qualifications. The Dutch Reformed Church placed greater emphasis on persuasion, but by 1943 it also authorized its ministers to exclude National Socialists from communion and confirmation at their discretion.[172]

In their attempt to provide ideological guidance, the churches took issue with the assertion of the occupying power that all Christians should help the Third Reich in its struggle against bolshevism. This argument had some persuasive power among the more fundamentalist conservatives, who were bitter enemies of communism on political as well as religious grounds. In May 1943 the Catholic Church reminded its members that "the only power to combat communism in essence is not national socialism but Christianity."[173] The Dutch Reformed Church in November 1943 likewise reaffirmed the incompatibility of the two concepts and rejected the National Socialist plea for cooperation.[174]

The churches enjoined their congregations to aid victims of Nazi persecution. In February 1943 they went so far as to ask their members to practice civil disobedience rather than to participate in hunting down Jews and young people. The declaration of the Dutch Reformed Church reasserted the Biblical injunction: " 'We must obey

God rather than men.' This commandment is the touchstone in all conflicts of conscience including those created by the [German] measures which have been taken. This word of God forbids participation in deeds of injustice through which one would come to share in the guilt for that injustice."[175]

The Catholic pastoral letter on this subject concluded with the words: "And should the refusal of this collaboration require sacrifices from you, then be strong and steadfast in the awareness that you are doing your duty before God and your fellow men."[176]

Subsequently, the Catholic Church outlined in detail the implications of this general directive for various situations. The Church advised leading officials in employment offices to resign, but permitted Catholic policemen to collaborate in the apprehension of strikers after the May strike, since these actions endangered the public order and security, which the police were obliged to maintain. However, the Church forbade collaboration in hunting down students or other labor draftees, veterans liable to reinternment, and Jewish citizens. In this connection the episcopacy redefined the concept of "duress" as a justification for continued collaboration. Only the threat of a concentration camp and the death penalty could be considered "duress." The loss of office and livelihood were not included in that category.[177] It was generally understood that persons who lost their income as a result of refusing collaboration would receive financial support from the Church.

In addition to providing guidance to their communicants, the churches acted as spokesmen for the entire Dutch community in confronting the Germans with certain moral and political questions. The first such instance was the protest of the Protestant churches in October 1940, requesting Seyss-Inquart to withdraw the regulation prohibiting the hiring of new Jewish employees and to abandon the plan for dismissing Jewish officials.[178] For the next two years the Jewish question remained the most important topic of exchanges between churches and the German authorities.

When Commissioner-General Schmidt announced the impending deportation of Jews in the summer of 1942, Catholic and Protestant churches immediately sent protest telegrams to the Reich authorities. They planned to have these messages read from the pulpit on a subsequent Sunday. The Germans threatened immediate deportation of Jewish Christians (i.e., converted Jews) if the churches persisted. The episcopacy refused to be intimidated and the protest telegram was read in the Catholic churches, with the result that Catholic Jews were deported.[179]

In May 1943 the churches again took issue with the Germans on behalf of the Jewish citizens. At that time the Germans gave those Jews married to non-Jews the choice between sterilization and deportation. The protest of the combined churches was worded in the sharpest language used so far:

> Sterilization . . . is the logical end result of an anti-Christian doctrine which supports human extermination. It is the result of a boundless self-glorification and an outlook on the world and life which renders a Christian and humane life impossible.
>
> . . . We entertain no illusions. We realize that we can hardly expect that Your Excellency [will listen to] the voice of the Church, the voice of the Gospel, the voice of God. But what we cannot humanly expect, we may still hope for as Christians . . . for the good of Your Excellency and of our suffering people.[180]

Eventually, the High Commissioner prohibited the sterilization of Jews in mixed marriages.[181]

The religious bodies did not limit themselves to the Jewish question in their pleadings with the authorities. In the first year of the occupation, the Protestant churches asked the Secretaries-General to do anything in their power to prevent the trend toward lawlessness, such as street riots and arrests of innocent citizens.[182] When it became clear that the Secretaries-General could not change the course of events, the Protestant churches allied themselves with the Catholic Church in asking for a personal interview with the High Commissioner. This interview took place in February 1942. In the memorandum prepared for Seyss-Inquart as the basis for the audience, the churches again protested against the anti-Jewish measures, the arbitrary arrests, and the attempt to impose national socialism on the Dutch people by force.[183] In practical terms, the interview was fruitless in changing the German course of action. But it served a purpose in pointing up the irreconcilable nature of the ideological conflict.[184]

The Catholic Church did a spectacular job in supporting those of its members who resisted the German regime on principle. When the Germans began to limit the means of livelihood of Jews in 1941, the Catholic Church held a special collection in June, to build up a "Fund for Special Emergencies." Originally this fund was to be used to help Catholic Jews. In August 1941, after the dissolution of the Catholic workers' union, it was decided that a regular collection would be made at all church functions for "the special needs of the archbishopric." To avoid German countermeasures, the specific purpose of this fund was not announced officially. Nor were further requests for contributions made after the first appeal. But the collections were taken up Sunday after Sunday throughout the occupation. The Fund grew beyond expectations. Its benefits were extended to all citizens who made sacrifices for the sake of Christian principles, such as resigning their jobs or giving up social security benefits. Catholic patriots who went into hiding after 1943 for political rather than religious or moral reasons generally received help through individual solicitations by priests from wealthy members of their parishes. It has been estimated that about fifteen million guilders were collected for the Fund between June 1941 and November 1944.[185] The Dutch Reformed Church also established a special fund, called the "Treasury for Mutual Assistance," which disbursed hundreds of thousands of guilders to victims of the German regime.[186]

The churches rejected all German attempts to interfere with their services. Traditionally, prayers for the Queen had been a part of the Sunday service of the Dutch Reformed Church. German authorities tried to stop this custom, but the leadership of the Church firmly refused to give in. It instructed its ministers to continue prayers for the Queen, but also to include prayers for the occupying power.[187] Individual ministers arrested for such prayers always could refer to orders from their superiors. By and large, the prayer for the Queen continued to be said throughout the occupation. In Catholic chapels, the Latin hymn *"Domine, salvam fac reginam nostram"* ("Lord, safeguard our Queen") also was sung regularly.

The resistance of the churches required numerous sacrifices. Hundreds of ministers and priests were arrested, although the higher Catholic clergy was not molested. Forty-three ministers of the two major Protestant denominations and forty-nine Catholic priests lost their lives in resistance to national socialism.[188] In addition, many prominent Protestant and Catholic laymen were sent to concentration camps and death.

Despite vacillations and hesitations, especially at the beginning, the churches grew stronger and more united during the occupation. They played a more vital part in the lives of their adherents and in national affairs than they had for many years.

CHAPTER NINE

The Response of the Jewish Population

In 1930 approximately 113,000 persons representing 1.4 percent of the population were registered as belonging to the Jewish faith.[1] After Hitler's rise to power in Germany, a number of German Jews settled in Holland, enlarging the existing community by about 10 percent. Most Jews lived in the big cities. Amsterdam had a neighborhood largely inhabited by Jewish people. In contrast to the situation in Germany and in most Western European countries, many Jewish Dutchmen engaged in manual labor and belonged to the low-income group. For example, they almost held a monopoly as grinders in the Amsterdam diamond industry. Many Amsterdam Jews such as street vendors belonged to the lowest stratum of urban society.

In contrast to eastern Europe and Germany, little active anti-Semitism existed before the German invasion, although rather definite social dividing lines prevailed between Jews and Gentiles just as between Protestants and Catholics.[2] Jewish scholars and officials occupied respected positions in public institutions. As part of the Erasmian and Nonconformist Protestant inheritance, and as a result of the need to accommodate the powerful Catholic minority, the principle of religious toleration became a cornerstone of Dutch civilization.

REACTION TO INITIAL GERMAN MEASURES, 1940–1942

As the military struggle drew to a close, on May 14, a number of Jews tried to escape from the Netherlands by ship. Since the Germans had already cut off Holland from Belgium, the North Sea remained the only way out. Therefore the port of Ijmuiden, near Amsterdam, the center of the Jewish population, was crowded with people who wanted to reach England. Few succeeded and some lost their lives crossing the Channel.

On the same day, and during the ensuing week, a number of Jews committed suicide. It may be estimated that approximately 200 Jews ended their own lives in 1940 to avoid persecution.[3] Many, but by no means all, were refugees from Germany who refused to face Nazi terror once more.

Dutch Jews began to relax in the weeks after the surrender, as did the rest of the population, because the anticipated measures against the Jews did not materialize as soon as expected. When the first anti-Jewish regulations were published in the late summer and autumn of 1940, the Jewish population complied. Practically all full Jews under the Nuremberg Laws registered in the special Jewish census of January 1941,[4] although it appears that a number of persons of mixed parentage failed to do so.[5] This special registration supplied the Germans with the basic data needed to implement the persecution which was to ensue. It is doubtful that the Germans could have established an accurate file in accordance with the regulations of the Nuremberg Laws without the cooperation of the Jews themselves.*

In February 1941 the only instance, during the occupation, of "armed" resistance or "fighting back" by Jewish groups took place. A few Amsterdam Jews of working-class background formed Action Groups (Knokploegen) in response to the provocative marches and attacks of Nazi storm troopers (W.A.). These Action Groups secured primitive weapons and fought pitched battles with members of the N.S.B., wounding a number of them and killing one. All further open resistance was stifled by ruthless German countermeasures, such as the well-known physical extermination, in the Mauthausen camp, of the young Jews arrested in February and June 1941.[6]

Consequently, the Jewish population continued to comply in 1941 and 1942 with German measures designed to segregate the Jews. Despite all difficulties, a renaissance of Jewish cultural life occurred

---

* Cf. [171], p. 18, for a contrary opinion. In this passage, Berkley maintains that failure to register would have been useless since the German administration could have secured the data from public files.

during this period. A number of monographs on topics relating to the Jewish tradition were published, and a new Hebrew dictionary and a few volumes of Hebrew poetry appeared. There was a resurgence of religious feeling, as evidenced by an increased demand for the religious instruction of children.[7]

THE DEPORTATIONS, JULY 1942–SEPTEMBER 1943

With the start of the deportations, the problem of physical survival and the effort to remain in Holland rather than be forced to leave for an unknown destination became paramount. When the Zentralstelle, the German office responsible for deportations,[8] informed the heads of the Jewish Council late in June 1942 that Jews would have to go to Germany to work under the supervision of the police (*polizeilicher Arbeitseinsatz*), there was great consternation among the Jewish population. This distress was intensified by the speech of Commissioner-General Schmidt on June 28, in which he had painted a bleak picture of the fate of the Jews, predicting that they would have to return to their country of origin, presumably Poland, as "poor and full of vermin" as they had left.[9]

In view of these statements, doubts and fears about the fate of the deportees were intense. Consequently, relatively few Jews who had been ordered to report to the Zentralstelle had appeared by July 14, the date set for the departure of the first group. The German police therefore arrested approximately 750 Jews in mass raids on July 14, holding them as hostages to force the departure of the first groups of persons assigned to deportation.[10] This strategy initially worked well. Over 6,000 Jews arrived in Westerbork between July 15 and July 31.[11]

However, the strategy lost its effectiveness when, on August 2, Commissioner-General Schmidt delivered another talk in which he described the fate of the Jews in even starker colors.[12] The turnout dropped and few Jews reported for the trains to Westerbork. Thereupon the German police had an extra issue of the *Joodse Weekblad* published, in which persons who refused to obey the summons to report for the "labor draft" were threatened with arrest and shipment to Mauthausen,[13] a threat that carried a connotation of certain death in view of past experience. In addition, the Germans conducted two raids in Amsterdam in which they caught thousands of Jews. Many were released, and others escaped at the staging point.*

Despite the threats of deportation to Mauthausen, and the deep impression created by mass raids, the turnout continued to be so poor that the Germans were forced to change their methods. Originally they had mailed a summons to individuals or families who were assigned to deportation. Soon the German police found themselves forced to capture Jews assigned to deportation in night raids on their dwellings, although the system of calling up persons was maintained in the provinces for some time and was never completely abandoned. The big night raids commenced in Amsterdam at the beginning of September. They were conducted almost daily, and approximately 300 to 500 Jews were captured each time.[14]

During September the Germans formalized their system of exemptions[15] by providing *Sperrstempel* (exemption stamps) in an elaborate variety of categories. A good *Sperrstempel* was the Jews' most highly prized possession during 1942–43.

In the summer and autumn of 1942 the Germans and the Jewish Council developed a routine for staging the departure of Jews from Amsterdam. In July and August, when the German police ordered deportees to report "voluntarily," special streetcars were run from Jewish neighborhoods to the Central Station, the main staging point at the beginning of the deportations. Individuals and families living in areas not covered by this service had to walk long distances to the station.[16]

The increasingly poor turnout forced the Germans to establish another staging point where deportees could be screened, exemptions granted, and other administrative problems met. At first, only the office of the Zentralstelle was used, but at the end of July a Jewish theater, the Joodse Schouwburg, was rented for these purposes. For some time after, arrestees were taken both to the Zentralstelle and the Schouwburg, but as procedures became more routinized, regular arrestees were taken increasingly to the Schouwburg for screening and staging.[17] Special cases, such as people whom the Germans wanted to process separately because of some transgression of regulations, continued to be taken to the Zentralstelle. At both points officials of the Jewish Council were present to keep order, to assist

* It appears that the officials of the Jewish Council stationed at the assembly point succeeded in helping many to escape ([145], p. 8).

with screening, and to minister to the many needs of the deportees.[18]

In October the Germans gave a reprieve to Amsterdam Jews and concentrated on the other big cities, especially Rotterdam, and on the provinces.[19] They also closed the work camps, most of which were located in the eastern part of the country. Previously, they had encouraged between 7,000 and 8,000 Jews to go to these work camps by creating the illusion that people in the camps would not be deported. This was simply a ruse, since Rauter intended to lock the Jews in the camps and deport them and their relatives, hopefully a total of 13,000 persons, during the autumn.[20]

Beginning in November, persons who had been granted exemptions because they were employed in factories working for the German armed forces were arrested at their places of work. Their families were also rounded up and sent to transit camps.[21]

In January, after a short "Christmas recess," raids and call-ups were resumed in full force in Amsterdam and elsewhere. Now a special effort was made to deport institutionalized persons, such as orphans, and the aged and sick. Exemptions were also canceled for German veterans of the First World War.[22] In March and April all Jews living outside of Amsterdam had to report, and special raids were conducted in the provinces.[23]

In early May there was a period of comparative rest in preparation for the mopping-up operations. On May 14 Jews living in Amsterdam, except those with exemptions, were ordered to leave by May 20.[24] Since only one-fourth of the number called up reported, the Germans ordered the Jewish Council to designate 7,000 of its own employees for deportation. This the Council did after much soul-searching.[25] Again only a fraction of the persons designated showed up at the appointed time on May 25.[26] Consequently the Germans conducted a mass raid in the center of Amsterdam on May 26, seizing 3,000 Jews.[27] They then assured the Jewish Council that no further raids would be conducted "for the time being,"[28] but small seizures continued. On June 20, in another mass raid in the southern and eastern part of Amsterdam, 5,700 persons were captured.[29]

The final blow came on September 29, the Jewish New Year, when 3,000 Jews, including the leaders of the Jewish Council, were arrested in Amsterdam and 7,000 Jews were seized elsewhere in simultaneous raids.[30] At that time the Jewish Council ceased to exist.

This was the end of the big raids, although throughout the rest of the occupation the police continued to track down Jews who had gone underground. From this point on, with the exception of people in hiding, only persons with very special exemptions, most of them partners in mixed marriages, were allowed to remain outside the camps.

A summary of Jewish reaction to the deportations shows a pattern of growing reluctance, which forced the Germans to use increasingly direct methods, starting with summons by mail, changing to piece-meal raids on designated persons, and culminating in large-scale man-hunts during which the police arrested every Jew in sight, respecting few exemptions.

However, despite the reluctance to report for the Westerbork train, only a minority of the Jewish population attempted to avoid deportation by going underground. It has been estimated that ap-proximately 20,000 Jews, or fewer than one out of six persons slated for deportation, went into hiding and that 8,000 of these survived,[31] half of them children.

Several individual Jews endeavored to save as many lives as pos-sible through clandestine action. An official of the Jewish Council, Walter Süsskind, with the aid of the resistance movement, managed to smuggle approximately 1,000 Jewish infants out of a nursery at the Joodse Schouwburg.[32] Other officials also helped individual Jews to escape from staging points in Amsterdam.

A Zionist Youth Group established an underground organization with the aid of non-Jews, designed to help its members go under-ground in Holland or France or to escape to Spain. Eighty succeeded in crossing the Pyrenees and 240 survived in hiding. The group suc-ceeded in saving the lives of almost half its members.[33]

A number of Jews individually attempted to escape from the Neth-erlands by land. Some of these remained underground in other oc-cupied territories, particularly Belgium and France, while others succeeded in reaching neutral territory and continuing on to Eng-land. Obstacles were many, so escape was tried mainly by younger persons, especially single men. Nevertheless, recent figures indi-cate that 2,000 Jews managed to save their lives by leaving Holland, which is half the number of adults who appear to have survived in hiding in the Netherlands.[34]

No specific Jewish resistance group was formed to obstruct the deportations through clandestine operations, with the exception of the Zionist Youth Organization. Individual Jews who decided to engage in resistance to the Germans joined other underground organizations. Not all resistance organizations were willing to accept Jews, since Jews were more exposed in many respects than Gentiles. It has been asserted that Dutch patriots tended to underestimate the role individual Jews played in the Resistance, while the Germans, victims of their own distorted propaganda, grossly overestimated this role. One leading authority claims that a larger percentage of the Jewish than of the Gentile population engaged in resistance activities.[35]

The life of the Jewish people during the period of the deportations is best conveyed in contemporary diaries, underground newspaper articles, and works of fiction in which the substance of the experience is relived. From these sources it is apparent that a semblance of "normal life" continued, albeit under the ever-darkening gloom of fear and despair. Jewish business establishments and restaurants remained open to serve a shrinking trade. Schools and vocational training institutions carried on, although more and more students and teachers disappeared after each raid. The Jewish Council provided "a way of life" for the swollen ranks of its employees.

But despite these semblances of "normalcy," the deportations threw an ever-lengthening shadow over the lives of most people. Many hours were spent waiting at the offices of the Jewish Council and the Zentralstelle in attempts to obtain exemptions, to appeal an assignment to the next train, or to wind up family and business affairs if the inevitable had been accepted.

Uncertainty and fear were never absent. Every time Jews went into the streets there was a danger they might be caught in one of the recurrent raids, since they were plainly marked by the Star of David and the "J" on their identity cards. Once caught, no *Sperrstempel* was reliable because German dignitaries were quite erratic in their respect for exemptions. At night, as Jews sat at home, fear was still with them. Every car might be a police van arriving for its quota of human beings. Each footstep might mean the approach of the S.S. coming to take them away. Children and adults alike became tense and quarrelsome in this climate of perpetual fear.

The inevitable end to the waiting at home came in a variety of ways, but for most people with the same result: the train to the East. A family might receive an order to report and decide to go, walking from the apartment to the waiting streetcar, which Jews were allowed to use only for this final ride to the train at the main railroad station, to a loading platform at the East Harbor, or to the Joodse Schouwburg.

Or, perhaps, a family would refuse to report and stay behind, waiting for the Germans to come and get them. Or they might never have received a summons and be hauled from their home because they were on the German list for the night, or because the police had decided to seize every Jew in a given neighborhood. Or Jews might be caught on the street in a day raid and taken to the staging points, to be dispatched by train to Westerbork or Vught.

The following description, taken from the September 1942 issue of an underground newspaper, may serve to portray a "typical raid":

> In the quiet streets of the Zuid [the southern part of Amsterdam] you hear suddenly the noise of many cars, the hated Green Police vans in which the Germans fetch their victims . . . They descend from the vans . . . The Green Police and their Dutch henchmen.
>
> In a short time . . . all streets between the skyscraper on the Daniel Willinkplein and the Scheldestraat have been occupied . . . And then it begins: on each corner stand German agents, rifles slung across their shoulders . . .
>
> And there they noisily climb upstairs: "Are any Jews living here?" And then the Jews of Holland are driven together on the street corner. Men and women and children . . .
>
> . . . There they stand on the corner of their own street, alone and abandoned. No, thank God, not abandoned, there are Christians, real Christians, human beings with a heart in their breasts who come to their aid. Look, they reason with the uniformed Germans, they plead with them, and no threats that they, too, will be taken along can stop them. They bring food and candy and warm clothes to the unfortunate Jews, and then run off to tell relatives who live in the neighborhood what is happening to their families . . .
>
> From the fourth floor a Jew leaps to his death rather than fall into the hands of the Germans. The Germans followed him up to the roof after they had searched closets and cellars, attics and tool sheds. A dog who defends his master . . . is shot down by the Germans. That is the only shot fired that night . . .
>
> And the public sees this and the heart turns to stone. Every-

body walking through the neighborhood is stopped at each corner and has to show his identity card. If he has the fatal J on his card he is lost. If not, he can walk on, until another policeman has to be satisfied at the next corner . . .

Then comes the end. The big green vans start their engines and begin to move. The engines keep roaring until a quarter to twelve . . . The vans bring their loads to the Gestapo Building, to the Joodse Schouwburg and elsewhere. And then the transports start leaving the city. It breaks your heart to see people like yourselves hauled away, calm, hopeful, and often dignified, the old nation of the Israelites. Crying women and children, everybody enters the train and departs . . . [36]

FACTORS EXPLAINING JEWISH REACTIONS

The description of the segregation and deportation of Jews in Holland raises the question why this group accepted its fate with comparative passivity. Why did so few Jews make a major effort to remove themselves from the German grip by securing false documents and going into hiding?

First, the basic fact that must be remembered is that the Jews did not "know" what the future had in store for the deportees. The extermination policy and its grisly details were unimaginable, particularly to the potential victims. Jews and Gentiles shared this limitation of the human imagination: they could not entertain seriously the concept that the Germans were determined to destroy the physical substance of the Jews.

The Germans succeeded well in their attempt to camouflage the destiny of the deportees. In public they spoke of "labor service in Germany" (*Arbeitseinsatz in Deutschland*), although the term "*Aussiedlung*" or "forced emigration" was used in internal communications. Even when it became clear that the majority of Dutch deportees went to Auschwitz, a former Polish town located in territory annexed to Germany in 1939 (which made it technically correct to speak of labor service in Germany), it was still unknown what went on in the camp. The misleading messages which the Germans arranged to have sent back from Auschwitz were carefully studied and analyzed in an effort to determine the consequences of deportation. These messages described the kind of work the senders were supposedly doing in Auschwitz.[37] They contributed a great deal to the deception of the Jews in Holland, since, despite doubts, they were essentially believed. The elaborate instructions on how to send mail to the deportees, which continued to appear in the *Joodse Weekblad* until September 1943, long after most of the deportees had been murdered, also reinforced the impression that survival was possible and that normal life continued in the East.

Second, fear played a crucial role in inducing the Jews to comply with German measures. Throughout the deportation period the Germans threatened that Jews who went into hiding or failed to report for deportation would be sent to Mauthausen. (In actuality, "punitive cases" were handled no differently from others after arrival at Auschwitz, although persons in this category were kept in separate barracks in Westerbork and promptly sent to the East.) The Germans deliberately deported Jews who possessed special strength and integrity, in order to eliminate potential opposition.[38] It was difficult and often dangerous to try to locate a hiding place, especially before May 1943. (The history of the extermination of the Dutch Jews might indeed read quite differently if the deportations had been initiated a year later, in the summer of 1943, when the spirit of anti-German resistance had spread into the countryside on a broad scale.) Many Jews had facial features that set them off prominently from their fellow countrymen in the northern sections of the Netherlands. Stories of Jews who had been caught in hiding or while trying to escape from Holland were widely circulated. But while these risks were real enough, it is clear in retrospect that the dangers of going into hiding were exaggerated and the dangers of deportation were underestimated.[39] This distortion of reality had a profound impact on decisions.

Third, it also must be remembered that almost from the start of the occupation the Dutch population as a whole, and the Jews in particular, sustained a fervent and, in retrospect, absurd belief in a sudden collapse of the Third Reich. Self-deception played a role, but Allied war propaganda and the tenor of some underground publications reinforced this illusion.*

---

* See below, pp. 176–77, for comments on the need for self-deception. It must be admitted, however, that any number of circumstances such as Hitler's death or an early success of the military conspiracy might have led to an unexpected sudden end of the war.

Fourth, love and courage and a reluctance to impose on others induced people to submit. Many did not want to endanger their Gentile friends. Others, who might have preferred to go into hiding, chose to stay with their families. (After all, the Germans had promised that families would be allowed to remain together!) In some instances, wives of men who had been arrested decided to join their husbands in Westerbork; in others, young men, exempted because they were employed by a factory working for the Germans, volunteered to join their parents.[40] Thus, the strong family ties typical of Jewish people induced some to submit more readily than they might have otherwise. In the same spirit, some men and women felt an obligation to share the fate of their race, rather than save their own lives.

Fifth, the Germans and the Jewish Council provided a basis for the illusion that there was some hope of escape from deportations, even at the last moment. The German police frequently released a certain percentage of the Jews it had arrested. Each group of those released was mentioned in the bulletins of the Jewish Council and circulated in Amsterdam, generating greater compliance.

The same illusion was maintained and the Jewish community split by encouraging a variety of groups, particularly in 1942, to believe that they would not be deported. At first, only young adults between sixteen and forty who were able to perform physical labor were asked to report, this being an attempt both to reinforce the pretense of labor service and to remove first from Holland the young adults most likely to give trouble. Therefore, older people could cherish the hope that they might not have to go. Then there were the "exempted categories" such as workers for the armed forces, employees of the Jewish Council, and the Portuguese Jews, to name only a few. The Germans permitted these categories to be artificially inflated as long as it suited their purposes.

Finally, it appears to the postwar observer that the cumulative effect of years of intimidation, segregation, deteriorating food and living conditions, and discouraging news from the theaters of war (at least until January 1943) all conspired to promote a mood of demoralization and fatalism. In this mood it was easier to choose the course of least resistance and to avoid decisions that might involve effort and immediate danger: "Very few persons immediately made the decision to go or not to go. Most of them remained undecided until the last moment."[41] At that last moment it usually was too late and submission came by default.

It can be asserted that the Jews behaved as any group would have behaved under similar circumstances and that they were simply helpless in the face of German persecution.[42] Evidence of behavior in concentration and internment camps of the Second World War and the Korean war suggests that the human being can stand only so much stress before his moral core disintegrates. The threat hanging over the Jews of Holland in 1942 and 1943 produced such disintegration.

While some of these factors, and others not listed, tended to induce most Jews to report or to wait at home for the police, the great shapeless fear of what could happen in the East induced a substantial minority to attempt to escape or to go into hiding. The specter of Mauthausen, the knowledge of what had happened to the hundreds of young Jews deported in 1941, while engendering fear, also made German assurances of resettlement seem dubious. There was also a great terror of Poland, intensified by Schmidt's speeches. Articles in underground papers asserting that deported Jews faced certain death,[43] and conceivably echoes of the vague statements about extermination camps made by British Foreign Secretary Eden in December 1942, intensified the existing sense of dread. The following diary entry of September 1942, written by a young woman who had chosen to go into hiding with her husband, exemplifies the state of mind of many Jews in this period:

> I knew well what I was doing when I made my decision to go into hiding with my husband instead of letting him go to a camp, because all Jews and even almost all non-Jews knew only too well the consequences of going to a work camp. I was fully conscious of the fact that this meant leaving [my parents] behind without knowing whether we should ever see . . . [them] again, something which I often doubt very much . . . [44]

These contradictory insights often were held at different levels of consciousness. Most persons in this situation brought all powers of rationalization into play in order to be able to believe that "things might not be so bad after all." The following statement made after the war by a high official of the Jewish Council illustrates the limitations of the human imagination: "I once heard later, toward the end of 1943, . . . on the Allied radio, that all Jews were being exterminated in the East. But no details were given and this report was considered propaganda . . . certainly there were pessimists during the occupation who asserted that none of the Jews would return, but there were also optimists who were of a different opinion . . . "[45] The human being, faced with complete physical destruction, will cling consciously to whatever rays of hope there are, and will reject insights that confirm the inevitability of death. This psychological mechanism "explains" the desire to believe German promises, to consider the messages from Eastern camps genuine, to view rumors and underground descriptions of extermination camps as war propaganda, and to expect a sudden defeat of Germany. On this conscious level most Jews maintained hope to the end.

But underneath these rationalizations and conscious beliefs, a great and profound fear prevailed, as well as, in many instances, in the opinion of this writer, a subconscious awareness of the threat of death and destruction. In the absence of psychological or psychoanalytical investigations it is necessary to base this hypothesis on descriptions of actions (as compared with verbalizations) in the face of impending deportation. The intensity with which exemptions and delays were sought, the despair that people expressed when faced with the final necessity to depart for the transit camps, and especially the traumatic terror that assignment to the Auschwitz trains caused at Westerbork and Vught,[46] all lead to the assumption that the deportees "knew," subconsciously, more about their ultimate destiny than they dared admit to themselves.

THE JEWISH COUNCIL

The Jewish Council played a crucial role in determining the response of the Jewish population to German persecution. From the beginning it had a dual function. The Germans saw it as an instrument through which they could impose their will on the Jews of Holland. Leaders of the Council saw it as an organization designed to maintain the life of the Jewish community in a time of crisis and to protect Jews from German persecution. The tragedy of the Jewish Council stems from the fact that the goals of the Germans and of the

Jewish leaders were incompatible, since the Nazis, in the long run, were determined to destroy the Jews physically, and had the power to accomplish this goal.

The Germans deliberately designated the Council as the exclusive intermediary between themselves and the Jewish population, to avoid having to deal with individual Jews and Jewish organizations. Jews were not permitted to approach German agencies directly.[47] The leaders of the Council accepted this role in the hope that the Council "could be a wall between the Germans and their own people."[48]

On this basis, the Jewish Council assumed the responsibility for announcing German regulations and threats. This usually was done through its weekly publication, *Het Joodse Weekblad,* but some of the most sinister announcements were passed on by word of mouth or through the mails or messenger services.

The Council did not remain exclusively an information agency, but lent such prestige as it had to the enforcement of these orders. Its first "assignment" was to admonish Jews to remain quiet during the February 1941 unrest in Amsterdam and to pass on the German threats of "punishment" for those who continued to resist.[49] *Het Joodse Weekblad* was full of such warnings and threats. The tone usually was urgent, and the admonition to comply was given in the supposed interest of the persons concerned, as in this appeal to non-Dutch Jews to register for emigration: " . . . in order to prevent a serious danger we are obliged to point out emphatically to all persons concerned, of course, exclusively in their own interest, that they must register . . . "[50]

The Council also appealed to the community spirit of the individual:

> The wrong action of the individual can hurt the entire community. We, for our part, are prepared to represent the interests of all Jews in Holland, without distinction. But we can do this only if we can count on the confidence and cooperation of each Jew without exception.[51]

Although some announcements and threats were attributed explicitly to German authorities, they usually carried the signatures and therefore at least implicit endorsement of the co-chairmen.

The Council also assisted the Germans in the administration of their policies. The flood of anti-Jewish regulations involved mountains of paper work, and the German police was so short-handed that it would have been difficult to accomplish these administrative chores with German personnel alone, although it might have been possible to find Dutchmen willing to assist.* But with the prodigious administrative and clerical labor performed by the Jewish Council, it became unnecessary for the Germans to seek additional help. The Council prepared a duplicate file of the Jews based on the 1941 registration.[52] It registered Jewish organizations before their disbandment.[53] It assisted in checking on individual registrations.[54]. It prepared requests for permission to emigrate from Holland.[55] It assisted with the administration of funds in blocked Jewish accounts.[56] It processed requests for travel and moving permits.[57] With the start of the deportations, it performed most of the paper work and processing of deportees, always, of course, in the hope of gaining relief for the persons involved.

When the system of exemptions was formalized in September 1942, applications were processed through the Jewish Council, which worked allegedly with lists prepared by the German police.[58] Surviving officials of the Jewish Council maintained after the war that they never furnished names of Jews to be deported to the German police and that the Zentralstelle assigned Jews to deportation not from the file prepared by Jewish Council employees in 1941 but from files furnished by the Dutch registration office.[59] There is no question, however, that the administrative machinery of the Council helped the Germans to keep lists and addresses up to date and provided many short cuts which would not have been possible otherwise.

In one instance the Jewish Council admittedly assigned a number of Jews to deportation. When it decided to comply with the order of May 21, 1943, to designate 7,000 of its own employees for the "labor draft," it sent the deportation announcement to certain employees, but, according to Professor Cohen's postwar statements, never gave the Germans the names of the persons so designated. Professor Cohen even justified this action in retrospect. He asserted that the German police would have conducted raids immediately if the Council had refused to cooperate. By calling up its employees, he claimed the Council provided them with time to go underground if they were

---

* In defense of his policy, Professor Cohen claimed in 1947 that the Germans could have used members of the N.S.B. for this administrative work ([142], p. 9).

prepared to do so, since they had a few days to make the necessary arrangements.*

The Council's claim that it endeavored to save as many Jewish lives as possible is not unjustified in fact. It attempted many times, usually unsuccessfully, to get the Germans to modify or lessen their demands. Administrative sabotage was committed,[60] although much less than might have been possible, and a few persons were given warning when police actions were being planned. On the whole, these efforts bore fruit only if the persons concerned made a determined effort to go underground, since most exemptions, except those for Jews in mixed marriages, turned out to be temporary.

The Jewish Council rendered many kinds of assistance to its clients. It gave advice to people seeking exemptions. Jewish Council personnel at the staging points provided meals and refreshments, helped persons obtain further delays if possible, carried messages, and furnished camp equipment where needed. Professor Cohen personally remained in the Schouwburg on the evenings of the big raids to answer questions and give advice.[61] The Council offices in Westerbork and Vught sought to assist camp inmates in their attempts to settle their affairs or seek postponement of deportation to the East.

Quite apart from its activities in connection with anti-Jewish measures, the Council was in many respects the center of Jewish community life. It was in charge of all social services for Jews, assisting the old, the sick, and the indigent. It operated employment and housing services for persons who had lost their jobs or been forced to leave their homes. It supervised distribution of food to the Jewish population and opened a public food service in Amsterdam in the winter of 1942–43.[62] Professor Cohen's claim that no Jew in Holland went hungry[63] probably was correct. In January 1943 the Council assumed the responsibility of making payments from blocked accounts.[64]

---

* [142], pp. 2–4. This defense is supported by the cryptic statement in a notation on the Council decision to obey the German demands of May 21, which reads as follows: ". . . we came . . . to the conclusion that we could not assume the responsibility for dangers [which might result from a refusal] . . . since it had appeared also outside of our circle, that representative bodies [usually] did not assume the responsibility for large-scale actions, but left the decision to each individual . . ." This may be an allusion to the failure of the churches and underground organizations to back the April–May strike. (Notation cited from [138].)

The Council also organized educational programs for young and old, including language and vocational training. Many young people prepared themselves for emigration to Palestine at the Council's Center for Vocational Training. In the autumn of 1942 the Council took over the management of Jewish schools from Dutch authorities.[65]

The publication of *Het Joodse Weekblad* was one of the most important activities of the Council. This house organ was started in April 1941, when the Germans suppressed other Jewish periodicals, and was published once a week until September 1943. The German police wanted such a medium in order to reach the Jewish population without having to publish its regulations and threats in the daily press, where the attention of other Dutchmen would be drawn to them. From the Council's point of view, a paper was equally desirable to publicize its activities and to provide a focus for the Jewish community.

The first page of *Het Joodse Weekblad* usually carried official announcements or editorials. Inside pages reported on cultural and educational activities and contained articles, stories, and poetry. The final pages were devoted to advertisements and "personals" such as birth and wedding announcements and a tragic array of obituaries. In the beginning *Het Joodse Weekblad* consisted of twelve pages (occasionally even more), but its contents decreased gradually until it became a two-page news sheet in May 1943.

Perusal of successive issues of *Het Joodse Weekblad* does not give the postwar reader an explicit description of the events of the period, although the many official announcements, appeals, and threats convey an implicit picture of the progressive destruction of the Jewish community. The reality and mood of the final months in 1943 are graphically conveyed by the repeated warnings that one's baggage should be packed and ready at all times because the "summons" might come at any moment.[66]

However, *Het Joodse Weekblad* contained no direct news of what was happening to the Jews. The June 1941 arrests of hundreds of young Jews went unreported, as did the start of the deportations, the big raids, and the self-dismemberment of the Council. Because of the selective nature of the material the Council was permitted to print, and because of the announcements of training courses and cultural activities which continued to appear until the very end, giving the appearance that a normal community life was being carried on, *Het Joodse Weekblad* has an eerie quality for the postwar reader familiar with the events of the period.

From the beginning, the role of the Jewish Council was controversial within the Jewish community. Strong antagonism against Asscher and Cohen was voiced at its first public function, the meeting in February 1941 at which the co-chairmen attempted to persuade the Jewish population of Amsterdam to stop fighting the N.S.B. on the streets.[67] The Communist and Socialist press promptly attacked the Council as a capitalist organization through which the Germans were attempting to subdue the Jewish proletariat.[68] The theme that the Council basically represented class interests and tended to protect middle-class Jews at the expense of the Jewish proletariat was repeatedly voiced during and after the war.

L. E. Visser, a leading Zionist and former President of the High Council (Supreme Court) of the Netherlands, also criticized the Jewish Council. He pointed out to Cohen as early as 1941 that, since German anti-Jewish measures violated international law, resistance to these measures was a moral duty even if it would not affect the outcome. To Cohen's objection that utilitarian considerations could not simply be pushed aside, Visser responded that the nature of the Jewish reaction to the persecution could not help but be a factor in shaping German policies, and that a refusal to cooperate with the Germans might force them to modify their approach. Visser emphatically maintained that cooperation with the kind of absolute evil embodied in German policies should be rejected on moral grounds. Otherwise, he correctly foresaw, the Council itself would be increasingly forced to adopt immoral and destructive policies.[69]

After the deportations commenced, most Jews who were not employees of the Council developed a peculiarly ambivalent attitude toward the organization. On the one hand, there was tremendous resentment over the willingness of the Council to collaborate with the Germans and to provide exemptions from deportations to its own employees. Bitter complaints were voiced about the bureaucracy and inefficiency of the organization. These complaints were often directed at the long hours of waiting in offices and the inadequate and antagonistic ways in which Council employees, working frequently under great emotional stress, dealt with their clients.

On the other hand, most Jews wholeheartedly took advantage of the machinery of the Council to secure favors and postponements for themselves. This reliance on the organization, although engendered by the nature of administrative arrangements dictated by the Germans, indicates that to a great extent the Jewish population was willing to accept the Council rather than try to circumvent German regulations through independent action.

In an account written after the war, Abel J. Herzberg, a former official of the organization and postwar legal counsel for Asscher and Cohen, has provided, in the opinion of this writer, the most balanced and complex appraisal of the Council to date.[70] According to Herzberg, the behavior of the co-chairmen was determined by their humanistic principles, and the Council was the instrument through which they hoped to help their people best. While Herzberg admits that history has shown the Jewish Council to have been almost entirely in the wrong,[71] he also points out that few Jews would have been willing to follow the path of "no compromise" recommended by Visser. He also reminds his readers that an earlier end to the war or a German exchange bargain with the Allies might easily have put the conduct of Asscher and Cohen in quite a different light.[72]

One of the most straightforward defenses of the Jewish Council was written by K. P. L. Berkley in April 1945, before the end of the occupation.[73] Berkley maintains that the Jewish Council succeeded in actually delaying the deportations and that the Germans could have secured data on Jews from existing government files. Like Herzberg, he stresses the point that many believed the war would be over in 1942 or 1943 and that, had this been the case, the Council's activities would have saved many.[74] The book contains no indication that the author knew anything about the nature of the extermination camps.

In a more critical appraisal of the Jewish Council, published in 1946, Sam de Wolff, a left-wing Socialist, admits that there could be little doubt of the good intentions of the Jewish leaders. De Wolff reproaches Asscher and Cohen, however, for their basic weakness "not to have dared to recognize . . . that resistance was the only alternative to becoming accomplices of the German measures."[75]

In a subsequent comment in 1947, De Wolff put the attitude of the Jewish Council into a broader perspective. While conceding that the policy of the Council was disastrous because the Jewish leaders failed to grasp that the Germans intended to exterminate the Jews, De Wolff maintains that the Council, in making this mistake, essentially represented middle-class Holland and its predominantly middle-class Jewish community with its fears and hesitations and its respect for any kind of legality. This being so, it seemed unfair to De Wolff to single out the co-chairmen for a reproach that could be made against an entire community.[76]

Disagreeing with De Wolff in this respect, a Jewish Court of Honor (Joodse Eereraad), sitting in judgment on Asscher and Cohen for their conduct as co-chairmen of the Jewish Council, condemned their administration in a decision rendered in December 1947. It reproached the chairmen particularly for (1) being willing to accept responsibility from German hands, (2) publishing *Het Joodse Week-blad* as the mouthpiece of the German authorities, (3) collaborating with German regulations and orders, especially the deportations, (4) threatening Jews with punishment and deportation for failure to obey regulations, (5) being willing to consign half of the Jewish Council employees to deportation.[77]

In making this judgment, the Court of Honor adopted the reasoning of L. E. Visser that cooperation with illegal and immoral actions was impermissible on grounds of principle.

This variety of judgments on the conduct of the Jewish Council reflects the doubts and divisions within the Jewish community. In the final chapter of this study an attempt is made to discuss more explicitly the conclusions of this writer.

♦

CHAPTER TEN

The Resistance Movement

The three previous chapters contain descriptions of many resistance activities undertaken spontaneously by unorganized Dutch citizens, or by groups with ties antedating the war. From the beginning of the occupation, however, new organizations were formed specifically to oppose the occupying power, most of which disbanded after liberation.

It will be useful to define three categories of "resistance." The terms "passive resistance" or "noncollaboration" will be employed to designate those attitudes and actions of opposition to national socialism and the Germans that did not involve major risks for patriots, such as the probability of imprisonment or death. The term "militant resistance" will be used to designate actions that did carry such risks but did not involve *primarily* the employment of military actions or other forms of destructive violence. The term "military resistance" will be reserved to designate actions serving essentially military ends such as espionage, sabotage, and what was known in other European countries as partisan warfare.

In one sense, one cannot speak of "the Dutch Resistance," since underground opposition to the German regime never grew into an effectively unified organization. In another sense, a certain unity did exist, spiritually if not organizationally, and most workers in the underground considered themselves part of one patriotic effort. Clandestine publications were full of references to The Resistance (Het Verzet) and The Illegality (De Illegaliteit), terms that referred to all secret groups struggling against the Germans and the N.S.B. In this chapter an attempt will be made to discuss a few of the most representative groups rather than to present an exhaustive catalogue of underground organizations.

The oldest important resistance group that managed to maintain an organization throughout the occupation was the Order Service (Orde Dienst, or O.D.). The Order Service was formed in the summer of 1940 and became a nationwide organization by November of that year.[1] The O.D. remained a relatively small organization in these early years, "a general staff without troops,"[2] most of its members being commissioned or noncommissioned officers.

The Order Service was organized along military lines, with a general headquarters and a tier of lower-level command posts.[3] During this early period many officers in the Order Service toyed with potentially antidemocratic ideas, wishing to set up a government after liberation. Throughout the war the O.D. remained politically the most conservative of the major underground organizations.

A few members of the organization originally engaged in reckless schemes of sabotage. After a number of arrests in 1941 and 1942,[4] a much sobered organization became more careful in its operations.[5]

The principal stated objective of the O.D. was to maintain order after a German collapse, until the arrival of the legal government. A secondary aim was to hasten the collapse of the German regime through military action at the appropriate moment and through espionage and sabotage activities, but the Order Service did not believe in massive military action until the German authority was sufficiently weakened for an underground "army" to be effective.[6] It also appears that after the arrests of 1941 the O.D. as an organization did not engage in sabotage, although individuals with O.D. connections participated in other resistance activities.

Although the emphasis of the Order Service was on the postwar transition period, it was not completely inactive during the occupation. One of the earliest attacks on a rationing office was organized by a local O.D. group.[7] It engaged in military espionage continuously from 1940. In 1943, through agents dispatched from England, it secured transmitters which functioned throughout the remainder of the war.[8] After September 1944 the Order Service was designated as one of the groups constituting the Forces of the Interior, and many of its officers were given responsible positions in the N.B.S. because they had military training. In the final winter of the war it collected arms dropped by the Allies and engaged in a number of sabotage actions. Since executive power was transferred directly from the

German to the Allied Command, the Order Service was never called upon to play the role it had envisioned for itself.

Relations between the Order Service and Allied and Dutch agencies in London were somewhat strained. The government-in-exile suspected the Order Service to be heavily infiltrated because of the 1941 arrests, and it feared its authoritarian tendencies. Moreover the Allies were not particularly eager to arm an organization that did not place its main emphasis on the struggle against the Germans. Also, the London government sometimes found the O.D. reluctant to accept orders. Only after the establishment of the Forces of the Interior did confidence in the O.D. begin to prevail.[9]

The Order Service was also unpopular among resistance organizations. Some underground groups resented the relative inactivity of the O.D., especially when contrasted to its alleged claim to leadership of the Resistance.[10] Others were suspicious of its political intentions. Liberal and left-wing groups accused it of a design to suppress a popular uprising at the time of the Liberation. There was even some question whether it would be prepared to take orders from the government-in-exile after the German collapse. A Socialist leader (K. Vorrink) went as far as to warn London that he would call a general strike after liberation if the O.D. tried to set up an authoritarian regime.[11]

In the postwar perspective, it appears likely that W. Drees, the later Prime Minister, was correct in his testimony before the Parliamentary Commission of Inquiry that there was no real problem of disobedience to the legal government, but that the Order Service would have been eager to "play government" if a vacuum of authority had occurred.[12] It also is clear that, despite some protestations to the contrary, the main preoccupation of the Order Service was with the terminal phase of the occupation, and that its somewhat rigid military and authoritarian complexion did not make it a suitable instrument for underground resistance, which required a great deal of flexibility, inventiveness, and personal initiative.[13]

ASSISTANCE TO PEOPLE IN HIDING

Assistance to "divers" (*onderduikers*—literally "people who go underwater"), as people in hiding were called,* was the main objective of two large related organizations, the National Organization for

* "Bikers" (*fietsers*) was another colloquial term for people in hiding in this country of many bicycles.

Assistance to Divers (Landelijke Organisatie voor Hulp aan Onderduikers, or L.O., as it was commonly called) and the National Action
Groups (Landelijke Knokploegen, or L.K.P.).

The L.O. was one of the largest organizations of the Resistance.
It came into existence as the result of a need for better coordination
of individuals and groups trying to assist Jews, underground workers,
and others who wished to go into hiding, especially those who wanted
to escape the labor draft and deportation to Germany. The organization was founded late in 1942 by a housewife, Mrs. H. Th. Kuipers-
Rietberg, a mother of five, who lived in the southeast of Holland near
the German border, and the Rev. F. Slomp, a Calvinist minister, who
had been forced to leave his pulpit because of his anti-Nazi preach-
ings and activities. It quickly spread across the Country. When Catholic groups working in the southern provinces joined forces with the
north in August 1943,[14] it had affiliates in every province of the Netherlands. Before the end of the war the L.O., according to its own
spokesmen, had approximately 15,000 collaborators.[15]

In the course of 1943 and 1944 the German police arrested a number of the group's leaders. Among these was Mrs. Kuipers-Rietberg,
who subsequently died in a German concentration camp. The total
loss of lives of the L.O. by the end of the war was estimated at
1,100.[16] Estimates of the number of divers under its care vary somewhat. It appears that the L.O. distributed approximately 220,000
ration books (*inlegvellen*) a month by the summer of 1944.[17] This
information suggests that the estimate by one of its spokesmen that
there were 200,000 to 300,000 divers by the summer of 1944 may be
close to the truth, although it is difficult to define what constituted
a "diver," since there were so many variations in arrangements.[18]
These figures indicate that the number of persons in hiding was of
the same order of magnitude as the number of Dutchmen working in
Germany at any one time.[19]

Most of the early members of the L.O. were devout Calvinists,
and religious motivations continued to play an important role even
after the organization had acquired collaborators of diverse backgrounds. Its Calvinist origins lent strength to the L.O., especially in
those villages where Reformed Churches were dominant, because it
could rely on contacts made through these churches and Calvinist
lay organizations. The Catholics who worked within the framework

of the L.O. could rely on the parochial organizational network of the Catholic Church.[20] However, as the war progressed and German demands and retributions grew harsher, religious and humanitarian motivations became increasingly overshadowed by patriotic considerations and by the wish to hurt and weaken the national enemy.[21]

The L.O. managed to operate with a small central committee responsible for the overall organization. Its great strength lay in local individuals and groups and in the countryside rather than in the cities. As compared with other resistance groups before September 1944, it was a mass organization, as it had to be in order to place the many tens of thousands who needed shelter, ration books, and food.[22]

Although the problems of the Jews had been among the preoccupations leading to the formation of the L.O., the organization as a whole preferred to refer these cases to specialized groups; yet many local groups did help Jews to find shelter and secure needed documents and food. The L.O. felt that aid to Jews involved special problems that a "mass" resistance organization seeking food and shelter for large numbers of divers could not handle.[23]

While assistance to adult Jews remained on a limited scale, the L.O., with its strong roots in the countryside, placed Jewish infants and children with local families, especially in the northeastern provinces. Where necessary, the L.O. paid the foster parents a small sum for board.[24] Some of the children smuggled out of the nursery of the Jewish Council by Walter Süsskind[25] were passed on to L.O. channels and consequently saved.

It is difficult to assess to what extent the hesitancy of the L.O. to become active in assistance to Jews was based on objective fact and how much was a reflection of the latent "Biblical" and traditional peasant anti-Semitism of its rural constituency. At any rate, by the time the organization had attained its full strength in the summer of 1943, most Jews were beyond redemption, in Westerbork or in the East.

In its efforts to assist divers, the L.O. faced changing problems. Until May 1943, its main effort went into locating hiding places, because not enough people were willing to take the risks involved in hiding patriots. After the April-May strike a sufficient number of hiding places became available. However, after May 1943 a critical

need for ration books developed, since people underground needed
these to buy food. After September 1944 the problem became mainly
one of procuring food, even for persons who had ration books and
stamps.[26]

The placement of divers with a "host" family, however, remained
a major concern of the L.O., at least until September 1944. In the
beginning, most placements were made on an informal basis, through
friends or acquaintances, or through churches and related lay organizations. But by early 1943 a more formal organization for the placement of divers in safe locations was developed. The first such *beurs*
("exchange"), held in January of that year,[27] met the need for organized placement so well that other similar meetings, once a week or
once a fortnight, were arranged on a regional basis. For a time in
1943 a national *beurs* functioned, but it was discontinued for security
reasons after the first big raid on the regional exchange in Hoorn in
October 1943. In its place a national committee of six members was
established as a coordinating and policy-guiding body.[28]

The *beurs* also provided an opportunity for the exchange of information and consultation on techniques and principles of underground work and for the formulation of policies to guide the work
of local L.O. groups. In this respect these meetings played a particularly important role in the first formative year of the L.O.

As mentioned earlier, arrangements for persons in hiding varied
greatly. Sometimes, chiefly in the case of Jews, entire families lived
in upstairs rooms, basements, or similar hideouts. A few outdoor
camps existed in remote parts of the country for varying lengths of
time.[29] But most arrangements were less dramatic. In many instances
the people taking refuge merely lived away from their homes, on
farms or at other residences in their home towns, under assumed
names and with false documents but pursuing regular jobs or other
useful activities.

In placing a diver with his host family, special caution had to be
taken in arranging the initial contact between diver and host, since
there was always the risk that the diver might not be reliable or that
the German police might have been shadowing him. According to
one postwar account, three methods of introducing divers and hosts
were developed. If the diver was not considered completely reliable,
the safest method was for the host and his guest to meet at a neutral

public spot in such a way that the diver was identified to the host but not the reverse. If security seemed less of a problem and if it was important to make a good match, a member of the L.O. might invite the diver to his house to become acquainted with him and to make a permanent assignment on the basis of this acquaintance. When there was no doubt about the reliability of the diver, the simplest and safest way was to give him the host address and ask him to check in with his host directly.[30]

The selection and matching of hosts and "guests" was complex and delicate, since they had to get along with each other under frequently trying and dangerous circumstances. Therefore a major effort was usually made to place divers with families who would be congenial by virtue of similar religious views, vocational training and interests, and general class background.

Obviously, it was not always possible to achieve an "ideal" match, and relations between host families and divers required wisdom and tact on both sides. The "Ten Commandments for Divers," published in the underground press, advised the diver to help his hostess with housework, to assist school-age children with their studies, and to be as amenable and unobtrusive as possible.[31] In general, the situation was easier in the country than in the cities: there was less need for all-day hiding, there was more space in which to move around, and the "guest" could frequently work as a farm laborer. Moreover, peasant families were used to having nonfamily members around the house, since many farmers relied on hired help.

The situation was quite different in the cities or small towns, especially for Jews and other particularly exposed persons. For these people it was advisable to remain indoors during the day and to avoid events and localities that were likely to be raided by the German police.

It often was unwise for the diver to let his own family know where he was, or to visit with them. Thus he was cut off from normal social life and had to rely on his own resources. The "Ten Commandments" advised people in hiding to keep a regular schedule, to take up a hobby, or to enroll in a correspondence course to maintain their emotional balance. But these were at best makeshift arrangements. Time was bound to weigh heavily on a person cut off from his usual activities, and it often took great self-discipline and a deep sense of purpose to sustain such a situation for months and, in many cases, years.[32]

Therefore it was only natural that in many instances diver and family did not get along and that the diver had to be moved to another shelter. As increasing numbers of young men went underground, the L.O. occasionally placed less worthy persons. Thefts, and incidents between divers and women and girls in the host families, occurred and sometimes it became necessary to abandon an untrustworthy diver.[33]

It also happened sometimes that a diver who had been arrested would betray his host family or his L.O. contacts, but according to one spokesman relatively few German agents moved in as divers,[34] partly perhaps because the German police was not as concerned with the destruction of the L.O. as with the fight against underground organizations specializing in "military resistance" such as sabotage and espionage.

After the start of the railroad strike in September 1944, the L.O. was asked by the Commander of the Netherlands Forces of the Interior to provide food for the Resistance and for the railroad workers on strike.

At this juncture the strength of the L.O. in the rural areas of the north once again proved to be advantageous. The northeastern provinces (Friesland, Groningen) and the northern end of the province of Noord-Holland turned out to be food-surplus areas. Relationships with peasants were so good that the L.O. soon found itself in a position to supersede official authorities in whom the peasants had lost confidence. The L.O. even instructed farmers on whether they should deliver food through legal channels and designated "legitimate" clandestine channels.

One of the greatest problems was to persuade peasants not to sell to the black market and to fix, without legal authority, prices at a "reasonable" level. Persuasion and appeals for the common cause usually sufficed, but occasionally the L.O. had to resort to threats and violence. In the fishing village of Volendam just north of Amsterdam it even became necessary to scuttle a few boats before certain fishermen could be prevailed upon to eschew the black market and provide fish at acceptable prices.

Most of the food was moved in barges (except during the frost period), but some was taken to the cities in automobiles of the Agricultural Control Service, with false papers and identification badges provided by the Resistance. In the cities the L.O. built up a separate organization for storage and distribution. Occasionally the L.O. even furnished food to the public food services, which were operating in the big cities during the final famine winter.[35]

Because of its mass base, the Calvinist spirit of self-reliance and sacrifice, and the nature of its work (some persons in hiding could fall back on savings and many did work for which they received pay), the L.O. had little trouble financing its work from within its own ranks. As a rule, it preferred to manage with as little aid as possible from the National Assistance Fund underwritten by the government-in-exile.[36] In the final year of the occupation it worked out a division of labor with the Fund, retaining financial responsibility for people in hiding in its care, but passing on to the Fund the burden of supporting the dependents of deported or deceased patriots.[37]

To do its job as efficiently as possible, the L.O. spawned a number of specialized organizations. In the autumn of 1943, when it became necessary to secure ration and identity cards on a large scale, it set up the "National Action Groups" (Landelijke Knokploegen, or L.K.P., as they were generally known).

By the beginning of 1944, the L.K.P. had grown into a country-wide organization with approximately 300 "official" members. After September 1944 its membership increased to approximately 1,500 men.

The primary task of the L.K.P. was to obtain ration cards and other official documents by force. In the summer of 1944 the organization decided to engage in sabotage in support of Allied operations.[38]

The use of violence in the struggle against the Germans posed a serious moral problem to the people of Holland, who had been traditionally law-abiding and respectful of government authority. The underground press tried to educate the public to approve and support the tactics of the Resistance. An article in the conservative *Trouw* pointed out that patriots who engaged in attacks on government offices or in sabotage activities were inspired by the desire to help their fellow men and to resist the enemy. It emphasized that they did not derive material advantages from their underground work and that ration books and identity cards were given free to all who could not pay the fee for them.[39]

Attacks on rationing offices began on a large scale soon after the May strike of 1943, although occasional attempts had occurred earlier. During the summer and autumn of 1943, these actions took place frequently, sometimes several times on the same day, in widely separated parts of the country. Some were planned for the seizure of ration books and identity papers with the necessary stamps and seals, while others were aimed at the destruction of such materials as population records which the Germans might use to track down men for the labor draft. Sometimes offices were broken into at night. Sometimes the robbery would take place in broad daylight while officials were held at bay by armed patriots. Occasionally a previous understanding was reached with the guards. In some cases, guards disappeared with the attackers, taking their rifles, weapons, and uniforms along. Sometimes ration books and similar documents were stolen in transit. In a number of instances, patriots used German, N.S.B., or Dutch uniforms to conceal their identities, as in the attack by a left-wing resistance group on the Amsterdam Bureau of Population Records in 1943, when files were destroyed by arson.

Occasionally Action Groups tried to liberate members of their organizations who had been arrested by the German police.[40] Sometimes such persons would be fetched by patriots wearing German uniforms or pretending to be Dutch police officials. On other occasions they would be abducted by force, or liberated while in transit from one prison to another. The largest successful enterprise of this kind was the liberation of over fifty political prisoners from the Arnhem prison in June 1944, including one of the founders of the L.O.* But these undertakings did not always succeed. In July 1944 an attempt to free a group of prisoners from an Amsterdam prison was betrayed by a German agent, and most of the assailants were arrested and executed.[41]

---

* [19] 7-A, 257, and 7-C, 207 (Testimony of L. Scheepstra, March 29, 1950). The majority of the almost 150 political prisoners in the Arnhem jail turned down the opportunity to escape for fear of reprisals against themselves and their families.

After becoming a part of the Forces of the Interior in September 1944, the L.K.P. collected arms and ammunition dropped by the Allies and engaged increasingly in outright sabotage.[42]

Since the L.K.P. was a creation of the L.O., its funds came from the parent organization and its actions were designed to meet the needs of the L.O. Moreover its membership came from the same background as that of the L.O. and shared the latter's religious and spiritual motivations. In spite of this, difficulties occurred, since the leaders of the L.K.P. sometimes felt the parent organization was trying to exercise close control over the Action Groups. In order to maintain liaison and minimize friction, the leadership of each organization included representatives of the other group.[43]

It was not enough, however, to supply only ration cards to persons in hiding. Other official documents were also needed, especially false identity cards that would survive official scrutiny. The "Identity Card Section" (Persoonsbewijs Sectie), which was largely composed of civil servants in hiding, specialized in the alteration of identity cards that had been taken from government offices by force or stealth. The "Office for Forgeries" (Falsificatie Centrale) specialized in the forging or alteration of other official papers. Liaison existed between all these organizations designed to support the L.O. through specialized techniques.[44]

The L.O. also received information from the "Central Intelligence Service" (Centrale Inlichtingen Dienst, or C.I.D.), an underground group formed primarily to gather information from official German and Dutch sources, which would have some bearing on the work for people in hiding, and items of information useful to other resistance groups and to the Allies. In the final winter of the war, the C.I.D. operated for a few weeks a direct telephone line to the liberated territory in the south.[45]

Relationships with independent groups operating in the same field as the L.O. (assistance to persons in hiding) often were somewhat tenuous. The L.O. had become the chief suppliers of ration cards, without necessarily laying claim to a monopoly in this field. Its original insistence on a strict accounting of the distribution of ration cards created conflict with some of the other groups. In a few instances the L.O. modified this demand and contented itself with spot checks; in others the independent group joined the L.O.[46] These relatively minor difficulties did not seriously interfere, however, with aiding persons in hiding.

The Council of Resistance in the Kingdom of the Netherlands (Raad van Verzet in het Koninkrijk der Nederlanden, or R.v.V.) was the underground organization most clearly identified with sabotage. The Council was founded just before the April-May strikes of 1943 by a group of patriots that had previously worked within the framework of the Order Service. These people felt that the Order Service was not sufficiently active in combating the Germans and that they must do more to hasten the end of the occupation.[47]

The first statement of purpose of the Council was couched in fairly exalted terms and included some rather wild statements about its own authority and the punishments to be meted out by the organization to black-marketeers, collaborators, and others who seemed too soft in their attitudes toward the Germans.[48] As time progressed, the statements and actions of the Council became more subdued, and by the summer of 1944 the Council had begun to ask the London government for policy guidance.[49]

One of the original purposes of the Council, as of a number of other underground groups, was to bring about unification or at least coordination of the many resistance groups that had sprung up by 1943. Although the Council did not succeed in this effort, it developed into one of the leading underground organizations.

The high command of the Council consisted of only a few persons. The Council was a nationwide organization, but contacts with local groups were relatively difficult to maintain. The Council, however, could fall back on a pool of approximately 2,000 persons for specific operations. It usually functioned through small groups of approximately three persons, especially on delicate assignments such as the liquidation of enemy agents.[50] The Council was originally self-supporting, but later received subsidies from the National Assistance Fund.

Sabotage of enemy installations, often ordered by the Allies, and of productive facilities useful to the Germans constituted the most important activity of the Council. The Council also operated transmitters and an espionage service which was in touch with Dutch agencies in England, and furnished political and economic information about the occupied territory. This channel was one of the best sources of domestic political news and reports from the underground press for the government-in-exile in 1943 and 1944.[51]

Especially in its early period, the Council was drawn into work designed to help divers, such as securing and distributing ration and identity documents.[52] After September 1944 the Council, together with the L.K.P., played a major role in the collection of arms dropped by the Allies. All in all, it was the most activist of the large underground organizations.

Throughout the occupation the political complexion of the Council was a subject of considerable discussion. The Council was widely suspected of being Communist-dominated. A substantial number of Communists were active in the organization; however, postwar evidence suggests that it was composed of patriots from a wide range of political backgrounds. As its chairman put it to the Parliamentary Commission of Inquiry after the war: "The military went into the Order Service. I always found religiously oriented people in the K.P., and everybody else joined the Council of Resistance, including the Communists."[53] After liberation, the Communist element in the Council in vain sought to perpetuate it as a political organization of the Resistance within the context of a popular front policy.[54]

Relationships with other underground groups were uneasy. *Vrij Nederland,* a leading clandestine publication, sent a rather negative report to London characterizing the leadership of the Council as immature, and imputing Communist leanings to it.[55] Relationships with the Order Service were very poor. The Council resented what it considered the relative passivity and leadership aspirations of the O.D., while the Order Service viewed the Council as a group of "wild" men with questionable political leanings and did not permit its members to join the Council.[56] Relationships with the National Committee of Resistance were also tenuous, owing to conflicting ambitions for underground leadership, but the Council often worked closely with the L.K.P. and the L.O.,[57] especially in matters relating to persons in hiding.

The government-in-exile was initially suspicious of the Council because of its "wild" actions and its alleged Communist leanings.

The London government's attitude had been strongly colored by the original flamboyant statements of the Council in 1943 and by the critical evaluation furnished by the *Vrij Nederland* group. It distinctly refused to regard the Council as the representative of the entire Resistance.[58] Gradually, however, the attitude of the London government became more favorable, especially after the arrival of Van Heuven Goedhart, an underground leader who subsequently became Minister of Justice in the London government.[59] In 1944 the growing appreciation by the London government and the Resistance of the Council's effectiveness led to the inclusion of its representatives in the committees established in 1944 and 1945 in order to achieve greater cooperation between resistance groups and to ease the transition to postwar "normalcy."

THE NATIONAL COMMITTEE OF RESISTANCE

The National Committee of Resistance (Nationaal Comité van Verzet) was founded in the wake of the April-May strike of 1943 by a group of government officials, students, and professional people who believed that the strike had proved the necessity for closer coordination within the Resistance. To achieve such coordination was the original aspiration of this group.[60] The National Committee introduced itself to the Resistance in a manifesto published in a number of underground papers. The manifesto presented the need for closer cooperation and called on resistance organizations to work with the National Committee in establishing greater unity.[61]

Other resistance groups, however, were less than eager to subordinate themselves to this new organization. The *Vrij Nederland* group prepared a critical report on the "pretensions" of the National Committee,[62] and Calvinist-oriented organizations, such as the L.O. and the L.K.P., also stood aloof.[63] The government-in-exile, on its part, regarded the National Committee as more representative and authoritative within the Resistance than it probably was in fact.[64]

Although failing to achieve the desired coordination, the National Committee became one of the cooperating resistance groups, gathering in its fold a number of middle-class patriots and providing useful liaison to the group of government officials and intellectuals with which it was associated. Numerically small but consisting of

men and women of high professional caliber, the National Committee
was at the moderate right politically. Although many discussions on
the spiritual and political aspects of postwar Holland were carried on
within the National Committee under the occupation, once liberation had arrived, the Committee, like the Council of Resistance, considered its task finished, and disbanded.[65]

THE NATIONAL ASSISTANCE FUND

The National Assistance Fund could trace its beginnings to the
first year of the occupation, when it became apparent that certain
groups of the population, which had lost their livelihood as the result of German actions, needed financial aid. In 1941 the wives of
Dutch sailors or merchantmen serving with the Allies were told that
they would henceforth be entitled to relief payments only.[66] In response to this reprisal the London government announced that it
would guarantee expenditures made to succor sailors' families.[67]
Thereupon, a certain Captain Filippo, former skipper of one of
Holland's great passenger liners, organized a special fund for sailors'
wives called the "Seamen's Pot" (Zeemanspot).[68] Other small groups
soon cooperated with this fund. Among these were a group in Eindhoven working under the leadership of I. J. van den Bosch, a former
navy officer working at the Philips factory, and a group in Amsterdam headed by Walraven van Hall, a banker. Walraven van Hall
devised an ingenious system of coded receipts in an attempt to operate on a sound business basis, despite the risks connected with
such a system.[69]

During 1942 it became obvious that financial assistance would
have to be extended to other victims of German persecution, such
as dependents of hostages and arrestees, Jews, underground workers,
and persons who wanted to go into hiding in order to escape the labor
draft. It was deemed advisable to establish a separate fund, called
the "Landlubbers' Fund" (Landrottenfonds), which was organized
in 1943 by Walraven van Hall and Van den Bosch.[70] Eventually, the
name of this fund was changed to "National Assistance Fund" (Nationaal Steunfonds, or N.S.F.). During 1943 the Fund secured the
cooperation of high government officials, including the former Director of the Netherlands Bank, L. J. A. Trip. He gave his assurance

that he would do his best after the war to see to it that the government reimbursed business establishments and institutions for loans made to the Fund.[71]

Despite security considerations, leaders of the Fund decided to continue operations on a business basis. Intricate records were kept, creditors were issued ingeniously coded acknowledgments, and receipts continued to be required of most recipients, in accordance with the system devised by Walraven van Hall.

The collaboration of tax officials, business establishments, and banks made it possible to secure large donations and loans from a comparatively small number of creditors. Minimum contributions were set at 25,000 guilders.[72] However, despite excellent cooperation, the number of people and organizations that needed financial assistance grew so rapidly that the Fund requested a formal guarantee from the government-in-exile through an intermediary, who made his way to London.[73]

In January 1944 the government authorized the disbursement of 30,000,000 guilders, 10,000,000 to be expended immediately.[74] In August 1944 the disbursement of the remaining 20,000,000 was authorized,[75] and this amount was further increased in the months before liberation. In its January 1944 authorization, the government empowered the Fund to use its judgment in rendering aid to organizations that assisted persons in hiding, and this authority was extended in August 1944 to include financial support to all underground organizations. Thus the National Assistance Fund became the "Banker of the Resistance."

In the summer of 1944 the archives of the Fund were stolen by a blackmailer, but were recovered after ingenious double-dealing.[76] In 1944 and 1945 a number of collaborators of the Fund were arrested, including two of the original founders. Both were executed by the Germans,[77] but their deaths did not interfere with the work of the Fund. During the final winter of the war, it disbursed larger amounts than before, extending assistance to railroad men, workers from industries lying idle because of lack of fuel, and persons in hiding who refused to submit to the labor draft.

Before liberation, the Fund spent 27,000,000 guilders directly, of which 4,700,000 went for assistance to Jews in hiding. A variety of groups assisting victims of German persecution were given 2,700,000 guilders, although the L.O., the largest organization in the field, received less than 600,000 guilders.[78] Assistance to dependents of seamen amounted to over 5,000,000 guilders, and aid to resistance organizations to 10,000,000. The largest single expenditure, 37,000,000 guilders, was made in support of the railway strike. Special arrangements with patriotic officials of the Netherlands Bank were necessary to secure this large amount. Altogether, including a variety of expenses for such items as administration and interest, 83,800,000 guilders were spent by the Fund before May 5, 1945.[79]

TECHNIQUES OF UNDERGROUND WORK

Since the lack of caution and techniques proved costly in the early years of the occupation, underground publications such as *Het Parool* frequently carried suggestions for illegal workers. In August 1943, J. H. Scheps, an influential underground publicist, issued the *Illegale Catechismus,* drawn up in a question-and-answer form. All but five of its 2,000 copies were confiscated by the German police, but the Catechism was reprinted by the clandestine press.[80]

The Catechism suggested that the key rule in illegal activity was to refrain from anything that might lead to the discovery of one's own work, or to compromising others. Therefore it was advisable to restrain one's natural curiosity and to learn as little as possible about illegal activities beyond the scope of one's own work. By the same token, it was obligatory to remain silent about one's own activities. This discretion extended to family and friends.

It was considered advisable to avoid normal channels of communication, such as the mail, since the Germans were liable to intercept such communications. For telephone conversations, it was preferable to use a public telephone booth in order to hide the identity of the caller, and to employ prearranged code terminology. Since possession of underground newspapers constituted a legal offense for which a person might be imprisoned, periodic disposal of clandestine papers and other compromising materials was recommended.

On the whole, it was considered important for resistance workers to continue a normal way of life insofar as possible, because every change of routine was liable to attract attention and because a definite schedule was psychologically necessary for maximum efficiency.

As far as work within a given organization was concerned, the principal rule was to engage in one kind of activity at a time, to protect the organization from discovery through detection of miscellaneous activities carried on by one person.

Also for security reasons, it was considered wise to memorize lists of addresses and telephone numbers whenever possible. If this proved impractical, such lists were to be written in code. Many organizations were destroyed because of lists of names found on arrestees. Unnecessary personal contacts were to be avoided, particularly with people whose reliability was in doubt. The penetration of Dutch resistance organizations by German agents was the largest single factor responsible for the destruction of underground groups.

The Catechism issued specific instructions on behavior for underground workers in case of arrests of fellow workers. It was important to remain calm and not to give the police cause for suspicion. It was imperative, however, to notify contacts of arrestees so they could change their addresses and cover names, and warn others. It was always best to assume that the third-degree methods of the German police would extract the desired information from their victims.

The Catechism also furnished advice to persons arrested by the Germans. It reminded its readers that the police often did not know much about their prisoners. Therefore it was wise to admit nothing until the Germans provided unmistakable proof of guilt. It was best to speak as little as possible, so that the police could not trap the arrestee in contradictions. The betrayal of the names of others was considered the worst offense of all, but it was well known that human endurance had its limits. In such a situation, it was important to gain time so that associates could be warned and appropriate measures be taken.[81]

SABOTAGE*

Spontaneous acts of sabotage began to occur soon after the capitulation. They were committed by individuals or by one of the few small underground groups that sprang up in the summer of 1940.

* Here a distinction is made between incidental violence, such as attacks on rationing offices, which has been described as "militant resistance" in the preceding section of this chapter, and "military resistance" through sabotage of the military machine of the enemy, which will be described in this section. It is true that some resistance groups engaged in both kinds of activities.

Most of these groups were discovered and arrested by the German police before they could accomplish much.

After the attack on the Soviet Union in June 1941, a Communist underground group became active in the field of sabotage. In 1943 it joined the Council of Resistance,[82] which became the main organization to concern itself with sabotage before September 1944. In the summer of that year the L.K.P. also decided to enter the field of sabotage.[83] After September all the groups in the Forces of the Interior (National Action Groups, the Council of Resistance, and the Order Service) engaged in sabotage and other forms of "military resistance," especially during the final two months of the war.[84]

Allied authorities in London stimulated sabotage activities in the occupied territory, primarily by using groups founded spontaneously in Holland. British strategy, until 1942, envisioned the liberation of the continent by comparatively small and highly trained invading armies supported by an uprising of armed patriots.[85] In preparation for this final assault, the British encouraged local sabotage activities in the occupied territories in order to soften up the enemy.*

This type of endeavor was so important to British thinking that a new agency was founded, the Special Operations Executive (S.O.E.), to stimulate underground resistance to the Germans. Dutch authorities in London organized a succession of services parallel to the S.O.E., with increasing attention to the establishment of underground organizations designed to assist Allied operations in the Netherlands and to stimulate sabotage activities.†

The Netherlands secret agencies in London labored under a number of handicaps. They were dependent on the British for the technical training of their agents, for transporting agents to the occupied

---

* In the long run, the American concept of a mass invasion of Western Europe, aimed at the heart of Nazi power in western and northern Germany, won out over the Churchillian predilection for peripheral enterprises (see [168], p. 28). But the British continued to encourage sabotage activities and the establishment of armed underground groups, which were expected to conduct military operations in support of Allied armies.

† The original "Office for the Preparation of the Return to the Netherlands and the Re-establishment of Lawful Rule" (Bureau voorbereiding van de terugkeer naar Nederland en het herstel van het wettig gezag aldaar, or B.V.T.) was supplanted in July 1942 by the "Office for the Military Preparation of Return" (Bureau militaire voorbereiding terugkeer, or B.M.T.), which began to concern itself with the dispatch of sabotage agents. This latter task became a primary assignment of the successor "Office for Special Assignments" (Bureau bijzondere opdrachten, or B.B.O.), which was established in March 1944.

territory, and for maintaining radio communications with them. Since the organizations devoted to sabotage were operating in a new field of warfare, they made costly mistakes before they succeeded in developing proper techniques. Adequate cooperation with corresponding British agencies was not achieved until early in 1944.

Original S.O.E. efforts in 1942 and 1943 to stimulate sabotage in the Netherlands and a grandly conceived plan to build up an underground army nucleus of approximately a thousand men to assist an Allied invasion were frustrated by German counterespionage agencies, through the so-called Englandspiel ("England Game").

Early in 1942 the German services captured a Dutch agent of the S.O.E. (Van der Reyden) from whom they learned a great deal about S.O.E. codes. By using this knowledge they induced another agent whom they had captured (Lauwers) to establish radio contact with England under German supervision. The S.O.E. officers did not realize that the Germans controlled the transmitter, although Lauwers had not betrayed his security checks, which were designed to provide protection against such an eventuality.[86] Lauwers made special efforts to warn the British that he was in German hands,[87] but the S.O.E. failed to comprehend or pay heed.[88]

Through Lauwers the Germans directed the British to drop additional sabotage agents at designated spots, where they were promptly arrested. Some of their transmitters were then put into service, enabling the Germans to operate a number of lines to England until early in 1944, although the S.O.E. had become increasingly suspicious after receiving a series of warnings from the occupied territory.

Within the framework of the Englandspiel the British dropped approximately fifty agents, who were captured. During this period, the S.O.E. directed its supposed contacts in Holland to commit a number of acts of economic and military sabotage. They also supplied the supposed agents with quantities of small arms. In August 1943 a few captured agents escaped and eventually made their way back to London. At first they were suspected of being German agents and were put in jail, but by the end of 1943 the British ceased to rely on the contaminated channels of communication.[89] On April 1, 1944, the Germans put an end to the Englandspiel with the following sarcastic message to the Allied officers they considered to be in charge of the sabotage operation:

MESSRS BLUNT BINGHAM AND SUCCS LTD LONDON IN THE LAST TIME
YOU ARE TRYING TO MAKE BUSINESS IN NETHERLANDS WITHOUT OUR
ASSISTANCE STOP WE THINK THIS RATHER UNFAIR IN VIEW OUR LONG
AND SUCCESSFUL COOPERATION AS YOUR SOLE AGENTS STOP BUT NEVER
MIND WHENEVER YOU WILL COME TO PAY A VISIT TO THE CONTINENT
YOU MAY BE ASSURED THAT YOU WILL BE RECEIVED WITH THE SAME
CARE AND RESULT AS ALL THOSE YOU SENT US BEFORE STOP SO LONG.[90]

The Englandspiel was a great success for the Germans. It enabled
them to block practically all important Allied-instigated sabotage
activities from 1942 to 1944 and to arrest approximately 400 patriots
engaged in underground work.[91] They did not succeed, however, in
what was probably their ultimate hope, to learn the date and location
of the impending invasion.[92]

The Soviet Union also sought to stimulate underground activity in
the occupied Netherlands by exhorting Dutch patriots by radio to
engage in "partisan work." Apparently the Soviets even sent one or
two underground agents to Holland.[93]

Most of the sporadic early underground activities were directed
against the German military machine. Cables and telephone lines
were cut and an occasional attack was made on railroad trains carrying troops or supplies for the Wehrmacht. Military traffic signs were
destroyed or misplaced, and parked military vehicles were disabled.

Resistance groups also attacked economic targets. In an attempt
to prevent the occupying power from extracting foodstuffs from the
Netherlands, patriots sometimes set on fire storage places containing agricultural produce. In a number of instances, agricultural
implements such as threshing machines were sabotaged.[94] In order
to impede the movement of supplies, resistance groups occasionally
destroyed key bridges.[95]

Perhaps more important than interference with agricultural production was industrial sabotage. Some of this could be carried on
quietly without discovery by the Germans. Sometimes it was difficult to determine whether or not a breakdown of machinery was accidental. In a few cases, however, resistance groups used more violent
methods, such as blowing up key equipment in industrial plants, or
trying to burn down important factories.

Along with these overt activities, underground organizations
quietly prepared themselves for the day of action, whether it might

prove to be an independent uprising or an action in support of an Allied invasion. Weapons stolen from the Germans or from Dutch police forces were hidden for this purpose. After September 1944 the Allies began to drop relatively large quantities of firearms and ammunition. At this point the job of collecting and hiding arms, and of training patriots in their use, consumed much of the attention of groups associated with the Forces of the Interior. These groups were aided in their efforts by approximately a hundred agents and military instructors who were dropped from England between March 1944 and the end of the war.[96]

With the approach of Allied armies in September 1944, the pace of sabotage operations quickened. Railroad lines were blown up frequently, especially during the fluid phase of the war, but the Germans always succeeded in restoring rail connections quickly. An attempt by the L.K.P. to join the Allied attack near Arnhem failed because of insufficient organization and equipment.

During the final winter of the war, groups in the Forces of the Interior were more active than ever before. Hundreds of German cars were destroyed, many important traffic routes and lines of communication were cut repeatedly, and explosives to be used for demolition purposes were rendered unusable. These actions constituted a considerable harassment to the enemy but did not affect the military situation in a major way. The most directly useful military contribution was made by N.B.S. groups in the east of the country, which harassed the German army during its retreat before advancing Allied troops in March and April 1945.[97] In the west the N.B.S. never was called upon to perform this function because German authorities decided to negotiate a surrender.

ASSASSINATIONS*

The early months of 1943 witnessed the start of a wave of assassinations, chiefly of Dutch National Socialist dignitaries. The first, on February 5, 1943, was the assassination of General Seyffardt, a sponsor of the Netherlands Volunteer Legion, but not a member of the N.S.B. Four days later, H. Reydon, the recently appointed Secre-

---

* Dutch patriots have preferred the more euphemistic term "liquidation."

tary-General of the Department of Propaganda and Arts, was shot and later died of his injuries.[98] In June, F. E. Posthuma, a former Minister of War and member of the Political Secretariat of State of the N.S.B., was assassinated.[99] These three assassinations were the work of an underground organization that cooperated with the Council of Resistance.[100]

The Council also carried out executions of German agents and Dutch traitors. The decision to kill an opponent was made only by the Council itself, usually after a report on the person to be liquidated had been presented to it. Most of the assassinations were justified on the basis that liquidation of the person in question was necessary to protect the lives of patriots. Many of the victims were policemen and informers.

The National Action Groups also liquidated a number of German agents. In many instances, the L.K.P. consulted with ministers or priests and with legal authorities before making the decision to kill a traitor.[101]

After the May strikes, the number of assassinations increased. N.S.B. officials of lower rank, especially party members in the police service, were among the targets. The heads of police at Nijmegen and Utrecht were liquidated.[102] In the eastern provinces, N.S.B. peasants were killed and their farms were burned. Altogether, over forty members of the N.S.B. were shot between February 1 and September 15, 1943.[103]

At his trial, Rauter claimed that the countermeasures instituted in the autumn of 1943, including the system of reprisal murders and the establishment of the Home Guard, stopped the assassination of Dutch National Socialists. Actually, it appears that over 300 political assassinations occurred in 1944 alone.[104] After September 1944, attacks on the Nazi Home Guard, police informers, and German personnel increased substantially.

Particularly at the beginning there was some disagreement among patriotic circles whether such extremes of violence as assassinations were justified, but as the brutality of the German police regime increased, opposition to liquidations lessened. In general, most resistance groups and underground papers sanctioned the execution of police spies and traitors who endangered the lives of patriots through their activities.

The clandestine journal *Vrij Nederland* accepted the turn of affairs as inevitable, while expressing regret that the situation had deteriorated to such an extent.[105] Left-wing publications, such as *Het Parool* and *De Vrije Katheder,* heartily approved the liquidation of traitors.[106] Radio Moscow advocated such assassinations, and Dutch Communists were active in this field.[107]

In a February 1943 radio broadcast, the government-in-exile disapproved political assassinations and warned patriots against taking justice into their own hands.[108] On the other hand, it appears that the S.O.E. ordered the assassination of leading members of the N.S.B. and that for this purpose it dropped revolvers equipped with silencers.*

Advocates of assassination as a method of dealing with the N.S.B. and the police generally maintained that the occupying power and the N.S.B. had declared total war on the civilian population of the Netherlands. In such a total war, the elimination of opponents, especially of police spies, through assassination was considered only one more way to harm the enemy. It was judged to be no more reprehensible than to kill an enemy soldier on the battlefield.

The opponents of assassination held that no person or agency except the legally constituted government had the right to take life except in self-defense. Furthermore, they pointed out that in a police state, large numbers of innocent persons usually had to suffer because of reprisals.[109]

Although this disagreement, particularly with regard to purely political assassinations, was never completely settled, patriots increasingly subscribed to the point of view expressed in *Het Parool* on the occasion of the trial of the killers of Seyffardt, Reydon, and Posthuma. This view held that the defendants "were brave soldiers of the Dutch army, and that those who could not or did not want to follow their example should bear witness that these soldiers on the domestic front have brought victory closer by their own actions."[110]

---

* Schreieder, "Nota," [19], 4-B, 52. Actually, it seems that the S.O.E. made these requests at a time when it suspected or knew already that the Germans controlled their radio contacts. The S.O.E. claimed it wanted to see how far the German counterintelligence agencies would go to satisfy British demands in order to maintain the radio contacts. It seems likely that no Dutch government agency in London at any time ordered the assassination of leading members of the N.S.B. (see testimony of Henricus Lieftinck, May 10, 1949, *ibid.,* 4-C, 1060).

ESPIONAGE

The Dutch espionage service had made no preparation before May 1940 against the eventuality that the country might be overrun and the struggle against the invader might have to be continued from abroad. It therefore became necessary to build an espionage system in Holland from scratch after the arrival of Dutch authorities in London in May 1940. For this reason, in July 1940 the government-in-exile established a new intelligence agency called the Central Intelligence Service (Centrale Inlichtingen Dienst, or C.I.D.).[111] In November 1942 this service was replaced by the Intelligence Bureau (Bureau Inlichtingen, or B.I.). Under the leadership of Major I. J. Somer, appointed head of the B.I. in July 1943, this agency operated with considerable success until the end of the war.[112]

The dependence of Dutch secret services on their counterparts in the British Secret Intelligence Service (S.I.S.) created many problems. At first the Dutch services had little control over the selection of agents to be dispatched to Holland, and they saw only those messages received in London that the S.I.S. chose to pass on. In addition, they were initially forced to depend on the British for technical evaluations, such as determining whether messages received were "genuine" or were sent by the Germans.

Policy and personality conflicts within Dutch government circles in London also interfered with the effectiveness of the C.I.D. Its first head was officially dismissed in August 1941, but, with the approval of the Prime Minister, continued to play a role in intelligence activities.[113] The administrative location of the C.I.D. was a further problem, resolved only with the establishment of the B.I. under the Minister of War, in November 1942. As a result of these conflicts, the effectiveness of the Dutch secret services during the first half of the war was far less than it might have been had there been better early planning and administration in London.

The first agent of the Central Intelligence Service, L. A. R. J. van Hamel, was dropped in Holland in August 1940 with orders to establish several independent groups, which were to gather and relay by radio items of military intelligence. Van Hamel did an excellent job setting up a number of groups equipped with transmitters. Most of these were soon discovered by the Germans, but a few continued to operate for some time. One of the groups developed into the Intelligence Service of the O.D. This service was liquidated by the Germans in 1941, but one of its survivors continued to transmit military reports, fifty of which arrived in London.[114]

Van Hamel himself was arrested in October 1940 during an attempt to return to England. He did not betray any of his collaborators and was executed in June 1941.[115]

The London C.I.D. dispatched approximately a dozen more intelligence agents to Holland before the summer of 1942. Half of these landed on the Dutch coast by boat. One, a woman, with permission from the Germans, entered Holland via Lisbon.[116] The others were dropped by air. Most agents were supplied with transmitters and were ordered to gather and transmit military intelligence. One had the assignment to bring back to England two patriots from the occupied territory, one a political figure, the other a military officer.[117] Most agents remained at liberty for only a few months before they were arrested, but while they were at liberty they managed to transmit information to England. Two agents managed to return to England, where they reported to their superiors and to the Queen,[118] who had always displayed a strong interest in interviewing new arrivals from the occupied territory. One lost his life in an attempt to cross the North Sea,[119] but all others were arrested by the Germans.

In summary, tenuous radio communications for the transmission of military intelligence existed between England and the occupied territory until October 1942. The arrests of the last C.I.D. agents in 1942 were already the outcome of the Englandspiel, since the C.I.D. agents had some of the same contacts as the sabotage agents dropped by the S.O.E. Espionage activities were therefore at their lowest ebb from the autumn of 1942 until the summer of 1943, when the reorganized Bureau Inlichtingen began to build up a new espionage network independent of the penetrated S.O.E. lines.

The line of communication between the occupied territory and the London government that was used most intensively was operated not by radio but by a courier service to Geneva, where a Dutch clergyman, W. A. Visser 't Hooft, happened to be living in 1940. Visser 't Hooft remained in touch with his friends in Holland, many of whom were associated with the underground publication *Vrij Nederland.* It soon appeared to the *Vrij Nederland* group that the London government and Radio Orange needed better information about conditions and opinions inside Holland. Therefore it began to dispatch reports and complaints concerning political, social, and economic conditions in the occupied territory to London through Visser 't Hooft, who frequently supplemented these with his own commentary. Since the German police occasionally allowed "reliable" Dutch businessmen to travel to Switzerland, Visser 't Hooft was in a position to check his own impressions with these compatriots. The government-in-exile sometimes sent replies to the comments received from Holland, which Visser 't Hooft passed on to his associates in the occupied territory, for discussion among underground political leaders. Visser 't Hooft visited London in 1942 and signed an agreement with Prime Minister Gerbrandy, which systematized this information service.

Early reports sent to Switzerland were usually sewn into books. Incidental couriers were also used. After July 1942, a regular woman courier took charge. She was also responsible for the collection of information in Holland. In October 1943 a relay service was established for transmittal of the increasingly well-organized and steadily growing quantity of information.

Since Visser 't Hooft was not concerned with military intelligence, such information was separated in the Swiss processing center and sent to London via the Netherlands Military Attaché. When the Order Service tried to censor political information, the *Vrij Nederland* group objected, and in 1944 a separate channel for military information was set up. The main limitation of the "Swiss Way" for military intelligence was its slowness.

In Holland a political commission was formed to discuss the problems brought up by the correspondence with Visser 't Hooft and the London government. The commission was closely associated with *Vrij Nederland* and played an important part in the formulation of postwar plans within the resistance movement.[120]

The other important channel for information from the occupied territory to London was the so-called "Swedish Way," organized in June 1942 by the Dutch Consul in Stockholm and A. L. Oosterhuis, a resistance leader in Delfzijl, the easternmost Dutch coastal shipping center. Oosterhuis had good connections with the captains of ships conducting coastal trade with Sweden, through which he had previously helped young patriots to escape. In June 1942 he felt the need to supply better information for Radio Orange and started a news line via the same channels to prevent Radio Orange from broadcasting "such nonsense."[121] He also used a secret transmitter, while sending bulky material, such as copies of underground publications, by ship. Among other information, he transmitted a detailed report of the arrest of the National Committee and a description of the German agent, A. van der Waals. In July 1943, Oosterhuis was betrayed and the Swedish Way became inoperative.[122]

Both the Swedish Way and the Swiss Way were comparatively ineffective in the field of military espionage because communication was slow and cumbersome at best. Radio contacts were the only feasible method for supplying military data promptly and for issuing day-to-day directives from London.

In 1943 the Netherlands Intelligence Bureau (B.I.) finally worked out effective procedures for dropping agents in Holland. The B.I. handled the selection and instruction of agents. The British provided the agents with technical training, supplied their equipment, and dropped them into the occupied territory. The B.I. usually assigned one agent to a specific underground group. Thirty-three such agents were dropped before September 1944. The majority of these were arrested eventually, but most of them succeeded in carrying out their tasks for sufficiently long periods to ensure unbroken radio communications between the occupied territory and London for the remainder of the war.[123]

The intelligence groups maintaining wireless contact with London usually limited themselves to the collection and dispatch of information without engaging in other types of resistance work. Exceptions to this were the Group Albrecht, which helped persons to cross the rivers into liberated territory after September 1944, the Fiat Libertas Group, which specialized in arrangements for the escape of Allied aviators, and the Secret Service of the Netherlands (Geheime Dienst Nederland), which dispatched military and political information.[124]

Within the field of intelligence there was a certain amount of specialization. The underground Central Intelligence Service distributed advance notice of police actions to resistance groups.[125] The Group Kees concentrated on transmission of military information and supplies to London with data about V-weapons. It also made an attempt to set up an espionage organization in Germany.[126] The Radio

Service was closely associated with the Council of Resistance (R.v.V.). It specialized in political news and aspired to serve other underground organizations. It established many small local stations for internal communications. After September 1944 this service proved particularly useful, since it furnished communication between liberated and occupied territory.[127] The Rolls-Royce Group aspired to be a "post office" for the resistance movement by providing courier services. It also trained resistance workers in underground techniques and for the eventuality of arrest.[128]

Another intelligence organization, the Packard Group, regularly transmitted meteorological data for Allied air forces, and supplied information about food and economic conditions obtained from patriotic Dutch government officials in The Hague. In the last winter of the war, the Packard Group transmitted messages for the Representatives of the Government.[129]

After the southern part of the country had been liberated, the work of all these intelligence groups was accelerated. Much of the information was passed on to the liberated territory by radio phones and couriers.[130] Thus in the last months of the war, Dutch government agencies in the south and Allied authorities were well furnished with up-to-date information on the occupied territory.

LEADERSHIP AND COORDINATION

In the first three years of the occupation, underground organizations usually started locally and only slowly established contacts with groups in neighboring towns or in other parts of the country.[131] Even after the major organizations had been created, progress toward coordination or unification was slow. In the first place, political and ideological distinctions remained discernible. The Communists on the left and the orthodox Protestants on the right were especially intent on maintaining their separate identity and independence. In the second place, the desirability of close coordination was questioned for technical and security reasons.* But most important, the founda-

* [50], 67 (June 19, 1944), p. 7. The Parliamentary Commission of Inquiry came to the conclusion that disagreements about techniques of resisting the Germans were more directly responsible for internal conflict within the Resistance than political differences [19], 7-A, 315, but this writer believes that political suspicions and the fear of losing ideological identity were at the base of the general hesitations with regard to coordination and unification.

tions of Dutch resistance depended to such a large extent on spontaneous associations growing from the ground up that it was difficult to superimpose from the top a degree of coordination alien to the pluralistic character of the movement. This was the main reason why the groups which aspired to achieve greater coordination in 1943, when most underground workers saw the theoretical need for both liaison and leadership, failed to achieve their goal and became separate organizations working alongside other underground groups.

A degree of liaison was achieved, however, on a fairly wide scale by a group of leaders of resistance organizations who, from early 1943, met regularly on Thursdays in Amsterdam under the name "The Nucleus" (De Kern). Most of the original groups represented were concerned with assistance to people in hiding, but gradually a wide variety of organizations joined. The underground press, however, refused to participate, fearing for its security and independence.

The meetings of De Kern were started originally to resolve technical questions such as the distribution of ration books and identity cards and the financing of underground activities, but the group also discussed broader policy questions of the Resistance. Its leaders, according to their testimony after the war, did not aspire for the Kern to become a "high command" of the Resistance, although some resistance groups felt concern on this score.[132] The collaboration of the constituent organizations was not always easy to obtain because each was jealous of its independence and individuality. The Kern did not play an important political role and concerned itself less with postwar politics than most other coordinating groups, since its main purpose was to facilitate the effectiveness of the constituent organizations in the wartime struggle against the Germans.

Security arrangements of the meetings of the Kern were extraordinarily well thought out. This caution, and good luck, made it possible for the organization to continue meeting regularly without the loss of a single person.[133]

Despite the liaison achieved by the Kern and the close cooperation of many groups on the local level, excessive rivalry and antagonism remained (especially between the large organizations), which was bound to decrease the effectiveness of any potential military support of the Allies. Therefore, with the approach of Allied forces in August 1944, unification of these organizations became an urgent matter. In September 1944, in response to requests received from the Resistance, the government-in-exile established the Netherlands Forces of the Interior (Nederlandse Binnenlandse Strijdkrachten, or N.B.S.), with Prince Bernhard as chief.[134] At this time, the government expected liberation of all the Netherlands within a few weeks, and the groups belonging to the N.B.S. were to contribute by giving aid to advancing Allied armies.[135]

The Order Service (O.D.), the Council of Resistance (R.v.V.), and the National Action Groups (L.K.P.) were made divisions of the N.B.S., and their members were given legal recognition as combatants. It was hoped that the Germans would recognize them as such rather than regard them as partisans. The Germans did indeed issue orders to treat members of the N.B.S. as combatant soldiers under certain conditions.[136] Many resistance organizations remained outside the N.B.S. although some of their members signed up with N.B.S. groups.

Establishment of the Forces of the Interior finally created the framework for a unified military command, which the constituent organizations themselves requested in September.[137] On October 20, 1944, Prince Bernhard appointed Lieutenant Colonel H. Koot Commandant of the Forces of the Interior, with the definite assignment to establish unity among the competing organizations of the Resistance.[138] Because of the limitation of communications with the headquarters of Prince Bernhard, Koot in effect had to act on his own judgment most of the time.

At first, the internal organization of the Forces of the Interior was based on the so-called "delta formation," in which the chiefs of the three constituent organizations formed the command, with the highest officer of the Order Service as the Commandant. The usefulness of this arrangement was hampered by the fact that the leaders of each organization continued to have the authority to issue orders to their subordinates.[139] Early in 1945 it was decided to divide the N.B.S. into a Combatant and a Noncombatant Division. The Combatant Division was to engage in sabotage and military action; the Noncombatant group was to serve after the German collapse.[140]

A final reorganization in late March 1945, creating a single chain of command, came too late to be of much use. Although local N.B.S. groups successfully harassed the Germans and supported Allied troops, the Forces of the Interior remained relatively ineffective in a military sense. This failure can be attributed in part to the unexpected freezing of the front after the collapse of the Allied offensive at Arnhem, which made it impossible for the N.B.S. to play the role of auxiliary to the Allied armies assigned to it originally, but it must also be blamed on the reluctance of the major resistance organizations to subordinate themselves to a common command.

Although operational unification of the entire Resistance was never achieved, political liaison and continuity were maintained to a considerable extent throughout the occupation. From May 1940 on, traditional political leaders saw a need for mutual consultation to discuss attitudes toward the occupying power and to prepare for the transition after the German withdrawal. These leaders created a number of committees which increasingly began to focus on postwar problems.

These groups were not primarily designed to promote or coordinate active resistance against the Germans, but they did provide focal points of political cohesion. The government-in-exile played a decisive role in the creation and strengthening of some consultative groups, since it needed representative contacts in the occupied territory both to make judgments about resistance groups and to consider post-liberation problems. In 1944 the traditional politicians and the new men of the Resistance came closer together through joint participation in coordinating groups established under pressure from London.

The first in a long series of consultative, politically representative committees was formed soon after the capitulation. This so-called "Political Convent" was at first chaired by former Prime Minister Colijn and included leaders of the six parties in the De Geer cabinet. The original intention of the Convent to form a national party bloc to oppose the N.S.B. and to negotiate with the German administration was abandoned after the formation of the Netherlands Union. After the summer of 1940, the Political Convent took as its chief function the guidance of party and government officials. Its advice to government officials usually was ignored. There was considerable turnover in the membership of the Political Convent because of arrests. All the original participants except one were imprisoned at some stage during the occupation.

The Political Convent established contact with a religious group headed by Professor P. Scholten. In the fall of 1941 the two groups, with the addition of a few other prominent men, formed the Great Citizens' Committee (Groot Burger Comité), composed of fifteen persons including Professor W. Schermerhorn and W. Drees, who were designated in 1945 to form jointly the first postwar cabinet. In 1942 this organization set up a working committee of five members called the National Committee (Nationaal Comité), the closest approach to a clandestine political High Command achieved until 1944. The National Committee had contacts with provincial commissioners and other leading figures. It made plans for the postwar reconstruction period and was prepared to serve as a temporary government immediately after the Liberation. The Committee as such did not concern itself with active resistance although most of its members were active in the underground movement.[141]

Unfortunately, the notorious undercover agent, the Dutchman A. van der Waals, gained the confidence of the National Committee and assumed responsibility for transmitting its messages to the London government. As a result of Van der Waals' activities the German police arrested most of the members of the National Committee, and its parent group, the Great Citizens' Committee, in April 1943. Fortunately, the Germans gave this group, which included some of the best-known Dutch political leaders, preferential treatment equal to that accorded the hostages taken in 1940 and 1942. Most of the arrestees returned safely after liberation.[142]

After the arrest of the National Committee, the government-in-exile encouraged the establishment of a new group of five persons, the Patriotic Committee (Vaderlands Comité),* which included one member from each of the major parties (Social Democrats, Catholics, and Antirevolutionaries) and two persons not identified with any party.[143] Eventually, W. Drees, a prominent Social Democrat who had sat with the Political Convent and the Great Citizens' Committee, became its chairman.

Essentially, this new group was a continuation of the original National Committee. It considered its main task to be the submission

---

* Originally the new group had considered itself a continuation of the Nationaal Comité, but it changed its name to Vaderlands Comité, to avoid confusion with the Nationaal Comité van Verzet Drees ([242], II, 114).

of advice on postwar problems to the London government. It refused to consider itself a transitional government because it did not expect its authority to be respected by the Resistance.[144]

The Patriotic Committee scored some important achievements, especially in connection with planning for a postwar government. Because it was dominated by old-line party leaders, its advice to the government-in-exile was, on the whole, conservative. It advocated close adherence to the Constitution in postwar reconstruction and advised against the concept of a unicameral legislature proposed in resistance circles. It suggested the reactivation of the States-General as a provisional legislature through the convocation of the parliament elected in 1937, rather than the use of a new extraconstitutional assembly drawn from the Resistance.[145]

The possibility of postwar conflict between the Resistance and traditional political elements became a major concern of a number of thoughtful patriots by 1943. Foremost among the underground leaders so concerned was Bosch Ridder van Rosenthal, the author of the Commentary on the Directives of 1937, who was also closely allied with circles of the underground publications *Vrij Nederland* and *Het Parool*.[146] In the spring of 1944, through a personal messenger, Bosch Ridder van Rosenthal and Drees emphasized to Prime Minister Gerbrandy the need for more coordination. In June 1944, partly in response to this message, the London government urgently requested the formation of a high-level advisory organization of the resistance movement to assist the government in formulating postwar plans.[147] This committee, called the Great Advisory Commission of the Illegality (Grote Advies-Commissie der Illegaliteit), included representatives of most major underground organizations and clandestine publications.[148] Since it was too large to meet safely as a whole, most of its business was conducted by a Contact Commission (Contact Commissie), which also functioned as the liaison with the Patriotic Committee.

In the Contact Commission the Resistance and prewar political elements worked together effectively. In its discussions, consent of the Resistance to postwar plans worked out by the Patriotic Committee was secured after certain modifications had been made, such as the provision that the underground movement would be consulted on appointments to fill vacancies in the provisional States-General.[149]

The main achievement of the Contact Commission was to moderate the demands of certain resistance groups for political power after liberation.[150]

In August 1944 the Gerbrandy government appointed a group of persons in the occupied territory as "Representatives of the Government" (Vertrouwensmannen der Regering). The chief task of this group was to act on behalf of the government-in-exile in the interval between the end of the German rule and the arrival of the proper Dutch and Allied authorities. The Committee consisted of seven members. Five of these, appointed by the government, had been prominent in political life before 1940 but had been active in the Resistance as well. The two remaining members were leaders of the Council of Resistance and the National Committee of Resistance. The Representatives were in close touch with the Contact Commission of the Great Advisory Commission of the Illegality and with the Patriotic Committee, an arrangement that was facilitated by the fact that Drees was a member of all three groups.

In its instructions, the government emphasized that the chief task of the Representatives was to maintain peace and order and to prevent a "hatchet day" during the transition period after the German surrender.

The Representatives devoted much of their attention to personnel matters and established the principle that no controversial public figure should continue to exercise his function after liberation until he had an opportunity to present his case to the proper authorities. As a rule, the Representatives tried to persuade the persons in question to suspend their official activities voluntarily. On his own initiative, Secretary-General Hirschfeld asked for a leave of absence, but Frederiks could not be persuaded to do so, and an order of suspension was therefore issued to him.[151]

In the autumn of 1944 the Representatives made arrangements for the Order Service to act as an auxiliary police under their general authority, but the establishment of the Forces of the Interior and of the Dutch Military Government superseded this arrangement.[152]

While concentrating primarily on problems of the transition period, the Representatives also supported the resistance to the German regime. For example, in December 1944 they urged the government-in-exile to instruct Dutch officials and citizens in unequivocal terms to refuse all collaboration with the final German labor drive. In a few instances, where high officials and managers in private industry asked for exemptions for their employees, the Representatives intervened successfully.[153]

Although surrender negotiations conducted by the Vertrouwens-mannen in April 1945 did not lead to an armistice, they were instrumental in slowing down the pace of executions and physical destruction and in laying the groundwork for emergency arrangements for food and medical relief. After the German surrender, the Representatives published a proclamation admonishing the population to maintain peace and order, but they never had to function as a transitional government, because military authorities arrived promptly. In order to prevent the loss of valuable materials on the history of the occupation, a State Office for the Documentation of the History of the Netherlands in Time of War was established three days after the German capitulation, under the authority of the Vertrouwensmannen.[154]

The smooth transition to legal government after the occupation, without the major conflicts that characterized the corresponding periods in France and neighboring Belgium, and the absence of major excesses against Germans and members of the N.S.B. must be attributed at least partially to the preparatory work of the Special Representatives.

CHAPTER ELEVEN

The Underground Press

FUNCTIONS

The underground press in many ways called forth and stimulated the Dutch Resistance by serving as the "conscience" of the nation. It was itself the oldest form of resistance and remained an integral part of the Resistance until the end.[1] Most collaborators of clandestine papers played a role in other phases of resistance work, and the ties of underground papers with ideologically related resistance organizations were often close.

Yet, while the underground press considered itself an integral part of the Resistance, individual publications were jealous of their organizational independence. Most publications were reluctant to participate in a coordinating council for fear that their editorial independence might be compromised. For the same reason many publications did not wish to accept payments from the government-subsidized National Assistance Fund unless they had no alternative. They wanted to maintain the "independence from the government which had historically distinguished the Dutch press."[2]

The main purpose and indeed the *raison d'être* for the underground press was the overriding necessity to warn the Dutch people against submission to the Germans and to encourage them to resist the enemy to the best of their ability. The warnings against ideological compromise were most important in the early years of the occupation before the realities of German rule had immunized the Dutch against ideological contamination. The call for active resistance became more urgent from 1942 on, when it became necessary to encourage patriots to assist Jews and divers and to defy the labor draft.

A second function of the underground press, closely related to the call for resistance, was to provide interpretation of, and commentary on, events at home and abroad. The staff of each paper discussed and analyzed the issues of the day. The most controversial topics, such as the justification of political assassinations, subsequently became subjects of "public" debate between different periodicals. Thus the underground press helped to create a national consensus of opinion, normally reached in peacetime through a free press and through the parliament.

In the third place, the underground press provided a forum for discussion of postwar problems, a function that became increasingly prominent toward the end of the war. Some underground editors were reluctant to participate in these debates, which they felt divided and weakened resistance to the Germans. There may have been some truth in this contention, but the compromises achieved as a result of these discussions certainly helped after the Liberation.

GROWTH AND DEVELOPMENT

The first hand-written "underground" bulletin appeared the day after the Dutch capitulation. By the end of 1940, over sixty clandestine periodicals had been started, some not surviving long. In December of that year the total circulation of the underground press was approximately 57,000 copies.[3]

During 1941 the number of publications almost doubled, since the last opportunity for open expression of opposition to national socialism had vanished. In 1942, since a number of smaller publications merged with the "big periodicals,"[4] fewer titles were published than in 1941, but the circulation of the clandestine press probably continued to increase.

Although the number of clandestine publications was small at the outset, the underground press reached a comparatively wide public because each issue usually was passed on to many readers or was reproduced in longhand or on the typewriter. Moreover some periodicals circulated in strategic spots, such as factories and universities, thus increasing their impact.

The events of May 1943 modified the character of the underground press in two important respects. In the first place, the confiscation of radio sets forced clandestine editors to provide more extensive news coverage. Many new publications, most of them straight "newspapers" which appeared two or three times a week, were issued to fill this need. Second, the apparent approach of liberation led underground editors to give more thought and space to discussion of postwar problems. Articles on this subject resulted in a growing emphasis on ideological differences, frequently along prewar party lines.

In the months after the May strike the clandestine press grew rapidly in circulation and bulk. In December 1943 the big periodicals alone published approximately 450,000 copies.[5]

After the events of September 1944 another major expansion of the clandestine press took place. Hundreds of thousands of daily news bulletins were published in the occupied part of the country, since the lack of electric power had deprived the population of radio news. Most of these news bulletins sprang up locally because normal traffic within the occupied territory had practically ceased.[6]

Between May 1940 and May 1945 almost 1,200 periodicals were at one time or another issued clandestinely.[7] During the last months of the war the underground press was more widely read than the regular press.

In this chapter a number of the major publications and a representative sample of the less important titles are discussed. A complete listing of clandestine periodicals and pamphlets has been made available by the Netherlands Institute for War Documentation in Amsterdam.[8]

EARLY TEMPORARY PUBLICATIONS

The earliest specimens of clandestine literature were the "snowball letters" which appeared as soon as the Germans occupied the country. These were typewritten sheets or bulletins which the recipients were expected to copy to pass on to their friends. The snowball letters consisted mostly of appeals not to be misled by the conciliatory tone of German statements but to be prepared to continue the battle against the enemy.

The first underground messages were the Reports of the Geuzen-actie,* which were written by Bernard Ijzerdraat, a tapestry ex-

---

* *Gueux* or *geus* ("beggar") was a derogatory name the Spaniards used for the Dutch patriots during the sixteenth-century struggle between the Dutch and Spain. The Dutch themselves adopted this term and wore the name with pride.

pert and teacher at a vocational school in Haarlem. Ijzerdraat had been living near the German border before moving to Haarlem, and had at that time become aware of the nature of the Nazi system. For this reason, he had a clearer perception than most of his fellow countrymen of the trials that German rule would bring to Holland. He wished to alert his countrymen to the dangers ahead and to shake their illusion that the struggle against the enemy had terminated with the Dutch capitulation. Therefore, on May 15, the day after the capitulation, he started to send out hand-written bulletins which were to be copied and passed on in chain-letter fashion. The second of these bulletins, dated May 18, is the earliest surviving example of underground literature. Although somewhat emotional in tone, the clandestine note predicted many of the coming disasters, such as rationing and the labor draft. It drew a parallel between the Eighty Years' War against Spain and the present struggle against Germany. One sentence struck a note that was to recur in many underground publications: "Our country shall not become a part of Germany."[9]

The bulletins appeared in hand-written or typed format one to three times a week until August 1940. During this period Ijzerdraat built up an underground sabotage organization, the Geuzenactie, which engaged in minor "wild" sabotage. He and most of his followers were arrested in November 1940. In March 1941, Ijzerdraat and fourteen of his associates were executed.[10] The history of the Geuzenactie is an early illustration of the close ties between underground journalism and "militant resistance."

More moderate documents were prepared and distributed by the Committee for Free Netherlands (Comité voor Vrij Nederland), which had been founded in August 1940. This group also combined clandestine journalism with "militant resistance" and sabotage. Its members were arrested in the winter of 1940–41, and the organization ceased to exist.

The Comité voor Vrij Nederland addressed an Open Letter to the High Commissioner in which it claimed that Germany was bound to lose in the end because the United States and the Soviet Union would enter the war eventually. The letter went on to say that the Dutch people were willing to cooperate loyally with a purely military occupation, but that cooperation would require the withdrawal of such unconstitutional measures as the changes in the judicial system, the anti-Jewish decrees, and the arrests of hostages. The letter concluded with the remark that the Dutch people hated the Germans far less than they hated the Dutch Nazis.[11]

Four thousand copies of this open letter were stenciled in Amsterdam. They were distributed throughout the country and reproduced in other underground publications.

The Committee also distributed an underground weekly, *De Vrije Pers* ("The Free Press") and a series of occasional "Communiqués" (*Mededelingen*).[12] One of these issues warned against changing the Dutch political structure under the occupation. The Dutch people were also asked to facilitate the expected withdrawal of the Germans in the event of an attack on Russia, and not to take the law into their own hands in dealing with the N.S.B. It suggested avoiding contact with Germans in daily life. It ended with the optimistic salutation: "Greetings, people of Holland, it won't be long now."[13]

Het Bulletin was the first clandestine publication that survived for more than a few months. It was published approximately once a month, in the province of Utrecht, from June 1940 to August 1941. Again the chief aim of the editors was to warn their readers against the danger of compromise with the Germans. To that end they concentrated on the publication of domestic news, frequently made available by patriotic government officials. *Het Bulletin* was the most important publication during the first year of the occupation, with a maximum circulation of 1,200 copies.[14]

THE FIVE BIG UNDERGROUND PERIODICALS

Three major groups can be distinguished among the publications issued periodically.

First, there were the "big periodicals," which had a nationwide impact on many groups because they had a high level of editorial sophistication and because they reflected the sentiments of substantial segments of the population.

Second, there were the "miscellaneous periodicals," which had a lesser editorial impact or which spoke for a more limited segment of the population than the "big" papers. This group included a wide variety of publications such as Trotskyite and left-wing Socialist publications and special periodicals for students, intellectuals, and artists.

Third, there were the straight news bulletins, which sprang up in sizable numbers after the confiscation of radio sets in May 1943, but especially after September 1944.

Vrij Nederland was the oldest of the big periodicals. Its first issue of 130 copies bore the date of August 31, 1940, the Queen's birthday, although it was actually published in September.[15] The following issues were published approximately once a month, in mimeographed form until December 1941, after which it was printed. This periodical was one of the few that managed to appear throughout the occupation on a regular basis and in approximately the same format.[16] By 1944 the total number of copies had risen to at least 40,000. After September 1944, local editions brought the total to 100,000. Daily news bulletins were also published by *Vrij Nederland* groups.[17]

Vrij Nederland was one of the most attractively printed underground papers. Its masthead showed two links of a chain, one enclosing the word *Nederland,* the other enclosing the name *Oranje,* symbolizing the interdependence of monarchy and country. Below the masthead was a verse by Vondel, Holland's national poet, in praise of "truth which cannot be suppressed."

The original editors were a group of young Calvinists who had earlier stenciled and circulated clandestinely General Winkelman's declarations on the alleged violations of Dutch neutrality and on the bombardment of Rotterdam, which the legal press had not been permitted to print. The editors "borrowed" the name of their paper ("Free Netherlands") from *La Libre Belgique,* an underground newspaper published in Belgium during the First World War.[18] During the first winter of the occupation, editorial direction was transferred to a group of older Calvinists.

In March 1941 the Germans arrested many collaborators of *Vrij Nederland.* Only a few members of the central staff managed to avoid arrest. The confusion of the following months was terminated when H. M. van Randwijk, a writer who had been director of an institute for homeless children, was designated editor in charge. In October 1941 the new management was organized and the paper acquired an editorial policy which it retained in essence until the end of the war.[19]

The paper suffered additional heavy losses in 1942. Van Randwijk and a number of his colleagues were arrested, though subsequently released by the Germans. In the autumn a large number of collaborators were caught and it became necessary to reorganize the paper once more.

Under these circumstances a conflict between Van Randwijk and the younger men who had become primarily responsible for the production and distribution of the paper led to a split in the organization. Two major issue were at stake. First, the group of younger Calvinists who opposed Van Randwijk wanted to separate the management of production and distribution from editorial responsibilities, while Van Randwijk preferred to retain total responsibility for the paper. Second, the younger group, which was closely allied to the Reformed Churches, found Van Randwijk's policies too secular and socialistic. Therefore they left *Vrij Nederland* and founded a new paper, *Trouw.*[20]

After the 1942 arrests and the resignation of the *Trouw* group, *Vrij Nederland* suffered few losses, none seriously affecting the publication. It has been estimated that over seventy persons lost their lives by working for *Vrij Nederland.*[21]

The German police had such respect for the paper that they attempted to bargain for the voluntary cessation of publication, in return for which they promised to spare the lives of collaborators held as prisoners. After much soul-searching, the Board of *Vrij Nederland* countered this offer with a set of conditions which the Germans did not accept. The Germans did, however, release a "hostage" who had taken the place of a prisoner whom they had released in order to carry on negotiations.[22]

During its first year, *Vrij Nederland* was a resistance paper, pure and simple, warning against compromise with and accommodation to the Germans and urging its readers to resist national socialism on religious and moral grounds. As the war progressed, the paper increasingly tended to reflect a liberal Protestant view, advocating humanistic principles and social responsibility on the basis of broadly conceived Christian ideals. Van Randwijk himself had been influenced by the Swiss theologian Karl Barth, who had been identified in Germany with Protestant opposition to national socialism.[23] In socioeconomic affairs *Vrij Nederland* held views close to those of the Socialists, including repudiation of denominationally organized political parties and voluntary associations. It advocated a postwar society characterized by a mixed economy and comprehensive social security.

Vrij Nederland was widely respected in Holland because of its editorial independence and its imaginative ideas about the postwar world. By maintaining contacts with groups on the right and the left it formed a link between Socialists and orthodox Protestants active in the Resistance.

Vrij Nederland sponsored a number of clandestine editions designed to discuss crucial issues of the day and of the future. Such editions contained an "Open Letter to Christiansen" about the persecution of the Jews, a discussion on annexation of German territory as compensation for war damages,[24] directions to employers on how to frustrate the selective labor draft of 1943–44, a report on the sea battle near Bali in 1942, and a set of underground songs with music.[25] After January 1944, *Vrij Nederland* published the *Internationale Informatiebladen*, containing articles from the world press intended to counteract the German attempt to cut off the people of the Netherlands from the rest of the world.[26]

Het Parool was another major clandestine publication that dated back to the early months of the occupation. In June 1940 its founder, the Socialist journalist Frans J. Goedhart, had started sending out a typed or mimeographed newsletter called *Nieuwsbrief van Pieter 't Hoen*. In *Het Parool*, which he started in February 1941, he retained his pseudonym, Pieter 't Hoen ("Peter the Chicken"), borrowed from a Dutch eighteenth-century publicist.

The paper appeared irregularly. In the beginning, and after September 1944, it was a weekly, but during the intervening period it was usually published only once or twice a month.[27] The Liberation number, published on May 7, 1945, the day Allied troops entered Amsterdam, was its hundredth issue.[28]

From the start, *Het Parool* had a relatively large circulation. Its first issue appeared in 6,000 copies. The demand for the paper was so great that it was soon decided to substitute the printing press for the mimeograph machine. Thus, in August 1941, *Het Parool* became the first printed underground paper.[29]

As a result of arrests of staff members, circulation dropped for a few months in late 1942 and early 1943, but soon picked up again and reached a total of 60,000 in 1944. Demand for the paper was greater than its circulation, but it seemed necessary to limit circulation for security reasons. Some large editions were printed in Amsterdam, but when distribution became too difficult and dangerous, increasing use was made of local print shops. After September 1944 local publication became the rule for *Het Parool*, as it did for most underground papers.[30]

The original staff of *Het Parool* was primarily but not exclusively Socialist. Frans Goedhart, the founder, had worked for a variety of publications. Some editors were former staff members of Social Democratic papers, but had also worked for independent periodicals or agencies. Until 1942, Koos Vorrink, Chairman of the Social Democratic Party (S.D.A.P.), also sat on the editorial board.

Many collaborators of *Het Parool* paid with their lives for their work on the paper. Twice during the war, in 1942 and in 1944, large groups were arrested and tried by German courts. Goedhart himself was caught while attempting to cross the channel to England, but the German police did not realize they had captured Pieter 't Hoen, although they knew that the prisoner had worked for *Het Parool*. To protect him, his colleagues continued to publish editorials under his pseudonym. The Germans sentenced Goedhart to death, but with the help of Dutch policemen whom he had informed of his identity he escaped in August 1943, just a few days before his scheduled execution. After his escape, Goedhart resumed his position on the editorial board of *Het Parool*.[31]

Four of the other main editors were executed or died in concentration camps, but two made their way to England. On request of the London government, one of them, G. J. van Heuven Goedhart, went to England to report on the resistance movement.[32] When he arrived in July 1944, he was appointed Minister of Justice.

Frans Goedhart's original motivation for publishing the *Nieuwsbrief van Pieter 't Hoen* had been his wish to educate his readers politically and to induce them to eschew the defeatism so common in 1940 and 1941. The original objectives were, however, broadened with the publication of *Het Parool*. It was established as a liberal and Socialist-oriented paper, without becoming an organ of the S.D.A.P. The paper aspired to be independent of party as "the spokesman of the best progressive and democratic ideas."[33] Goedhart tended to be critical of the prewar parliamentary system and to air this criticism in

Het Parool. This became a source of conflict with Koos Vorrink, who objected to public criticism of prewar parliamentary democracy, which he considered inopportune and detrimental to the fight against the Germans. This conflict, plus differences of opinion about technical aspects of publication, continued for some time, ending with Koos Vorrink's resignation in 1942. After his resignation from *Het Parool,* Vorrink continued to publish miscellaneous clandestine pamphlets and papers.[34]

In general, *Het Parool* advocated policies somewhat to the left of those of *Vrij Nederland,* with which close contact was maintained. It pledged loyalty to the House of Orange and reprinted the speeches of the Queen, but it placed less emphasis on the role of the monarchy than *Vrij Nederland* or other papers to the right. It carried definite but basically constructive criticism of the government-in-exile. For postwar reconstruction it advocated a planned economy, partial nationalization of means of production, and comprehensive social security. It also advocated autonomy (but not independence) for the Dutch East Indies.[35] Many of these ideas were set forth in a joint *Manifesto* with *Vrij Nederland,* published in April 1944 in anticipation of the Liberation.[36]

In September 1944 *Het Parool* began to publish daily news bulletins all over the country. The daily, country-wide circulation of these bulletins approached 100,000.[37] After the Liberation *Het Parool* continued publication as an independent newspaper.

The third of the major clandestine periodicals, *Je Maintiendrai,* took its title from the emblem of the House of Orange, which bore the motto of William the Silent in his battle against Spain. This motto, "I will stand fast," had acquired new significance under the German rule.

Je Maintiendrai was started in March 1943. It was the result of a fusion of a local group which had published a resistance paper called *B.C. Nieuws* and a group of former members of the Netherlands Union in Utrecht who felt the need to reach a wider audience through a clandestine publication. By October 1943 *Je Maintiendrai* had grown from a small mimeographed sheet produced in the attic of the International Court of Justice in The Hague to a well-planned, printed periodical with a circulation exceeding 20,000 copies. From the middle of 1943, *Je Maintiendrai* appeared approximately twice a month. In 1945 it became a weekly.[38] Its circulation rose to 40,000 copies per issue before the end of the war.[39]

After May 1943 the editorial board of *Je Maintiendrai* was largely made up of people who had been active in the Netherlands Union or sympathetic to its political concepts. Some of the collaborators were Catholics, but on the whole *Je Maintiendrai* included a diverse group of people, Protestants, Catholics, and "humanists," who worked together in harmony. Professor W. Schermerhorn, the first postwar Prime Minister, also contributed to *Je Maintiendrai*.[40]

The paper suffered two major blows. A number of distributors were arrested in July 1943, but the most important of these were freed from prison. In August 1944, however, the Germans managed to seize two of the founders and key editors. These men were executed in October.[41]

Je Maintiendrai made an effort to provide news coverage as well as political guidance and discussion. Its political orientation was somewhat to the right of *Vrij Nederland*. It was colored by the concepts of the Netherlands Union. The paper toyed with the idea of a single party, embodying all democratic elements of the political spectrum, and a single trade union, representing the interests of the working class. It opposed the denominational divisions of prewar Holland, and hoped to carry the new-found unity of the Resistance into the postwar world. It emphasized the role of a strong government and a strong monarchy as the expression of national unity.[42] In line with its pronounced "royalism" *Je Maintiendrai* gave special attention to editions published on birthdays of members of the House of Orange and sometimes printed photographs of the royal family. *Je Maintiendrai* advocated maintaining control over Dutch colonial possessions and retaining armed forces capable of defending them.[43]

Like *Vrij Nederland*, *Je Maintiendrai* addressed itself to an educated audience. Much of its space was devoted to commentary concerning postwar reconstruction. It was more restrained than *Het Parool* in its call for resistance and in its criticism of the government-in-exile. In March 1943 it allotted the major part of an issue to a discussion of the different kinds of opposition to the Germans, recommending firm passive resistance.[44]

Perhaps the outstanding feature of *Je Maintiendrai* was the quality of its editorship. Tastefully printed and illustrated, it carried thoughtful commentaries and editorials, which took a comparatively calm and judicious view of even the most urgent questions of the day.

The fourth major underground paper, *Trouw*, was started by a group of resistance workers who had split from *Vrij Nederland*. The group was led by Wim Speelman, a former university student who had been in charge of the distribution of *Vrij Nederland*. It joined forces with the underground organization of the Antirevolutionary Party, which had cast about for some time for a publication of its own that would present more distinctly than *Vrij Nederland* the points of view of the Antirevolutionary Party and of the Calvinist segment of the population. The first issue of this new publication was called *Oranjebode* ("Messenger of Orange") in honor of the birth of the youngest granddaughter of the Queen. Subsequent issues were called *Trouw* ("Loyalty").[45]

The circulation of *Trouw* increased rapidly during 1943 and reached 60,000 copies in August. With approximately sixty local and regional editions it became one of the largest and, because of the high quality of its editorial comment, most influential underground papers.[46]

The publishers of *Trouw* maintained a sharp separation between the editors and the men responsible for production and distribution. This was done for reasons of security and in order to avoid the kind of internal conflict that had occurred within the *Vrij Nederland* organization.[47]

In the summer of 1944 the German police tried to blackmail the staff of *Trouw* into stopping publication by promising to spare the lives of a large number of *Trouw* arrestees. The *Trouw* leadership, at the insistence of Wim Speelman, refused to make a bargain with the S.D. Thereupon the German police executed twenty-three of the prisoners.[48] Wim Speelman himself was arrested (for the second time) and executed early in 1945. A total of approximately 120 persons lost their lives in connection with their work on *Trouw*.[49]

In order to evolve a clear editorial line, regional leaders of the organization met regularly in "weekend seminars." These seminars helped create a spiritual unity which permitted regional publishers of *Trouw* to follow the same editorial policies.[50]

Some of the editors were members or functionaries of the Antirevolutionary Party and of the Reformed Churches, but the underground Antirevolutionary Party had no formal control over the policies of the publication. *Trouw* aimed to represent all orthodox Protestants. At one time the editors hoped to bring about a fusion of the Christian Historical Union and the Antirevolutionary Party, but this attempt failed. *Trouw* had close ties with the National Organization for Assistance to Divers (L.O.) and the National Action Groups (L.K.P.). Some Catholics also worked for the organization, especially in the south.[51]

Politically, *Trouw* represented the right wing of the underground press. It advocated a return to the prewar political and social system. It pleaded for a strong colonial policy and a politically authoritative government which would not interfere in religious or cultural life. It expressed opposition to the "better world" optimism which it attributed to the government-in-exile and to liberal and left-wing groups in Holland.[52]

After September 1944, *Trouw* groups published local editions of the national paper and news bulletins on an extraordinarily large scale. By January 1945 the total weekly circulation of these bulletins amounted to approximately 2,000,000 copies.[53] After the Liberation *Trouw* continued as the organ of the Antirevolutionary Party.

De Waarheid ("The Truth") was the main clandestine publication of the Communist Party. It was named after the Soviet daily, *Pravda*. When the Party was forced underground in the summer of 1940 it decided to establish a clandestine paper, but preparations delayed the appearance of the first issue until November.[54] The main edition of *De Waarheid* was issued in Amsterdam and distributed to local groups in the capital and elsewhere, which either re-mimeographed the paper or prepared their own local edition based on the original issue. For reasons of security these local editions sometimes bore a different name. *De Waarheid* was published less regularly than many other clandestine papers because the German police inflicted unusually heavy casualties on the Communists. Since the printing process entailed more risks than mimeographing, *De Waarheid* did not appear in print until the last winter of the war.

Within a few months after its start, *De Waarheid* had an estimated circulation of 7,000 copies in Amsterdam and 3,000 to 4,000 elsewhere. German arrests cut into the staff to such an extent that total circulation had to be reduced to approximately 3,000 in 1943. By the end of 1944, when the paper was printed as a weekly in Amsterdam and Rotterdam, the total circulation may have risen to as high as 100,000 copies.[55]

When the Party was forced underground in 1940, P. de Groot, a member of the executive committee of three which formed the new clandestine leadership,[56] was assigned responsibility for the publication of *De Waarheid*. In 1943 this assignment was taken over by A. J. Koejemans, who remained editor until the end of the war.[57]

De Waarheid basically followed the party line as laid down by Moscow and interpreted by the underground leadership. Apparently secret contact existed between Moscow and the C.P.N. during the occupation. After the war, De Groot denied the existence of such contact,[58] but L. de Jong of the Institute for War Documentation considers it certain that it did exist at the beginning of the occupation.[59] At any rate, the broadcasts of Radio Moscow which could be received in Holland clearly conveyed the current party line.

In the period before the invasion of the Soviet Union *De Waarheid* condemned the war as an imperialist conflict inherent in a world of economic competition between capitalist countries. While maintaining that an Allied victory would only result in the return of an antilabor capitalist government in Holland, it also fiercely attacked the Germans, national socialism, and particularly anti-Semitism.[60] In his postwar testimony, De Groot maintained that the leaders of the Party had never doubted that a German-Soviet nonaggression pact was purely temporary and that the Soviet Union would eventually enter the war against Germany.[61] Communist publications of that period do not bear out his contention, but it must be acknowledged that *De Waarheid* and other Communist propaganda instruments were indefatigable in their attacks on national socialism even before June 1941 and that the Party played a major role in triggering the February strike of 1941.[62]

After the invasion of the Soviet Union *De Waarheid* called the struggle against the Germans a "War of Liberation." In order to reach as wide a section of the Dutch population as possible, it now accepted the constitutional monarchy,[63] and reprinted the Queen's speeches and messages. In line with the Popular Front policy of the Soviet Union, it also called for a united front of the Dutch Resistance. Until 1943 there was little contact with other groups, partly for security reasons and partly because of mutual distrust. From 1943 on, more contact developed. *De Waarheid* contributed to the pamphlet *Om Neerlands Toekomst* and was represented in the Great Advisory Commission. It also collaborated with the Council of Resistance and allied sabotage groups were transferred to that organization.[64]

Although De Groot declared after the war that *De Waarheid* attempted to be a resistance paper primarily and to avoid political controversy which might divide the Resistance,[65] it did participate with increasing frequency in political discussions during the last two years of the occupation, when Koejemans was editor. It attacked the idea of a strengthened postwar government proposed by *Je Maintiendrai*[66] and advocated a unified nondenominational trade union (*eenheidsvakbeweging*). *De Waarheid* continued after the Liberation as the organ of the Communist Party.

"MISCELLANEOUS" CLANDESTINE
PERIODICALS

The non-Stalinist Communist parties also issued a number of publications during the first two years of the occupation, before the German police broke up most of the small left-wing underground groups. In 1941 the leader of the Revolutionary Socialist Workers' Party (Revolutionnair-Socialistische Arbeiders Partij), H. J. F. M. Sneevliet, and his associates issued the *Bulletin van het Marx-Lenin-Luxemburg-Front* and the fortnightly *Spartacus*. These poorly mimeographed sheets were full of doctrinaire discussions of Marxist theory, and their attacks on the Soviet Union were as violent as those on the German Reich and on the political parties of prewar Holland. These periodicals showed little sympathy for other resistance groups or underground journals, and continued to call the Second World War a "War of Imperialism," even after June 1941. They advocated a world-wide proletarian revolution as the only way of ending the war.[67] These periodicals ceased publication early in 1942, when Sneevliet and his associates were arrested, although survivors published a variety of pamphlets and periodicals later in the war.[68]

De Vonk ("The Spark") began publication in January 1941 as the organ of the Internationale Socialisten Bond (International Socialist League), another left-wing splinter group made up primarily of intellectuals and artists. The first issue had been preceded by a series of "Open Letters" written by Henriette Roland Holst, a well-known Socialist and pacifist poet and writer. Initially *De Vonk* was published as a monthly, but in February 1943 it was converted to a fortnightly periodical. Its early circulation was only 2,000 copies, but it rose to 20,000 toward the end of the war.

In 1942 two successive groups of editors were arrested, and publication of *De Vonk* was interrupted. Later, a new editorial group reactivated the publication in a number of provincial towns, primarily in the east and north of the country.[69]

De Vonk was primarily a resistance paper for left-wing intellectuals and workers outside of the C.P.N. It advocated a nonviolent revolution of the working class all over the world as the means to end the war, and an anarchistic system of social organization in time of peace. The *Vonk* group sought contact with like-minded Germans and, in the last year of the war, published pamphlets and handbills encouraging German soldiers to desert.[70] In line with *De Vonk's* pacifist and humanist convictions, Henriette Roland Holst cautioned against the flood of hatred she saw rising among patriots under the occupation.[71] The *Vonk* group also disapproved of armed attacks on rationing offices. It believed the necessary documents could be secured by the Resistance through administrative arrangements.[72]

The *Vonk* group published independently a number of literary essays and political pamphlets. When Jews were required to wear the Star of David, the group circulated 300,000 Jewish stars with the inscription: "Jews and Non-Jews Are One." Some of these stars were dumped from the roof of the biggest department store in Amsterdam.[73]

The Social Democratic Workers' Party did not publish its own clandestine paper during the first four years of the occupation, partly because Socialist views were already presented by *Het Parool* in general terms. Toward the end of the occupation, however, some members of the Party considered it desirable to present their own points of view. To this end, the weekly *De Baanbreker*, among others, appeared in August 1944. It justified its existence by observing that Social Democratic views should be represented in a period when much clandestine writing was addressed to problems of postwar reconstruction.[74]

Despite its large circulation, *Ons Volk* ("Our Nation") is included among the "minor" periodicals because it did not affect "public opinion" to the extent of the five "major" papers. *Ons Volk* simply aspired to be a resistance paper without a political or "opinion-forming" function beyond the call for resistance.

Ons Volk was the largest underground paper under the occupation, having an initial circulation of 55,000 and increasing to 120,000. It was organized in the autumn of 1943 by a group of former university students who felt that the underground press appealed primarily to intellectuals without reaching the masses. For this reason the founders designed *Ons Volk* somewhat along the lines of a tabloid newspaper. It was the first underground periodical to carry current photographs and cartoons. The paper had special appeal because it published a good deal of inside information leaked to it by friends in government circles. It reprinted articles from the world press and devoted considerable space to military events.

Ons Volk appeared in print from the start. At first it was a monthly, but in September 1944 it became a weekly. In 1945, after a final Liberation issue, it ceased publication.[75]

Christofoor was originally published in 1942 in the town of Ijselstein near Nijmegen as a small local paper to encourage Catholic resistance. Its early issues were mimeographed in the city hall and in the rectory. The original staff was broken up by the German police, but after a few months it was reconstituted with the help of former members of the Netherlands Union. Between the autumn of 1943 and September 1944 circulation grew to 25,000, but it dropped back to 10,000 after the liberation of the south.[76]

In August 1944 the German police again broke up the *Christofoor* group, arresting seventy to eighty persons, including the main editors. A number of these arrestees lost their lives in Germany.

Early in 1944 an agreement was made between *Je Maintiendrai* and *Christofoor* that the latter publication would make a special effort to propagate the concepts of the Netherlands Union among Dutch Catholics, placing particular stress on the need to break through denominational barriers in political and social life.[77] *Christofoor* therefore opposed the reconstitution of the Catholic Party. In this it represented the feelings of the younger Catholics who cherished the bonds with Protestants which they had developed in the Resistance.

Je Maintiendrai and *Christofoor* merged in September 1944, but in November a conflict led to a renewed separation.[78] After the Liberation *Christofoor* continued publication as a weekly for liberal Catholics.

De Geus onder Studenten ("The *Gueux* Among Students") is an example of a clandestine paper written primarily for a "professional" segment of the population. Although it was designed primarily for students, it was read by others for its judicious writings.

The editors and publishers of *De Geus onder Studenten* were the two Drion brothers, students at the University in Leiden. In the summer of 1940 the Drions saw a need for a student publication designed to counteract German propaganda and the authoritarian and corporative ideas bandied about by the Netherlands Union. They believed that a resistance paper for university students might be particularly valuable, since students could afford to take more risks than their elders. The Drions deliberately limited their paper to discussions of theoretical and practical aspects of the occupation, especially student resistance. They avoided a consideration of postwar problems.[79]

At first the Drions wrote most of the paper themselves, but they gradually widened the circle of contributors. From 1942 on, *De Geus* became the organ for the "Council of Nine," a group of students who coordinated resistance at Dutch universities. It played a particularly active role in the agitation over the loyalty oath in 1943.

The first issue of *De Geus* was mimeographed in October 1940 and had a circulation of 250. From November 1942 it was printed, and circulation rose to 8,000. After May 1943, copies were distributed among students in Germany. Until the closing of the universities in 1943, *De Geus* appeared approximately once a month. During the last winter of the war only one issue was published, since the brothers did not see a need for a separate student paper after universities had been closed and student resistance had merged with the general resistance movement.[80]

De Vrije Katheder was another underground paper designed primarily for students. Its subtitle (the main title of the first three issues) read: "Bulletin for the Defense of the Universities." It was published by a group of left-wing students in Amsterdam but was soon distributed in other university towns. The first issue appeared in November 1940. Thereafter it was published approximately twice each month. From an original few hundred copies it developed into a periodical with a maximum circulation of 5,000 copies, appealing to left-wing intellectuals outside of the universities.

Many of the editors were arrested during the course of the occupation. One of these, the psychiatrist H. Katan, was executed in October 1943 for his part in the assassination of prominent members of the N.S.B. early in 1943. Despite these individual arrests, the organization was never destroyed by the Germans.

Some of the editors were Communists, and the publication often followed the Communist line. It was, however, not a Stalinist publication, and criticism and debates took place in its columns that were not possible in *De Waarheid*.[81]

After the closing of the universities in 1943, the editors enlarged the scope of the paper by discussing a variety of political, social, and economic topics from a "progressive" point of view. As the end of the war drew closer, postwar topics were increasingly debated.[82]

De Vrije Kunstenaar ("The Free Artist") was published in Amsterdam by a group of artists to strengthen the resistance of those artists who refused to join the Nazi *Cultuurkamer*. Owing to a large number of arrests among its staff, *De Vrije Kunstenaar* appeared irregularly between May 1942 and August 1943. In August it appeared as a printed monthly and continued as such until liberation. During this latter period it had a circulation of 3,000 to 5,000 copies per issue.

The staff of *De Vrije Kunstenaar* consisted largely of artists who were oriented toward the far left. In August 1942 the paper collaborated with *De Waarheid* in a manifesto protesting Jewish deportations. This political orientation, however, did not come to the fore as much as it might have, since the paper was primarily concerned with encouraging resistance to nazification of the arts. In 1944 it published a strong attack on the world-famous conductor Willem Mengelberg, who had been a collaborationist by any standard, demanding that he not be allowed to exercise his profession after the war.[83] Toward the end of the occupation, it devoted much of its attention to the place of the arts in postwar society.[84]

The association of Indonesian students in Holland (Perhimpunan Indonesia) started publishing a clandestine paper, *De Bevrijding* ("The Liberation"), in Leiden and The Hague in May 1944. This was the successor to a number of short-lived publications put out irregularly by the same group since May 1940. It was published two or three times as a mimeographed periodical until March 1945, after which time it appeared as a printed weekly. It was designed primarily for Indonesians living in Holland. For this reason it concentrated on foreign news reports and commentary, mostly about Asia. *De Bevrijding* participated in a broadly based study group on the future of Indonesia.[85]

Exemplifying the increasing concern over the future which was felt after Stalingrad were two periodicals, *De Ploeg* ("The Plow") and *De Toekomst* ("The Future"), which devoted themselves almost entirely to a discussion of postwar problems. *De Ploeg* was founded in July 1943 by a group of students from Groningen who, as they expressed it in the masthead of their paper, wanted "to arouse [their countrymen] to a consideration of [Holland's] postwar task." *De Ploeg* appeared as a monthly, with a circulation increasing from 500 to 4,000. It contained articles written by university professors and people who had been active in public life before the occupation. Each issue contained a review of articles that had appeared in the underground press. In 1944 *De Ploeg* published an anthology of clandestine articles on postwar problems.[86] The organization also stenciled selections from E. H. Carr's *Conditions of Peace*, which had been smuggled into occupied Holland.[87]

De Toekomst was published by the same organization that issued *Ons Volk* but addressed itself more to the intellectuals than to the masses.[88] Its theoretical and philosophical discussions were among the most independent and thoughtful in the underground press. In October 1944, during one of the darkest periods of the war, it questioned the decision of the government-in-exile to introduce retroactive legislation in order to punish Nazis and Nazi collaborators.[89]

The weekly *Op Wacht* ("On Guard"), like *Ons Volk*, was primarily a resistance paper. It was published in The Hague beginning in January 1944 by two young army veterans who had gone into hiding. They wished to emphasize the religious basis of resistance and to stress loyalty to the House of Orange.[90] They hoped to use the income from the paper to alleviate the burdens of divers and their families. For security reasons they decided to continue mimeographing the paper even though it reached a total circulation of

12,000. For this purpose they established "mimeograph stations" over the country. The paper devoted much space to military analysis. The tone of its exhortations was more emphatic than that of many other underground publications.[91]

This same strident tone was characteristic of *De Oranjekrant* ("The Journal of the House of Orange"), which characterized itself in its masthead as "intolerable reading for Germans and members of the N.S.B."[92] The paper was started in January 1942 by a journalist, Johan Doorn, who considered it important to discuss political issues, including postwar problems, in order to protect the Dutch population against political apathy. Its editorials were polemic and frequently attacked the government-in-exile. In 1942 the *Oranjekrant* appeared once a month, in 1943 once every two weeks. In February 1944 the editor, who had in the meantime joined the Council of Resistance, was arrested, and from that time on the paper appeared only irregularly, being published by his collaborators.[93] Doorn escaped from the Amersfoort concentration camp, but perished in November 1944 on his way to the liberated south.

FORGED EDITIONS

A few times during the occupation regular newspapers were printed and distributed as "free" publications, an undertaking that had been tried previously in Belgium.[94] In April 1944 a group of underground workers seized the plant of the *Schoonhovense Courant* in Schoonhoven in the province of Zuid-Holland and at gunpoint forced the personnel of the paper to print the underground copy supplied by the resistance group. The paper was then distributed under armed guard. The group escaped after its work was accomplished.[95]

The success of this enterprise was an incentive for a similar venture undertaken in June 1944, when an imitation of the *Haarlemse Courant* was printed by an underground group outside of Haarlem. The contents of this issue were not those of a serious underground paper, but were designed as a parody on the speeches and actions of German officials and dignitaries of the N.S.B. In its masthead, the June 5 issue of the *Haarlemse Courant* announced sarcastically that it was being published outside the sphere of responsibility of its regular editors.[96] It included a report on the underground publication of the *Schoonhovense Courant,* an article ostensibly written by Josef Goebbels for the fictitious *Vierte Reich,** and a proclamation in Orwellian vein attributed to Rauter, imposing a special curfew on dogs and ducks as punishment for their anti-German activities. It also produced a Last Order of the Day by the Fuehrer, to be published on the day of the German capitulation. On its last page the *Haarlemse Courant* carried a composite photograph contrasting the promises made by the N.S.B. early in the war and the realities of the German Nazi regime.[97]

The June 5, 1944, issue of the *Haarlemse Courant* caused special consternation among the Germans because they thought the underground had known the date of the Normandy invasion and had deliberately timed publication of the *Haarlemse Courant* to fall on the date of the invasion. As a matter of fact, this was pure coincidence.[98]

A similar satirical imitation of the *Friesche Courant,* a Leeuwarden daily, was printed by the *Trouw* group in Friesland. The paper was delivered just ahead of the regular *Friesche Courant* on September 7, 1944. Again, the accidental publication date, two days after "Mad Tuesday," created a special effect.[99]

In May 1944 a local group around *Ons Volk* published an illegal copy of *De Gil,* a satirical, illustrated magazine published by the propaganda division of the High Commissioner's office as "counterpropaganda" against the underground press. The clandestine copy of *De Gil* was distributed in Amsterdam under the guise of a special issue of the legal *De Gil.* It was sold out in less than an hour, before the Germans got wind of what had happened.[100]

The Germans also produced fake issues of clandestine papers in order to create confusion and promote Nazi propaganda by making the underground press look ridiculous. In 1942 they published a forged edition of *Vrij Nederland,* placing a large question mark after the title. In 1943 and 1944 the Germans produced these imitations by forcing typesetters and printers imprisoned in the Vught concentration camp to print the issues. Forged copies of *Ons Volk, Het Parool, De Vonk,* and *De Waarheid* were reproduced in quantities of 10,000 to 20,000 copies per issue. To maintain the illusion that the forged issues were genuine, most of the original copy of each under-

---

* This was a satirical variation on the name of Goebbels' weekly *Das Reich.*

ground paper was reproduced faithfully, but a few phrases were changed to distort the meaning or convey an intention opposite to that of the original writing.[101]

In the early years of the war the clandestine press did not need to furnish comprehensive news coverage because a sufficient number of patriots listened to the British and Dutch radios to keep the population supplied with reliable information on world events.

The confiscation of radios after May 1943 and the increasingly exciting news following Stalingrad and the Allied advances in the Mediterranean induced the clandestine press to concern itself more and more with the publication of straight "news sheets" or newspapers. These "news bulletins" essentially contained information taken from the radio, and accounted for a large share of the 150 clandestine publications that made their appearance in 1943.[102] Most of these papers consisted of two to eight pages of mimeographed material. They usually were published locally a few times a week. One of the few nationally distributed and probably the best edited of these news bulletins was *De Vrije Nieuwscentrale* (later *V.O.D.: Voorlichtingsdienst van Je Maintiendrai*), published by the editors of *Je Maintiendrai*. Originally this publication was designed to keep the staff of *Je Maintiendrai* and a selected number of readers informed, but it was later distributed more widely, eventually reaching a circulation of 3,000 copies per issue.[103]

After the Normandy invasion in June 1944 the thirst for current news was greater than ever. Therefore many more local news sheets made their appearance, approximately one hundred between June and September.[104] Most of these newspapers were published independently of the national periodicals, but in September the need for prompt publication of war news and of official announcements and instructions became so urgent that many national papers took a hand in publishing daily bulletins. The national papers often cooperated in this venture. The *Oranje Bulletin*, which was published in Amsterdam under joint sponsorship of *Ons Volk*, *Het Parool*, and *Vrij Nederland*, was such a publication. The special purpose of the *Oranje Bulletin* was to circulate announcements of the Dutch government and of Allied military authorities.[105]

In Rotterdam, six underground papers joined to publish a common newspaper, *De Vrije Pers*, which appeared approximately three times a week, attaining a circulation as high as 55,000 copies in Rotterdam alone. Other newspapers also called *De Vrije Pers* appeared in a number of cities under the joint sponsorship of national periodicals.[106]

Between September 1944 and January 1945, 350 news bulletins made their appearance, reaching a cumulative circulation of millions of copies. By the end of the war, 500 news bulletins had been published, almost half the total number of clandestine periodicals listed by the Institute for War Documentation.[107]

PUBLICATION AND DISTRIBUTION

The need for secrecy made the task of publishing clandestine papers exceedingly complex. Traditional organizational patterns no longer applied. In the case of small papers, one person was often editor, publisher, and distributor. With larger papers, division of labor was necessary, but during the occupation it usually was based on expediency rather than on traditional patterns of organization. Publishers usually had to devote far more attention to production and distribution than would have been necessary under "normal" conditions.[108]

News sources were many and varied. Domestic news was gleaned from the "official" press. "Behind-the-scenes" information was leaked by patriotic government officials. Frequently the underground press quoted verbatim from secret memorandums. In 1943 *Vrij Nederland* even considered it necessary to admonish other underground editors to be more careful with such quotations lest they incriminate cooperating officials.[109] For a while during the last winter of the occupation, the clandestine press was furnished information by a central news-gathering agency which tapped official telephone and teletype lines.[110]

Since much domestic news was based on hearsay and rumor, it was natural that some of the information in clandestine newspapers was erroneous. This was true especially in the early years of the war. Most papers, however, made an honest effort to stick to the truth.

Foreign news was secured primarily via radio. Good linguists who could take down broadcasts from Allied radio stations were required for this assignment. Patriots with a knowledge of "rare" languages such as Russian and Japanese were particularly valuable.[111]

After September 1944, when electricity was cut off in many areas, clandestine workers had to find alternative sources of power for radios. Storage and flashlight batteries and generators powered by gasoline engines were pressed into service. The underground press also used battery-powered radios, dropped by Allied planes, and crystal sets with earphones, put together by amateurs.[112]

Some underground papers received copies of periodicals published in Allied or neutral countries, such as the Dutch weekly *Vrij Nederland,* published in London, and the Swiss *Die Weltwoche,* through special couriers and air drops, but these materials were more useful for background information than for day-to-day news, which had to be secured by radio.

Production of underground papers required the cooperation of many individuals and organizations. First, it was necessary to secure newsprint. Second, mimeograph machines or printing presses were needed. Third, a system of distribution had to be organized. Finally, financing for the entire operation had to be arranged.

Wholesale paper concerns were the most important source of newsprint. By working hand in hand with officials in the government offices responsible for paper rationing, these concerns usually were able to deliver sufficient paper to the underground press, but sometimes it became necessary to seize newsprint by force or stealth. Many smaller publications managed to secure sufficient newsprint from their readers, from retail stores, or from friends in local newspapers or publishing concerns.[113]

The changes in methods of production reflected the growth of the underground press. Until the end of 1942 most underground publications were mimeographed, although some papers such as *Het Parool* and *Vrij Nederland* had already switched to printing. During 1943 more and more national papers began to appear in print. Papers with a circulation of more than a few thousand copies usually tried to find a printer, while smaller publications generally preferred the safer and quicker mimeographing method. News bulletins that attempted to carry current news also usually appeared in mimeographed form in order to avoid delay.

Some underground "publishers" experienced difficulty in locating enough mimeograph machines, since the supply of such machines had not been plentiful in prewar days. Sometimes machines were "borrowed" from their rightful owners "for the duration."[114] Where mimeograph machines were unavailable more primitive methods of reproduction were employed.

Because secrecy was of paramount importance, special efforts had to be made to hide equipment such as radio receiving sets and mimeograph machines. Radios were hidden under floor boards or built into walls or telephone directories. Mimeograph machines were put into attics, evacuated apartments, and other obscure locations. In Friesland, the news bulletins of *Trouw* were produced in a haystack replete with radio, typewriter, and mimeograph machine.[115]

Printing was the most complex and dangerous method of production because typesetting machines and printing presses could not be hidden or moved about easily. It was often difficult to find local typesetters and printers. Type sometimes had to be transported a long distance after it had been set and the printed paper had to be shipped back for distribution. Transportation of type was particularly difficult because of its weight. *Trouw* even trained a special crew of "strongmen" for this chore.[116]

Because of the scarcity of available print shops, some establishments printed more than one underground paper, others printed both legal (even German or N.S.B.) and underground papers. Much of the work was done at night, but that too involved risks because the noise of the machines could be heard outside. With the cutting off of fuel and electricity, special efforts had to be made to secure power. Electricity lines were secretly tapped, gasoline-driven generators were installed, and even outboard motors were used.[117]

Despite all precautions, many clandestine printers and typesetters were arrested and executed. Papers often were forced to change their format or cease publication because their operation had to be moved.

Distribution and final delivery were also highly dangerous. One of the safest means of delivery was the regular mail service, using envelopes bearing the letterhead of government agencies or fictitious return addresses. More common was shipment by truck, railroad, or barge. It was possible to use official cars or the railroad delivery system if patriotic officials could be persuaded to cooperate. The most common delivery, however, was by couriers who carried the papers in suitcases. After September 1944 girls were used as couriers almost exclusively. They were advised to observe the rules of caution required in all resistance activities.

Local distribution often was accomplished by milkmen and others who delivered the daily necessities of life.[118] Occasionally a local resistance group acted as distributor.[119]

In order to increase the circulation of the necessarily limited number of copies, underground publications urged their readers to peruse issues and pass them on promptly. Almost every clandestine paper carried a slogan to this effect, inveighing against readers who kept underground publications as souvenirs, or were afraid to pass them on. *Het Parool* sarcastically advised those of its readers who had the collector's instinct to collect German revolvers rather than keep clandestine publications from the many patriots eager to read them.[120]

Methods of financing underground publications differed from one paper to the next, but most papers had to obtain financial support from patrons until 1944, when the National Assistance Fund began to help. Despite the security risks involved, many underground papers accepted contributions from their readers and acknowledged these contributions through codes suggested by the donors. Other periodicals preferred to rely on large contributions from wealthy patrons. This became the major way of financing clandestine papers from 1943 on. In 1944 the National Assistance Fund began to subsidize publications represented in the Great Advisory Commission. By May 1945 the Fund had contributed approximately half a million guilders to the underground press. One-half of that amount went to *Vrij Nederland* and one quarter to *Het Parool*.[121] *De Waarheid* and *Trouw*, on the other hand, did not use the N.S.F. because they believed readers and patrons had a responsibility to sustain their publications. The *Trouw* management believed government should not become involved in the support of the press.[122]

In most instances it appears that underground papers had little trouble financing themselves from their own circles. Some clandestine publications were even started as a means of raising funds for victims of German persecution. Reliance on outside subsidies through the N.S.F. became general only after September 1944, when the mushroom growth of daily news bulletins imposed an unprecedented financial strain on resources.[123]

THE APPEAL FOR RESISTANCE

In its attempt to induce the Dutch people to resist the enemy, the underground press from the very beginning sounded a few basic themes. It held that the war was by no means over and that the Germans were bound to lose it eventually.[124] It asserted that the Germans would plunder and subjugate Holland economically.[125] It stressed over and over that ideological compromise with national socialism was possible only at the expense of national character, religion, and loyalty.[126] In short, the underground press exhorted its people to remember that the Netherlands was at war with Germany, that the Germans were the enemy,[127] and that violation of international law and decency by the Germans made it the duty of patriots to resist in whatever way they could.[128]

Apart from these broad themes, the underground press used many techniques to awaken and reinforce in the Dutch people the will to resist. One of its devices was to emphasize the evil of the German regime. To that end, clandestine papers carried detailed reports on arrests, executions, and conditions in concentration camps. For the same reason they reported continuously on the persecution of the Jews and on the economic pillage of the country.

A second device was the use of sarcasm in portraying the enemy. Clandestine papers often carried stories about the moral and financial corruption of German and Dutch National Socialists, the tensions and competition within the enemy camp, and their cowardly behavior in the face of approaching defeat. The most cutting expressions, however, were reserved for Anton Mussert, whose name was rarely mentioned without a belittling or derogatory appositive.

In recognition of the truth of Pascal's observation that "courage is the only sentiment that is almost as contagious as fear,"[129] the underground press, as a third device, continuously cited instances of successful resistance on the part of individuals and groups such as students and physicians. It proudly relayed the accomplishments of Action Groups and of other underground organizations. In January

1944, *Vrij Nederland* published a special supplement on the 1942 sea battle near Bali in which Dutch sailors had participated, so that "their deeds may be an example for us all, as civilians, . . . to do our duty, just as our countrymen at Bali did theirs."[130]

The more moderate publications soon learned they had to be discriminating in their appeals for resistance. When Communist pamphlets continued to call for work stoppages after the February strike of 1941, *Het Parool* warned its readers to use the strike weapon sparingly and only under conditions where it would do the most good.[131] After the May strike, most underground publications outside the Communist orbit limited themselves to advocating passive resistance, aid to divers, and, after September 1944, aid to the Allied forces.

During the first three years, the appeal for assistance to Jews was one of the major themes of the underground press. In July 1942, *Het Parool* devoted its lead editorial to this appeal. It claimed that if German designs prevailed, the deportation of Jews would be only a prelude to the forced deportation of millions of Dutch citizens to the East. It asked its readers to provide shelter, food, and money to all victims of German persecution.[132]

In October, *Vrij Nederland* issued this urgent call for assistance to Jewish citizens: "People of Holland! In your midst the defenseless cry out, the weak call for rescuers, the persecuted have no shelter, the innocent die! . . . We must aid where assistance is possible. There is still opportunity to render such help."[133] Late in 1943, as the deportation of Jews approached its end, many papers commented sadly on the insufficient assistance rendered.

By the beginning of 1943, frustrating the German labor draft became the most important preoccupation of the clandestine press. Even in 1940 and 1941, clandestine papers had warned workers against accepting employment in Germany. In 1942, when the Germans required that employers ask permission to hire new workers, *Vrij Nederland* urged that this order be sabotaged.[134] The underground papers repeatedly appealed to government officials to refuse collaboration with the labor draft, or to sabotage it quietly. *Het Parool*, among others, stressed that collaborating officials would be held responsible after the Liberation.[135]

Most clandestine publications were emphatic in denouncing collaborationist officials. *Je Maintiendrai,* however, which had close ties with patriotic government officials, took a more judicious view of the motivations and complexities involved. Frederiks, Verwey, and Hirschfeld were favorite targets of clandestine editors. Hirschfeld particularly was violently attacked for collaborating in the issuance of the second ration books in 1944.[136]

After the April-May strikes, clandestine papers advised army veterans against reporting for reinternment even if they possessed valid exemptions. In a special edition, *Het Parool* pointed out that it would be difficult for the Germans to arrest 300,000 former soldiers, and that the men could afford to wait for the police to come and get them.[137]

As early as February 1943, *Het Parool* carried reports on the impending action aimed at the deportation of eighteen- to twenty-four-year-olds.[138] *Je Maintiendrai* reported on it in April, appealing to the young men concerned to disregard the draft calls. It compared compliance with the labor draft to the signing of the ancestry forms of 1940, which had led to deportation of the Jews.[139]

From 1943 on, the clandestine press warned all potential labor draftees against asking for any kind of exemption, because all exemptions involved registration, which eventually would enable the Germans to seize the persons concerned. In support of this assertion, *Het Parool* published the text of a circular by Seyss-Inquart, in which it was pointed out that German authorities could fall back later on the people who had registered and secured exemptions.[140]

After September 1944, when the German authorities began direct raids on men of military age, the clandestine press urged its readers to prepare hiding places and to be cautious in public. After the big November raid in Rotterdam, underground publications criticized the meek submission of Rotterdam men and called on the inhabitants of other cities to do better. They reprinted an appeal by the Commandant of the Forces of the Interior in which he asserted that the dangers of going into hiding were far less than those of working near the front lines, or of being deported to Germany.[141]

The underground press likewise opposed compliance with the final labor draft announced late in December 1944. It reprinted declarations of the London government that enjoined government officials against collaboration with the new draft order.[142] Throughout the remaining months of the occupation, clandestine papers were full of slogans directed against people who were willing to ask for exemptions or to work on German fortifications in the hope of getting adequate food.

In 1940 the forerunners of the responsible underground publications already had published directions for Dutch conduct during a British invasion. In June 1942, *Vrij Nederland* reprinted the official Allied announcement warning civilians in the occupied territories not to confuse small-scale commando raids with the real invasion.[143]

After the Normandy invasion, major resistance papers printed the directives of Allied authorities to the population of the occupied territories. These instructions called for continued passive resistance, but cautioned patriots against overt actions except upon direct orders from the Allies. In July the underground press published a *Manifesto to the Netherlands People*, sponsored by a wide range of clandestine publications. The manifesto urged that passive resistance be continued and that instructions of Allied authorities and of the government-in-exile be obeyed.[144]

The clandestine press published in special bulletins the order for the railroad strike and asked the population to support the railway men. After the failure of the Arnhem offensive, underground publications urged railroad workers to continue the strike in accordance with orders of the government-in-exile. *Het Parool* called upon the Resistance to supplement the strike by acts of sabotage against rail installations and garages servicing German road transport.[145]

COMMENTARY AND INTERPRETATION

The responsibility of the underground press to provide commentary on conditions under the occupation assumed great importance because the press quickly became the only available forum for free discussion. In the first years of the occupation, this discussion was concerned largely with a reassertion and clarification of traditional values as part of the defense against National Socialist ideology. But editorials and reflections increasingly turned to an interpretation of life under the occupation, and to the debate on postwar conditions.

In the summer of 1940 the more perceptive underground writers recognized a serious danger to democratic values and institutions in the Netherlands Union, with its emphasis on authoritarian government and its avowed willingness to collaborate loyally with German authorities.[146] *Het Parool* warned against the rejection of parliamentary democracy, and reminded its readers of the deeper spiritual unity of the Dutch people, a quality considered more lasting than the national "unity sausage" (*eenheidsworst*) of the Union.[147]

In view of the strong anti-Communist sentiments of the majority of Dutch people, many underground writers considered it necessary to admonish their readers to reject the German appeal for assistance in the battle against bolshevism. In July 1941, *Het Parool* expressed certainty that the Russians would be able to inflict heavy casualties on the German armies, but hoped that the "two repulsive political systems might drag each other into the abyss."[148] In June 1942, after a change of editors, *Het Parool* expressed a kindlier view of the Soviet Union, now referring to it as a special type of social democracy.[149] Ambivalence toward the Soviet Union characterized a large section of the underground press throughout the war.

The underground press formed a vital link between the population in the occupied territory and the Queen and the government-in-exile. On the one hand, it reported and usually printed verbatim the major speeches and announcements of the authorities in London. On the other hand, it conveyed to the Queen and the Dutch officials in England impressions of events and trends of thought in the occupied territory. From 1942 on, microfilms of major underground publications were smuggled to England via the Swiss Way.[150] In November 1943, Queen Wilhelmina expressed her gratitude to the underground press for keeping her and the government informed of developments in the occupied territory.[151]

With the exception of a few extreme left-wing publications, the underground press was unanimous in its praise of the Queen. *Het Parool* praised her for her "understanding of the distress of our people, which was as sharp as it was sensitive, and, even more important, [for her understanding] of the desire for social change, which revealed itself among our people during the growth of oppression. The Dutch people recognized her as one of its best and most reliable leaders."[152]

The attitude of the clandestine press toward the government-in-exile was more divided. In the early years of the war there was much criticism of the lack of leadership from London. In 1943 and 1944, initial plans for a transitional military government were sharply criticized, but after further clarification of the temporary nature of the military government, most papers declared themselves satisfied. At no time did underground papers question the basic authority of the London government.

In the later years of the war a number of clandestine publications tried to evaluate the underlying significance of the occupation experience. In 1944, *Je Maintiendrai* drew up a balance sheet of the shortcomings and achievements of the Dutch people since May 1940. The failure to save more Jews from deportation, the compliance of thousands with the labor draft, and the continued collaboration of many government officials were cited as shortcomings. The great strikes and the fact that the people were not corrupted by the ideology of national socialism were considered important achievements.[153]

Toward the end of the war, some clandestine papers became increasingly concerned over basic questions of morale. *Vrij Nederland*, in its criticism of excessive self-pity, suggested that the Dutch should not feel so sorry for themselves, since millions had perished in the war, and many people, especially those in eastern Europe, had suffered even more than the Dutch.[154]

The corruption of morals also became a topic of concern. The underground press pointed to the growth of juvenile delinquency and to the vandalism and black-market dealings of teenagers. After September 1944, it turned against the black market, which it had supported hesitantly as an aid in the struggle against German exploitation. Papers urged black-market dealers and peasants to sell their goods at fair prices, and commented sadly on the increasing tension between city and country.[155] Racketeers were threatened with postwar prosecution.

As the occupation neared its end, many people in the underground wondered what motivations had engendered the resistance movement. A controversy on this question broke out in the clandestine press when *Trouw* published a declaration claiming that Christianity had been the main inspiration for resistance to the German regime.[156] Such papers as *Vrij Nederland* and *Het Parool* replied that humanistic or political considerations had provided motivation for many

underground fighters. They deplored the fact that *Trouw* had published a statement which, in their opinion, could only serve to divide
the Resistance.[157] This controversy was an indication that the normal
pluralism of Dutch life had begun to reassert itself.

POSTWAR PROBLEMS

One of the foremost topics in the discussions of postwar problems
was: who should govern after liberation?[158] At first some feeling was
expressed that the Resistance should assume power.[159] The more responsible publications, however, never shared this idea. In February
1945, *Het Parool* specifically declared itself to be against the establishment of a unified resistance party.[160] The paper advised resistance
fighters to participate in the revival of regular political parties.[161]
De Geus onder Studenten pointed out that the persons best fitted for
conducting underground resistance might not necessarily be best
qualified for running the government in times of peace.[162] All papers
welcomed the decision of the Queen to consult with the Resistance
on the formation of a new cabinet.

The sentiment for a unity party, which had led to the establishment of the Netherlands Union, weakened after 1941, although *Je
Maintiendrai* tried to keep alive the concept of increased political
unity. Most clandestine papers recognized that differences of political opinion needed institutionalized channels.

De Waarheid advocated the formation of a Popular Front working-class party.[163] The democratic groupings and publications remained cool toward the Communist Party while professing admira-
tion for its resistance activities. No underground publication opposed
legal reestablishment of the Communist Party.

There was considerable disagreement on whether the religious
divisions of prewar days should resume influence in social and economic life. *Trouw*, as the mouthpiece of the Calvinist element, advocated the return of denominational organizations and institutions.[164]
Among the Catholics there was a division on the issue. The more
conservative Catholic politicians felt that denominational organizations should return but that there should be closer interdenominational cooperation in social and economic matters. The more liberal

Catholics, such as the editors of *Christofoor*, hoped that there would be fewer denominational organizations and that trade unions would be unified, with special provisions for programs of different denominations.[165] *Het Parool* advocated crystallization of public life along political rather than religious lines, and in November 1944 commented sarcastically on the apparent reconstitution of denominational organizations in the liberated south.[166] Many clandestine contributors commented with elation and wonderment on the *rapprochement* between Protestants and Catholics in the Resistance and expressed the hope that this closeness would not be lost in the postwar period.[167]

Differences on postwar social policy among clandestine publicists were relatively minor. The Communists advocated nationalization of the means of production.[168] Most Socialist editors favored only selective nationalization of industry,[169] but advocated for everybody genuine social security, including the right to work.[170] They called for elimination of collaborationist industrialists, such as the mine owners, and consideration of complete nationalization of the mines.[171] The position of *Vrij Nederland* was close to that of *Het Parool*.[172] *Je Maintiendrai* advocated a limit on income from investments, since all citizens were considered to have a moral duty to perform socially useful work.[173]

Most clandestine publications, including even *De Waarheid*, professed identical opinions concerning the treatment of war criminals and members of the N.S.B. They called for orderly processes of arrest and internment, and judgment by legally constituted courts.[174]

The underground press, from *De Waarheid* to *Trouw*, studied the question of the future of Indonesia through a special study committee. This committee, speaking on behalf of the entire Dutch Resistance, published a statement in April 1945 calling for the early liberation of Indonesia by Dutch forces and for the right of Indonesians to determine their own future. The declaration expressed the hope that the Indonesians would decide to remain within the bounds of a Netherlands Commonwealth, adding that this would have to be by free choice. Anticipating the conflict that was to develop, the declaration stated that decisions about Indonesia's future would have to be arrived at by mutual consent and not by arbitrary decision of the Indonesians alone.[175] The course of history was to be otherwise.

Clandestine publishers printed not only periodicals but also a variety of pamphlets and books. In a few instances they reprinted material smuggled into the Netherlands from abroad. *Juggernaut over Holland,* a report by Eelco van Kleffens, the Dutch Foreign Minister, on the diplomatic exchanges and events leading up to, and including, the invasion of the Netherlands, was smuggled into the country,[176] and allegedly was reissued in thousands of copies.[177]

Two copies of a pamphlet on the postwar reconstruction of the Netherlands, published in London in 1942 by J. G. de Beus, secretary of Prime Minister Gerbrandy, under the pseudonym "Boisot" and entitled *De Wedergeboorte van het Koninkrijk* ("The Rebirth of the Kingdom"), also were brought into occupied territory and republished many times.[178] *Vrij Nederland* asserted that more copies might have been published clandestinely than in England.[179] Both *Je Maintiendrai* and *Vrij Nederland* expressed satisfaction over the fact that Boisot's thinking, stressing the need for a strong postwar government, tended to agree with that of the underground workers in the occupied territory. This was taken as a hopeful indication that the Free Dutch group in London and the people living in the occupied territory had not grown as far apart in their points of view as other evidence had led many patriots to believe.[180]

A secret pamphlet entitled *Bezettingsrecht* ("Occupation Law"), published in February 1942, examined the German claim that the population was legally obliged to submit to the decrees of the occupying power. The author asserted that the Dutch did not owe obedience to laws and regulations of an occupying power that were in conflict with the established laws and morality of the Kingdom.[181] On the contrary, the pamphlet claimed that under such conditions, resistance to the unjust German rule was "legally" required of each citizen.[182]

One of the most courageous underground publicists was J. H. Scheps, who described himself as a "religious Socialist."[183] In 1940 he began to publish pamphlets in which he attacked National Socialist ideology. For a while, apparently, Scheps issued these pamphlets openly without reprisals. Later he went underground and continued to publish clandestinely. After the war he was elected to the parliament, and he has been described as one of its most eloquent members.

Through this entire series, Scheps reiterated the thesis that it was wrong to enter into any kind of compromise with the enemy for reasons of expediency. He asserted that decisions should be based on the inherent right or wrong of a given situation rather than on utilitarian considerations.[184]

At first, Scheps concerned himself chiefly with the problems of the working class. He claimed that national socialism and genuine socialism were incompatible because socialism could exist only in a democracy.[185] For this reason he urged the officials of the Netherlands Federation of Trade Unions to abandon their collaboration with Woudenberg and, if necessary, to resign from their positions.[186]

In 1942, Scheps turned to other groups facing conflicts with the Germans. He described the physicians' opposition to the attempt to force them into a National Socialist chamber as an exemplary instance of resistance on grounds of principle.[187] Adhering to his basic contention that all collaboration with totalitarianism was reprehensible, he refuted De Geer's thesis that the Dutch people should come to a compromise with the German Reich for reasons of expediency.[188] In a pamphlet published in 1943, Scheps berated local officials who remained in office because they thought "they could do more good" that way.[189]

One of the most influential clandestine pamphlets of the war was *Om Neerlands Toekomst* ("For the Sake of the Future of the Netherlands"), first published in 1943. It was the product of a study group that had met repeatedly under the leadership of Bosch Ridder van Rosenthal.[190] The pamphlet aimed to present the views of all major resistance groups and of the traditional political parties toward postwar problems under three headings: "Democracy," "Personal Freedom," and "National Economy."[191] Thousands of copies circulated throughout the country and created much discussion.

In addition to titles dealing with political problems, clandestine publishers printed nonfiction, novels, and poetry.[192] In 1943 a collection of resistance poems entitled *Geuzenliedboek* was issued in memory of the songs of the *gueux* in the sixteenth century.[193]

These pamphlets and books appeared not only in Dutch but also in other languages, notably in English and French. Apparently, almost sixty French titles were produced secretly by eighteen different printing establishments.[194] In keeping with the temper of the times, and forecasting the rise of existentialism, lyric poets such as Mallarmé, Baudelaire, and Rimbaud, who dealt with the tragic quality of human existence, were widely printed and read.[195]

PART FOUR

Summary and Conclusion

CHAPTER TWELVE

The Dutch Reaction
to the Occupation

The ensuing discussion is based on the commonly accepted humanistic value judgments set forth in such documents as the Declaration of Independence, derived from Judaeo-Christian assumptions of the uniqueness and brotherhood of man and rejecting biological teleologies of human destiny. Since national socialism repudiated this universalist philosophy, the Second World War is regarded here not only as a conflict of sovereign states but also as a "just war" in which the survival of basic human values, such as those present in Judaeo-Christian civilization, depended on the victory of the Allies over the Axis powers.

This chapter is concerned first with the classification of German activities which were outlined in Part Two, in terms of their impact on the attitudes and actions of the Dutch people. Second, it summarizes the reaction to the Germans and attempts to delineate differences in the responses of the groups within Dutch society which have been described in Part Three. Finally, it presents a hypothesis which is designed to identify the sources of these differences.

CHARACTERIZATION OF GERMAN ACTIVITIES

The self-interest of the Third Reich, if analyzed rationally, required, first of all, victory over its wartime enemies. Therefore, the main objectives of the German occupation of the Netherlands were to ensure (1) that Dutch resources would be exploited in such a way as to make a maximal contribution to German victory and (2) that no disturbance of peace and order would interfere with the prosecution of the war. These goals were stated clearly in Seyss-Inquart's First Report to Hitler, but did not consistently control German occupation policies.

On the whole, German authorities were successful in the realization of these primary goals. The skillful use of the Dutch administration, the conciliatory tone of early German pronouncements, and the disciplined behavior of German occupation troops helped to minimize tensions inherent in an occupation in which foreign personnel control a subject population. Until 1943, German police succeeded in suppressing most underground activities affecting the German war effort and, with the exception of the February strike of 1941, in preventing major public disturbances.

Up to a point, the German administration was also successful in its economic exploitation of the Netherlands. With the help of appropriate Dutch authorities, the German administration exported a substantial amount of raw materials and foodstuffs. Until September 1944 the domestic supply of food remained at a tolerable though declining level, and physical conditions were bearable. Dutch factories were put to work for the German war machine without much opposition. Until 1943 the German administration was similarly effective in inducing, without large-scale use of its police or armed forces, substantial numbers of Dutch citizens to work in Germany.

The above measures were the logical outcome of military occupation at the stage of technological development that obtained during the Second World War. Once resentment over the unprovoked invasion had subsided, German economic exploitation failed to arouse the kind of indignation that could propel large numbers of men and women into active resistance, provided there was enough to eat and the police did not force men to work in Germany.

German policy in Holland was, however, affected by a secondary set of objectives. The Nazi vision of a postwar Europe required conversion of the Germanic peoples to national socialism and the enslavement, or elimination from Europe, of racial groups that were seen as inherently antagonistic and inferior. Since the Dutch were regarded as an outstandingly Nordic race, their conversion was of special importance. Since the Jews were viewed as implacable enemies of the Germanic races, their elimination was a prime necessity. These secondary ideological measures aroused more emotional opposition during the first three years of the war than the primary pursuit of military victory.

The effort to impose National Socialist concepts and institutions on Dutch society turned out to be an error because national socialism had no historical roots in the Netherlands. The failure of this ideology to make a significant number of converts illustrates the point that "the structure of a language may make it difficult to understand —that is to make the desired responses to—concepts that have originated in another culture."[1] Despite deceptive superficial similarities between German and Dutch culture and languages, National Socialist ideology and vocabulary were full of such concepts as the leader's principle and blood-and-soil theories, which not only failed to elicit the desired emotional resonance but frequently provoked ridicule when attempts were made to translate them into Dutch and to transplant them into Dutch life. At the Nuremburg trial, Seyss-Inquart admitted that the occupying power had erred in assuming that it could "form" the political will of the Dutch people and that authoritarian public organizations were superior to the voluntary ones they replaced. With considerable understatement, Seyss-Inquart concluded that "maybe it was due to a lack of imagination that these organizations were . . . similar to their prototypes in the Reich."[2]

It can be argued that the ideological conflict was intensified beyond original German intentions by the N.S.B. Some of the pressure to establish Nazi organizations came from the N.S.B. rather than from German authorities. Although the N.S.B. furnished valuable manpower to the German cause, it was in some respects more of a liability than an asset to the occupying power. After the Liberation, Max Blokzijl, the foremost N.S.B. propagandist, went as far as to claim at his trial that all good patriots owed him gratitude because he had done more than any other citizen to evoke involuntarily the sentiment of resistance among the Dutch people.[3] While this unexpected side-effect offers no excuse for Blokzijl's conduct or that of his party, a similar paradox applies to the role of the entire Dutch National Socialist Movement.

The ideologically inspired persecution of the Jews was, however, the main irritant around which deeply felt hostility to the Germans and the beginnings of large-scale active resistance crystallized.[4] For many patriots this persecution caused a violent and emotional rejection of the entire occupation regime, which expressed itself later in resistance activities that had in themselves nothing to do with the persecution of the Jews.

The arbitrary and terrorist conduct of the German police, which was sanctioned by Nazi ideology and state policy, was another cause of deep emotional revulsion against the regime. Patriots would take it for granted that the police would attempt to suppress resistance activities, but reports about third-degree methods, beatings, torture, and annihilation of persons in concentration camps, shootings of hostages, and reprisal murders aroused a moral indignation and hatred that often led to participation in active resistance.

Thus by April 1943 the attempt to impose national socialism by force, the persecution of the Jews, and the terrorism of the police had created the moral climate for a country-wide response to an action, such as the reinternment order, affecting a large segment of the population. The decision of the Germans to disguise what was basically a labor draft as a punishment for patriotic activities illustrates their failure to sense the mood of the population. Far from making the labor draft more palatable, the political garb of the reinternment order galvanized and mobilized the latent indignation over nazification and the persecution of the Jews. A draft based purely on the need for labor would have aroused the Dutch less than the alleged retribution for resistance activities.

THE CHARACTER OF THE DUTCH RESPONSE:
THE POPULATION AT LARGE AND SPECIAL GROUPS

To a large extent, the conduct of the Dutch under the occupation was a reaction to German measures. It is therefore appropriate to examine the attitudes and actions of the Dutch in terms of the two conflicting German objectives outlined in the preceding section: the economic exploitation and the ideological conquest of Holland.

Without major reservations it can be stated that the population at large did not fall victim to the blandishments of national socialism. The traditional loyalties and the commitment to democratic and humanitarian principles of the great majority of the population remained unshaken.

It must be admitted, however, that the Dutch did not remain completely untouched by the ideological crosscurrents of the times. Dissatisfaction with parliamentary democracy ran high, at least in the months after the capitulation, although it can be argued that the "common people" showed sounder political instinct than some of their "leaders." The membership of the Netherlands Union, for instance, did not fall for the authoritarian concepts of the Union leadership. The people at large recognized the ideological implications of the Nazi-inspired Winter Help more accurately than government officials and other notables willing to serve on sponsoring committees. The popular repudiation of the N.S.B., as evidenced in the street fights of 1940 and 1941, demonstrated an almost "instinctive" response to this alien ideology.

It does appear, however, that anti-Semitism made some inroads on the population during the occupation. Such elements of anti-Semitism as had existed before the war were reinforced by Nazi propaganda and by the not always admirable conduct of Dutch Jews in the face of persecution. While most Gentile Dutchmen fully sympathized with the fate of their Jewish countrymen, and while hundreds risked, and many incurred, imprisonment and death for their willingness to assist Jews, Dutch feelings about Jews frequently were ambivalent. Individual Dutchmen who fully condemned German anti-Jewish measures often harbored mixed feelings such as those reflected in a diary entry by a Gentile inhabitant of Amsterdam written in June 1943: "What suffering [the deported Jews] have to go through, separated from wives and children. Granted they are not a pleasant kind of people. But after all, they are human beings."[5]

In balance it appears that anti-Semitism as well as revulsion against all forms of racism were stronger in Holland after the Liberation than they had been before the war because Nazi ideology and persecution had polarized pre-existing attitudes and tensions.

The response of the Dutch people to the German attempt to exploit the Netherlands economically was less clear-cut than their resistance to nazification. Most Dutchmen intensely disliked serving the German war machine and acted accordingly where opposition could be practiced without serious risk or financial sacrifice; hence the prevalence of clandestine butchering while surplus meat was believed to be exported to Germany, and the almost universal refusal to hand in coins and metal. The response was less certain and more divided when refusals to serve the German war effort entailed financial sacrifice or personal risk. Most Dutch men were prepared, albeit unhappily, to work for the German war effort, especially if such work could be performed in Holland. Only after May 1943, when hiding places became available more freely and life in Germany under increasing Allied bombardment more and more dangerous, did a great many men, by 1944 perhaps even a majority, prefer to go underground rather than to work in Germany.

Although many Dutchmen were willing to take minor risks such as reading underground newspapers and passing them on to friends or listening to the Allied radio, the bulk of the population as elsewhere in occupied Western Europe did not participate in resistance activities, and the number of persons who gave up their normal way of life for full-time underground work remained small. Schreieder, chief of the German police counterespionage service, estimated after the war that fewer than 1,200 patriots gave their entire time to underground activities before June 1944,[6] but it should be borne in mind that these cadres could call on thousands of volunteers for specific ventures.

Thus the attitude of the Dutch population under the occupation can be summarized as having been uncorrupted by Nazi ideology, but as being ambivalent in respect to employment beneficial to the Germans and with regard to underground activities. The general dislike and hatred of the Germans, and the desire to harm the enemy and to avoid doing anything that might benefit him, were in a dynamic balance, for most people, with concern over the physical safety and economic security of self and family. For this reason, among others, participation in "militant resistance" activities remained limited to a small but ever widening section of the population.

The conduct of the three main Secretaries-General who remained in office during most of the occupation, Hirschfeld, Frederiks, and Verwey, was characterized by expediency, despite differences between them in motivation, policy, and personal stature. The Secretaries-General saw their responsibilities primarily in administrative terms and failed to comprehend fully, or give sufficient weight to, the implications of such actions as sponsorship of the Winter Help and, in the case of Frederiks and Hirschfeld, the publication of the antisabotage proclamation of 1941. On the one hand, they quite happily used the political power bestowed upon them in their new roles of quasi-ministers, into which the accident of history and the will of the occupying power had thrust them, but, on the other hand, they did not seek, and even disregarded, the advice of former political leaders. Nor did they pay much attention to directives issued by the government-in-exile.

There is no doubt that the Secretaries-General believed that their attempt to continue the operation of governmental services and to maintain control over them would primarily benefit the Dutch people. But it appears to this writer that they underestimated the extent to which the occupying power would avail itself of this governmental machinery in its attempt to nazify the Dutch people and to place the resources of the occupied territory at the disposal of the German war effort. Nor did they fully understand the deleterious effect on national morale of their apparent acquiescence in German measures, from the economic spoliation of the country to the persecution of the Jews and the forced deportation of men of working age.

It has remained a moot question whether this course of action, in the language of the Directives of 1937, "benefited the population more than the occupying power." Whether such a weighing of tangible "profit and loss" was a proper basis for decision under the conditions the Germans forced on the Dutch is discussed below.

The conduct of most government officials followed the pattern set by the three principal Secretaries-General, and the results were therefore characterized by the same ambivalence. On the one hand, thorough nazification was prevented and incumbents were protected in their positions, so that few permanent employees had to work in Germany. The administrative machinery remained intact and thus made possible a relatively high degree of normalcy in civilian life until quite late in the war. Within this administrative machinery, patriotic officials were able to obstruct such German measures as the use of the second ration card for tracking down persons in hiding, and they were able to cooperate with the Resistance in a variety of ways. On the other hand, this same bureaucracy gave substantial assistance to the German war effort and made it possible for Seyss-Inquart to govern and exploit Holland with a minimum of German manpower.

The Dutch judiciary, at its apex, displayed the same lack of political acumen as the heads of the administration. The High Council let its moment in history pass by default in January 1942, when it refused, probably on perfectly valid legal grounds, to use the opportunity to denounce the decrees of the occupying power. It also is difficult to accept the reasons given for its failure to protest in 1940 the dismissal of its President and of other Jewish officials. It must be said, however, that the lower courts showed more courage and political responsibility than the High Council, as evidenced by the inquiries into conditions in prison camps and by the denunciation of these conditions by the Leeuwarden court.

Prewar political parties could not do a great deal to protect the ideological integrity of the Dutch people, since the parties were deprived of their natural forum, the national parliament, and since meetings were soon outlawed and their organizations were dissolved in June 1941. Moreover, many of their parliamentary representatives were arrested by the Germans. Before the end of the occupation most former representatives of the Antirevolutionary, Social Democratic, and Communist parties in the Second Chamber had been seized.[7]

Within the limits of the possible, the prewar political leaders accomplished more than they were given credit for at the time. Meetings of the Liberal and Protestant parties and the continued consultation of party leaders until 1943 helped to lay a basis for ideological resistance and political continuity. The refusal of the S.D.A.P. in July 1940 to have anything to do with its German-appointed Commissioner and its immediate self-dissolution frustrated the N.S.B. attempt to gain the adherence of the working class to a Nazi-inspired bogus socialism. Moreover, the organizational connections of the outlawed Communist, Socialist, and Antirevolutionary parties were useful in the development of underground organizations and activities of former members of these groups.

It must be noted, however, that Colijn and De Geer, leaders of their parties, displayed questionable attitudes of defeatism, though Colijn only for a very brief period immediately after the capitulation. The Catholic Party as such played no role in the resistance to the Germans (although the bishops and Catholic lay organizations did). Instead, it encouraged its members in the summer of 1940 to join the Netherlands Union, which they did *en masse.* Some of them contributed heavily to the corporative leanings among the leadership of the Union.

In retrospect, the wartime criticism of the political parties for their failure to solve the economic problems of the thirties and to provide leadership during the occupation seems exaggerated. None of the Western democracies really recovered from the depression, and political parties by their very nature could not be effective under an occupation by a totalitarian enemy. The basic strength of Dutch political parties and the degree to which they accurately reflected the basic structure of, and belief of the Dutch people in, a democratic system were demonstrated by their re-emergence, with only minor modifications, at the end of the occupation, and by the great political stability after the Liberation.

The response of organized labor to the Nazi efforts to subvert its organizations for the purpose of advancing national socialism was divided. The denominational trade unions, which could profit from the experience of a year of occupation, refused to compromise with national socialism and dissolved themselves when they were put under Nazi tutelage in 1941. The leadership of the Socialist Netherlands Association of Trade Unions, however, which was put to the test during the first summer of the occupation, reacted in a fashion similar to that of the top echelon of government bureaucracy. It accepted Nazi leadership in order to save the union organization with its many social institutions and benefits.

The rank and file of labor was in many respects more militant than its leaders. The Nazi Commissioner of the N.V.V. frequently was booed or drowned out by labor audiences. In February 1941 the workers of Amsterdam were the ones to set off the first large-scale defiance of the German regime. In April 1943 another section of labor in the eastern Netherlands provided the spark that kindled a flame of nationwide protest against the German regime. The readiness of the railroad workers to go on strike in September 1944 also indicated clearly how little headway Nazi ideology had made among labor.

There is not much evidence on the extent to which organized labor, or what was left of labor union leadership on the local level after 1942, influenced workers in their decisions whether to sabotage the enemy war effort through slow-downs, sabotage of machinery, and refusal to work in Germany. The best-documented case of union influence is that of the railroad organization, where representatives of former labor unions were retained in the Personnel Council after the dissolution of the unions in 1941 and 1942. Union leaders and members apparently did not basically question the necessity of performing such chores as running trains carrying deportees and goods to be used in support of the German war effort. In line with this collaboration, union leaders fully supported management policy to keep the trains running during the April-May strikes of 1943, despite a spontaneous rank-and-file walkout at railroad headquarters in Utrecht. However, once it was decided to plan for a strike to be called at the order of the government-in-exile, labor leaders on the Personnel Council fully supported the concept. When the strike was called, labor leaders worked wholeheartedly for its success.

The position of the leadership of the railroad unions can be considered symptomatic of a general attitude in the nondenominational branches of labor: on the one hand, the desire to maintain the organization as long as feasible and the willingness to serve the German war effort, if this could be done in Holland on one's regular job; on the other hand, the readiness to finally oppose the Germans, when pushed too far or when supported by established authority (government and management).

Dutch university students were among the first groups to become sensitive to the dangers of ideological contamination and to encourage the growth of resistance. The protest strikes against the dismissal of Jewish faculty members in November 1940 constituted the earliest instance of organized open resistance under the occupation, and may have provided a stimulus for the February strike in Amsterdam. The students' mass refusal to sign the loyalty declaration in 1943 may have been partly responsible for the outbreak of the April-May strikes. Especially after the events of April and May, 1943, large numbers of students became leaders and workers in the Resistance. The history of the underground press is full of instances in which former university students were the originators of new clandestine publications.

The medical resistance also was an outstanding example of vigorous opposition to the imposition of National Socialist principles and institutions. The entire population took courage from the doctors' resistance, especially since many of the messages issued by the Medical Contact were widely circulated.

The medical profession stood firm in its refusal to assist the Germans in their war effort. The Medical Contact advised physicians against collaboration with the labor draft and warned them against going to Germany under any pretext. The action of the medical profession may be considered an almost perfect example of noncooperation with the German war effort, made possible by the near-unanimous attitude and excellent organization of its members and by the fact that physicians were irreplaceable and their wholesale imprisonment would have been a major disaster from the German as well as from the Dutch point of view.

Important as the contributions of the students and physicians were, the most pervasive and widely influential opposition to Nazi ideology came from the Dutch churches. From the first year of the occupation until almost its end, the churches spoke out in defense of Christianity and humanitarian principles.

They counseled their communicants to stand by these principles, to reject National Socialist ideology, and to combat attempts to impose this ideology and the institutions that went with it on the Dutch people. Since the Germans were reluctant to risk a frontal conflict with the churches, the latter could become and remain centers of spiritual opposition without running the risk of being closed although many individual ministers and priests were persecuted and lost their lives.

The attempt of the churches to caution the Germans in their actions, especially with respect to the persecution of the Jews, could not be effective, since the German course of action in major matters of this kind was determined by the Reich leadership. The churches never succeeded in impressing the German leaders with the depth and universality of the spiritual revulsion against the Nazi regime.

The role of the churches was of course more crucial in spiritual and ideological matters than in practical resistance designed to harm the German war effort. But the churches played an important role indirectly in the awakening of an attitude of intransigence toward German demands, reflected in individual decisions about such actions as the labor draft. Moreover, many churches stood ready to lend material and moral support to groups and individuals who had decided on the basis of principle to go underground rather than to work for the Germans. Individual priests and ministers went even further than the religious bodies as a whole in encouraging, and even participating in, resistance activities.

Jewish leaders, as represented on the Jewish Council, adopted a line of conduct similar to that of high government officials and non-denominational trade union leaders. Their major goals were "reasonable cooperation" with the Germans and, by 1942, maintenance of the Council's machinery, which ensured temporary postponement of the deportation of thousands of Council officials and their families. The failure of the Council's policy of "reasonable cooperation" was more disastrous than the failure of similar policies of other groups because the stakes were higher and the Jews had no room to negotiate.

The Jews were not subjected to Nazi propaganda because the Germans and the N.S.B. were interested not in their conversion but in their submission. A tiny Jewish Fascist splinter group headed by a certain De Leon did not gain a foothold in the Jewish community. However, descriptions of the conduct of the German-Jewish police in Westerbork suggest that Nazi attitudes, if not Nazi ideology, had made some headway among these men. Moreover the Nazi terror and the threat to life were such that the Jewish community as a whole, despite many personal exceptions, was forced into submitting to the will of the occupying power to a larger extent than any other population group outside of the prisons and concentration camps.

The Jews were in no position to interfere with the German war effort. To the contrary, the all-pervasiveness of the threat to life itself was such that Jews as a rule were quite willing to work for the Germans if by doing so a semblance of security could be obtained. They volunteered for factories producing for the German military and sometimes reported voluntarily to labor camps in Holland.

TREASON, SUBMISSION, AND "REASONABLE COLLABORATION"

The preceding review of conduct under the occupation brings us to an examination of the general problem of wartime collaboration with the enemy. Three categories of collaboration can be identified.

The first of these categories, voluntary collaboration with the Germans to the detriment of humanitarian considerations or Dutch national interest, motivated by National Socialist convictions or by a desire for personal gain, may be classified as "treason," regardless of whether it fell within the legal definition of this term. It can be condemned without qualification.

The second category of collaboration was submission to German demands on the grounds of "superior force." This category may be designated as "accommodation." In many instances, the situation required such "accommodation," and resistance would have been suicidal. In other instances dangers were not as great as imagined and the plea of "superior force" was made by persons who simply did not have enough courage to take moderate risks.

No nation is composed predominantly of heroes, and for many citizens the necessity of making this choice never presented itself. It is sufficient to say, therefore, that individual Dutchmen who had to face such often heart-breaking alternatives, whether to work in Germany or to go into hiding, whether to offer shelter to Jews, or whether to join a resistance group, arrived at their decisions probably with the same mixture of heroism, cowardice, and common sense that other persons would display under similar circumstances, except that the sense of responsibility for one's fellow men was probably stronger in Holland than elsewhere because of the vigor of religious life. Because each instance of "accommodation" has to be judged on its own merits, it is impossible to make a generalized judgment with respect to this category of collaboration.

The third category of collaboration presents the most controversial response to the alternatives posed by the occupying power. This response was characterized by the assertion that "reasonable collaboration" with the Germans was required in the interest of the general population or of special groups. This attitude frequently was taken by persons in positions of administrative responsibility. Thus, Secretary-General Frederiks argued that it was important to remain in office as long as possible in order to protect individuals and to prevent the execution of worse measures by persons who would be willing henchmen of the occupying power. From this standpoint, it was logical for the Secretaries-General to implement inevitable German regulations, such as those pertaining to the segregation of the Jews, the confiscation of supplies, and the institution of the labor draft, as long as they had any chance to soften some measures and to prevent others from being put into effect. On the basis of these assumptions, members of the High Council could believe that they should continue to collaborate with the occupying power in order to prevent complete nazification of the courts. This principle strengthened the argument of university administrators and faculty members that the universities should be kept open at almost any price to protect students from the labor draft and to provide a supply of qualified men for postwar reconstruction. Members of the Jewish Council could argue that through their collaboration with the German administration, a part of the Jewish population might be saved.

In the eyes of ideological intransigents, this doctrine was a faulty one. Scheps, who can be considered a spokesman for the anticollaborationist attitude, asserted that "in the final analysis even the saving of precious human lives is not the ultimate criterion . . . but the preservation of the eternal values . . . "[8] In condemning the collaboration of the Jewish Council, the former chairman of the High Council, L. E. Visser, took the same view when he reprimanded his friend Cohen, in December 1941, for his opportunism, which "could do no good because it lacked principles and ethical standards."[9]

If saving individual lives and minor interference with German measures is taken as the criterion for action, then Frederiks' position was valid, and the maintenance of administrative services for the population and his success in saving the lives of a few hundred prominent Jews outweighed the indirect harm he did by keeping the national administration at the disposal of the Germans. In the case of the Jewish Council, it has been argued that its efforts might have been judged more favorably if the war had ended earlier, or if one of the major exchange undertakings which Reich authorities considered at various stages during the war had materialized.

This writer, however, accepts the argument of Scheps that any collaboration with the absolute evil represented by National Socialist principles, policies, and institutions, backed up by the police power of the totalitarian state, was bound to corrode the good intentions of all collaborating individuals or groups. On this basis, the refusal of

Social Democratic Party leaders, in July 1940, to have any dealings with Rost van Tonningen appears to have been an early realistic appraisal of the existing situation, and the self-dissolution of the confessional trade unions in 1941 seems commendable. By the same token, the collaboration of the leaders of the Netherlands Association of Trade Unions in 1940 for the sake of preserving the institution and its material benefits must be questioned. In this perspective, the collaboration of Secretaries-General Frederiks, Verwey, and Hirschfeld cannot be justified. The decision of the High Council to refuse the review of German legislation appears as a legalistic act of spiritual compromise. From this point of view, collaboration on all levels with the labor draft after 1943 and with the issuance of the second ration card must be deplored.

The policy of "reasonable collaboration" for humanitarian reasons was carried to its logical extreme and its ultimate self-defeat and self-destruction by the Jewish Council. It is possible that no alternative course of action would have saved more lives, in view of the German determination to exterminate all European Jews. But deportation and death might have come with more pride and dignity, and the German cause might have been hurt more decisively, if a refusal of the Jewish leaders to have anything to do with the Germans had forced the police to more direct and brutal action in full view of the local population. And it is even conceivable—although not germane to this line of reasoning—that more lives might have been saved if the Jewish Council had not counseled the Jewish community to submit.

THE RESPONSE OF THE RESISTANCE AND
OF THE UNDERGROUND PRESS

The Resistance and the underground press emerged in response to the German attempt to nazify and exploit Holland and to deport its Jewish citizens. The most important original task of the underground press was to alert the Dutch people to the ideological challenge and to urge them to resist the Germans and the N.S.B. whenever possible.

The underground press performed this task well. Even though its circulation was relatively small in the crucial years of 1940–42, when basic attitudes toward the occupation were being formulated, its influence reached further than the mere number of copies circulated might suggest. It was the one free forum where unembellished truth could be spoken without the caution that even the churches usually were forced to employ. Together with the churches the underground press played a decisive role in immunizing the Dutch against Nazi ideology and in encouraging them to resist.

In its attempt to fight the Germans, the Dutch Resistance faced a number of limitations. Geographical conditions did not encourage guerrilla warfare and made military operations almost impossible until the approach of the Allies in September 1944. The absence of a common frontier with Allied or neutral territory deprived the Dutch Resistance (until September 1944) of many of the advantages that the French and Norwegian underground movements enjoyed. Thus the struggle was carried on primarily "within the confines of ordinary social life."[10]

The military espionage carried out from 1940 on by the Order Service and other groups received praise from Allied authorities, but, as has been shown, only a fraction of the intelligence gathered could be transmitted to the Allies before 1943. In 1944 espionage activities assumed greater importance and after September many channels of communication were available.

The sabotage activities of different resistance groups remained scattered and relatively ineffective until September 1944. From then on, especially in conjunction with Allied military advances in September 1944 and March–April 1945 (in the eastern part of the country), relatively effective sabotage of rail and road communications was carried out by a number of groups, but the extent to which all these scattered activities hurt the Germans is unknown.

The most significant contribution of the Dutch Resistance to the Allied cause was its assistance, largely through the L.O. and its allied organizations, to patriots refusing to work in Germany. It furnished shelter and papers to these patriots, and through this effort German factories and other productive facilities were deprived of the labor of many tens of thousands of Dutchmen at a time when the German war economy depended to a large extent on imported slave labor. In less tangible ways, Dutch resistance, like that of other West European occupied nations, provided moral encouragement to the Allies in their preparation for the invasion of the continent.

FINAL REMARKS

The foregoing study has made it clear that German National Socialist ideology failed to gain a foothold among the Dutch people and invited the growth of opposition and active resistance. The cardinal mistake of the German regime, in the opinion of this writer, lay in its insistence on introducing National Socialist principles and institutions into the occupied territory before the war had been concluded. The decision to do so was probably unavoidable for a number of reasons.[11] First, National Socialist ideology had been responsible for German aggression in Europe, so it was natural that its proponents should have tried to impose it on captive populations, especially Germanic peoples. Second, in 1940 and 1941 the German leadership was so sure of early victory that nazification of the occupied territory seemed to involve no major risks. Third, extermination of the Jews, an intrinsic part of the nazification process, seemed possible only under conditions of wartime secrecy and fanaticism. Fourth, the desire of the N.S.B. to gain more power forced the German administration to go further in giving support to local National Socialists than some German leaders would have preferred.

Through the persecution of the Jews and the insistence on nazification, German authorities forced a conflict with the most deep-seated patriotic, religious, moral, and ideological sentiments of the Dutch people, without ever fully understanding the strength of these sentiments. The Germans could have continued economic exploitation of the Dutch people and recruitment of men for the war effort, and they could have dealt firmly with sabotage and espionage, without arousing the religious and moral conscience of the nation to the extent to which they did. Once victory was won, they could have imposed their ideology and institutions without encountering effective opposition, because no resistance of significant proportion is feasible without the hope of success. Thus it must be concluded that the ideological dynamics of the German regime actually interfered with the immediate military and economic considerations of the war effort.

The imperviousness of the Dutch people as a whole to National Socialist contamination must be credited chiefly to the basic characteristics of Dutch society rather than to external circumstances. Foremost was the fact that in Holland the family and the churches had not abdicated their character-shaping and opinion-forming functions to the state and to political groupings to the same extent as in most other industrialized countries. The primary family group and the churches were comparatively inaccessible to the new ideology and could not be made to conform as easily as groups and organizations with a greater dependence on the state.

Furthermore, no antecedent existed for totalitarian institutions, since in modern times the authoritarian tradition had remained weak in a country politically dominated by its commercial middle class. An absolute monarchy had never developed in Holland and parliamentary democracy had evolved steadily and without major upheavals in the nineteenth century. Parliamentary democracy had gained almost universal acceptance, which, as history has shown, was only temporarily shaken in 1940. The Dutch army carried little prestige and there was no enthusiasm for military service. Formation of the W.A. and the S.S. therefore had no military tradition on which to build.[12]

Moreover, national socialism conflicted with the patriotic sentiments of the Dutch, since it continued to be considered an alien ideology forced upon the nation by a foreign enemy. The postwar history of Central Europe under Soviet domination has shown the comparative instability of ideologies forced upon captive nations by a foreign power.

Finally, Holland possessed a symbol of national identity in its Royal House. The House of Orange had been an integral part of the national history for so many centuries that it served well in its "deferential function,"[13] and provided an emotional rallying point for the patriotic sentiments of the Dutch people. Much credit for this must be given to Queen Wilhelmina, who admonished and encouraged the population of the occupied territory in her radio speeches, and so became a respected and beloved national leader.

The hesitancy of the population at large to engage in "militant resistance" needs further explanation, although no nation consists entirely of intransigents. This cautious attitude of the Dutch people was due partially to the fact that Holland had not been involved in any war for over a hundred years and in recent times had not known the bitterness of an enemy occupation as had Belgium, France, and

Poland. German policies in Holland, except for the persecution of the Jews, were relatively mild and restrained, if compared with German conduct in eastern Europe. Moreover there had been many historical ties between Germany and the Netherlands, and sentiments toward the German people had been quite friendly until the rise of national socialism. But the spirit of accommodation shown in 1940 and afterwards was also due to the essentially middle-class character of the Dutch people. This was responsible for a certain cautiousness, a reluctance to adopt easy enthusiasms, and a willingness to go as far as seemed morally feasible in adjusting to the occupation regime. These attitudes were valuable in the ideological defense against national socialism, but they inhibited the growth of resistance. In this sense, Secretary-General Frederiks, as the personification of the white-collared government official, was more representative of the population at large than was Pieter 't Hoen, the underground editor, with his appeal for total resistance.

With the moderation and "accommodation" of the general population in mind, it is important to observe why certain groups in Holland became active and effective in resistance while others did not. It appears to this writer that groups that excelled in effective resistance were voluntary organizations independent of state control that were conveyers of religious or ethical norms. The moral implications of Christian doctrine motivated the resistance of the churches. An awareness of the intellectual consequences of national socialism and a certain sense of responsibility to provide leadership were largely responsible for the resistance activities of university students. The necessity for upholding the humanitarian standards of the medical profession, as expressed in the Oath of Hippocrates, urged the physicians into action. The strength of their belief in a Jewish homeland enabled young Zionists to endure persecution and concentration camps more successfully than their co-religionists.

Groups that were dependent on the government and lacked an internal ethos could not be effective sources of opposition. Government officials did not have a common set of values, except perhaps that of efficiency and respect for bureaucratic process and established authority, which made it harder for them to oppose the occupying power. The legal profession, with its commitment to the concept of government by law, might have been expected to possess the integrative force necessary for effective resistance. But it must be assumed that the skeptical spirit and the civil service character of the Dutch legal profession, as well as the absence of a tradition of judicial review of legislation, tended to put the response of lawyers and judges on a par with that of government officials.

The Jews of Holland present a special case in this analysis. The Jewish religion and the common ethnic identity might have provided a common bond and an ethos conducive to joint resistance. The course of events showed that they failed to do so. The accident of inadequate leadership may have played a role, but on a more basic level the Jewish community, despite its distinct and separate identity typical of all religious communities in Holland, was too secularized and fragmented to permit religious and ethnic identity to be an effective mainspring of resistance. This lack of an operative common ethos was, in the opinion of this writer, the main reason for the absence of Jewish group resistance (as distinguished from the resistance of individual Jews).

Other factors contributed to this failure. The Jews alone, among the targets of German persecution, were persecuted not because of actual opposition to the German regime, freely decided upon, but simply because of their birth and ethnic identity. Only in the case of the Jews were wives and children automatically subject to the same threat as men. And that threat, even though probably not consciously perceived as such, was universal extermination of the biological substance of the group. The threat itself was more paralyzing and therefore the capacity to resist it was less vigorous than for other groups. By contrast, non-Jews persecuted by the Germans usually had chosen the path of resistance by virtue of some religious or ideological allegiance, and were less threatened in an ultimate sense because the Germans usually did not interfere with the families of men who were executed or consigned to a concentration camp.

Subsidiary reasons may have played a supplementary role. Since the Maccabees, the entire Jewish religious and cultural tradition had been essentially one of adjustment and submission to persecution and segregation. Being primarily urban, the Jews lacked the military tradition frequently developed from a feudal agrarian past. The customary divisions of social life along religious lines lessened the incidence of social contact with Gentiles which might have catalyzed the potential will and capacity to resist and go into hiding. Finally, the high concentration of Jews in Amsterdam, deliberately intensified by the Germans, increased the physical isolation from the rest of the population, especially from Gentile families in small towns and in the country who were in a better position to offer hiding places than families in urban centers.

Giving due consideration to all these contributing factors, it nevertheless appears that the lack of a deeply felt common ethos was the most fundamental reason for the failure of the Jewish community to display a higher degree of "militant resistance."

The nature of the basic motivation of individuals in the Resistance was discussed frequently in the underground press. It is now apparent that many different motivations went into the Resistance, since it was composed of people from all walks of life. Patriotic sentiments may be regarded as the most common binding factor, as expressed by the renewed devotion to the Queen and the dynasty as the living symbols of national identity, and by the hatred of the Germans and the contempt for their Dutch supporters in the N.S.B. Religious motivation, especially on the part of Catholics and orthodox Protestants, played a larger part in Holland than in resistance movements elsewhere. But many underground workers joined for primarily humanitarian, political, or patriotic reasons, or simply, as the Resistance poet Jan Campert put it, because "the heart . . . could not do otherwise" ("[om] het hart, dat het niet laten kon").[14]

Less noble considerations undoubtedly played a part. Psychological motivations, such as hatred of authority and rebellion against the prevailing patriarchal family structure in Holland, have been mentioned in this category.[15] There is no doubt that the desire for adventure also had its influence. By 1943 it had become socially unacceptable among many groups of young people to comply with the labor draft and similar regulations. For some, therefore, opposition to the Germans became a subjective necessity to preserve standing with the peer group. But in many reports the impression is given that despite differences in motivations, a sense of exaltation was common for most underground workers, and that, to many, clandestine activities brought a sense of elation and usefulness which made them speak later of their years in the Resistance as "the most glorious period of our lives."[16]

The religious and humanitarian element in the motivation behind the underground movement helped it preserve its primary character as an instrument of "militant resistance" until, in the autumn of 1944, the state of military affairs provided justification for outright action aimed at the military and police apparatus of the enemy. It seems to this writer that apart from espionage activities, "militant resistance," such as aid to persons seeking refuge from the German police and publication of underground papers, was the most appropriate activity for the Dutch Resistance, given the circumstances prevalent during the first four and one-half years of the occupation. The primary practical accomplishment of the underground movement must therefore be sought not so much in the actual military damage it inflicted on the enemy as in the extent to which it saved victims of Nazi persecution and deprived German factories of manpower by enabling patriots to go into hiding. But the most profound significance of the Resistance was that it helped the Dutch people to preserve with a steady heart their self-respect and their allegiance to common democratic and spiritual loyalties.

Notes

Notes

In the following notes, bracketed numbers refer
to sources listed in the Bibliography, pp. 318–30.

1. [18], pp. 7–8.
2. [13], p. 314.
3. [18], pp. 8–14.
4. [13], p. 265.
5. [86], p. 9.
6. [117], pp. 79–81.
7. [19], 2-A, 38.
8. [117], pp. 88–89.
9. [182], pp. 92–93.
10. [194], p. 27.
11. [10], I, 209.
12. Address of Adolf Hitler to Commanders in Chief, November 23, 1939, *ibid.*, XXVI, 334–35.
13. Document 072-C, *ibid.*, XXXIV, 284–97.
14. [106], p. 79; [19], 1-A, 110.
15. [106], pp. 87–88.
16. *Ibid.*, pp. 91–92; "The German Memorandum to the Dutch and Belgian Governments, May 10, 1940," [9], pp. xxii–xxviii.
17. Address of Adolf Hitler to Commanders in Chief, November 23, 1939, [10], XXVI, 335.
18. [194], pp. 30–31.
19. Reproduced in [125], pp. 270–71.
20. [267], pp. 65–74. See [194] for a detailed description of the military events following the German invasion. [214] is a presentation in English of the military events of the invasion by a Dutch General Staff officer.
21. [179], p. 13.
22. [242], IV, 605; [106], pp. 154–55. The official history of the Dutch General Staff does not mention the original intention to proceed to Zeeland ([194], pp. 40–41).
23. [27], pp. 3–5. The Foreign Minister and the Minister of Colonies had left for London on May 10.
24. [106], pp. 158–59; [125], pp. 277–78.
25. [133], p. 295; [188], pp. 644–46; [232], pp. 111–14.
26. Statement of Netherlands Government, [10], XXVII, 544.
27. [194], pp. 42–43; "Bedingungen für die Uebergabe der Niederländischen Wehrmacht," Bijlage VI, [194], pp. 228–29.
28. According to the records of the Centraal Bureau voor de Statistiek, 2,109 members of the armed forces and 1,683 civilians lost their lives in the entire year of 1940 because of war activities ([15], pp. 24–25). The report of the General Staff of the Army lists 2,067 military fatalities as the

result of hostilities in May 1940 ([194], p. 22). Dr. L. de Jong, Executive Director of the Netherlands State Institute for War Documentation, stated in 1958 that 2,500 military personnel had lost their lives in May 1940 ([257], p. 380).

CHAPTER TWO

1. [179], pp. 126–27.   2. *Ibid.*, p. 199.
3. *Ibid.*, pp. 137–41.   4. Cf. *ibid.*, pp. 170–97.
5. *Ibid.*, pp. 219–27.
6. [164], September 9, 1944, p. 200; [19], 7-B, 35.
7. [29], pp. 3–6.
8. [28], pp. 1–3.
9. *Ibid.*, p. 12.
10. [193], I, 44–45. Actually the famine teams did not cross the German lines until after the general surrender took effect.
11. [164], May 12, 1945, p. 456.

CHAPTER THREE

1. [216], p. 85; cf. [151], p. 26.
2. [216], pp. 69–70, 540; [172], pp. 98–99; [231], p. 3.
3. [174], p. 219.
4. "Verslag September 1940, door Van Geelkerken" (Doc. 4), [23], p. 318.
5. [267], p. 5.
6. [134], pp. 949–51.
7. "Sonderbestimmungen für die Verwaltung und Befriedung der besetzten Gebiete Hollands, Belgiens und Luxemburgs," [10], XXX, 212.
8. Entry of May 17, 1940, [99], IV, 15.
9. Testimony of H. M. Hirschfeld, June 14, 1946, [10], XVI, 218.
10. "Seyss-Inquart's First Report of the Situation in the Occupied Netherlands, Including Measures Introduced by the Occupying Power between 29 May and 19 July 1940," *ibid.*, XXVI, 413. Cf. Entry of November 16, 1940, [99], V, 25.
11. Entry No. 46 (July 25, 1942), [135], p. 122. For these same reasons, Seyss-Inquart made special provisions for the illegitimate offspring of German personnel stationed in the Netherlands.
12. [134], p. 947.
13. [135], pp. 446–47.
14. William L. Langer, ed., *An Encyclopedia of World History* (Cambridge, Mass., 1948), pp. 379–80.
15. [267], p. 3.   16. [23], p. 87.
17. *Ibid.*, p. 191.   18. [10], I, 339.
19. [242], II, 262–63; [229], p. 153.
20. [258], pp. 19–24.
21. Entry No. 13 (March 28, 1942) and Entry No. 36 (June 27, 1942), [135], pp. 57–58, 101.
22. Entry No. 7 (February 3, 1942), *ibid.*, pp. 49–50.

23. Entry No. 18 (April 5, 1942), *ibid.*, p. 67; [157], II, 13–14 (November 1947), pp. 171–72.

24. [8], 1/1940.

25. Interview of L. de Jong with Hanns Rauter, January 31, 1947, [157], IV, 1 (March 1949), p. 21.

26. "Aus Anlass der Uebernahme der Regierungsgewalt," May 29, 1940, [147], pp. 9–10.

27. "Versammlung der AO der NSDAP," July 26, 1940, *ibid.*, p. 28.

28. [8], 2/1940 and 3/1940; [184], p. 18.

29. [8], 4/1940.

30. *Ibid.*, 3/1940.

31. *Ibid.*, 1/1940.

32. Entry No. 116 (May 20, 1942), [135], p. 243; [96], pp. 426, 475.

33. See interview of De Jong with Rauter, January 31, 1947, [157], p. 21.

34. Judgment, [10], I, 330; [257], p. 381.

35. [10], XLI, 551.

36. [95], p. 399.

37. G. M. Gilbert, "Seyss-Inquarts Persoonlijkheid," [157], IV, 4 (December 1949), p. 15.

38. A. E. Cohen, "Rauters Positie en Bevoegdheden," [157], IV, 1 (March 1949), pp. 12–13; cf. [24], pp. 9–12.

39. [10], XV, 646; cf. [157], p. 15.

40. [24], pp. 16–17, 126.

41. *Ibid.*, p. 14.

42. [10], XV, 646.

43. L. de Jong, "Hanns A. Rauter—Persoon en Daden," [157], IV, 1 (March 1949), p. 3.

44. *Ibid.*, p. 4.

45. *Ibid.*, p. 22.

46. *Ibid.*, p. 4.

47. [179], pp. 53–54.

48. [24], p. 21.

49. "Verloop van de Zaak Rauter," *ibid.*, pp. xxxv–xxxvii.

50. Notation of Ministerialrat Luther, October 8, 1942, to A. Steengracht, reproduced in [253], II (1962), 49.

51. See [157], III, 4 (June–July, 1948), pp. 8–15, on theories concerning the causes of Schmidt's death.

52. [210], pp. 28–29.

53. [93], p. 16.

54. [179], pp. 42–47.

55. Affidavit of Generaloberst K. Student, January 30, 1947, [22], pp. 236–37.

56. See below, p. 59.

57. [22], pp. 9–11.

58. "Seyss-Inquart's First Report," [10], XXVI, 417.

59. [165], p. 63.

60. [179], p. 32; [97], pp. 16–19.

61. "Seyss-Inquart's First Report," [10], XXVI, 419; [93], p. 8; Frederiks' testimony [19], 7-A, 73.

62. [8], 211/1940.

63. "Anordnung betreffend Aufteilung der Funktionen des früheren Ministeriums für auswärtige Angelegenheiten," June 11, 1942, [165], pp. 79–80.

64. [8], 23/1940.

65. *Ibid.*, 193/1940.

66. *Ibid.*, 22/1940.

67. [93], p. 67.

68. [8], 152/1941.

69. *Ibid.*, 67/1941.

70. [184], p. 21.

71. [242], I, 460.

72. [17], pp. 95–105.

73. [157], I, 19–20 (December 28, 1946), p. 8. These figures are taken from a statistical summary prepared by a German official.

74. [8], 52/1940.

75. [242], I, 528–29.

76. [8], 2/1941.

77. [10], XV, p. 650.

78. [242], I, 531.

79. [8], 62 /1943.

80. *Ibid.*, 156/1941.

81. [243], pp. 11–15.

82. [8], 71/1941.

83. [242], I, 497–98.

84. [8], 56/1941.

85. *Ibid.*, 130/1941.

86. *Ibid.*, 187/1940.

87. *Ibid.*, 3/1940.

88. [216], pp. 544–46; [231], p. 12.

89. [24], p. 21.

90. [198], pp. 14–15.

91. [196], pp. 9–11.

92. [242], I, 522; [228], pp. 14–15.

93. [267], pp. 117–20.

94. [8], 147/1942.

95. [242], I, 424–26.

CHAPTER FOUR

1. "Seyss-Inquart's First Report," [10], XXVI, 413.

2. See below, pp. 133–36.

3. See below, p. 104.

4. "Seyss-Inquart's First Report," [10], p. 427.

5. [8], 152/1940.

6. [97], p. 63.

7. *Ibid.*, p. 87.

8. [164], June 28, 1941, p. 675.

9. Seyss-Inquart's testimony, June 11, 1946, [10], XVI, 9–10.

10. [267], p. 44.

11. [8], 120/1941.

12. See below, p. 268.

13. [8], 145/1940 and 41/1941.

14. [267], p. 57.

15. [8], 211/1941.

16. *Ibid.*, 196/1941.

17. [164], October 16, 1943, p. 356; [242], II, 636; [229], pp. 105–6.

18. [8], 47/1942.

19. [13], p. 299.

20. [8], 186/1940.

21. Letter of General Winkelman, June 26, 1940, [179], p. 27.

22. *Ibid.*

23. [8], 97/1941.

24. [13], p. 313; [229], pp. 108–9.

25. [164], February 8, 1941, p. 43.

26. [75], IV, 8 (first November issue), pp. [3–4], and IV, 9 (Christmas issue, [December 1943]), p. [15]; [141], pp. 54–56.

27. [8], 73/1941.
28. *Ibid.*, 5/1942.
29. [139], p. 73.
30. *Ibid.*; [8], 95/1942 and 96/1942; cf. [242], III, 274.
31. [242], I, 409.
32. "Seyss-Inquart's First Report," [10], XXVI, 423–24.
33. [267], pp. 50–51.
34. [164], August 22, 1942, p. 110; [77].
35. [261], pp. 58–59.
36. [267], p. 51.
37. [8], 83/1941.
38. [242], II, 152–54; Befehlshaber der Sicherheitspolizei und des SD für die besetzten niederländischen Gebiete, "Jahresbericht 1942 über den Einsatz der Aussenstelle Amsterdam," [157], I, 5 (June 7, 1946), p. 21; [251], pp. 47–50.
39. [122], p. 17.
40. [8], 49/1941.
41. [242], p. 179.
42. *Ibid.*, p. 183; [173], p. 52.
43. [8], 160/1940. In November 1940 the film industry was placed under the supervision of the newly established Department of Propaganda and Arts (*ibid.*, 211/1940).
44. *Ibid.*, 132/1941.
45. *Ibid.*, 165/1941.
46. [242], p. 172.
47. *Ibid.*, p. 178.
48. [147].
49. [164], June 14, 1941, p. 622.
50. "Zur Einsetzung des niederländischen Kulturrates," February 11, 1942, [147], p. 94.
51. [267], pp. 53–54.
52. Reproduced in [97], p. 27.
53. E.g., [250]; this illustrated sixty-four-page pamphlet probably was issued by the Propaganda Section of the High Commissioner's office. [160], November 5, 1943, p. 9.
54. [266].
55. [8], 197/1940.
56. Rauter to Himmler, September 27, 1943, [157], IV, 1 (March 1949), p. 8.
57. Rauter to Himmler, January 13, 1944, *ibid.*, p. 10.
58. See [109], pp. 5d–5e, for a description of the methods used by officials in the eastern Netherlands to frustrate German designs.
59. [89], pp. 96–103, and *passim*.
60. [24], pp. 58–60, 300–301.
61. [8], 188/1940.
62. *Ibid.*, 6/1940 and 155/1941.
63. S. H. A. M. Zoetmulder, *Onze Vernedering*, Part I of [274], III, 82–84.
64. *Ibid.*, pp. 88–89.
65. [8], 25/1943; [164], April 10, 1943, p. 324.
66. [8], 232/1940, 26/1941, 138/1941, and 1/1943.
67. *Ibid.*, 222/1941.
68. *Ibid.*, 48/1943.
69. L. de Jong estimates that 90 percent of all political prisoners were dealt with in this fashion (interview with L. de Jong, September 1, 1961).
70. [8], 94/1941.
71. *Ibid.*, 138/1941.

72. *Ibid.*, 195/1941.
73. *Ibid.*, 55/1942.
74. *Ibid.*, 1/1943.
75. *Ibid.*, 55/1941.
76. *Ibid.*, 1/1943.
77. *Ibid.*, 15/1944. Under special mitigating circumstances, a minimum penalty of ten years in prison could be imposed.
78. [158], September 5, 1944, p. 1.
79. Document 669–PS, [10], XXVI, 245–49.
80. "Bekämpfung von Terroristen und Saboteuren in den besetzten Gebieten; Gerichtsbarkeit," [24], p. 152.
81. *Ibid.*, p. 45.
82. [179], pp. 33–35.
83. See below, pp. 74–75.
84. [209], pp. 50–52.
85. [153], July 25, 1940, p. 1.
86. [8], 7/1941.
87. Plea of prosecutor, [24], p. 237.
88. [8], 75/1942.
89. Rauter's testimony, July 21, 1948, [22], pp. 21–22.
90. *Ibid.*, p. 26.
91. [158], November 23, 1942 (Avondblad A), p. 1.
92. [22], pp. 49–53.
93. See below, pp. 206–7.
94. [24], pp. 188–89.
95. *Ibid.*, p. 199.
96. *Ibid.*, pp. 163, 169.
97. *Ibid.*, p. 183.
98. Reproduced in [97], p. 254.
99. [24], p. 153.
100. Testimony of Fritz Wilhelm Hermann Fullriede, quoted in [22], pp. 212–13.
101. [242], I, 702; Tj. Wouters speaks of forty-four survivors ([128], p. 289).
102. [164], November 4, 1944, p. 450.
103. [257], p. 404.
104. [213], pp. 45–48.
105. *Ibid.*, pp. 51–61.
106. In 1948 the Centraal Bureau voor de Statistiek reported that 2,800 persons were executed under the occupation ([15], pp. 24–24).
107. [204]. This summary represents the collective judgment of the staff of the Rijksinstituut voor Oorlogsdocumentatie as of May 1960.
108. [15], pp. 24–25. At the Nuremberg trial, the prosecution submitted a report of the Restoration Service of the Military Command, dated December 20, 1945, estimating that more than 4,000 Dutch citizens had been executed ([10], XXXVI, 705). This figure probably is too high.
109. The figures for 1945 include executions that took place in preceding years, but were not reported previously.
110. [113], p. 11.
111. [94], pp. 17–18.
112. [24], pp. 53, 394.
113. Cf. [157], III, 6 (November–December, 1948), pp. 73–83, and IV, 1 (March 1949), p. 5; Rauter's testimony, [24], p. 145.
114. [219], pp. 80–83.
115. Judgment, [10], XXII, 493.
116. [265], p. 94.
117. [93], p. 72; Wimmer's testimony, June 13, 1946, [10], XVI, 192.
118. Rauter's testimony, [24], p. 46.

119. *Ibid.*

120. Memorandum of Wilhelm Harster, Commander of the Security Policy, *ibid.*, pp. 44–45.

121. Declaration of Harster, *ibid.*, p. 312.

122. [8], 6/1941.

123. *Ibid.*, 189/1940 and 48/1941.

124. *Ibid.*, 102/1941.

125. [219], pp. 330–31. (Wielek, [124], p. 57, states that the second group included 274 young men.)

126. [219], pp. 331–32.

127. [24], p. 36.

128. [200], pp. 4–6.

129. *Het Joodse Weekblad*, August 7, 1942, in [124], p. 152; also p. 58.

130. [219], p. 23.

131. [190]; [124], pp. 35–36.

132. [219], p. 332.

133. [8], 27/1941 and 28/1941.

134. *Ibid.*, 199/1941.

135. [153], April 29, 1942, p. 1.

136. [8], 1948/1941.

137. *Ibid.*, 154/1941.

138. *Ibid.*, 198/1941.

139. [124], pp. 82–83.

140. *Ibid.*, p. 151.

141. Decrees reproduced in [24], pp. 24–25.

142. For a more detailed description of German methods of rounding up Jews, see below, pp. 167–70.

143. [124], pp. 239–43.

144. [177], pp. 185–94.

145. [124], p. 170.

146. *Ibid.*

147. Rauter to Himmler, March 2, 1944, [24], p. 33.

148. [242], III, 128–30; see also Seyss-Inquart's testimony, June 11, 1946, [10], XVI, 45–46.

149. [93], pp. 74–79.

150. [242], III, 140–42.

151. [26], p. 18.

152. *Ibid.*, p. 34.

153. All figures for mixed marriages mentioned after 1941 are substantially below that of the 1941 registration. A notation of the Rijksinspectie van de Bevolkingsregisters [146], dated November 5, 1942, reports that 7,217 applications for exemption from deportations had been received from Jewish men or women in mixed marriages with children, or from childless Jewish women in mixed marriages, who also were exempted from deportations. A postwar study by the Commissie voor Demografie der Joden in Nederland ([175], p. 10) assumes that approximately 4,000 Jewish men were living in childless mixed marriages. It is probable that some Jewish persons who registered as living in mixed marriages in 1941 were divorced, died, went underground, or were deported before September 1942, or failed to register; but none of these explanations accounts for the large gap between the 1941 and 1942 figures. The 1961 inquiry assumes that an involuntary statistical error in the 1941 registration inflated the figure reported by the Bevolkingsregister ([175], pp. 9–10). The present writer also considers it likely that many Jews in mixed marriages preferred to take their chances by "passing" for Gentiles once the trend of anti-Jewish measures emerged, especially after June 1941.

154. [175], p. 10.

155. [130], pp. 3–4.

156. [175], p. 9. Most of the survival figures quoted in this study were originally furnished by A. E. Cohen, then of the Netherlands State Institute for War Documentation.

157. This figure does not include deaths in Holland from natural causes or through suicide or executions. Nor does it include all deaths in prisons and concentration camps in Holland or Germany, where many Jews were sent as punishment for illegal activities. While these casualties may be substantial, they do not fully explain the discrepancy between the 1941 registration figure and the number of persons accounted for after the war.

CHAPTER FIVE

1. "Seyss-Inquart's First Report," [10], XXVI, 413.
2. [267], p. 243.
3. *Ibid.*, p. 246.
4. Speer's testimony, June 20, 1946, [10], XVI, 458–61.
5. Friedrich Wimmer's testimony, June 13, 1946, *ibid.*, p. 195; [229], pp. 59–61.
6. Seyss-Inquart's testimony, June 10, 1946, [10], XV, 647.
7. [257], pp. 382–83.
8. "Seyss-Inquart's First Report," [10], XXVI, 420.
9. [13], p. 159. Actually these figures do not give the complete picture, since they do not show the exports that were not registered with the customs services, such as many military and clandestine purchases.
10. [8], 1/1942.   11. [210], pp. 66–68.
12. [13], p. 323; [274], II, 58–60.   13. [88], pp. 6–7.
14. [192], pp. 88–89.
15. [247], pp. 21–23, and *passim.*
16. Rauter's testimony, [24], p. 79.
17. See above, p. 69; [13], p. 15; cf. Rauter to Himmler, August 10, 1943, [24], p. 55, and Speer's testimony, June 25, 1946, [10], XVI, 460–61.
18. [13], p. 5.   19. *Ibid.*, pp. 18–19.
20. *Ibid.*, p. 5.   21. [242], II, 620.
22. [13], pp. 96–98.   23. [242], p. 617.
24. [13], p. 7.   25. [207], p. 538.
26. [240], p. 18. Before March 1942, this agency was called Geschäfts-gruppe Soziale Verwaltung.
27. [8], 166/1940. The decree establishing the Rijksarbeidsbureau was published in September 1940, but went into effect on May 1, 1941 [13].
28. "Rapport van Reichsamtsleiter Liese aan de Reichspropaganda-leiter Goebbels," November 16, 1944, [209], pp. 256–58.
29. [240], pp. 116–17.
30. [140]; cf. [158], June 28, 1940, p. 2, and [221], p. 119. Actually this regulation had been in force before 1939, when it was withdrawn be-cause of the outbreak of the war.
31. [8], 42/1941.   32. *Ibid.*, 26/1942.
33. *Ibid.*, 15/1942.   34. *Ibid.*, 32/1942.
35. [13], p. 290.   36. [240], pp. 132–36.
37. [13], p. 305. All figures on the labor draft have to be treated with

caution, primarily because of the inadequacies of wartime statistics and their political implications, and because the large number of workers who returned illegally from Germany is also unknown. (See note 56, this chapter.)

38. [8], 30/1943; interview with L. de Jong, September 1, 1961.

39. [158], April 29, 1943, p. 1.   40. [195], pp. 15–16.

41. [207], p. 781.   42. [8], 43/1943.

43. [13], p. 302.   44. [240], p. 179.

45. *Ibid.*, pp. 196–98.   46. *Ibid.*, p. 203.

47. [13], p. 305.   48. [209], p. 54.

49. See above, pp. 56–57.   50. [209], p. 16.

51. *Ibid.*, p. 13. Sijes assumes that actually only 52,000 persons were taken away.

52. [13], p. 331; [158], December 27, 1944, p. 1. In the eastern part of the country the upper age limit was fifty years ([207], p. 1090).

53. *Ibid.*, p. 1135.

54. *Ibid.*, pp. 1091–92.

55. Statement of L. de Jong, December 23, 1947, [24], p. 65.

56. According to official figures supplied by the Central Office for Statistics and the State Employment Office, 388,000 persons were at work in Germany in July 1944. However, it is probable that these figures are approximately 20 percent too high, since the Dutch and local German agencies tended to pad their figures in order to please their superiors, and since many workers returned clandestinely without reporting to the employment offices ([13], pp. 305–6). L. de Jong estimated in December 1947 that at least 300,000 persons were deported for labor purposes before September 1944, while approximately 100,000 were taken during the actions of the last winter of the war ([24], p. 65). Bauer also places the total number of deportees at between 350,000 and 400,000 ([240], p. 310).

57. De Jong to author, January 2, 1962. This is a tentative figure. It is likely that the exact number of Dutch workers who perished in Germany will never be established. Earlier estimates had been higher than the figure furnished by De Jong which is cited in the text. (Cf. [204].)

58. [240], p. 299.

59. Speer's testimony, June 20, 1946, [10], XVI, 486.

60. Seyss-Inquart's testimony, June 11, 1946, *ibid.*, p. 12.

61. [192], p. 52.

62. "Statement of the Netherlands Government on the Prosecution and Punishment of German Major War Criminals," [10], XXVII, 562.

63. [192], pp. 155–56.

64. [242], IV, 360. Earlier figures reported that approximately half of the inundated land was covered with salt water ([13], p. 2).

65. [192], p. 222.

66. [11], p. 35. An earlier estimate by Philip J. Idenburg, Director of the Central Office for Statistics in June 1945, placed the total cost of the occupation at 15 billion guilders at the 1938 price level ([164], June 23, 1945, p. 659).

67. [242], II, 622.   68. [17], p. 422.

69. [13], p. 250.   70. *Ibid.*, p. 259.

71. [193], I, 79.   72. [13], p. 259.
73. Seyss-Inquart's testimony, June 11, 1946, [10], XVI, 14; cf. Hirschfeld's testimony, June 14, 1946, *ibid.*, pp. 213–14.
74. "Statements, 7 and 10 April 1946, by von der Wense, former Chief of the Main Department Food and Agriculture with the Reich Commissioner for the Occupied Dutch territories . . ." (Doc. Seyss-Inquart 105), *ibid.*, XLI, 364–79. See also Seyss-Inquart's testimony, June 12, 1946, *ibid.*, XVI, 68.

75. [180], pp. [4]–[8].   76. [13], pp. 244–46.
77. [193], I, 79.   78. [13], p. 249.
79. *Ibid.*, p. 261.   80. *Ibid.*, p. 226.
81. *Ibid.*, p. 194.   82. *Ibid.*, p. 197.
83. *Ibid.*, p. 210.   84. [8], 64/1940.
85. *Ibid.*, 218/1940.
86. *Ibid.*, 115/1942; [217], pp. 43–45.
87. [13], p. 264.   88. [8], 217/1940.
89. *Ibid.*, 114/1942.   90. [13], pp. 292–93.

CHAPTER SIX

1. [259], p. 130.
2. Befehlshaber der Sicherheitspolizei und des SD, "Jahresbericht 1942 über den Einsatz der Aussenstelle Amsterdam," [157], I, 5 (June 7, 1946), p. 2, and I, 7 (July 5, 1946), p. 2.
3. [270], pp. 26–29.
4. [164], December 27, 1941, p. 685.
5. [23], p. 53.
6. *Ibid.*, pp. xi-xii.
7. Cf. *De Waag*, October 3, 1940, quoted in [274], I, 29–30.
8. [242], II, 45.
9. Mussert, "Nota over de Bond der Germaanse Volkeren," August 27, 1940, [25], pp. 21–23. "Overzicht van de Strijd der N.S.B.," December 4, 1940, *ibid.*, p. 136.
10. [23], pp. 56–57.
11. [12], pp. 50–51; cf. [235], pp. 216–23.
12. [242], II, 50.
13. [23], p. 72.
14. See Rost van Tonningen's complaint in his letter to Seyss-Inquart of August 24, 1940, [157], II, 11–12 (September 1947), p. 147; also Mussert's 1936 letter to the Pope, reproduced in [253], II, 21.
15. [162], May 24, 1940, p. 7.
16. *Ibid.*, August 2, 1940, p. 2.
17. [262], p. 14.
18. [23], pp. 80–81. The German authorities prevented Robert Van Genechten, the N.S.B. Attorney-General, from instituting criminal proceedings against one of these men ([21], pp. 55–56).
19. [242], II, p. 71.
20. [162], May 24, 1940, p. 7.
21. Mussert, "Nota over de Politieke Ontwikkeling in Nederland," October 26, 1943, [25], pp. 84–85.

22. E.g., [270], pp. 39–40.

23. [220], pp. 236–47.

24. Seyss-Inquart's testimony, June 10, 1946, [10], XV, 646.

25. [262], pp. 19–20.   26. *Ibid.*, p. 32.

27. *Ibid.*, p. 37.   28. [162], June 28, 1940, p. 2.

29. *Ibid.*, July, 5, 1940, p. 1.   30. *Ibid.*, June 14, 1940, p. 1.

31. *Ibid.*, November 29, 1940, p. 3.

32. See [242], II, 73.   33. [267], p. 46.

34. [23], p. 219; [242], II, 44.   35. [257], p. 380.

36. [23], p. 41.   37. [262], pp. 42–44.

38. See [248], p. 399, for the view of the N.S.B. concerning this function of the W.A.

39. Rauter to Himmler, February 20, 1941, [157], V, 1 (March 1950), p. 41.

40. In 1942 the name was changed to Germanic S.S. in the Netherlands (Germaanse S.S. in Nederland).

41. [162], September 20, 1940, p. 3.

42. Mussert, "Nota over de politieken Toestand in Nederland," May 17, 1943, [25], p. 69; [242], II, 57.

43. [262], p. 45. See below, pp. 90–91.

44. Feldmeijer, "De Nederlandse S.S.," [162], September 27, 1940, p. 5. The oath of loyalty to Hitler was a sore point with Mussert, about which he complained bitterly to the Fuehrer. (Mussert, "Nota over de Ontwikkeling der N.S.B. sinds September 1940," July 4, 1941, [25], pp. 53–54.)

45. Mussert, "Nota over de politieken Toestand in Nederland," May 17, 1943, *ibid.*, p. 70.

46. [160], March 2, 1945, pp. 1–2.

47. [162], March 1944, p. 2.   48. [8], 110/1943.

49. [242], II, 61.   50. [23], p. 146; [242], II, 65.

51. Seyss-Inquart's testimony, June 10, [10], XV, 648.

52. Mussert, "De Ontwikkeling der N.S.B. sinds September 1940," [25], p. 52.

53. [158], July 10, 1941, p. 1.

54. [242], II, 59; see also [211], pp. 47–49.

55. [8], 24/1943. At first this organization bore the name of Landwacht, which was changed to Landstorm in October 1943 ([8], 103/1943).

56. [242], II, 59.

57. Quoted in plea of prosecutor, [23], p. 74. These figures are undoubtedly too high, since Van Geelkerken tried to impress the Germans, but they serve as an indication of how deeply the N.S.B. was involved in the conduct of the war.

58. [257], p. 380.

59. [204], p. 1.

60. [157], II, 11–12 (September 1947), p. 160.

61. L. de Jong, "Himmlers Vertrouwensman," *ibid.*, p. 145.

62. "Seyss-Inquart's First Report," [10], XXVI, 416.

63. Cf. above, p. 44.

64. Cf. [159], July 12, 1947, pp. 3–6.

65. [13], p. 319; [158], March 26, 1941, Avondblad A, p. 1.

66. [199], p. 2.
67. See below, pp. 94–95.
68. [157], II, 11–12 (September 1947), p. 160.
69. [242], II, 65.
70. [157], II, 11–12 (September 1947), pp. 146, 160.
71. See Rost van Tonningen's articles in *De Waag* of December 1, 1944, and January 26, 1945, quoted in the plea of the defense attorney, [23], p. 96.
72. Mussert's defense plea, *ibid.*, p. 137.
73. Mussert, "Nota over de Bond der Germaanse Volkeren," August 26, 1940, [25], pp. 19–32.
74. Van Geelkerken, "Verslag September 1940" (Doc. 4), [23], p. 318.
75. "Seyss-Inquart's First Report," [10], XXVI, 416.
76. Mussert, "De Ontwikkeling der N.S.B. sinds September 1940," July 4, 1941, [25], p. 50; [23], p. 193.
77. [162], July 11, 1941, p. 1.
78. E.g., *ibid.*, October 17, 1941, pp. 4–5.
79. "Protocol van de Eedsaflegging op 12 December 1941," [25], p. 6.
80. [197], p. 9.
81. "Het Verslag van Reichsleiter Bormann," December 14, 1942, [157], II, 13–14 (November 1947), p. 171.
82. "Verslag Reis van de Leider 8–11 December 1942 naar het Führerhoofdkwartier en zijn Onderhoud op 10 December 1942 met de Führer" (Doc. 8), [23], p. 326.
83. "Aus Anlass der 11. Jahresfeier der N.S.B.," December 3, 1941, [147], p. 112.
84. [8], 10/1943.
85. [242], II, 51.
86. Seyss-Inquart's testimony, June 10, 1946, [10], XV, 644.
87. "Verslag van het Onderhoud van Mussert met de Führer in het Führerhoofdkwartier op 2 December 1943" (Doc. 9), [23], pp. 330–31.
88. Mussert, "Kerneuropa," November 17, 1944, [25], pp. 98–110.
89. [157], I, 11–12 (September 5, 1946), p. 6.
90. Mussert, "Proclamatie" (Doc. 11), [23], pp. 343–44.
91. *Ibid.*, p. 120.
92. See above, p. 26.

CHAPTER SEVEN

1. [14], p. 10.
2. [15], p. 17. These figures apply to the year 1939.
3. [15], p. 94.
4. [60], November 1, 1944, pp. 5–6.
5. [164], November 22, 1941, p. 521, and March 7, 1942, p. 172.
6. [15], p. 403.
7. [13], pp. 329–31.
8. *Ibid.*, p. 261; see above, p. 80.
9. [167], p. 17.

10. [13], p. 238.

11. [166], p. 3 and *passim.*

12. This figure is based on the May 1961 estimate prepared by the Rijksinstituut voor Oorlogsdocumentatie [204], which suggests that 241,-000 persons lost their lives as a result of war action. This estimate is a slight increase over the 1947 figure of 235,000 furnished by the Centraal Bureau voor de Statistiek ([13], pp. 230–31).

13. "Versammlung der AO der NSDAP," July 26, 1940, [147], pp. 21–22.

14. [15], pp. 24–25. Some of the above material is based on the personal observations of the writer, who lived in Holland until March 1941.

15. [208], p. 4.

16. [157], III, 4 (June–July, 1948), pp. 1–7.

17. The term "symbolic resistance" used by J. Meulenbelt is cited in [169], p. 14.

18. See below, p. 134.   19. [169], p. 13.

20. [162], August 2, 1940, p. 4.   21. [164], August 3, 1940, p. 2.

22. [189], pp. 44–45.   23. E.g., [97], p. 124.

24. E.g., diary entries of engineer's wife and of women office workers, of January 22 and March 2, 1945, on pp. 509, 545–52 of [143].

25. [255], I, 279.

26. See above, p. 57.

27. [208], p. 20.

28. Befehlshaber der Sicherheitspolizei und des SD, "Meldungen aus den Niederlanden," No. 33 (February 18, 1941), *ibid.,* p. 21.

29. *Ibid.,* pp. 70–71.

30. *Ibid.,* p. 78.

31. Rauter to Himmler, February 20, 1941, [157], V, 1 (March 1950), p. 4.

32. See above, pp. 63–64.   33. [208], pp. 101–4.

34. *Ibid.,* pp. 109–14.   35. *Ibid.,* p. 151.

36. *Ibid.,* p. 148.

37. "Rauters Rapport van 4 Maart 1941," *ibid.,* p. 213. Two more persons were killed in the town of Zaandam.

38. *Ibid.,* p. 170.

39. *Ibid.,* p. 174.

40. *Het Parool* [50], 4 (March 4, 1941), in [144], p. 98.

41. Cf. above, p. 65.   42. [210], pp. 66–68.

43. [274], VI, 43.   44. [13], p. 295.

45. [50], 51 (April 5, 1943), p. 2.

46. See above, pp. 74–75.

47. [195], pp. 20–21.

48. B. A. Sijes, "De April-Mei-Stakingen in Twente," Bijlage I, *ibid.,* pp. 221–28.

49. *Ibid.,* pp. 25–26.

50. *Ibid.,* p. 102.

51. *Ibid.,* pp. 28–31.

52. Sijes, "De April-Mei-Stakingen in Twente," *ibid.,* pp. 248–53.

53. *Ibid.,* pp. 136–38.   54. *Ibid.,* pp. 35–37.

55. *Ibid.*, p. 448. 56. [50], 4 (May 28, 1943), p. 3.
57. [179], p. 40. 58. See below, p. 152.
59. Rauter to Himmler, July 15, 1943, [24], pp. 86–87.
60. [42], V, 3 (August issue, 1944), p. 7.
61. Radio Address of Prime Minister Gerbrandy, May 19, [164], May 29, 1943, p. 562. Cf. Radio Address of Gerbrandy, February 4, 1943, *ibid.*, February 13, 1943, p. 67.
62. See above, pp. 52–53, 75.
63. [157], I, 11–12 (September 5, 1946), pp. 1–3; [115], pp. 5–13; [104], pp. 48–49.
64. See below, pp. 141–46.
65. E.g., [127], p. 33.
66. [104], pp. 48–49; [110], pp. 276–81. Many of the reports on underground activities, which were published in great numbers immediately after the Liberation, contained stories of such assistance rendered to advancing Allied units, some of them exaggerated.
67. [169], pp. 36–37.

CHAPTER EIGHT

1. See [19], 7-A, 38–45, for the text of the Directives.
2. [242], I, 387–94.
3. *Ibid.*, pp. 395–97; [50], 55 (June 25, 1943), pp. 4–5.
4. [50], 61 (November 20, 1943), p. 2. It appears that Gerbrandy did not even know until 1943 about the existence of the Directives of 1937 ([19], 7-A, 65).
5. [271], p. 16.
6. [50], 55 (June 25, 1943), p. 2.
7. [242], I, 410.
8. Frederiks, Hirschfeld, and Six (Colonies).
9. [19], 7-A, 114. 10. See above, p. 66.
11. [93], p. 55. 12. [242], I, 408.
13. [202], pp. 2–3.
14. [50], 67 (June 19, 1944), p. [3].
15. *Ibid.*, 63 (January 10, 1944), p. 4.
16. [202], p. 3. 17. [19], 7-C, 620.
18. *Ibid.*, 7-A, 101–2. 19. [242], III, 422.
20. [19], 7-C, 624. 21. [242], III, 394.
22. *Ibid.*, p. 421. 23. [19], 7-A, 116–17.
24. *Ibid.*, p. 85; also 7-C, 623. 25. [19], 7-C, 624.
26. [242], III, 384–85. 27. [19], 7-C, 624.
28. *Ibid.*, p. 625.
29. [50], 67 (June 19, 1944), p. 3; [93], pp. 23–24.
30. [93], p. 99.
31. *Ibid.*, p. 54.
32. [97], p. 217.
33. [164], January 29, 1944, p. 9.
34. Circular of the Director-General of Police, September 23, 1943, reproduced in [242], I, 431; cf. [24], pp. 100–104. At his trial, Rauter

claimed that this order was in effect only for a few months in the autumn of 1943 ([24], p. 103).

35. See above, pp. 38–40.

36. [91], pp. 42–43.

37. "Judgment by the High Council of the Netherlands," January 12, 1942 (Doc. Seyss-Inquart 96), [10], XLI, 360–63; cf. [170], pp. 53–55.

38. See [91], pp. 17–27. 39. *Ibid.,* p. 52.

40. *Ibid.,* p. 61. 41. *Ibid.,* p. 9.

42. See [119], *passim.* 43. [242], I, 499–503.

44. "Translation of a Letter to the Secretary-General of the Netherlands Ministry of Justice," March 15, 1943, [10], XXVII, 521–23.

45. [242], I, 504.

46. "Copy of Judgment by the Court of Appeal of Leeuwarden . . . ," February 25, 1943, [10], XXXVIII, 695–97.

47. [19], 7-A, 181–82.

48. [242], II, 8–10; [120], pp. 66–68.

49. [19], 7-A, 140–41.

50. See above, p. 44.

51. [67]. This report was circulated clandestinely in many copies at the time.

52. [242], II, 29; [63], August 22, 1941, p. 2.

53. [19], 7-A, 140.

54. Joseph Schreieder, "Nota over het England-Spiel, geschreven ten behoeve van de Enquêtecommissie," March 10, 1949, [19], 4-B, 50.

55. See "Seyss-Inquart's First Report," [10], XXVI, 424–25.

56. [245], *passim.*

57. Interview with L. de Jong, September 1, 1961.

58. [19], 7-A, 186.

59. See [114] for a description of Colijn's internment, written by his wife.

60. [27], pp. 7–14.

61. Bene to Wimmer, April 15, 1942, [157], I, 19–20 (December 28, 1946), p. 3.

62. [19], 7-A, 142, 206.

63. [208], pp. 43–45.

64. [19], 7-A, 205–6; see below, pp. 233–35.

65. [50], 94 (April 17, 1945), p. 2.

66. See [242], II, 78.

67. "Programma van de Nederlandse Unie," [161], first issue, August 1944, p. 12.

68. [161], February 22, 1941, p. 1.

69. [242], II, 100–101.

70. E.g., [161], September 14, 1940, p. 1, and January 11, 1941, pp. 1–2.

71. *Ibid.,* October 12, 1940, p. 3; [242], II, 97.

72. [161], January 18, 1941, p. 1.

73. *Ibid.,* November 23, 1940, p. 1.

74. *Ibid.,* March 22, 1941, pp. 1–2.

75. *Ibid.,* July 3, 1941, p. 1. 76. [242], II, 105–8.

77. [14], p. 305.
78. [242], III, 373–74.
79. [217], pp. 63–65.
80. *Ibid.*, p. 68.
81. [221], pp. 80, 101.
82. "Herderlijke brief van de Nederlandse Bisschoppen," July 25, 1941, [222], pp. 199–202.
83. [221], p. 112. This figure was provided by German sources.
84. [274], VI, 71–74.
85. [195], p. 136.
86. [15], p. 204. The railroad officials themselves usually talk about "40,000 employees." This latter figure may include temporary employees.
87. [205], pp. 7–8.
88. *Ibid.*, pp. 11–12.
89. *Ibid.*, p. 23.
90. *Ibid.*, p. 49.
91. *Ibid.*, pp. 24, 102.
92. *Ibid.*, pp. 84–85.
93. Testimony of Godert Joustra, August 19, 1953, [19], 7-C, 704.
94. [205], pp. 117–19, 136–39.
95. *Ibid.*, p. 139.
96. [19], 7-A, 390, 369–73.
97. [205], p. 117. The report of the *Enquêtecommissie* ([19], 7-A, 369–73) indicates that there were no instances of outright refusal.
98. [205], pp. 131–32. The general concept of a mass railroad strike was discussed throughout the occupation. *Het Parool* mentioned a railroad strike in July 1942 as a "fatal stab in the back of the collapsing German power," ([50], July 25, 1942, pp. 6–7).
99. [205], pp. 161–64.
100. *Ibid.*, p. 176.
101. *Ibid.*, p. 170.
102. *Ibid.*, p. 220.
103. [176], p. 354.
104. [205], pp. 226–27.
105. *Ibid.*, pp. 242–44.
106. *Ibid.*, pp. 278–79.
107. *Ibid.*, pp. 279–80.
108. *Ibid.*, pp. 399–401.
109. *Ibid.*, p. 419.
110. See below, pp. 199–201.
111. [205], pp. 363–67.
112. *Ibid.*, pp. 373–75.
113. *Ibid.*, pp. 363–64.
114. *Ibid.*, p. 300.
115. *Ibid.*, p. 374.
116. *Ibid.*, pp. 274–76.
117. *Ibid.*, p. 257.
118. *Ibid.*, p. 260.
119. *Ibid.*, p. 416.
120. *Ibid.*, p. 407.
121. *Ibid.*, p. 469.
122. [19], 7-A, 391.
123. [14], p. 78.
124. *Ibid.*, p. 18.
125. [242], II, 301, 303–4.
126. *Ibid.*, p. 302; [16], p. 27; [39], 27 (July 11, 1944); [144], p. 264.
127. [242], II, 310.
128. [217], pp. 119–22; [71]; reproduced in [98], pp. 129–34.
129. [74]; reproduced in [144], pp. 78–80.
130. [217], p. 122. Cleveringa was released in August 1941.
131. [98], pp. 34–35; [13], p. 321.
132. A. E. Cohen, "Frontuniversität Leiden," [157], III, 2 (March 1948), p. 1.
133. [98], pp. 135–36.
134. [242], II, 320.
135. [217], p. 125.

136. Cohen, "Frontuniversität Leiden," [157], III, 2 (March 1948), pp. 2, 10–13.

137. [217], p. 125.

138. [98], p. 9.

139. [242], II, 325.

140. [157], I, 6 (June 21, 1946), p. 1.

141. [242], II, 325.   142. [24], p. 94.

143. [8], 27/1943.   144. [217], p. 126.

145. [242], II, 335. The Germans took revenge for this "reconsideration" by arresting the Rector, who died later in a concentration camp (*ibid.*).

146. [98], pp. 55–57.

147. [164], October 7, 1944, p. 343.

148. [157], I, 19/20 (December 28, 1946), p. 81.

149. [158], May 5, 1943, p. 1.

150. [24], pp. 98–99. Apparently half of the girl students called up for work in Germany in the summer of 1943 also reported ([242], II, 336).

151. [164], March 18, 1944, p. 231.

152. *Ibid.*, July 15, 1944, p. 772.

153. [242], II, 336. Kollewijn ([217], p. 127) even claims that "by far the greater number" of Dutch students who were sent to Germany returned before the end of the war.

154. "Aan de Secretaris-Generaal van het Departement van Opvoeding, Wetenschap en Cultuurbescherming te Apeldoorn," [98], pp. 148–51.

155. Letter of F. Wimmer, May 26, 1941, [233], pp. 9–11.

156. *Ibid.*, pp. 16–17.

157. After a consolidation, there were seven districts spread over the eleven provinces.

158. [233], p. 80.   159. *Ibid.*, pp. 86–88.

160. *Ibid.*, p. 24.   161. *Ibid.*, pp. 45–51.

162. [8], 51/1943.

163. Letter of June 23, 1943, to Seyss-Inquart, [233], pp. 242–43.

164. *Ibid.*, pp. 51–57.

165. *Ibid.*, p. 52; [30], I, 82; [31], p. 3. The 1926 figures for the United States are the closest in time to the 1930 Netherlands census available to the author.

166. Samuel Macauley Jackson, ed., *The New Schaff-Herzog Encylopaedia of Religious Knowledge* (New York, 1908–14), IX, 428–29; V, 319.

167. [224], I, 35; [173], pp. 8–9.

168. [259], p. 121.

169. [217], p. 149. Before 1942 this group was called the Convent of Churches (Convent der Kerken).

170. "De Nationaal-Socialistische Beweging—Herderlijke Brief en Instructie aan de Geestelijkheid van de Nederlandse Bisschoppen," January 13, 1941, [222], pp. 183–86.

171. "Loyaliteitsverklaring van de Studenten—De Aartsbisschop aan de Secretaris-Generaal van het Department van Opvoeding, Wetenschap en Cultuurbescherming (Van Dam)," April 13, 1943, *ibid.*, p. 276.

172. "Pastoral about the National-Socialist Philosophy" (1943), [149], p. 76.

173. "Arbeiders-Deportatie—Herderlijke Brief van de Nederlandse Bisschoppen," May 12, 1943, [222], p. 279.

174. "Pastoral about the National-Socialist Philosophy" (1943), [149], pp. 74–75.

175. "Declaration and Letter on Forced Labor" (February 1943), *ibid.*, pp. 53–54.

176. "Joden-Deportatie; Studentenjacht. Herderlijke Brief van de Nederlandse Bisschoppen," February 17, 1943, [222], p. 267.

177. "Richtlijnen voor de Arbeidsbureaux en de Politiebeambten—Instructie aan de Geestelijkheid van het Aartsbisdom Utrecht," May 13, 1943, *ibid.*, pp. 280–82.

178. "Letter on the Dismissal of Jewish Officials," October 24, 1940, [149], pp. 23–24.

179. "Declaration on the Deportation of the Jews" (July 1942), *ibid.*, pp. 47–50; "Joden-Deportatie—Herderlijke Brief van de Nederlandse Bisschoppen," July 20, 1942, [222], pp. 249–51.

180. "Letter on the Question of Sterilization" (May 1943), [149], p. 58.

181. See above, p. 66.

182. "Letter to the General Secretaries" (March 1941), [149], pp. 26–28.

183. "Memorandum to the Authorities" (January 1942), *ibid.*, pp. 42–45.

184. [224], II, 70–77; *ibid.*, I, 100–103.

185. [222], pp. 142–47.

186. [224], I, 272–74.

187. "Prayer for the Distress of Christendom," [149], p. 25.

188. [263], p. 14.

CHAPTER NINE

1. [14], p. 52.

2. [121], p. 69.

3. [15], pp. 24–25; [242], III, 11. This figure is based on the assumption that almost all of the excess of suicides in 1940 over the preceding and following years must be attributed to Jews.

4. [131], p. 3; author's conversation (August 11, 1961) with Professor Jacob Presser, Municipal University of Amsterdam, author of the forthcoming history of the Jews under the occupation, sponsored by the Institute for War Documentation.

5. *Statistisch Jaarboek der Gemeente Amsterdam* (XXX, 71), cited in [242], III, 50.

6. [242], III, 96–98.

7. *Ibid.*, p. 170.

8. See above, p. 65.

9. [153], June 29, 1942, p. 2.

10. [242], III, 107.

11. [124], p. 150.

12. [153], August 3, 1942, p. 1.

13. [155], August 7, 1942, reproduced in [124], p. 152.

14. [137], *passim*. The perusal of these information sheets, prepared for Jewish Council officials every day or every other day, gives a detailed picture of the number of people called up or arrested in Amsterdam each night and, to some degree, in other cities.

15. [145], p. 7.

16. Interview with J. Presser, August 11, 1961.

17. [137], October 15, 1942.

18. [145], pp. 9–12; see also [137], *passim*, for numbers of persons taken to the Zentralstelle and the Joodse Schouwburg, respectively.

19. [137], October 1942.

20. Rauter to Himmler, September 24, 1942, reproduced in [24], p. 29.

21. [137], November 1942.

22. *Ibid.*, December 1942 and January 1943.

23. *Ibid.*, March 1943 and April 1942; cf. [153], April 10, 1942, p. 1; [242], III, 119.

24. [242], III, p. 113.

25. [138]; [145], p. 15; [142], pp. 3–4.

26. [145], pp. 15–16.   27. [242], III, 115.

28. [137], May 28, 1943.   29. [242], III, 115.

30. *Ibid.*, p. 117.

31. *Ibid.*, p. 245; interview with L. de Jong, September 1, 1961.

32. [263], p. 15.

33. [242], III, 173–76; [237], p. 84.

34. [175], p. 9.

35. Interview with J. Presser, July 25, 1961.

36. *Verzet*, I, 4 (September 1942), reproduced in [144], pp. 157–60.

37. E.g., [137], August 14, 1942; December 6, 1942; March 26, 1943; and *passim*.

38. Interview with J. Presser, August 11, 1961.

39. E.g., [137], August 25 and September 2, 1942; [242], III, 245; [124], p. 147; interview with J. Presser, August 11, 1961.

40. [137], November 11, 1942.

41. [124], p. 147.

42. Interview with L. de Jong, September 1, 1961.

43. E.g., the Communist *De Waarheid* [65]: "A certain death faces these unfortunates" (December 12, 1942); see also [144], *passim*.

44. Diary entry of teacher, twenty-two years old, September 22, 1942, [143], p. 193.

45. [145], p. 6.

46. Cf. [267], pp. 57–58.

47. [155], October 31, 1941, and February 5, 1943.

48. [142], p. 4.   49. [208], pp. 91–94.

50. [155], January 12, 1942.   51. *Ibid.*, February 20, 1942.

52. [145], p. 6.   53. [155], April 11, 1941.

54. *Ibid.*, June 13, 1941.

55. *Ibid.*, August 22, 1941.

56. *Ibid.*, September 5, 1941.

57. *Ibid.*, October 24, 1941, and *passim*.

58. [145], p. 6; [142], pp. 1–2.   59. [142], p. 4.

60. [145], p. 10.
61. [142], p. 6; [145], p. 16.
62. [155], January 1943.
63. [142], p. 8.
64. [155], January 1, 1943.
65. [242], III, p. 185.
66. E.g., [155], April 9, 1943, and *passim*.
67. [242], III, 89.
68. [65], No. 5, February 1941, p. 2; [58], No. 6, end of February [1941], p. 3.
69. Visser to Cohen, November 18, 1941, in [242], III, 146–47.
70. Abel J. Herzberg, "Kroniek der Jodenvervolging," in [242].
71. [242], III, 151.
72. *Ibid.*, pp. 160–61.
73. [171].
74. *Ibid.*, pp. 95–96.
75. [237], p. 68.
76. [238].
77. [148], pp. 3–4.

CHAPTER TEN

1. [19], 7-A, 247.
2. *Ibid.*, p. 239.
3. Report of G. A. Dogger, April 17, 1942, *ibid.*, p. 241.
4. *Ibid.*, 7-C, 442.
5. L. de Jong to author, February 12, 1962.
6. [19], 7-A, 240–46.
7. *Ibid.*, p. 250.
8. *Ibid.*, 4-A, 405–7.
9. *Ibid.*, pp. 547–51.
10. *Ibid.*, 7-A, 256.
11. *Ibid.*, p. 253.
12. *Ibid.*, p. 256.
13. See *ibid.*, p. 254.
14. [19], 7-A, 215.
15. *Ibid.*, p. 217.
16. *Ibid.*
17. [242], III, 710.
18. [106], II, 601, and [242], III, 689. In his appearance before the Parliamentary Commission of Inquiry, Van Riessen testified that there may have been between 200,000 and 400,000 persons in hiding ([19], 7-A, 217). The upper limit is probably too high, but these estimates suggest an order of magnitude similar to Rauter's estimate, as early as September 1943, that 250,000 people had gone underground (Rauter to Himmler, September 27, 1943, [24], p. 57).
19. See above, p. 77.
20. [242], III, 697.
21. *Ibid.*, p. 704.
22. [19], 7-A, 215–16.
23. *Ibid.*, p. 217.
24. [164], March 3, 1945, p. 132, and June 16, 1945, p. 621.
25. See above, p. 170.
26. [242], III, 710.
27. *Ibid.*, p. 697.
28. *Ibid.*, p. 701.
29. Rauter to Himmler, August 10, 1943, [24], p. 54, and [242], III, 707–8.
30. [19], 7-A, 702.
31. [50], 51 (April 5, 1943), p. 6.
32. [120], pp. 129–34. Maurits Dekker's *Jozef duikt* [90] tells of the vicissitudes of a young Jewish diver in an Amsterdam boarding house. Anne Frank's *The Diary of a Young Girl* [92], which relates the story of two Jewish families in hiding, has since become a world-wide best-seller.
33. [242], III, 704.
34. *Ibid.*, p. 705.
35. *Ibid.*, pp. 719–20.
36. [19], 7-A, 219.

37. *Ibid.*, p. 229.   38. *Ibid.*, p. 257.

39. [56], II, 3 (end of March 1944); [144], pp. 256–58.

40. [120], p. 122.

41. For a detailed account of this attempt, see [112], pp. 146–74.

42. *Ibid.*, pp. 14–18.   43. [19], 7-A, 220.

44. *Ibid.*, pp. 221–22.   45. *Ibid.*, 4-A, 435–37.

46. [242], III, 714–15.   47. [19], 7-C, 262.

48. *Ibid.*, pp. 267–68.   49. *Ibid.*, p. 316.

50. *Ibid.*, pp. 260–63.   51. [164], June 23, 1945, p. 650.

52. [19], 7-A, 260.

53. See testimony of Gerben Wagenaar, December 19, 1951, *ibid.*, 7-C, 476. Wagenaar was the one Communist member of the inner circle of the Council of Resistance. See also testimony of Jacob van der Gaag, March 31, 1950, *ibid.*, p. 234.

54. *Ibid.*, 7-A, 261–62.   55. *Ibid.*, p. 267.

56. *Ibid.*, p. 264.   57. *Ibid.*, pp. 263–64.

58. "Regeringsverklaring naar Aanleiding van Aanslagen op Leden van Mussert's Schimmenkabinet," February 13, 1943, *ibid.*, 7-B, 30.

59. *Ibid.*, 7-A, 265, 269.

60. *Ibid.*, pp. 231–32.

61. Reproduced in *ibid.*, pp. 232–33.

62. Reproduced in *ibid.*, pp. 234–36.

63. *Ibid.*, p. 233.

64. *Ibid.*, p. 316 (conclusions of the Commission).

65. *Ibid.*, p. 237.   66. [158], April 1, 1941, p. 2.

67. [19], 7-B, 31.   68. [206], pp. 2–3.

69. *Ibid.*, pp. 5–6.

70. [157], III, 1 (January–February 1948), p. 4. This issue of the periodical issued by the Rijksinstituut voor Oorlogsdocumentatie contains an excellent preliminary summary of the work of the N.S.F., which, however, has been superseded by the Sanders study [206].

71. [206], pp. 18–19.

72. *Ibid.*, p. 18.

73. *Ibid.*, pp. 24–25; [19], 7-A, 230–31.

74. [19], 7-A, 225; facsimile reproduction in [206], opp. p. 38.

75. [19], 7-A, 226; facsimile reproduction in [206], opp. p. 39.

76. [206], pp. 54–60.

77. *Ibid.*, pp. 148–49, 151–52.

78. *Ibid.*, pp. 100–101; see above, p. 348.

79. [206], p. 180.

80. [157], IV, 2 (June 1949), p. 29.

81. [164], September 11, 1943, pp. 197–98.

82. [19], 7-A, 264.   83. *Ibid.*, p. 258.

84. [201], p. 20.   85. See [226], pp. 55, 99–100.

86. [19], 4-A, 874.   87. *Ibid.*, p. 844.

88. *Ibid.*, p. 852.   89. *Ibid.*, pp. 655–85.

90. *Ibid.*, p. 878. (The wire is quoted in the original English, precisely as it was sent.)

91. [201], p. 28.

92. *Ibid.*, p. 29; [19], 4-A, 873.
93. [19], 4-B, 34; [201], p. 33.
94. [50], 59 (October 15, 1943), p. 8.
95. [164], July 4, 1942, p. 714.
96. [201], p. 29.
97. *Ibid.*, pp. 18–20. Cf. [109], pp. 9B–9L.
98. [162], February 19, 1943, p. 2; [97], p. 178.
99. [162], June 11, 1943, p. 1.
100. [19], 4-A, 555–57.
101. De Jong to author, February 12, 1962.
102. [97], pp. 178, 188.
103. [24], p. 280.
104. See [15], pp. 24–25. This figure represents a minimum estimate. All forms of murder (except executions) are reported in *Jaarcijfers* under one heading. From 1939 to 1941, the average annual number of homicides was 42.3. In 1942 it rose to 60, in 1943 to 124. Since 509 persons were murdered in 1944, the estimate of a minimum of 300 political assassinations is conservative, allowing for the violence prevalent during that period.
105. [64], III, 7 (February 21, 1943), in [144], p. 193.
106. [50], 56, July 30, 1943, p. 7; [59], IV, 1 (October 6, 1943), in [144], pp. 248–49.
107. [164], February 27, 1943, p. 153, and October 16, 1943, p. 381; [123], p. 55.
108. [19], 7-B, 30 (Bijlage 15, broadcast of Radio Oranje, February 13, 1943).
109. See *ibid.*, 7-A, 258–59.
110. [50], 59 (October 15, 1943), pp. 1–2.
111. [19], 7-A, 15.
112. *Ibid.*, pp. 17–18.
113. *Ibid.*, p. 118.
114. *Ibid.*, p. 79. Schreieder, the chief of counterespionage for the German police, placed the liquidation of the O.D. Intelligence Service in the summer of 1942 ([118], p. 297).
115. [118], pp. 5–16; [19], 4-A, 47–49.

116. [19], 77.	117. *Ibid.*, p. 119.
118. *Ibid.*, pp. 53, 121.	119. *Ibid.*, p. 54.
120. *Ibid.*, pp. 197–99, 244–47.	121. *Ibid.*, p. 174.
122. *Ibid.*, pp. 192–94.	123. *Ibid.*, pp. 456, 460.

124. *Ibid.*, pp. 422–25, 408–12, 393–94.
125. J. A. H. S. Bruins Slot, "The Resistance," [217], p. 147; [112], p. 203; [19], 4-A, 436.

126. [19], 4-A, 412–16.	127. *Ibid.*, p. 430.
128. *Ibid.*, pp. 439–40.	129. *Ibid.*, pp. 418–22.
130. *Ibid.*, pp. 423–25, 433–35.	131. [118], pp. 49, 333.
132. [19], 7-A, 272–73.	133. *Ibid.*, pp. 269–72.

134. "Koninklijk Besluit," September 5, 1944, reproduced in [19], 7-A, 322. Actually Prince Bernhard had been appointed Commander of all Dutch land forces two days earlier (Bijlage 24, Koninklijk Besluit, September 3, 1944, *ibid.*, 7-C, 35).

135. *Ibid.*, 7-A, 364.
136. [179], p. 246.
137. [19], 7-A, 320.
138. [179], p. 250.
139. *Ibid.*, p. 241. Cf. [19], 7-A, 365.
140. [19], 7-A, 364–65.
141. *Ibid.*, p. 187; "Proclamatie," quoted in [242], II, 123.
142. [242], p. 113; [19], 4-A, 668–72.
143. [19], 7-A, 167–68; [242], II, 114.
144. [19], 7-A, 168.
145. [242], II, 116–17.
146. [19], 7-A, 169.
147. *Ibid.*, p. 289.
148. [132], pp. 21–23; [87], pp. 419–21.
149. [242], II, 113–18.
150. [19], 7-A, 293.
151. [29], pp. 3–7.
152. *Ibid.*, pp. 13–14.
153. *Ibid.*, p. 24.
154. "Besluit van de Secretaris-Generaal van het Ministerie van Onderwijs, Kunsten en Wetenschappen, houdende Instelling van een Rijksbureau voor Documentatie van de Geschiedenis van Nederland in Oorlogstijd," [29], pp. 47–48. The Military Government revoked this decree, but the Institute was soon re-established as the Rijksinstituut voor Oorlogsdocumentatie.

CHAPTER ELEVEN

1. [19], 7-A, 190.
2. *Ibid.*, p. 314.
3. [212], p. 20.
4. *Ibid.*, pp. 22–23.
5. *Ibid.*, p. 28.
6. *Ibid.*, p. 34.
7. *Ibid.*, p. 7; [144], p. 47. This number includes publications that were issued only once or a few times.
8. [212].
9. "Geuzenactie Bericht no. 2," [157], I, 4 (May 24, 1946), p. 3; [144], p. 54.
10. [212], p. 124.
11. [72]. This Comité voor Vrij Nederland has no connection with the clandestine publication *Vrij Nederland,* which will be discussed below.
12. [212], pp. 174–76, 352.
13. [73].
14. [212], pp. 96–97.
15. [19], 7-A, 194. It is necessary to distinguish between the weekly *Vrij Nederland* [164] which appeared in London, the clandestine *Vrij Nederland* [64] published under the occupation, and its legal continuation which was issued in Amsterdam after the Liberation [163].
16. [164], April 22, 1944, p. 392; [212], p. 322.
17. [19], 7-A, 197.
18. [212], pp. 322–23.
19. *Ibid.*, pp. 324–26.
20. *Ibid.*, pp. 327–28; [19], 7-A, 196.
21. [212], p. 330.
22. *Ibid.*
23. *Ibid.*, p. 328.
24. *Ibid.*, p. 331.
25. [41], No. 4–5 (April–May, 1944), p. 16.
26. [163], May 17, 1945, p. 10.

27. [50], 67 (June 19, 1944), p. 7, and V, 103 (May 10, 1945), p. 1; [212], p. 227.

28. [212], p. 237.

29. *Ibid.*, pp. 227–28.

30. *Ibid.*, pp. 235–36.

31. [164], December 15, 1945, p. 655; [144], p. 402; [212], pp. 232–34.

32. See [101] for a lively description of the two-month trip from Holland to England through Belgium, France, and Spain.

33. [50], V, 111 (May 18, 1945), p. 1.

34. [19], 4-A, 100, and 7-A, 191–92; [212], p. 229.

35. [212], p. 235.

36. "Manifest van *Het Parool* en *Vrij Nederland*," April 15, 1944, [144], pp. 305–11.

37. [212], p. 236.

38. [185]; [42], Liberation issue (May 1945), p. 2.

39. [212], p. 140.

40. *Ibid.*, p. 142.

41. *Ibid.*, p. 141.

42. [42], Liberation issue (May 1945), p. 2.

43. [212], p. 142.

44. [42], III, 37 (March 31, 1943), pp. 1–4.

45. [212], pp. 287–89.

46. *Ibid.*, p. 293; [164], November 27, 1943, p. 552, and April 22, 1944, p. 392.

47. [19], 7-A, 199.

48. [212], p. 291.

49. *Ibid.*, pp. 293–94.

50. *Ibid.*, p. 289.

51. *Ibid.*, pp. 289–90.

52. [19], 7-A, 200.

53. [212], p. 293.

54. [19], 7-A, 204–5.

55. [212], p. 367.

56. See above, pp. 132–33.

57. [144], pp. 364, 368–70.

58. [19], 7-A, 204.

59. [201], p. 33; De Jong to author, February 23, 1962.

60. *De Waarheid* [65], 1 (December 7, 1940), in [144], pp. 75–77.

61. [19], 7-A, 205–6.

62. See above, pp. 107–8.

63. [144], p. 38.

64. [201], p. 32.

65. [19], 7-A, 204.

66. [42], V, 3 (August issue, 1944), p. 5.

67. E.g., [53], 1 (end of January 1941), pp. 2–3.

68. Befehlshaber der Sicherheitspolizei und des SD für die besetzten niederländischen Gebiete, "Jahresbericht 1942 über den Einsatz der Aussenstelle Amsterdam," [157], I, 5 (June 7, 1946), p. 2; [212], pp. 98–99.

69. [212], pp. 315–16.

70. *Ibid.*, p. 315.

71. "Tegen Haat en Wraak," Bijlage bij *De Vonk*, July 1941, [144], pp. 115–18.

72. [19], 7-A, 208–9.

73. [212], p. 315.

74. [32], February 14, 1945, p. 1; [212], p. 84.

75. [212], pp. 210–11.

76. [212], pp. 100–101; [19], 7-A, 203.
77. [19], 7-A, 201.   78. [212], pp. 101–2.
79. [19], 7-A, 200–201.   80. [212], p. 123.
81. [19], 7-A, 206-7.   82. [212], pp. 347–48.
83. [60], November 1, 1944, pp. 6-8.
84. [212], pp. 349–51.   85. *Ibid.*, pp. 91–92.
86. [136], p. 76.   87. [212], pp. 245–46.
88. *Ibid.*, p. 275.
89. "Te nonchalant," *De Toekomst* [55], No. 7 (October 1944), in [144], pp. 368–70.
90. [46], April 7, 1944, pp. 1–2.
91. [212], p. 213.
92. [164], October 17, 1942, p. 367.
93. *Ibid.*, April 22, 1944, p. 393; [212], p. 221.
94. [223], pp. 237–40.
95. [212], pp. 256–57.
96. Title page reproduced in *ibid.*, opp. p. 129.
97. [40], June 5, 1944.   98. [212], p. 129.
99. *Ibid.*, p. 118.   100. *Ibid.*, p. 125.
101. *Ibid.*, pp. 67–69.   102. *Ibid.*, p. 28.
103. *Ibid.*, pp. 351, 313–14. 104. *Ibid.*, p. 32.
105. *Oranje Bulletin No. 1*, September 5, 1944, *ibid.*, reproduced opp. p. 32.
106. *Ibid.*, pp. 351–57.
107. *Ibid.*, p. 34.
108. [242], III, 657–58, 665–67.
109. [64], II, 13 (April 24, 1942), p. 1.
110. [164], June 3, 1945, p. 557; [212], p. 35.
111. [212], pp. 45–46.   112. *Ibid.*, pp. 46–47.
113. *Ibid.*, pp. 57–59.   114. *Ibid.*, pp. 47–48.
115. *Ibid.*, p. 48.   116. *Ibid.*, pp. 52–53.
117. *Ibid.*, pp. 50–51.   118. *Ibid.*, pp. 53–55.
119. [104], pp. 32–34.
120. [50], 67 (June 19, 1944), p. 5.
121. [212], pp. 59–61.
122. *Ibid.*, p. 60.
123. [19], 7-A, 211.
124. E.g., *Circulaire No. 1 van het Comité "In Verdrukking één,"* June 29, 1940, [144], p. 55; Nieuwsbrief van Pieter 't Hoen, no. 1, July 25, 1940, *ibid.*, p. 61.
125. "De Weg naar Vrede en Vrijheid," *De Waarheid*, no. 1 (December 7, 1940 [?]), *ibid.*, p. 77.
126. E.g., "Nederlandse Unie," *De Geus Onder Studenten*, no. 2, October 1940, *ibid.*, pp. 71–75.
127. E.g., "Wij zijn nog altijd in Oorlog," *De Geus*, no. 1, October 4, 1940, *ibid.*, pp. 63–65.
128. E.g., "Staat de Nederlandse Justitie in Duitsen Dienst," *Slaet op den Trommele*, no. 4 (July 1940), *ibid.*, pp. 112–13; "De misleidende Proclamatie," *Vrij Nederland* (cland.), II, 6 (November 1941), *ibid.*, pp. 124–27.

129. Quoted in [39], 6 (February 15, 1941), p. 1.

130. January 1944 Supplement, p. 1, distributed with [64], IV, 8 (January 24, 1944).

131. *Het Parool* [50], 4 (March 4, 1941), in [144], p. 99.

132. [50], 40 (July 14, 1942), pp. 1–2.

133. [64], III, 3 (October 10, 1942), p. 2.

134. *Ibid.*, II, 13 (April 24, 1942), p. 3.

135. [50], 49 (February 17, 1943), p. 2.

136. *Ibid.*, 62 (December 18, 1943), p. 3.

137. *Ibid.*, 53 (May 1943), pp. 1–2.

138. *Ibid.*, 48 (February 10, 1943), pp. 1–2.

139. [42], III, 38 (April 25, 1943), pp. 5–6.

140. [50], 56 (July 30, 1943), pp. 10–11.

141. E.g., [42], I, 6 (first December issue [1944]), p. 3.

142. [54], II, 36 (June 4, 1945), p. 1.

143. [64], II, 16 (June 23, 1942), p. 1.

144. E.g., [42], V, 2 (second July issue, 1944), pp. 4–5.

145. [50], 71 (October 1944), p. 1.

146. [39], 2 (October 1940), pp. 1–3.

147. [50], 2 (February 17, 1941), p. 1.

148. *Ibid.*, 16 (July 16, 1941), p. 5.

149. *Ibid.*, 39 (June 17, 1942), pp. 1–3.

150. [212], p. 25.

151. *Ibid.*, p. 30; [164], December 4, 1943, p. 578.

152. [50], 56 (July 30, 1943), p. 1.

153. [42], IV, 17 (first May issue, 1944), pp. 1–2.

154. [64], 2e Extra Uitgave voor Zuid-Holland (December 10, 1944), pp. 1–2.

155. E.g., [50], 84 (February 6, 1945), pp. 1, 4.

156. *Trouw* [56], II, 18 (December 1944), in [144], pp. 370–72.

157. [50], 80 (January 9, 1945), pp. 1–2.

158. See [136], *passim*.

159. [144], pp. 44–45.

160. [50], 86 (February 20, 1945), pp. 2–3.

161. *Ibid.*, 69 (August 8, 1944), pp. 4–5.

162. Quoted in [42], IV, 13 (first March issue, 1944), p. 1.

163. *De Waarheid* [65], 117 (March 31, 1944), in [144], pp. 303–5.

164. *Trouw* [56], I, 7 (June 23, 1943), in [144], pp. 271–72.

165. [37], II, 4 (May 1944), pp. 6-8, and II, 7 (November 1944), pp. 3–4; [76], pp. 50–51, 54–55.

166. [50], 74 (November 21, 1944), pp. 1–2.

167. E.g., [76], pp. 38–39.

168. *Ibid.*, p. 73.

169. *Ibid.*, p. 67.

170. [50], 63 (January 10, 1944), p. 3.

171. *Ibid.*, 80 (January 9, 1945), p. 2.

172. See [150], pp. 6–7.

173. [42], V, 4 (first November issue, 1944), p. 4.

174. [64], II, 16 (June 23, 1942), p. 1; *Het Parool,* June 5, 1943,

quoted in [164], October 2, 1943, p. 295; *De Waarheid*, quoted in *ibid.*, June 17, 1944, p. 645.

175. "De Strijd voor de Bevrijding van Indonesie," *Vrij Nederland* (cland.), V, 21 (April 30, 1945), in [144], pp. 389–90; also reproduced in [34], 221 (April 28, 1945), p. 1, and in other underground papers.

176. [103], p. 28.

177. [164], June 13, 1942, p. 621.

178. E.g., [69]. Boisot's work aroused so much discussion that the S.S. weekly *Storm* reprinted a two-page summary as part of the attempt to refute its thesis ([160], December 24, 1943, pp. 7–8).

179. [64], IV, 5 (October 21, 1943), p. 8.

180. *Ibid.*; [42], IV, 7 (second October issue, 1943), pp. 5–6.

181. [68], pp. 17–19.   182. *Ibid.*, p. 23.

183. [79], p. 13.   184. [82], p. 87.

185. [81], pp. 12–19.   186. [82], pp. 87–88.

187. [78]. This pamphlet is a reprint of the earlier edition, which was published in 1942.

188. [180], pp. 19–20.

189. [83]. This pamphlet is a reprint of the earlier edition, which was printed in 1943 but confiscated by the German police.

190. [97], p. 228.   191. [76], *passim*.

192. [100], p. 38.   193. [131], p. 3.

194. [1], p. 25.   195. *Ibid., passim*.

CHAPTER TWELVE

1. [191], p. 415.   2. [10], XV, 645.

3. [20], pp. 44–45.   4. [109], p. 2a.

5. Diary entry, June 8, 1943, commercial traveler, Amsterdam, [143], p. 305.

6. [118], p. 50.

7. [19], 7-A, 181–82.

8. [83], p. 14.

9. Visser to Cohen, December 30, 1941, Herzberg, [242], III, 148.

10. De Jong to author, July 26, 1962.

11. See [252], p. 7.

12. At least one Dutch National Socialist theoretician, Krekel, foresaw this failure as early as 1940 ([187], pp. 23–25).

13. See [239], pp. 105–7.

14. From [129], p. 46.

15. See [50], 90 (March 17, 1945), pp. 1–2.

16. [112], p. 15.

Glossary

This glossary contains translations and brief descriptions of selected Dutch and German terms.

AANWIJZIGINGEN VAN 1937. Directives of 1937. Instructions issued by the Colijn cabinet to provide government officials with guidelines for their conduct in the event of a foreign occupation.

AKTION SILBERTANNE. Operation Silver Fir. Code name used internally by the German police to designate its campaign of reprisal murders instigated in 1943.

ANJERDAG. Carnation Day. June 29, 1940, Prince Bernhard's birthday. The day on which many Dutchmen demonstrated their loyalty to the House of Orange, often by wearing carnations, the favorite flower of the Prince.

ANTI-REVOLUTIONNAIRE PARTIJ (A.R.). Antirevolutionary Party. The largest Protestant party. Conservative with regard to domestic policy and in favor of a strong colonial policy. Closely related to the Reformed Churches. Its leader, Hendrik Colijn, was Prime Minister for many years before the war.

ARBEIDSINZET. Labor Draft. The Dutch translation of the German term *Arbeitseinsatz* for the utilization of Dutch workers for the German war effort. Often synonymous with "deportation to Germany."

AUSWEIS. Exemption Certificate. A certificate stating that a person had been exempted from the labor draft. Also more specifically refers to the exemption certificates issued in 1945 in connection with the final German defense effort.

BEAUFTRAGTER. Representative. Local or provincial representative of the High Commissioner.

BEVOLKINGSREGISTER. Bureau of Population Records. The branch of the government charged with keeping records and vital statistics. Before the war, local offices were part of the municipal administration, but the central office in The Hague was part of the national administration.

BUREAU INLICHTINGEN (B.I.). Intelligence Bureau. The intelligence agency of the Dutch government, which started to function early in 1943.

CHRISTELIJK HISTORISCHE UNIE (C.H.U.). Christian Historical Union. The second largest Protestant party, closely related to the Dutch Reformed Church. Its leader, De Geer, was Prime Minister at the time of the invasion.

CHRISTELIJK NATIONAAL VAKVERBOND (C.N.V.). Christian National Trade Union. The Protestant trade union.

COMMISSARIS DER KONINGIN. Commissioner of the Queen, or Provincial Commissioner. Government officials appointed by the crown to represent the national administration in the eleven provinces. The Commissioner served as the executive head of the provincial administration.

COMMUNISTISCHE PARTIJ NEDERLAND (C.P.N.). Communist Party of the Netherlands. The Dutch Communist party, which had been started after the First World War. In 1937 it captured 3.4 percent of the vote. Its main strength was in Amsterdam.

DOLLE DINSDAG. Mad Tuesday. September 5, 1944. The day on which exaggerated reports of Allied advances led to premature victory celebrations and to the flight of Germans and Dutch Nazis to the East.

ENDLÖSUNG (DER JUDENFRAGE). Final Solution (of the Jewish problem). Euphemistic term used by the Germans to camouflage the policy of exterminating European Jewry.

GENERALKOMMISSAR. Commissioner-General. Title of the four main administrative assistants to Seyss-Inquart who were responsible for the supervision of the Dutch administration and for the execution of non-military German policies.

GRÜNE POLIZEI (DUTCH: *groene politie*). Green Police. Colloquial name (after the characteristic green uniforms) for the *Ordnungspolizei* (Order Police), the executive branch of the German police services.

GULDEN (abbrev.: f.). Guilder or florin. A unit of Dutch currency. The exchange equivalent of fifty-three United States cents in April 1940.

HOGE RAAD. High Council. The Netherlands supreme judicial organ.

JOODSE RAAD VAN AMSTERDAM (J.R.). Jewish Council of Amsterdam. An organization created by the Germans as a means of implementing their anti-Jewish policies. Responsible for all aspects of Jewish life, superseding previously existing Jewish organizations except the religious bodies. The Council was active throughout the Netherlands.

KNOKPLOEG (K.P.). Action Group. Dutch name for street gangs. Also applied to action groups formed during the 1941 unrest in Amsterdam, later to all underground groups, especially those attacking ration offices and population registries.

LANDELIJKE KNOKPLOEGEN (L.K.P.). National Action Groups. The resistance organization formed in 1943 to secure ration books and identity cards for divers through direct action. Closely allied to the L.O. (see below).

LANDELIJKE ORGANISATIE VOOR HULP AAN ONDERDUIKERS (L.O.). National Organization for Assistance to Divers. The underground organization chiefly responsible for the placement and care of people in hiding.

LANDSTORM. Territorial Guard. A militia formed by the Germans to defend Dutch territory against Allied attack.

LANDWACHT. Home Guard. An auxiliary police force formed to combat underground activities and to protect Dutch Nazis.

NATIONAAL-SOCIALISTISCHE BEWEGING DER NEDERLANDEN (N.S.B.). National Socialist Movement of the Netherlands. The Dutch Nazi party headed by A. A. Mussert.

NATIONALSOZIALISTISCHE DEUTSCHE ARBEITERPARTEI (N.S.D.A.P.). National Socialist German Workers Party. The German Nazi party.

NATIONAAL STEUNFONDS (N.S.F.). National Assistance Fund. The clandestine fund which financed many Resistance operations.

NEDERLANDSE ARBEIDSDIENST (N.A.D.). Netherlands Labor Service. An organization modeled on the German *Arbeitsdienst,* in which young Dutchmen were required to serve for six months, receiving physical training and performing manual labor.

NEDERLANDSE ARBEIDSFRONT (N.A.F.). Netherlands Labor Front. The Nazi labor organization (modeled on the German *Arbeitsfront*) which was established in 1942 to supersede the N.V.V. (see below).

NEDERLANDSE BINNENLANDSE STRIJDKRACHTEN (N.B.S.). Netherlands Forces of the Interior. The official organization of recognized Dutch resistance forces set up by the Netherlands government-in-exile under the command of Prince Bernhard.

NEDERLANDSE UNIE. Netherlands Union. A political movement founded in the summer of 1940 to oppose the N.S.B. and to provide opportunities for the expression of patriotic sentiment.

NEDERLANDS VERBOND VAN VAKVERENIGINGEN (N.V.V.). Netherlands Association of Trade Unions. The largest Dutch labor union. Allied to the Social Democratic Party.

ONDERDUIKERS. Divers. Colloquial term for persons in hiding.

OPBOUWDIENST. Construction Service. An organization established in 1940 to clean up destruction caused during the invasion and to prevent a sudden rise in unemployment as a result of the release of men from military service.

ORDE DIENST (O.D.). Order Service. An underground organization formed by military personnel largely devoted to the maintenance of order after German withdrawal.

PERSOONSBEWIJS (P.B.). Identity Card. The identity card which every Dutchman was required to carry with him.

RAAD VAN STATE. Council of State. Organ of government responsible for the appointment of a regent in the event of a vacancy on the throne, and for a number of other governmental functions.

RAAD VAN VERZET IN HET KONINKRIJK DER NEDERLANDEN (R.v.V.). Council of Resistance in the Kingdom of the Netherlands. A resistance organization devoted to espionage, sabotage, and other forms of direct action.

RADIO ORANJE. Radio Orange. The official Dutch radio service in London, broadcasting to the occupied Dutch territories.

REICHSKOMMISSAR FÜR DIE BESETZTEN NIEDERLÄNDISCHEN GEBIETE. High Commissioner for the Occupied Dutch Territories. The chief executive civilian German official in the occupied Netherlands.

HET RIJK. The Realm. Dutch term for the Kingdom of the Netherlands and the national administration.

RIJKSINSTITUUT VOOR OORLOGSDOCUMENTATIE (R.v.O.). Netherlands State Institute for War Documentation. The official government institute for the study of the history of the Netherlands and the Dutch East Indies during the Second World War.

ROOMS KATHOLIEKE STAATSPARTIJ (R.K.S.P.). Roman Catholic State Party. The Dutch Catholic party, the largest party in parliament in the years before the war.

ROOMS KATHOLIEK WERKLIEDENVERBOND (R.K.W.V.). Roman Catholic Workmen's Association. The Catholic trade union, second largest in the country.

SCHUTZSTAFFEL (S.S.). Security Squad. The security organization of the German Nazi party which became the heart of the Nazi totalitarian state under Himmler. The Dutch S.S. copied the initials of the German organization (Nederlandse S.S. or Germaanse S.S.) although the letters "S.S." had no meaning in Dutch.

SECRETARIS-GENERAAL. Secretary General. The permanent civil service administrative head of each ministry.

SICHERHEITSDIENST (S.D.). Security Service. The intelligence service of the German police and S.S.

SOCIAAL-DEMOCRATISCHE ARBEIDERS PARTIJ (S.D.A.P.). Social Democratic Workers Party. The Dutch Socialist party.

STATEN-GENERAAL. States-General. The Dutch parliament, consisting of an upper house (Eerste Kamer—"First Chamber") elected by the provincial legislatures and a lower house (Tweede Kamer—"Second Chamber") elected by universal suffrage under a system of proportional representation. The lower house played a role similar to that performed by the House of Commons in England.

VERTRAUENSMANN (V-Mann). Undercover agent. A Dutch agent of the German police.

VERTROUWENSMANNEN DER REGERING. Representatives of the Government. A group of persons designed by the government-in-exile in 1944 to act as its representatives during the transition from German to Allied rule.

HET VERZET. The Resistance. The most common Dutch term for the Resistance.

VRIJWILLIGERSLEGIOEN NEDERLAND. Volunteer Legion Netherlands. A military volunteer unit formed to fight with the German army in the Soviet Union.

WAFFEN-S.S. Armed S.S. The military branch of the S.S.

WEER-AFDELING (W.A.). Defense Troop. The uniformed but unarmed auxiliary of the N.S.B. designed to "conquer the streets."

WINTERHULP. Winter Help. The Nazi-inspired public charity organization modeled on the German Winterhilfe.

ZENTRALSTELLE FÜR JÜDISCHE AUSWANDERUNG. Central Agency for Jewish Emigration. The special office of the German police for the organization of the deportation of Jews from Holland.

Bibliographical Notes for English Readers

Since most works on the German occupation of the Netherlands have appeared in Dutch, the reader who is unfamiliar with Dutch will find available materials somewhat limited. For this reason an attempt is made in this section to list a few publications written in English or containing English summaries for those who wish to pursue further their interest in the occupation.

Readers who wish general background information on prewar Holland will find B. Landheer's *The Netherlands* [259] a useful description of political, economic, and social conditions before the Second World War.

The only comprehensive treatment of the occupation in English is the May 1946 issue of the *Annals of the American Academy of Political and Social Sciences* entitled *The Netherlands during German Occupation* [217], edited by N. W. Posthumus. The work consists of a series of articles written by prominent Dutchmen, most of whom had played important roles in the Resistance. The articles contain much useful information, but suffer from the fact that they were written quickly and at a time when the authors' emotions were too close to the occupation for an objective and dispassionate treatment of the period.

During the war Louis de Jong, who was at that time connected with the official Netherlands Radio Service in London, published in Dutch a four-volume year-by-year account of the German occupation of Holland (and of events in the Dutch East Indies) under the title *Je Maintiendrai* [255]. An adaptation of the first two volumes of this series, up-dated to include events to December 1942, was prepared and translated into English by Joseph W. W. Stoppelman. This adaptation was published in 1943 as *The Lion Rampant. The Story of Holland's Resistance to the Nazis* [256]. De Jong also prepared in English an abbreviated account of the occupation covering the period from May 1940 to February 1941 under the title of *Holland Fights the Nazis* [254].

These two English volumes, as well as the Dutch series on which they are based, draw on contemporary Dutch official and clandestine newspapers and periodicals, German publications, monitored German-controlled radio broadcasts, and reports from escapees from the occupied territory. Despite their propagandistic intent and the emotional climate in which these volumes were written, they give a vivid picture of life in Holland under the occupation, subject of course to the limitations of the materials available at the time of writing.

Most of the publications of the Netherlands State Institute for War Documentation contain English summaries. Therefore, they constitute the most valuable single group of reference works for the English reader. *Nederland in Oorlogstijd* [157], a periodical published by the Institute between 1946 and 1950, contains articles and source materials of great interest to a student of the occupation. Sometimes entire issues were given over to special topics such as the National Assistance Fund, Carnation Day, or a series of interviews with Rauter, the head of the German police. The Institute also published trial records of a number of Dutch Nazis (Mussert, Blokzijl, Van Genechten) and of Rauter and General Christiansen, the German military commander in the Netherlands [20–24].

The Institute issued two volumes on the underground press. A selection of articles from the clandestine press published under the title *Het Woord als Wapen* ("The Word as a Weapon") [144] and edited by R. S. Zimmerman-Wolf can be supplemented by a catalogue of the clandestine publications in *De ondergrondse Pers* [212], edited by L. E. Winkel. The introduction to this latter volume contains an excellent summary of the history of the underground press.

Among the monographs on specialized aspects of the occupation, B. A. Sijes' account of the February strike of 1941 (*De Februari-Staking, 25–26 Februari 1941* [208]) and of the Rotterdam raids (*De Razzia van Rotterdam, 10–11 November 1944* [209]), P. J. Bouman's account of the April-May strike of 1943 (*De April-Mei Stakingen van 1943* [195]), A. J. C. Rüter's fascinating re-creation of the railroad strike against the background of the social history of the Dutch railroads (*Rijden en staken. De Nederlandse Spoorwegen in Oorlogstijd* [205]), and P. Sanders' description of the National Assistance Fund (*Het Nationaal Steunfonds: Bijdrage tot de Geschiedenis van de Financiering van het Verzat* [206]) may be selected as being of the most general interest.

Documents pertaining to the resistance of the Protestant churches were recorded in wartime by W. A. Visser t' Hooft in a collection published in 1944 under the title *The Struggle of the Dutch Church for the Maintenance of the Commandments of God in the Life of the State* [149]. A monograph by J. H. Boas, *Religious Resistance in Holland* [173], published in London in 1945, attempts to render a more comprehensive survey of the struggle of the churches.

Among the personal memories of the occupation period, Anne Frank's *Diary of a Young Girl* [92] is the most widely known because of its literary quality and its world-wide impact. Jacob Presser's *Breaking Point* [268] is a fine fictionalized account of the persecution of the Jews and of the Westerbork concentration camp. It has a ring of authenticity although it is garbed as a novel.

In concluding this section, it may be useful to list four key publications in Dutch for the reader whose knowledge of related languages may enable him to use a Dutch text. First of these is the eight-part report of the Parliamentary Commission of Inquiry (*Enquêtecommissie*) into the conduct of the Dutch government during the war (*Verslag houdende de Uitkomsten van het Onderzoek* [19]), which contains much basic documentary material and testimony of witnesses. *Onderdrukking en Verzet* [242], edited by J. J. van Bolhuis and others, and published in four volumes between 1947 and 1955, provides a comprehensive canvass of the occupation through articles written by individuals who frequently had participated in the events described in their writings. Many of these articles are source material rather than monographs based on research, but the collection contains comparatively more balanced, sophisticated, and authentic views than the articles in *The Annals*. *Dagboek Fragmenten* [143], edited by T. M. Sjenitzer–van Leening, is an invaluable source collection containing excerpts of diaries kept during the occupation.

Finally the attention of the reader should be drawn to a series of books by L. de Jong, which is being published at this writing under the title *De Bezetting* [253]. These soft-cover editions reproduce the text of television broadcasts on the occupation by Dr. de Jong and contain documents and photographs from the files of the Institute and elsewhere. Even though the broadcasts are obviously addressed to a popular audience, they embody the collective judgment of the staff of the Institute and the gist of the staff's most sophisticated consensus and interpretation reached at the time.

Bibliography

BIBLIOGRAPHIES

[1] Jong, Dirk de. *Bibliographie des éditions françaises clandestines imprimées aux Pays-Bas pendant l'occupation allemande, 1940–1945.* La Haye, 1947.
[2] ——. *Het vrije Boek in onvrije Tijd: Bibliografie van illegale clandestine Belletrie.* Leiden, 1958.
[3] Nederlands Comité voor geschiedkundige Wetenschappen. *Repertorium van Boeken en Tijdschriftartikelen betreffende de Geschiedenis van Nederland verschenen in het Jaar 1941,* comp. by Aleida Gast. Leiden, 1945.
[4] ——. *Repertorium van Boeken en Tijdschriftartikelen betreffende de Geschiedenis van Nederland verschenen in de Jaren 1942–1944,* comp. by Aleida Gast. Leiden, 1947.
[5] Netherlands. Regeringsvoorlichtingsdienst, 's Gravenhage. *Bibliographica Neerlandica 1940–1945.* The Hague, 1951.
[6] United States. Department of the Air Force. *Guide to Captured German Documents,* comp. by Gerhard L. Weinberg, War Documentation Project, Study No. 1. Maxwell Air Force Base, 1952.

GOVERNMENT DOCUMENTS

(See also Documents and Sources, below)

[7] ——. Germany. *Reichsgesetzblatt 1942.* 2 vols. Berlin, 1942.
[8] ——. *Verordnungsblatt für die besetzten niederländischen Gebiete.* Den Haag, 1940–45. 5 vols. Citations are of decree number and date: thus "152/1940" refers to decree 152 in the year 1940.
[9] ——. Auswärtiges Amt. *Allied Intrigue in the Low Countries: Further Documents concerning the Anglo-French Policy of Extending the War: Full Text of White Book No. 5.* New York, 1940.
[10] International Military Tribunal. *Trial of the Major War Criminals.* 42 vols. Nuremberg, 1947–49.

Netherlands

[11] *Memorandum van de Nederlandse Regering inzake de door Nederland van Duitsland te eissen Schadevergoeding.* N.p., 1945.

[12] *Staatsalmanak voor het Koninkrijk der Nederlanden 1940.* 's Graven-hage, 1939.

[13] Centraal Bureau voor de Statistiek. *Economische en sociale Kroniek der Oorlogsjaren, 1940–1945.* Utrecht, 1947.

[14] ——. *Jaarcijfers voor Nederland 1940.* 's Gravenhage, 1942.

[15] ——. *Jaarcijfers voor Nederland 1943–1946.* Utrecht, 1948.

[16] *Statistisch Zakboek 1944–46.* Utrecht, 1947.

[17] Departement van Algemene Zaken. *Bestuursalmanak voor het be-zette Nederlandse Gebied 1943–1944.* 's Gravenhage, 1943.

[18] Departement van Buitenlandse Zaken. *Netherlands Orange Book,* Leyden, 1940.

[19] Enquêtecommissie Regeringsbeleid 1940–45. *Verslag houdende de Uitkomsten van het Onderzoek.* 8 vols. 's Gravenhage, 1949–56. This report was published in eight volumes, each relating to an issue or area of inquiry identified in the original parliamentary decision to appoint the Commission of Inquiry. Each of these volumes or parts is subdi-vided into three parts: the report of the Commission (A), the support-ing documents (B), and the text of the hearings (C).

[20] [Ministerie van Onderwijs, Kunsten en Wetenschappen.] Rijksinsti-tuut voor Oorlogsdocumentatie. *Max Blokzijl.* Serie Bronnenpublica-ties Nr 1, Processen Nr 1. Amsterdam, n.d.

[21] ——. ——. *Van Genechten.* Serie Bronnenpublicaties Nr 2, Pro-cessen Nr 2. Amsterdam, n.d.

[22] ——. ——. *Het Proces Christiansen.* Bronnenpublicaties, Processen Nr 4. 's Gravenhage, 1950.

[23] ——. ——. *Het Proces Mussert.* Serie Bronnenpublicaties Nr 4, Processen Nr 3. 's Gravenhage, 1948.

[24] ——. ——. *Het Proces Rauter.* Bronnenpublicaties, Processen Nr 5. s' Gravenhage, 1952.

[25] ——. ——. *Vijf Nota's van Mussert aan Hitler over de Samenwerk-ing van Nederland en Duitsland in een Bond van Germaanse Volkeren, 1940–1944.* Serie Bronnenpublicaties Nr 3. 's Gravenhage, 1947.

[26] Rijksinspectie van de Bevolkingsregisters. *Statistiek der Bevolking van Joodsen Bloede in Nederland.* 's Gravenhage, 1942.

[27] Rijksuitgeverij. P. S. Gerbrandy. *Eenige Hoofdpunten van het Re-geringsbeleid in Londen.* s' Gravenhage, 1946.

[28] Vertrouwensmannen der Regering. *Het Duitse Aanbod tot een Be-ëindiging der feitelijke Vijandelijkheden in het nog bezette Nederlandse Gebied van April 1945.* 's Gravenhage, 1946.

[29] ——. *Verslag van de Werkzaamheden van Vertrouwensmannen der Regering aangewezen bij Besluit van Harer Majesteits Regering van 2 Augustus 1944.* 's Gravenhage, 1946.

[30] United States. Department of Commerce. Bureau of the Census. *Religious Bodies: 1926.* 2 vols. Washington, D.C., 1930.

[31] ——. ——. Bureau of Foreign and Domestic Commerce. *Statistical Abstract of the United States: 1930.* Washington, D.C., 1930.

[32] *De Baanbreker: Sociaal-democratisch Orgaan,* editie voor Zuid-Hol-land, February 14, 1945–May 1945. 's Gravenhage.

CLANDESTINE PERIODICALS*

[33] *Berichtenblad van Christofoor en Je Maintiendrai,* October 13, 1944–Christmas 1944. Amsterdam.

[34] *De Bevrijding,* Uitgave voor Zuid-Holland [May 1944–May 1945. Leiden].

[35] *Bulletin,* June 14, 1940–August 14, 1941. Maartensdijk (Utrecht).

[36] *Bulletin van het M.L.L.-Front* [Marx-Lenin-Luxemburg-Front]: *Door Klassestrijd en Internationalisme naar het Socialisme,* July 1940–February 1942. Amsterdam.

[37] *Christofoor: Voor God en Vaderland,* 1942–May 1945. Ijselstein-Nijmegen-Amsterdam.

[38] *Friesche Courant,* September 7, 1944. Leeuwarden.

[39] *De Geus onder Studenten,* October 4, 1940–May 1945. 's Gravenhage.

[40] *Haarlemse Courant: Buiten Verantwoordelijkheid van Mees, Peereboom en Derks,* June 5, 1944. Hillegom.

[41] *Internationale Informatiebladen van "Vrij Nederland,"* January 1944–May 1945. Amsterdam.

[42] *Je Maintiendrai,* January 1943–May 1945. Utrecht-Amsterdam.

[43] *"Het Nieuws,"* 1943–May 1945. s' Gravenhage.

[44] *Nieuwsbrief van Pieter 't Hoen,* July 25, 1940–April 10, 1941. Amsterdam.

[45] *Ons Volk: Den Vaderlant ghetrouwe,* October 7, 1943–May 1945. Utrecht-Amsterdam-'s Gravenhage.

[46] *Op Wacht: Voor God-Nederland-Oranje,* January 1944–May 1945. 's Gravenhage.

[47] *Oranje-Bode,* end of January 1943. Meppel.

[48] *Oranje-Bulletin: Bulletin ter Verspreiding van de letterlijke Tekst van Regeringsverklaringen, Bevelen van het Geallieerd Opperbevel, Aanwijzigingen van het ondergronds Verzet, en Hoofdzaken van het Nieuws,* September 15, 1944–November 30, 1944. Amsterdam.

[49] *De Oranjekrant: Vivere militare est,* January 1942–March 1945. [Zeist (?)]

[50] *Het Parool: Vrij onverveerd,* February 10, 1941–May 1945. Amsterdam-'s Gravenhage-Utrecht-Amsterdam.

[51] *De Ploeg: Wil opwekken tot Bezinning op onze na-oorlogse Taak,* July 1943–May 1945. Groningen-Ijselstreek-'s Gravenhage.

[52] *Schoonhovense Courant,* April 14, 1944. Schoonhoven.

[53] *Spartacus (Spartakus): Orgaan van het Marx-Lenin-Luxemburg Front (van het derde Front),* January 1941–February 1942. Amsterdam.

[54] *Telex Bulletin,* September 1944–April 1945. 's Gravenhage.

[55] *De Toekomst,* October 15, 1943–May 1945. 's Gravenhage.

* The publication data in this section are based on information provided by L. E. Winkel in *De ondergrondse Pers* [212]. The inclusive dates of publication are given. As in the text, all titles are given in italics even though many clandestine issues were mimeographed. No distinction between printed and mimeographed issues is made.

[56] *Trouw*, January 20, 1943–May 1945. Meppel-Amsterdam.

[57] *V.O.D.: Voorlichtingsdienst van "Je Maintiendrai,"* April 1944–May 1945. Utrecht-Hilversum.

[58] *De Vonk: "Uit de Vonk zal de Vlam oplaaien"* (Poesjkin), January 1941–May 1945. Amsterdam.

[59] *De Vrije Katheder: Bulletin ter Verdediging van de Universiteiten,* November 1940–May 1945. Amsterdam.

[60] *De vrije Kunstenaar: Religieus en politiek onafhankelijk Orgaan van de Nederlandse Kunstenaars, waarin opgenomen de Brandarisbrief,* May 1, 1942–May 1945. Amsterdam.

[61] *De vrije Nieuwscentrale*, June 6, 1943–March 7, 1944. Utrecht.

[62] *Vrij Goes*, September 15–December 3, 1944. Goes.

[63] *Vrijheid*, spring 1941–end of January 1942. 's Gravenhage.

[64] *Vrij Nederland: Nederland-Oranje,* August 1940–May 1945. Amsterdam.

[65] *De Waarheid*, November 23, 1940–May 1945. Amsterdam.

CLANDESTINE BOOKS, PAMPHLETS, AND
MISCELLANEOUS PUBLICATIONS

[66] Baanbreker, pseud. *Spartakus ontwaakt! Het Derde Front marcheert.* [Amsterdam] 1941.

[67] "Beknopt Verslag van het Onderhoud tussen de heer Rost van Tonningen en de gewezen Voorzitter der S.D.A.P. van 23 Juli 1940." Typewritten MS, Hoover Library.

[68] *Bezettingsrecht.* 2d ed. [1942].

[69] Boisot, pseud. [G. J. de Beus.] *De Wedergeboorte van het Koninkrijk.* [Tilburg, 1943 (?)]

[70] [Burger, J. A. W.] *Perspectief van onze Tijd, opgedragen aan het Nederlandse Volk door een Engelandvaarder die thans een Regeringsfunctie in Engeland bekleedt.* [1944 (?)]

[71] Cleveringa, R. P. "Rede." Typewritten MS, Hoover Library.

[72] Het Comité voor vrij Nederland. "Brief aan Z. Exc. de Heer Rijkscommissaaris Dr. Arthur Seyss-Inquart." Typewritten MS, Hoover Library.

[73] ——. "Mededelingen." Typewritten MS, Hoover Library.

[74] [Holk, L. J. van.] "Nederlands geestelijke Vrijheid en de Jodenvervolging." Typewritten MS, Hoover Library. [1940 (?)]

[75] *Je Maintiendrai*, editors of, *Bloemlezing uit 25 Nummers van Je Maintiendrai.* [Amsterdam, 1944 (?)]

[76] *Om Neerlands Toekomst.* 2d ed. 1944.

[77] "Photostats of Articles Published in the *Nationale Rotterdamse Courant* [sic] and Other Papers of the Quisling Press during 1941." Hoover Library.

[78] Scheps, J. H. *De Artsenstrijd is Neerlands Strijd.* Den Dolder, 1945. (Reprinted from original clandestine edition published in 1942.)

[79] ——. *Gerechtigheid en Volkseer.* Den Dolder, 1941.

[80] ——. *Jhr. Mr. D. J. de Geer's "De Synthese in de Oorlog," beantwoord.* Rotterdam (?), 1942.

[81] ——. *Het Misverstand der Ned. Soc. Werkgemeenschap.* Den Dolder. [1940.]

[82] ——. *Het N.V.V. in de Branding.* Den Dolder, 1941.

[83] [——,] Jan Ronduit, pseud. *De Verstrakking van het gemeentelijke Bestuursapparaat.* Den Dolder, 1945. (Reprinted from original clandestine edition published in 1943.)

DIARIES AND REMINISCENCES

[84] *Albrecht meldt zich.* N.p., n.d.

[85] Bergh, S. van den. *Deportaties.* Bussum, n.d.

[86] Best, S. Payne. *The Venlo Incident.* London, 1951.

[87] Boven, Adriaan van, pseud. [Walter van der Kampen.] *Jan Jansen in bezet Gebied: Oorlogsdagboek van een Ambtenaar.* Kampen, 1945.

[88] Clercq, G. de. *Amsterdam tijdens de Hongerperiode.* Amsterdam, 1945.

[89] Dekker, C., *et al. 1940–1945: Een Analyse van het Verzet: Verzetsgroep TD.* Amsterdam, 1945.

[90] Dekker, Maurits. *Josef duikt.* Leiden, 1946.

[91] Dries, N. C. M. A. van den. *De Hoge Raad der Nederlanden tijdens de Bezetting.* Leiden, 1945.

[92] Frank, Anne. *The Diary of a Young Girl.* New York, 1952.

[93] Frederiks, K. J. *Op de Bres, 1940–1944: Overzicht van de Werkzaamheden aan het Departement van Binnenlandse Zaken gedurende de Oorlogsjaren.* 's Gravenhage, 1945.

[94] Gijzel, B. H. v.d. *St. Michielsgestel: Herinneringen uit het Gijzelaarsleven.* Bussum, 1945.

[95] Gilbert, G. M. *Nuremberg Diary.* New York, 1947.

[96] *The Goebbels Diaries.* Ed. Louis P. Lochner. Garden City, 1948.

[97] Graaff, F. A. de. *Op. Leven en Dood: Kroniek van Oorlog en Bezetting, 1940–1945.* 2d ed. Rotterdam, 1946.

[98] Groot, A. W. de. *De Universiteit van Amsterdam in Oorlogstijd.* Amsterdam, n.d.

[99] Halder, Generaloberst Franz. "Tagesbuch" [*sic*]. Mimeographed. 7 vols. Copyright 1946 by the Attorney General of the United States. [Washington, D.C. (?)]

[100] Hendriks, Jan. *Vijf Jaar Drukkunst "in het Verborgene."* Utrecht. [1945.]

[101] Heuven Goedhart, G. J. van. *De Reis van "Colonel Blake."* Utrecht. 1945.

[102] Hirschfeld, H. M. *Herinneringen uit de Bezettingstijd.* Amsterdam, 1960.

[103] Kammeijer, J. H. D. *5 Jaar onder Duitse Druk.* Laren, 1946.

[104] Karhof, Nic. J. *Bezet, Verzet, Ontzet: Goes en Omgeving in de bewogen Jaren 1940–1944.* Goes, 2d ed.; n.d.

[105] Kleffens, Eelco Nicholaas van. *Juggernaut over Holland.* New York, 1941.

[106] LO-LKP Stichting. *Het Grote Gebod: Gedenkboek van het Verzet in LO en LKP.* 2 vols. Kampen, 1951.

[107] Loon, K. van. *Verzet in en om Dordt.* Den Haag, 1947.

[108] *The Memoirs of Dr. Felix Kersten,* ed. Herma Briffault. Garden City, N.Y., 1947.

[109] Netherlands. Nederlandse Binnenlandse Strijdkrachten, Afdeling Ommen. *Aan de Bronnen van het Verzet: De Strijd der Gemeente Ommen tegen de Duitse Overheersing, 1940–1945.* Ed. by Jef Last. Amsterdam, n.d.

[110] Nie, J. A. van. *"Bericht voor Grote Jan."* 's Gravenhage, 1946.

[111] *Nooit Vergeten.* Comp. by the editors of *Het vrije Volk.* Amsterdam, n.d.

[112] Norel, Karel, *et al. De Vijand wederstaan: Historische Schetsen van de Landelijke Organisatie voor Hulp aan Onderduikers, Landelijke Knokploegen en Centrale Inlichtingendienst.* Wageningen, 1946.

[113] Peereboom, Robert. *Gijzelaar in Gestel.* Zwolle, 1945.

[114] Puchinger, G., ed. *Dagboek van Mevrouw Colijn.* Kampen, 1960.

[115] Raatgever, J. R., Jr. *Van Dolle Dinsdag tot de Bevrijding.* Amsterdam, n.d.

[116] RR [Rolls Royce]. *Ontstaan en Werken van de Koeriers- en Inlichtingendienst R.R.* Amsterdam, 1945.

[117] Schellenberg, Walter. *Memoiren.* Köln, 1959.

[118] Schreieder, Joseph. *Das war das Englandspiel.* München, 1950.

[119] Seinen, K., ed. *Nederland gedenk: Gedenkboek van het Nederlandse Concentratiecamp Erika te Ommen.* Den Haag, 1946.

[120] Snoep, J. *Nederland in de Branding: Oorlog, Bezetting en Bevrijding, (1940–1945).* 2d ed. Groningen, 1946.

[121] Veterman, Eduard Necker. *Keizersgracht 763.* Amsterdam, 1946.

[122] Vogt, Willam. *Hoe het de Omroep verging: Een Verhaal over de Omroep in Bezettingstijd.* Amsterdam, 1945.

[123] Vries, G. J. P. de. *Achter de Schermen: De ondergrondse Strijd voor onze Bevrijding: Onthullingen over de Werkzaamheid der illegale Organisaties tijdens de Duitse Bezetting.* Rotterdam, 1946.

[124] Wielek, H. *De Oorlog die Hitler won.* Amsterdam, 1947.

[125] Wilhelmina. *Eenzaam maar niet alleen.* Amsterdam, 1959.

[126] Wind, E. de. *Eindstation . . . Auschwitz.* Amsterdam, 1946.

[127] Woude, Johan van der. *Arnhem: Betwiste Stad.* Amsterdam, 1945.

[128] Wouters, Tj. *Het Drama van Putten: Terreur over een Nederlands Dorp: October 1944.* Laren, 1948.

DOCUMENTS AND SOURCES
(See also Government Documents, above)

[129] Braaksma, J. B., ed. *Gedichten uit de bezette Nederlanden.* Brussel, 1945.

[130] Cohen, A. E. "Hoofd van de Afdeling Bronnenpublicaties, Rijksinstituut voor Oorlogsdocumentatie to Ministerie van Buitenlandse Zaken, attention A. J. Th. Hofman, November 24, 1958." Typewritten MS, Doos 27, Nr 3, Rijksinstituut voor Oorlogsdocumentatie.

[131] *Geuzenliedboeck 1940–1945.* [Amsterdam, 1946.]

[132] Grote Advies-Commissie der Illegaliteit. *Witboek over de Geschie-*

denis van het georganiseerde Verzet voor en na de Bevrijding. Amsterdam, 1950.

[133] Hasselt, W. J. C. van, comp. *Verzameling van Nederlandse Staatsregelingen en Grondwetten.* 7th ed. Schoonhoven, 1909.

[134] Hitler, Adolf. *Mein Kampf.* New York, 1939.

[135] *Hitlers Tischgespräche im Führerhauptquartier, 1941–1942.* Ed. Gerhard Ritter. Bonn, 1951.

[136] *De illegale Pers over na-oorlogse Problemen.* Ed. by the editors of *De Ploeg.* Assen, 1945.

[137] Joodse Raad voor Amsterdam. "Interne Mededelingen," August 14, 1942–June 18, 1943. Typewritten MS, Rijksinstituut voor Oorlogsdocumentatie.

[138] ——. "Onderhoud met den Heer SS. Hauptsturmführer aus der Fünten door de Heren A. Asscher, Prof. Dr. D. Cohen, Dr. E. Sluzker op Vrijdag 21 Mei 1943 des Morgens te 10 Uur." Typewritten MS, Doos 13, Nr 38, Rijksinstituut voor Oorlogsdocumentatie.

Netherlands

[139] *Het Onderwijs in 1941.* 's Gravenhage, 1942.

[140] Departement van Sociale Zaken. "Steunregeling Werklozen, betreffende: Het Werken van Nederlandse Arbeiders in Duitsland." Circular of the Acting Secretary-General, Nr 732 A.B. Afd. W.V. en A.B., June 25, 1940. Typewritten MS, Rijksinstituut voor Oorlogsdocumentatie.

[141] Dienst Voorlichting Bijzondere Rechtspleging, Bijzonder Gerechtshof Amsterdam. *Documentatie: Status en Werkzaamheid van Organisaties en Instellingen uit de Tijd der Duitse Bezetting van Nederland.* N.p., n.d.

[142] Directoraat-Generaal voor Bijzondere Rechtspleging, Politieke Recherche-Afdeling, Amsterdam. "Proces-Verbaal, David Cohen, April 19, 1947." Typewritten MS, Doos 24, Rijksinstituut voor Oorlogsdocumentatie.

[143] Ministerie van Onderwijs, Kunsten en Wetenschappen. Rijksinstituut voor Oorlogsdocumentatie. *Dagboek Fragmenten, 1940–1945.* T. M. Sjenitzer–van Leening, comp. Bronnenpublicatie, Serie Diversen Nr 2. 's Gravenhage, 1954.

[144] ——. ——. *Het Woord als Wapen: Keur uit de Nederlandse ondergrondse Pers, 1940–1945.* Ed. R. S. Zimmerman-Wolf. Bronnenpublicaties, Diversen Nr 1. 's Gravenhage, 1952.

[145] Rijksrecherche by het Bijzonder Gerechtshof de Amsterdam. "Proces-Verbaal, Edwin Sluzker, April 29 and May 4, 1948." Typewritten MS, Rijksinstituut voor Oorlogsdocumentatie.

[146] "Overzicht van de ingekomen Verklaringen betreffende Gemengd Huwelijk." Typewritten MS, Map Calmeyer, Rijksinstituut voor Oorlogsdocumentatie.

[147] Seyss-Inquart, Reichminister [Arthur]. *Vier Jahre in den Niederlanden: Gesammelte Reden.* Amsterdam, 1944.

[148] "Uitspraak van de Joodse Ereraad." *Nieuw Israëlitisch Weekblad,* December 26, 1947. Amsterdam.

[149] Visser 't Hooft, W. A., ed. *The Struggle of the Dutch Church for the Maintenance of the Commandments of God in the Life of the State.* London, 1944.

[150] *Wat zei VN er van? Citaten uit bijna vijf ondergrondse Jaargangen.* Comp. by the editors of *Vrij Nederland.* Amsterdam, 1945.

NEWSPAPERS AND PERIODICALS

[151] *Die Aktion,* October 1940. Berlin.

[152] *Algemeen Handelsblad,* 1940–45. Amsterdam.

[153] *Deutsche Zeitung in den Niederlanden,* 1940–45. Amsterdam.

[154] *De Gil: Periodiek verschijnend Orgaan voor nuchter Nederland.* [1944 (?)]

[155] *Het Joodse Weekblad,* 1941–43. Amsterdam.

[156] *Het Nationale Dagblad,* 1936–45. Leiden.

[157] *Nederland in Oorlogstijd,* 1946–50. Amsterdam. (Published by the Rijksinstituut voor Oorlogsdocumentatie.)

[158] *Nieuwe Rotterdamse Courant,* 1940–45. Rotterdam.

[159] *De Stem van Nederland,* 1947. Amsterdam.

[160] *Storm: Weekblad der Germaanse S.S. in Nederland,* 1941–45.

[161] *De Unie,* 1940–41. 's Gravenhage.

[162] *Volk en Vaderland,* 1933–45. Amsterdam.

[163] *Vrij Nederland,* 1945. Amsterdam.

[164] *Vrij Nederland,* 1940–46. London.

MONOGRAPHS AND SPECIAL STUDIES

[165] Althaus, Ernst. *Die Behandlung der Personalangelegenheiten in den besetzten niederländischen Gebieten.* 2d ed. Den Haag, 1943.

[166] Amsterdam. Gemeentelijk Bureau voor Lijkbezorging. *De Begrafenismoeilijkheden in 1945 te Amsterdam.* Amsterdam [1946].

[167] ——. Gemeentelijk Bureau voor Pers, Propaganda en Vreemdelingenverkeer. *Amsterdam tussen Invasie en Bevrijding, Juni 1944–Mei 1945.* Amsterdam, n.d.

[168] Baldwin, Hanson. "Churchill Was Right," *The Atlantic Monthly,* CXCIV, No. 1 (July 1954), 23–32.

[169] Bartstra, J. S. *Vergelijkende Stemmingsgeschiedenis in de bezette Gebieden van West-Europa 1940–1945.* Mededelingen der Koninklijke Nederlandse Akademie van Wetenschappen, Afdeling Letterkunde. Nieuwe Reeks, Deel 18, Nr 6. Amsterdam, 1955.

[170] Bellefroid, J. H. P. *Beknopt Overzicht der Staatsinrichting van Nederland tijdens de Bezetting.* 2d ed. Nijmegen, 1942.

[171] Berkley, K. P. L. *Overzicht van het Ontstaan, de Werkzaamheden en het Streven van de Joodse Raad voor Amsterdam.* Amsterdam [1945].

[172] Best, Werner. *Die deutsche Polizei.* Darmstadt, 1941.

[173] Boas, J. H. *Religious Resistance in Holland.* London, 1945.

[174] Bracher, Karl Dietrich, *et al. Die nationalsozialistische Machter-greifung. Studien zur Errichtung des totalitären Herrschaftssystems in Deutschland 1933/34.* Köln, 1960.

[175] Commissie voor Demografie der Joden in Nederland. *De Joden in Nederland na de Tweede Wereldoorlog.* Amsterdam, 1961.

[176] Fock, C. L. W. "De Nederlandse Regering in London en de Spoorwegstaking," *De Gids* (Utrecht), CXXVIII.

[177] Gerstein, Kurt. "Augenzeugenbericht zu den Massenvergasungen," *Vierteljahrshefte für Zeitgeschichte* (München), I (1953).

[178] Hartog, J. L. "Het Bombardement van Rotterdam op 14 Mei 1940," *De Gids* (Utrecht), April 1959.

[179] Hilten, D. A. van. *Van Capitulatie tot Capitulatie.* Leiden, 1949.

[180] Hirschfeld, H. M. *De Centrale Reederij voor de Voedselvoorziening.* Overdruk Maandschrift *Economie,* April 1946.

[181] Jacobsen, Hans Adolf. "Der deutsche Luftangriff auf Rotterdam," *Wehrwissenschaftliche Rundschau* (Frankfurt), VIII, 5 (May 1958).

[182] Jong, Louis de. *De Duitse Vijfde Colonne in de Tweede Wereldoorlog.* Arnhem [1953].

[183] ———. *The German Fifth Column in the Second World War.* Chicago, 1956. Translation of [182].

[184] Kitz, Wilhelm, and Heinrich Gross. *Die Organisation der niederländischen Verwaltung.* Düsseldorf, 1941.

[185] "Kort Rapport over het Weekblad *Je Maintiendrai,* Illegale Periode." Typewritten MS, Hoover Library.

[186] Kranenburg, R. *Het Nederlands Staatsrecht.* 7th rev. ed. Haarlem, 1951.

[187] Krekel, Hendrik. "Holland und die neue Wirklichkeit," *Die Aktion* (Berlin), October 1940.

[188] Landheer, Bartholomew. "The Legal Status of the Netherlands," *Michigan Law Review,* XLI (1943).

[189] Meerloo, A. M. *Total War and the Human Mind.* New York, 1945.

[190] Melkman, J. "Bij de Dood van Abraham Asscher," *Nieuw Israël-itisch Weekblad* (Amsterdam), May 5, 1950.

[191] Moore, Barrington, Jr. *Soviet Politics: The Dilemma of Power: The Role of Ideas in Social Change.* Cambridge, Mass., 1950.

Netherlands

[192] Departement van Economische Zaken en Arbeid. E. van Konijnenburg. *Organized Robbery.* The Hague, 1949.

[193] Departement van Sociale Zaken. *Malnutrition and Starvation in Western Netherlands, September 1944–July 1945.* 2 vols. The Hague, 1948.

[194] Generale Staf. *Beknopt Overzicht van de Krijgsverrichtingen der Koninklijke Landmacht, 10–19 Mei 1940.* Leiden, 1947.

[195] Ministerie van Onderwijs, Kunsten en Wetenschappen. Rijksinstituut voor Oorlogsdocumentatie. P. J. Bouman. *De April-Mei-Stakingen van 1943,* Monografieën Nr 2. 's Gravenhage, 1950.

[196] ———. ———. A. E. Cohen. "Een onbekende Tijdgenoot: De laatste

Befehlshaber der Sicherheitspolizei in Nederland." Notities voor het Geschiedwerk, Nr 71. Mimeographed, Amsterdam, n.d.

[197] ——. ——. A. E. Cohen. "Eenige formele Gegevens betreffende Hitler's Bemoeienis met Nederlandse Aangelegenheden." Notities voor het Geschiedwerk, Nr 73. Mimeographed, Amsterdam, n.d.

[198] ——. ——. A. E. Cohen. "Schuldig Slachtoffer: De derde Befehlshaber der Sicherheitspolizei und des S.D. in Nederland." Notities voor het Geschiedwerk, Nr 90. Mimeographed, Amsterdam, n.d.

[199] ——. ——. E. Fraenkel-Verkade. "Correspondentie van M. M. Rost van Tonningen." Notities voor het Geschiedwerk, Nr 67. Mimeographed, Amsterdam, n.d.

[200] ——. ——. A. Hiemstra-Timmenga. "In 1941 en 1942 naar Mauthausen en Ravensbrück gedeporteerde Joden." Notities voor het Geschiedwerk, Nr 97. Mimeographed, Amsterdam, n.d.

[201] ——. ——. L. de Jong. "The Allies and Dutch Resistance, 1940–1945." Report for the Second International Conference on the History of European Resistance, 1939–45, Milan (26–29 March 1961). Notities voor het Geschiedwerk, Nr 106. Mimeographed, Amsterdam, 1961.

[202] ——. ——. L. de Jong. "Verslag eerste Kwartaal 1961, Auteur Geschiedenis van Nederland in de Tweede Wereldoorlog." Mimeographed, Amsterdam, April 17, 1961.

[203] ——. ——. A. J. van der Leeuw. *Huiden en Leder, Bijdrage tot de economische Geschiedenis van Nederland in de Tweede Wereldoorlog.* Monografieën Nr 7. 's Gravenhage, 1954.

[204] ——. ——. "Personele and Materiële Verliezen van Nederland in de Tweede Wereldoorlog." Mimeographed, May 1960.

[205] ——. ——. A. J. C. Rüter. *Rijden en staken. De Nederlandse Spoorwegen in Oorlogstijd.* Monografieën Nr 8. 's Gravenhage, 1960.

[206] ——. ——. P. Sanders. *Het Nationaal Steunfonds: Bijdrage tot de Geschiedenis van de Financiering van het Verzet, 1941–1945.* Monografieën Nr 9. 's Gravenhage, 1960.

[207] ——. ——. B. A. Sijes. "De Arbeitseinsatz in Nederland, 1940–1945" (tentative title). Typewritten MS. Rijksinstituut voor Oorlogsdocumentatie.

[208] ——. ——. B. A. Sijes. *De Februari-Staking, 25–26 Februari 1941.* Monografieën Nr 5. 's Gravenhage, 1954.

[209] ——. ——. B. A. Sijes. *De Razzia van Rotterdam, 10–11 November 1944.* Monografieën Nr 4. 's Gravenhage, 1951.

[210] ——. ——. L. J. A. Trip. *De Duitse Bezetting van Nederland en de financiële Ontwikkeling van het Land gedurende de Jaren der Bezetting.* Kleine Serie Geschriften Nr 1. 's Gravenhage, 1946.

[211] ——. ——. E. Verkade. Dienstneming van Nederlanders bij de Vijand." Notities voor het Geschiedwerk, Nr 39. Mimeographed, Amsterdam, n.d.

[212] ——. ——. L. E. Winkel. *De ondergrondse Pers, 1940–1945.* Monografieën Nr 6. 's Gravenhage, 1954.

[213] ——. ——. P. H. Winkelman, *Heusden geteisterd en bevrijd.* Monografieën Nr 3. 's Gravenhage, 1950.

[214] Regeringsvoorlichtingsdienst. P. L. G. Doorman. *Military Opera-*

tions in the Netherlands from 10th–17th May, 1940. London, 1944.

[215] ——. New York. *A Nation at War.* New York, n.d.

[216] Neumann, Franz. *Behemoth: The Structure and Practice of National Socialism, 1933–1944.* 2d rev. ed. New York, 1944.

[217] Posthumus, N. W., ed. *The Netherlands during German Occupation.* Vol. CCXLV (May 1946) of *The Annals of the American Academy of Political and Social Science.*

[218] Posthumus Meyjes, H. C. *De Enquêtecommissie is van Oordeel . . . Een Samenvatting van het parlementaire Onderzoek naar het Regeringsbeleid in de Oorlogsjaren.* Arnhem, 1958.

[219] Reitlinger, Gerald. *The Final Solution: The Attempt to Exterminate the Jews of Europe, 1939–1945.* London, 1953.

[220] Sannes, H. W. J. *Onze Joden en Duitsland's Greep naar de Wereldmacht.* Amsterdam, 1946.

[221] Stokman, S. *De Katholieke Arbeidersbeweging in Oorlogstijd.* Utrecht, 1946.

[222] ——. *Het Verzet van de Nederlandse Bisschoppen tegen Nationaal-Socialisme en Duitse Tyrannie.* Utrecht, 1945.

[223] Tanham, George Kilpatrick. "The Belgian Underground Movement, 1940–1945." Unpublished doctoral dissertation, Stanford University, 1951.

[224] Touw, H. C. *Het Verzet der Hervormde Kerk: Geschiedenis van het kerkelijk Verzet.* 2 vols. 's Gravenhage, 1946.

[225] Trevor-Roper, H. R. "Himmlers Leibarzt," *Der Monat,* XCVIII (November 1956). Berlin.

United States

[226] Department of the Army. Maurice Matloff and Edwin M. Snell. *Strategic Planning for Coalition Warfare, 1941–1942.* Washington, D.C., 1953.

[227] Office of Strategic Services, Research and Analysis Branch. *Education in the Netherlands.* R & A No. 1995. Washington, D.C., 1944.

[228] ——. "German Military and Police Tribunals in Occupied Territories," Part II, Vol. III, of *German Military Government over Europe.* R & A No. 878.2. Washington, D.C., 1943.

[229] ——. "The Netherlands," Part III, Section II, Vol. I, of *German Military Government over Europe.* R & A No. 2500.6. Washington, D.C., 1944.

[230] ——. *Problems of the Netherlands Government-in-Exile.* R & A No. 2386. Washington, D.C., 1944.

[231] ——. "The S.S. and Police in Occupied Europe," Part II, Vol. II, of *German Military Government over Europe.* R & A No. 2500.22. Washington, D.C., 1945.

[232] Vernon, Manfred Claude. "The Cabinet in the Government of the Netherlands." Unpublished doctoral dissertation, Stanford University, 1948.

[233] Vries, Ph. de. *De Geschiedenis van het Verzet der Artsen in Nederland.* Haarlem, 1949.
[234] Warmbrunn, Werner. "The Netherlands under German Occupation: The Attempt at Conciliation, May 1940–January 1941." Master's thesis, Stanford University, 1948.
[235] Wijthoff, W. F. *De Staatsinrichting van Nederland.* 7th ed. Haarlem, 1953.
[236] Wisliceny, Dieter. "Von Madagaskar bis zur Endlösung," in Leon Poliakov and Josef Wulf, eds., *Das Dritte Reich und die Juden.* Berlin, 1955.
[237] Wolff, Sam de. *Geschiedenis der Joden in Nederland: Laatste Bedrijf.* Amsterdam, 1946.
[238] ———. "De Joodse Raad: Wij richten niet," *De Vlam* (Amsterdam), November 14, 1947.

BOOKS, PAMPHLETS, AND POSTERS

[239] Bagehot, Walter. *The English Constitution.* New York, 1897.
[240] Bauer, August Johan Herman. *De openbare Arbeidsbemiddeling gedurende de Bezettingstijd (1940–1945).* Delft, 1948.
[241] Besgen, Achim. *Der stille Befehl.* München, 1960.
[242] Bolhuis, J. J. van, C. D. J. Brandt, H. M. van Randwijk, B. C. Slotemaker, eds. *Onderdrukking en Verzet: Nederland in Oorlogstijd.* 4 vols. Arnhem, 1947–55.
[243] Carp, J. H. *Een half Jaar Rechtspraak van het Vredegerechtshof.* Utrecht [1942].
[244] [Cleveringa, R. P.] *De Hooge Raad: Antwoord aan Mr. N. C. M. A. van den Dries.* Amsterdam, 1945.
[245] Colijn, H. *Op de Grens van twee Werelden.* Amsterdam, 1940.
[246] C. P. N. [Communistische Partij Nederland.] *De Waarheid over de Februari-Staking: B. A. Sijes vervalst de Geschiedenis.* Amsterdam, August 1954.
[247] Doelman, C. *Arnhem: Stad der Bezitlozen.* Arnhem, 1945.
[248] Geelkerken, C. van. *Voor Volk en Vaderland: Tien Jaren Strijd van de Nationaal-Socialistische Beweging der Nederlanden, 1931–1941.* 2d ed. [Utrecht] 1943.
[249] Geer, D. J. de. *De Synthese in de Oorlog.* Rotterdam, 1942.
[250] [Germany. Reichskommissar für die besetzten niederländischen Gebiete, Hauptabteilung Volksaufklärung und Propaganda (?)] V 1918–1943 ?. N.p. [1943 (?)]
[251] Goedhart, H. A., ed. *De Pers in Nederland.* Amsterdam, 1943.
[252] [Grote Advies-Commissie der Illegaliteit.] *Weerbare Democratie.* [Amsterdam, 1946.]
[253] Jong, Louis de. *De Bezetting.* 5 vols. Amsterdam, 1961–.
[254] ———. *Holland Fights the Nazis.* London. [1941 (?)]
[255] ———. *Je Maintiendrai.* 4 vols. London, 1941–45.
[256] ———, and Joseph W. F. Stoppelman. *The Lion Rampant. The Story of Holland's Resistance to the Nazis.* New York, 1943.

[257] ——. *Nederland in de Tweede Wereldoorlog*, Vol. XII of *Algemene Geschiedenis der Nederlanden.* Utrecht, 1958.

[258] Keuchenius, Pieter Emiel. *Oostland als Lotsbestemming.* Amsterdam, 1942.

[259] Landheer, Bartholomew, ed. *The Netherlands.* The United Nations Series, ed. Robert J. Kerner. Berkeley, 1943.

[260] Linthorst Homan, J. *In vaderlandse Zin.* Haarlem, 1940.

[261] Mussert, Anton A. *De Bronnen van het Nederlandse Nationaal-Socialisme.* [Utrecht (?)] 1937.

[262] Nationaal-Socialistische Beweging der Nederlanden. *Dit moet Gij weten over de Nationaal-Socialistische Beweging der Nederlanden.* Amsterdam, 1943.

[263] Netherlands. Ministerie van Onderwijs, Kunsten en Wetenschappen. Rijksinstituut voor Oorlogsdocumentatie. "Draaiboek: De Bezetting V–X. Mimeographed, Amsterdam, 1961–62. (Draft of [253].)

[264] ——. Regeringsvoorlichtingsdienst, New York. *Geographical Digest of the Netherlands*, Vol. X, No. 1A, of *Netherlands News.* New York, 1944.

[265] Poliakov, Leon, and Josef Wulf, eds. *Das Dritte Reich und die Juden: Dokumente und Aufsätze.* Berlin, 1955.

[266] Poster 95, 15–30 April [1944 (?)]. Poster Collection, Hoover Library.

[267] Prel, Max du, ed. *Die Niederlande im Umbruch der Zeiten.* Würzburg, 1941.

[268] Presser, Jacob. *Breaking Point.* New York, 1958. Translation of [269].

[269] ——. *De Nacht der Girondijnen.* Amsterdam, 1957.

[270] Reymer, P. J. *Het eigen Recht van het Staatsgezag.* Maastricht, 1942.

[271] Schrieke, J. J. *Bezet Nederland en het Haagse Landoorlogsreglement van 1907.* Amsterdam, 1944.

[272] Sweers, B. M. *Vrije Meningen in een vrij Land.* Amsterdam, 1946.

[273] Wilde, J. A. de, and C. Smeenk. *Het Volk ten Baat: De Geschiedenis van de A. R. Partij.* Groningen, 1949.

[274] Zoetmulder, S. H. A. M., *et al*, eds. *Nederland in de Oorlog zoals het werkelijk was.* 6 vols. Utrecht, n.d.

Index

DATE DUE
